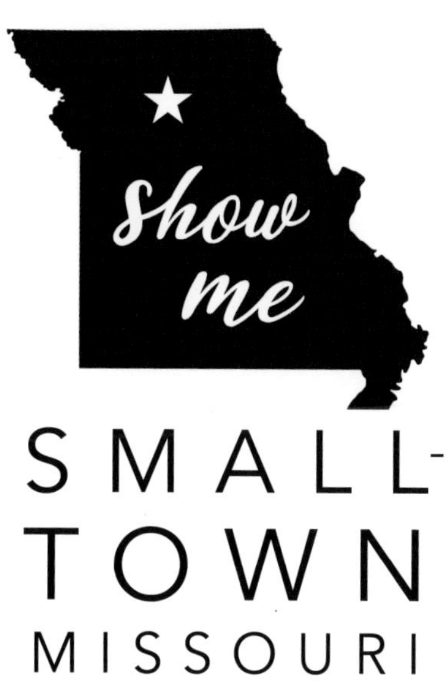
show me
SMALL-
TOWN
MISSOURI

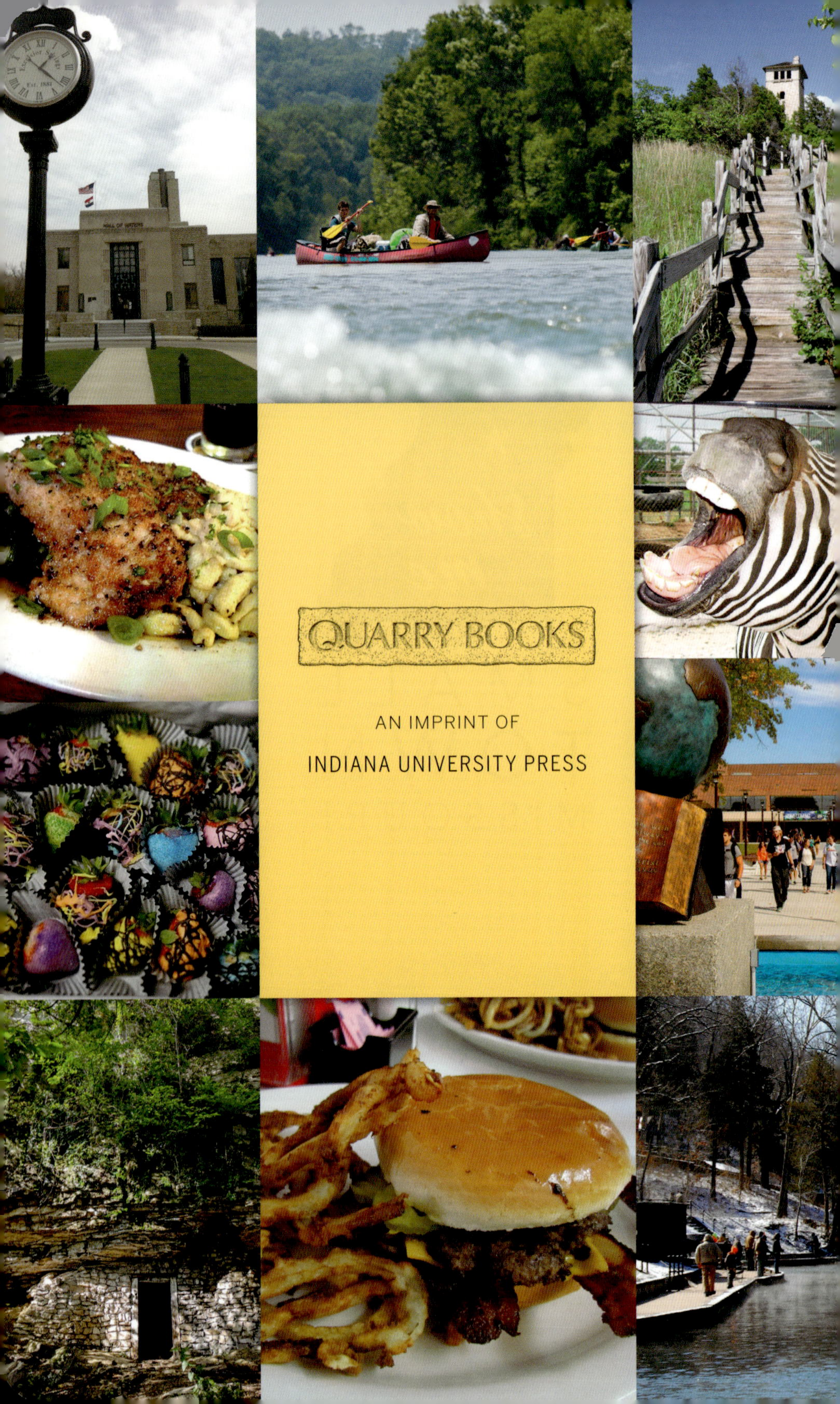
QUARRY BOOKS
AN IMPRINT OF
INDIANA UNIVERSITY PRESS
HALL OF WATERS

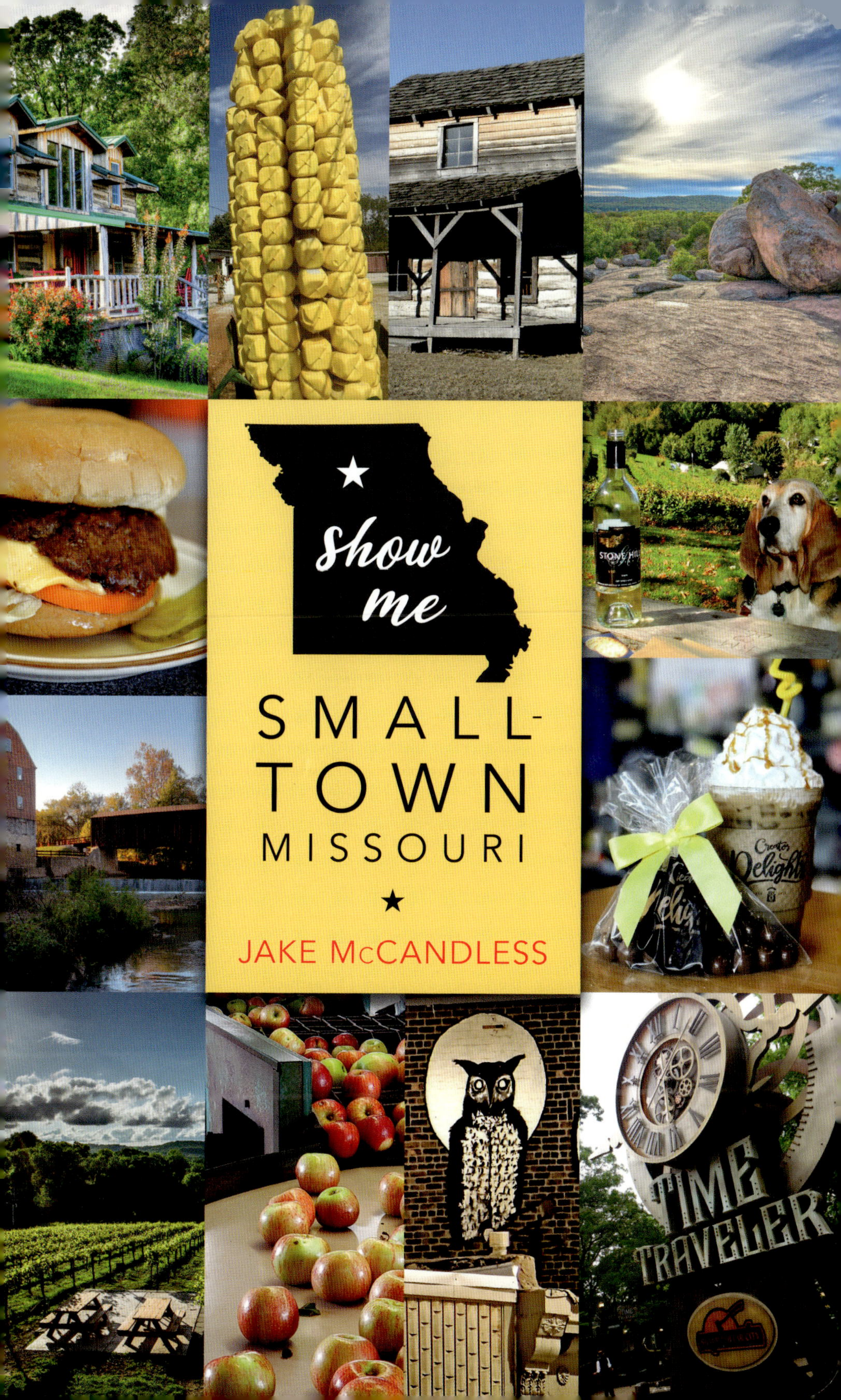
show me
SMALL-
TOWN
MISSOURI
JAKE McCANDLESS
STONE HILL
Creator Delights
TIME
TRAVELER

This book is a publication of

*Quarry Books*
an imprint of

INDIANA UNIVERSITY PRESS
Office of Scholarly Publishing
Herman B Wells Library 350
1320 East 10th Street
Bloomington, Indiana 47405 USA

iupress.indiana.edu



This book is printed on acid-free paper.

*Manufactured in China*

First printing 2020

ISBN 978-0-253-04948-3 (paperback)

*This book would not be possible without parents who instilled in me a sense of adventure—a mom who made everything a special occasion and a dad who spurred on the adventures—and now a wife who isn't afraid to hop in the truck to see what's out there.*

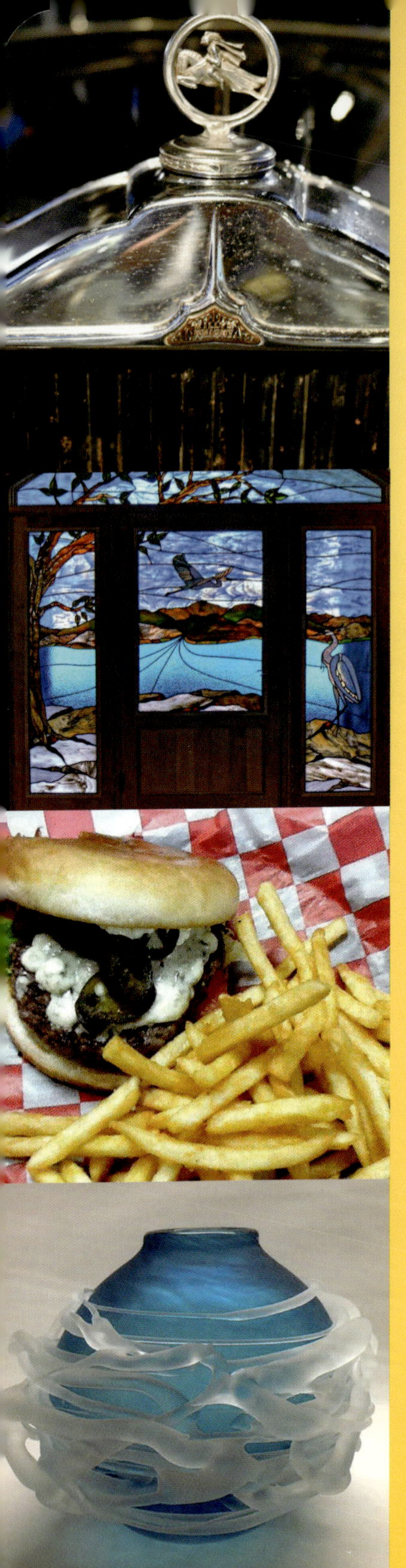

# Contents

## THE OZARKS ACROSS THE SOUTH



## THE LOWLANDS IN THE BOOTHEEL

# Acknowledgments

The thank-yous have to start with Amanda, Andrea, and Addison. Amanda, for putting up with this crazy project and joining me on this small-town odyssey as well as making sure I tried desserts, too, not just the main course. Andrea and Addie, thank you for letting Daddy work on his Missouri book—we've still got more places to see.

Thank you to Mom, Dad, Poppa, Kylie, Jesse, Kyanne, and Grayson for being great writing-retreat hosts, and thank you Rodney, Melinda, Amanda, and Linda for helping with the kiddos.

My agent, Cyle Young, is the man. Thanks for all you are doing to move me along as an author. I'm not sure whether to thank you or curse you on this one! Ashley, thank you for putting up with my inability to understand how much time each step of this journey was going to take and for your extreme patience. A big thank-you to Indiana University Press and Quarry Books. Thank you for the opportunity. And thanks to the whole Indiana University Press team.

And a big thank-you to my coworkers, collaborators, and partners in other projects for picking up all the slack while I sought out the best grub in the state—especially Christopher Mantei.

This book would not have been possible without such a great team of photographers who helped us capture the best Show Me State small-town images. Thanks for jumping on board. And special thank yous to the amazing business owners, restaurant owners, dreamers, and world changers out there who not only run their business or restaurant, hotel, or attraction, but who have created something special in their town. I hope this book does your hard work and your dreams justice.

And most of all, I want to give credit where credit is due. Many of the wonders found in Missouri small towns are in nature. The glory and praise for those wonders should go to the Creator who made them. The other noteworthy sights may be the creations of man, but they would be impossible without the creativity placed within them and the freedom to express it.

# Introduction

## MOTTOS AND GATEWAYS

US Congressman Willard D. Vandiver said Missourians were common-sense people who needed evidence and must be shown, not told. And of course, Missourians know best, so in making a pitch for our small towns to an outside world, it's not enough to simply say that these towns are special—full of life, tradition, history, beauty, and fun. Rather, the evidence has to be shown. True evidence has to be presented to those from the outside world or from the next town over. That is why this book is called *Show Me Small-Town Missouri.*

We'll look at the uniqueness of the small towns dotting this twenty-fourth state of the union. We'll see the major highlights. The must-see stops. The must-eat grub. The must-shop stores. The must-stay lodging. The must-know history. You from outside of Missouri have opened a guide to help you explore the state. It offers insider tips for those of you who live in the hustle and bustle of Kansas City and St. Louis and seek a weekend adventure. This book is also for those who love their small hometown—it's a chance to celebrate the wonder you already enjoy but fellow Missourians a county over have never experienced.

Although the phrase "show me" originated on that congressional floor and described what is needed for a Missourian to be convinced, the phrase "show me state" has now come to be about the bragging rights we have in our state. Our small hometowns are full of life and need to be celebrated. Therefore, like any good Missourian, this book will *show off* our small towns—which are clearly the best in the country.

"Show Me State" isn't the only Missouri motto that's branded in my mind. "Gateway to the West" is another. Of course, this refers to St. Louis's role in the westward expansion of the United States. When settlers headed west, their travel took them across the Mississippi River and often into St. Louis. This proverbial gateway is represented by the large arch in St. Louis today.

Missouri was the gateway to all of the adventures, excitement, and opportunity that lay beyond the settled lands of the eastern United States. This book is meant to serve in that same capacity—each entry is a gate to more for you to explore and know. Flip the pages and you'll see—you'll be shown—the wonder of small-town Missouri, and you'll enter the gateway for your next adventure.

You who are native to one of these Missouri small towns already know how much there is to enjoy, as do all of you who are small-town residents across the nation, but I fear some readers might be skeptical. Might be left questioning just how much life could be had in a Midwestern small town. Let me show you—it's a lot.

## FULL OF LIFE

With my eyes closed, I could mentally drive you through my hometown—a small town. Tell me which way you want to enter—north, east, south, or west. From the north, after the population sign and No Jake Brake sign, you could turn right and take the path on which I took many driver education trips or turn left toward the neighborhoods where I spent my summers mowing yards. You should continue south, though. On the right, a trailer park, then a muffler shop, next a vehicle air-conditioning shop, a forestry service, the highway department, and finally the community college. On the left, there was that house with the circular driveway, the propane place, the Nazarene church, houses, an apartment complex, and the former daycare. All this before we would pass the old restaurant—John Boy's. I loved their chopped pork barbecue sandwiches.

All through town, I could tell you each and every building and landmark that existed the two decades I lived there. On top of that, I could add commentary on the missing landmarks and past events of the two decades before my birth, as I recount each story my dad told me while we passed. Remembering the tales of my grandparents, I could relay the stories of the two decades before those. If you're counting, we're already six decades back. We could travel all the way back to when my great-grandfather rode a wagon into town.

In writing these words, I'm instantly transported to a classic blue Oldsmobile with my grandparents. Or to an old white Blazer with a standard transmission or that brand-new 1986 Ford Taurus, both belonging to my parents. Ghosts of the people they told me about bounce and weave through the now forsaken downtown or the abandoned junior high school.

Even more familiar are the scenes that pass through my mind like a movie of my life lived in that hometown. It's standing in front of the Christmas light–covered courthouse for the annual Christmas parade. The familiar face at the drugstore window. The shady park where our end-of-the-year school picnic took place. The church that transformed my life. The woods where my best friend, Caleb, and I built forts. The one-of-a-kind burger or famous Randy Dandy sandwich from the local burger joint that I still visit each trip I take home. My hometown meant so much to me. So much so that even after living away from it longer than I lived there, I still subscribe to the local newspaper and tune in to see how the Panthers did under the lights on Friday night.

With my hometown having such an impact on my life, you'd think I would know how much life could happen in a small town. But when I left the larger city where I went to college to take a job in an even smaller town than what I grew up in, I was reluctant—downright resistant. My hometown had a population of five thousand, but this new place only had a few hundred. I felt I had moved to the middle of nowhere, and I guess I had. But I soon found out that there was so much life in that town. Life I loved and now cherish. Even with an all-in-one feed store, gas station, massage therapy, video rental, grocery store, pizza place, and restaurant, this small town was full of life, as is each of the ninety you will read about. But what am I doing telling you that there is life there? I should show you.

# *The Prairie in the North*

Spanning from the Missouri River on the west to the Mississippi on the east and covering all land north of the Kansas City to St. Louis run of the Missouri River.

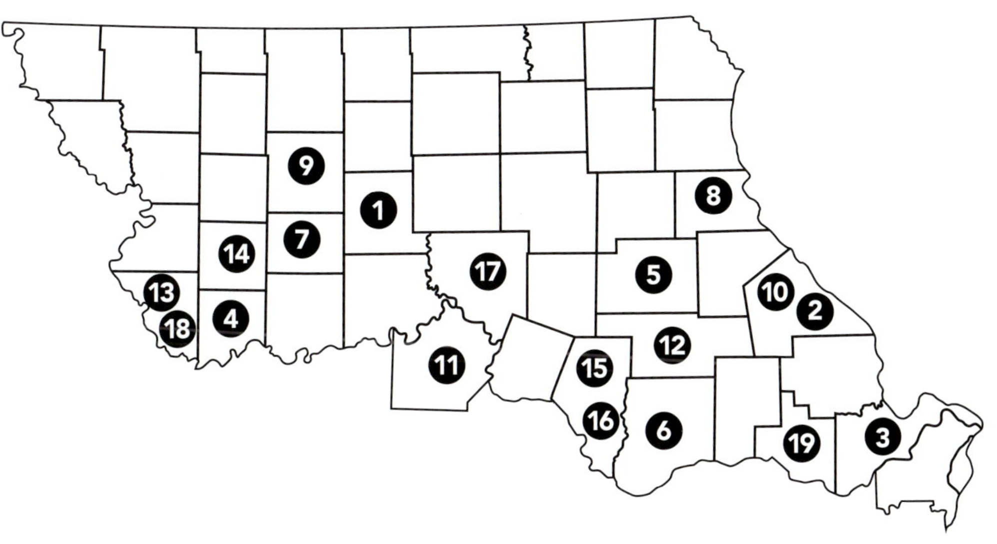


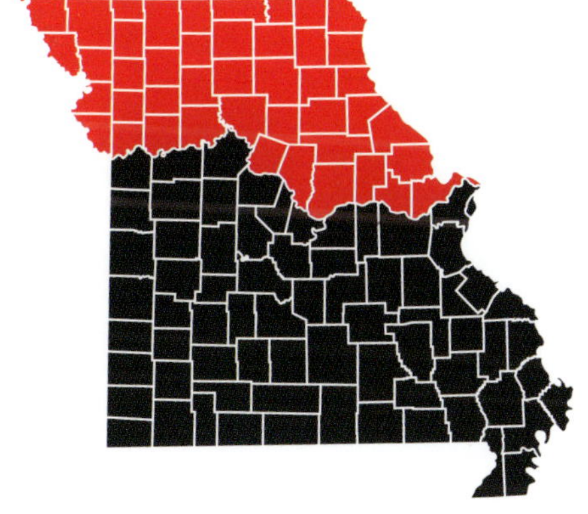

## The Prairie in the North

1. Chillicothe
2. Clarksville
3. Defiance
4. Excelsior Springs
5. Florida
6. Fulton
7. Hamilton
8. Hannibal
9. Jamesport
10. Louisiana
11. Marshall
12. Mexico
13. Parkville
14. Plattsburg
15. Rocheport
16. Sturgeon
17. Sumner
18. Weston
19. Wright City

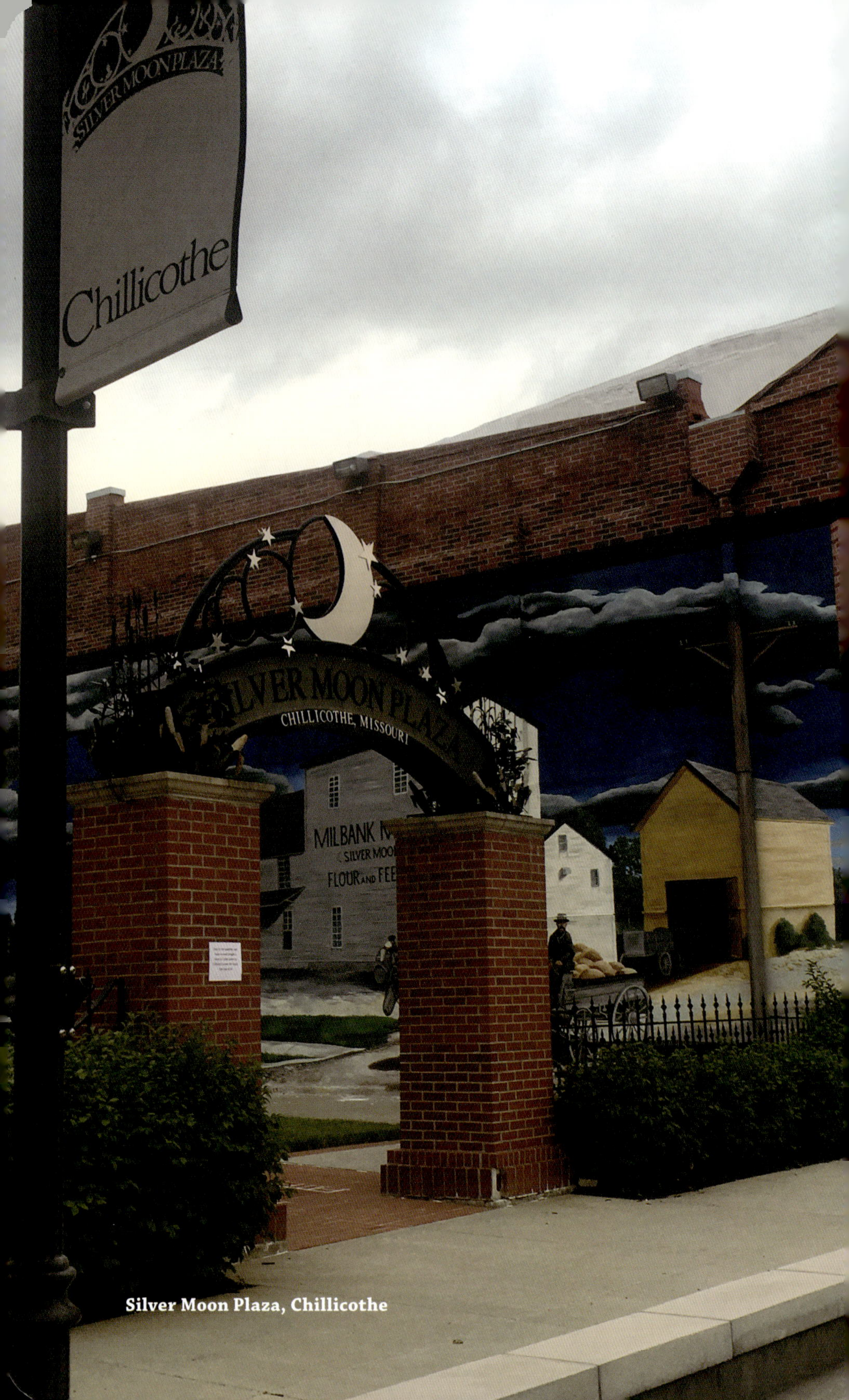

Silver Moon Plaza, Chillicothe

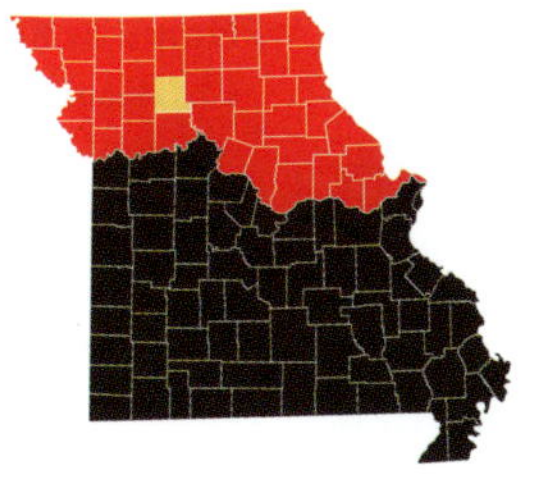

# 1

# Chillicothe

Surely you've heard the phrase "That's the best thing since sliced bread." The overused saying falls on deaf ears today, but there was a time when purchasing sliced bread wasn't even on the radar. So, if sliced bread is great, then certainly the town in which it was first sold must also be great. That town is Chillicothe.

Chillicothe became the home of sliced bread on July 6, 1928, when Frank Bench, founder of Chillicothe Baking Company, took a chance on a new invention by Otto Rohwedder. Twelve years before Bench's purchase, Rohwedder sold his three St. Joseph jewelry stores to devote his time to his bread-slicing idea. Persevering through multiple failed attempts, Rohwedder eventually had the patent to not only a bread-slicing machine but also one that packaged the sliced bread. Bench's purchase paid off, with his sales increasing 2,000 percent within the first year. By 1933, the sale of sliced bread eclipsed unsliced bread in the United States, and sales of pop-up toasters also soared. Ironically, the toaster was invented before the bread slicer.

Chillicothe has close to ten thousand residents and is the county seat of Livingston County. The name is from the Shawnee language and means "big city." A big Shawnee town in the area dates back to 1774. Before belonging to the Shawnee, the location was Osage territory.

Chillicothe became incorporated in 1851. Though the city has a rich history, it's not resting on that history, it's moving forward. In 2000, Main Street Chillicothe, a team formed by the Chillicothe Development

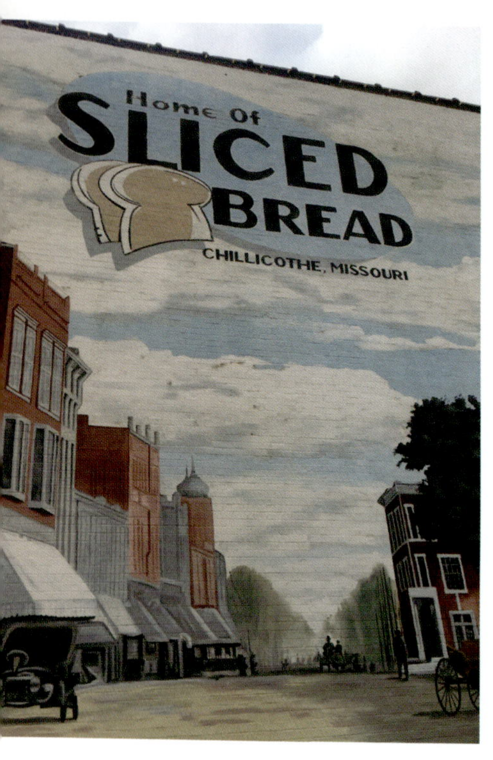


**Home of Sliced Bread Mural, Chillicothe**

Corporation, began earnest work to revitalize the downtown area. And their work is paying off: downtown is now beautiful, clean, and inviting. In 2019, downtown venue and gathering place Silver Moon Plaza won the Great Public Space award from the American Planning Association. Chances are, a special event or concert will be happening at the plaza when you're in town.

## MUST DO

Revitalization efforts have produced not only the plaza but also over twenty murals along with a couple of ghost signs to adorn downtown. The murals are stunning portrayals of generations past in the Midwest. Local artist Kelly William Poling, who has works displayed in the MGM Grand in Las Vegas and in Omaha's Joselyn Art Museum, was commissioned for the project. You can take a self-guided mural tour utilizing a downloadable map from the Downtown Chillicothe website, and you can also stop in Kelly's own art gallery in Chillicothe.

If your mural tour leaves you needing a break, stop in at the Sip, a gathering spot offering unique wine and craft beer. Their signature drink is wine slushies, offered year round. *Laid-back* is the keyword for this downtown place. Think bar-meets-coffee-house with the environment of a family reunion or *Seinfeld* episode occurring each afternoon. Every town needs to have such a place. Also, check their calendar—they often host live music or a special event.

## MUST SHOP

Historical murals aren't the only features downtown; the revitalization has brought in new businesses. Highlighting the shopping are the treasures at Nostalgia on Elm Street (not as scary as it sounds), along with Father and Daughter Antiques and Collectibles. If a stop at the Sip didn't relax you, treat yourself to Essential Kneads Day Spa, which offers salon services, massages, manicures, and pedicures. The name itself earns them points. A must-stop is Boji Stone Café and Bookstore, where one can find books and fun gifts.

## MUST EAT

Boji Stone has an atmosphere comparable to the Sip and adds a much deeper menu. Baristas serve freshly brewed coffee, steaming hot lattes, cappuccinos, frozen frappuccinos, and fruit smoothies. Along with the drinks, their menu includes pasta dishes, grilled sandwiches, salads, wraps, and quiche. Yet it's the desserts that make one's jaw drop. They offer homemade cheesecake, homemade ice cream, and much more. The clean and inviting atmosphere calls for one to prop open a laptop or fire up a tablet, use the free Wi-Fi, and savor the goodies. There's even a stuffed monkey named Mocha you'll have to meet.

Being "Boji-stoned" is not the only option or highlight for dining in town. Nico'Z Catering and Eatery is a unicorn for not just small-town Missouri but small-town America. Almost every small town across the Midwest has a café that serves dinner-plate lunches and has a special of the day. Some are better than others, and you'll read about the ones that set themselves apart in this book. Nico'Z is one of these—something different—boutique, high-end, gourmet dining combined with the

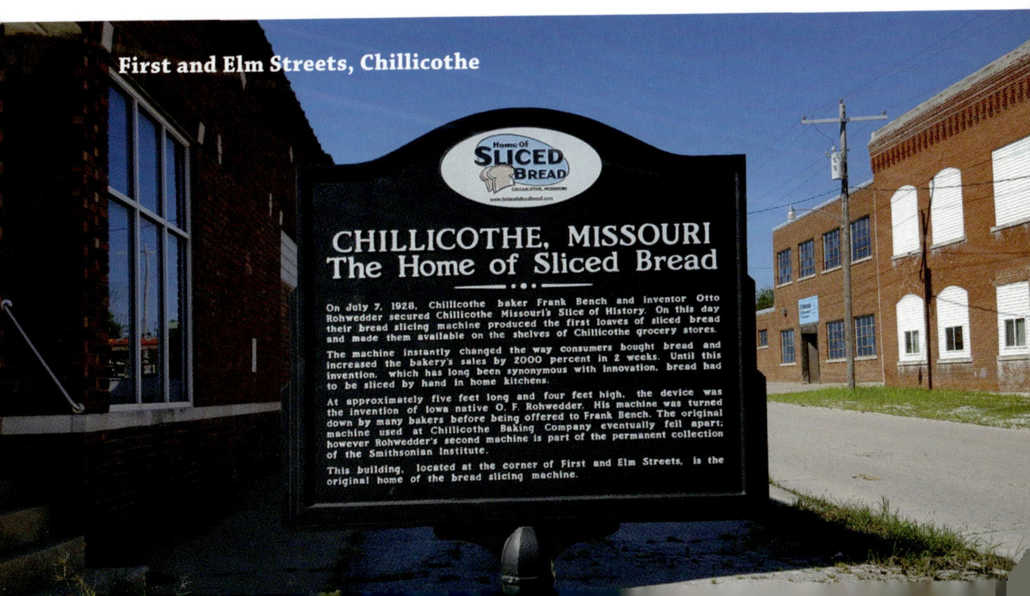


**First and Elm Streets, Chillicothe**

authenticity and relatability of a local diner. A place that could be an extension of your home while also a restaurant worthy of a special occasion.

Nico'Z is owned and operated by Nicole Booth, who moved back to her hometown of Chillicothe after working in the hospitality industry in Las Vegas. She adds an upscale and healthier touch to already proven dishes. Nicole has created an operation schedule that meets the needs of the town while also making meal times into special moments. There is a rotating quarterly menu that keeps food choices fresh for the regular Tuesday–Friday lunchtime. Special dinner times are offered on Wednesdays and Fridays. Wednesday is "Hump Day Happy Hour," with a festive menu of specialty pizzas. Friday dinner is an upscale, high-end experience that one formerly would have to travel to a big city to enjoy.

Another heavier-hitting eatery is Wabash BBQ, which is respected statewide for its smoked meats and award-winning ribs. Chillicothe is its second location, with the original being in Excelsior Springs.

## MUST NOTE

An evil but fascinating note that casts a shadow on the home of sliced bread is the account of Ray and Faye Copeland. They are the oldest couple ever sentenced to death in the United States. Faye was sixty-nine, and Ray was seventy-six. Ray had a criminal past and was well known as a fraud, which meant he could not buy and sell cattle. To get around this, he picked up hitchhikers or drifters, employed them, had them buy cattle with a hot check, sold the cattle before the check bounced, and killed the witness. The Copelands were found guilty of five murders, but are suspected of seven more. All of this happened near Chillicothe in Mooresville. Many crime shows and books have mentioned the Copelands.

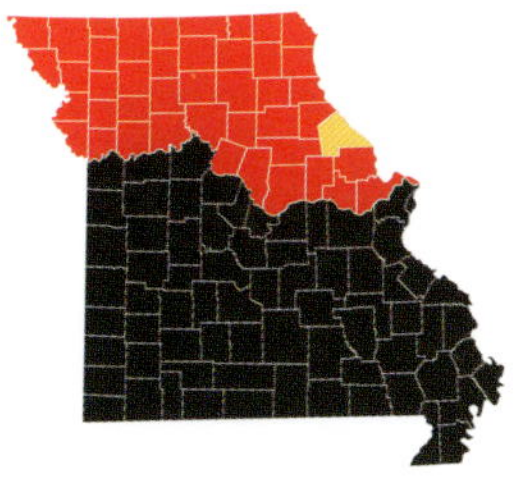

# 2

# Clarksville

Throughout this odyssey, through these ninety towns, are a handful of Hallmark-movie towns. You're probably familiar with the typical Hallmark scenario—fate takes a busy, big-city professional to a quaint, isolated, and romantic Thomas Kincaidish town where they're reminded of what matters the most and magically fall in love. There's no promise of you falling in love (you probably need to bring that significant other with you), but these towns are indeed quaint, isolated, and magical.

Clarksville is one such town. Here you can "Touch the Mississippi"—it's one of the only remaining towns not separated from the river by a levee or concrete wall, allowing for an unforgettable scene when one stands at the corner of Howard and Second. A line of historic downtown buildings leads straight to an archway serving as a door to the mighty river. The nostalgic Mark Twain steamboat lore that captures one's imagination in St. Louis, Cape Girardeau, or Hannibal is also present in Clarksville.

The river is the town's lifeblood, and Clarksville was established here because it was the best steamboat landing north of St. Louis. Several of the first settlers in 1812 were massacred by Native Americans, causing the rest to retreat to nearby forts. Eventually the area was resettled, and it was platted for the first time in 1819. The first steamboat landed less than a year later. Clarksville was named after William Clark of the Lewis and Clark expedition. The new port brought mills to the area, but flooding made industrial endeavors difficult. In 1960, an attraction opened

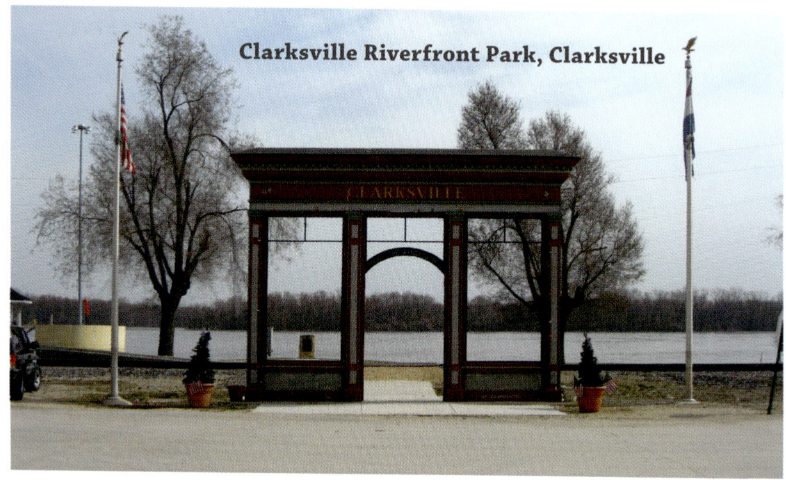

Clarksville Riverfront Park, Clarksville

that boosted tourism significantly: the Sky Ride, a ski lift that carried visitors up to the highest point on the entire Mississippi River bank. Unfortunately, the Sky Ride has closed down (although there are rumors that could change), but there is still plenty to experience and enjoy.

## MUST DO

Not only does the town's vibe give it that Hallmark feel, but a couple of its bed-and-breakfasts could be straight out of one of those movies, or maybe a Jane Austen book. A truly surprising oasis, the Inns at Overlook Farm offer a retreat that transports a couple into a real-life romantic novel and provides a complete departure from the hustle and bustle of life, as does the Village of the Blue Rose.

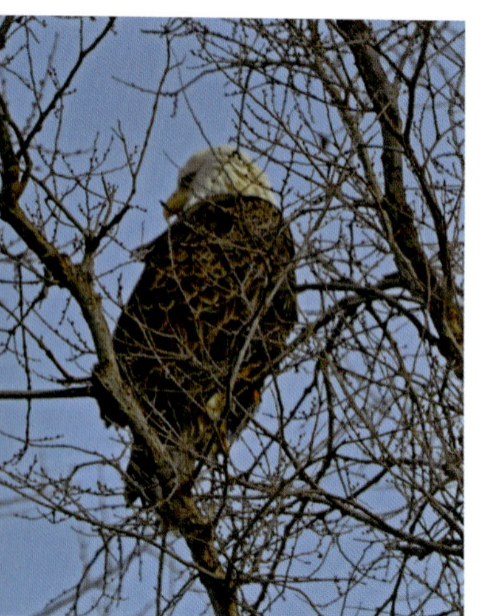

State Game Refuge, Clarksville

The bed-and-breakfasts are attractions and destinations themselves, but nearby are more adventures to be had. Take in the views that riverboat travelers of the 1800s enjoyed by driving the Great River Road, Highway 79, which has been designated a National Scenic Byway. Keep your eyes open for birds, especially bald eagles in winter months. The

National Audubon Society has designated Clarksville an Important Bird Area. Every late January the town celebrates Eagle Days, and there are many opportunities to see our national bird. In the fall is another celebration—Apple Fest.

## MUST SHOP

Downtown Clarksville is also a true working artisan community. With the river in view, you can stroll through antique stores, artists' workshops, and other specialty businesses. One can shop and watch the craftsmen work, whether it's making furniture from M & M Greenwell or Windsor Chairs, pottery from Great River Road Pottery and Wood Shop, natural-ingredient skin care and beauty products from Bee Naturals, lampworking and fused glass, woven wearable art, jewelry, or photography.

## MUST STAY

Overlook Farm is a longtime working farm with five distinct overnight escapes on the property, each providing top-shelf amenities, scenic views, beautiful gardens, and a quick walk to downtown. On-site chefs provide gourmet meals made with ingredients grown on the farm. Another nearby bed-and-breakfast is the Village of the Blue Rose, which sits atop Macintosh Hill and has a splendid view of the river. At the Blue Rose, you can have a great experience and do good, as it is a nonprofit that provides housing and employment for adults with developmental disabilities. It's a great experience for anyone and also encouragement for families of special-needs children.

## MUST EAT

Both Overlook Farm and the Village of the Blue Rose have restaurants open to the public. Another recommended stop is downtown facing the river, Tubby's Grub and Pub, which offers hearty comfort food and provides the combined vibe of the historic downtown and Riverwalk.

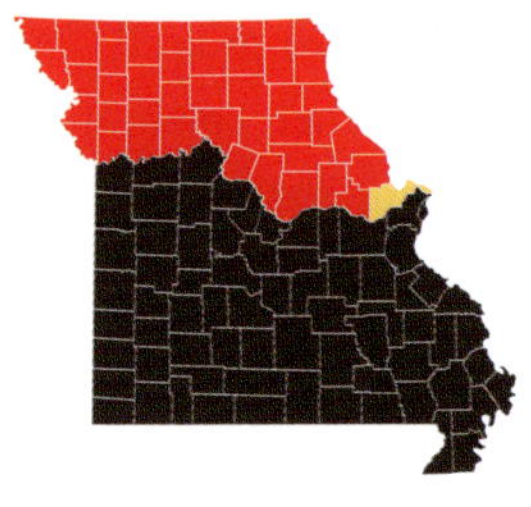

# 3

# Defiance

Defiance's original settlers were explorers seeking their fortunes and new adventures. Although slightly removed from those roots, Defiance is still a place for those looking for something new and wanting to be free from the hustle and bustle of the city, especially St. Louis, which is only an hour away. The most famous early settler of Defiance was the legendary frontiersman Daniel Boone. Boone left Kentucky to avoid financial and legal trouble and was granted land by the Spanish in 1799. He lived out his last two decades in Femme Osage Valley, just on the outskirts of modern-day Defiance. The larger-than-life folk hero's home is preserved and open to visitors. Remarkably, the Daniel Boone House is not the town's highlight or the reason most people come to the area. And believe it or not, Boone's trailblazing past had nothing to do with the town's name.

Defiance was originally named Parsons, but when the Katy Railroad added a stop in town, the name had to be changed since there was already a Parsons on the rail line. Settlers decided on Defiance to commemorate their battle with nearby Matson to become the chosen rail stop, which is one of best origin stories.

But today the true draw of Defiance is being the gateway to Missouri wine country. Stretching from Defiance down Route 94 through the Missouri River valley is the Missouri Rhineland, called such because of its resemblance to central Europe's Rhineland. German and Italian

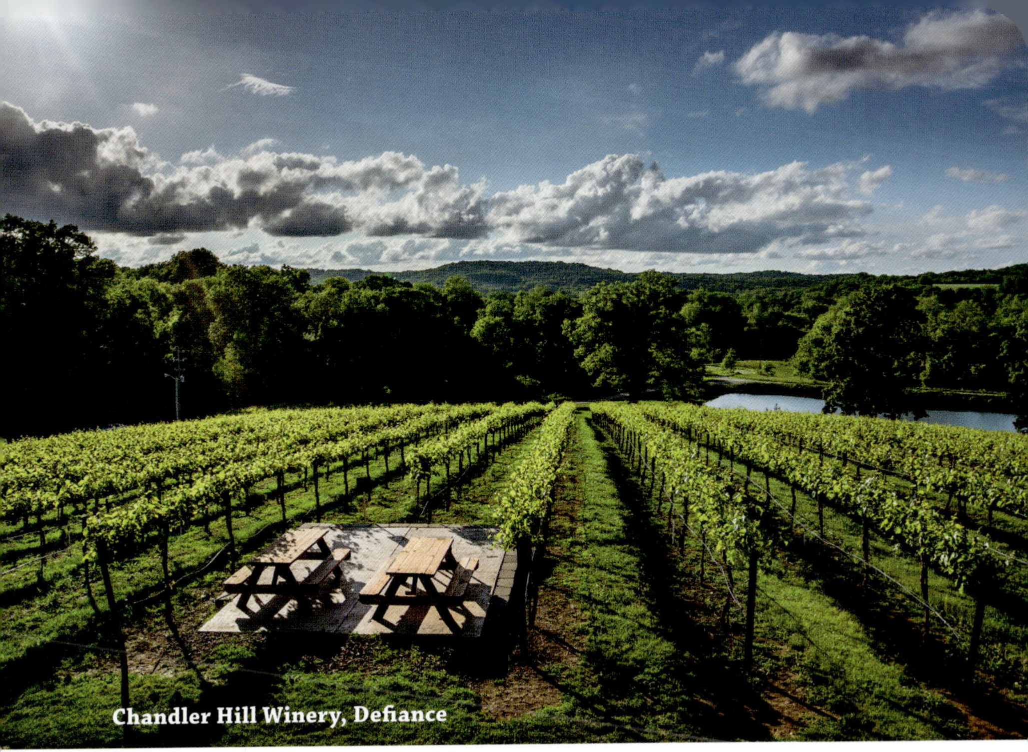
Chandler Hill Winery, Defiance

immigrants shaped this stretch of vineyards and wineries. The Defiance-Augusta-Dutzow wine country is the oldest in the United States.

## MUST DO

Defiance Ridge Vineyards and Chandler Hill Vineyards are both located in town. All of the wineries in this historic stretch offer spectacular views, though Chandler Hill may be the most picturesque. It's also one of the most elegant. Along with offering their Missouri wine, they offer wines from their vineyards in Napa Valley, the Willamette and Columbia Valleys, and the legendary Central Coast. Defiance Ridge offers panoramic views of the Missouri River from its ridgetop location. Both wineries have full menus and are home to weddings and special events.

The rolling hills, laid-back atmosphere, and setting along the river make the area a peaceful escape, but there's also adventure for the adventuresome. Katy Trail, America's longest recreational trail, converted from the railway of the same name, has its entrance in Defiance. The trail's 237 miles cross nearly all of Missouri and are used for hiking, running, and cycling. For those who like their adventure on the water, you can find outfitters for kayaking, canoeing, or rafting on the Missouri River.

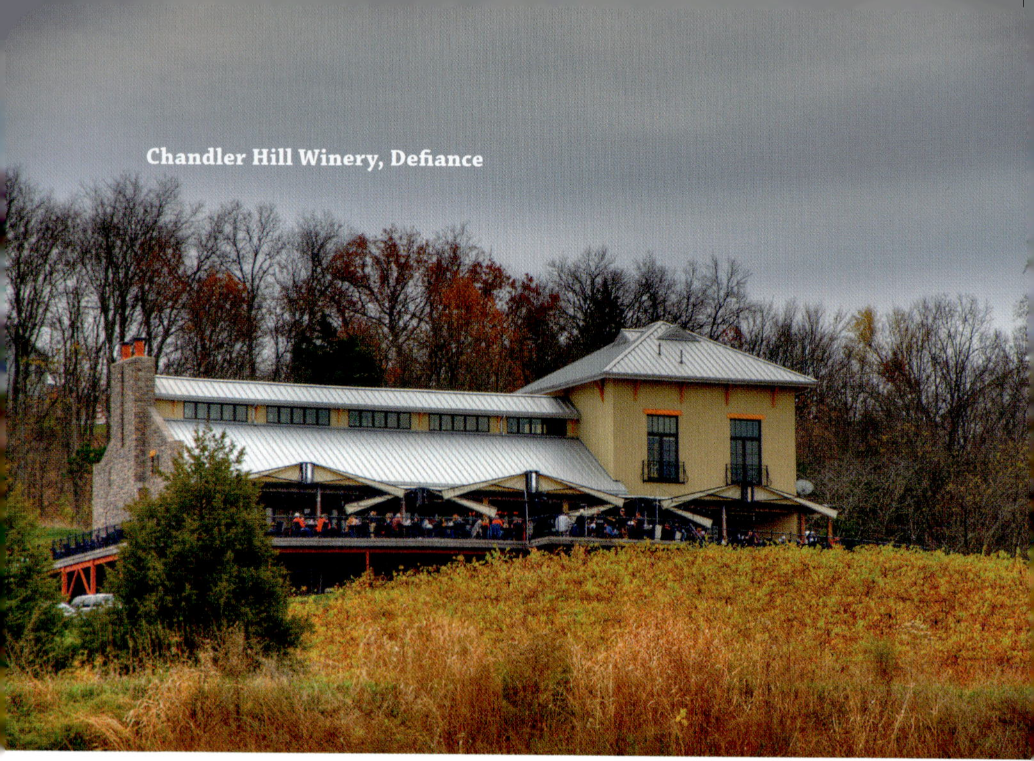
Chandler Hill Winery, Defiance

Defiance is not only a stop for nonmotorized bikes but also a rallying point for motorcyclists. Defiance Roadhouse and the adjacent Terry and Kathy's Bar and Grill are must-stops that cater to bikers. They both regularly offer live music and special events.

## MUST EAT

Defiance Roadhouse offers casual dining and American cuisine. Terry and Kathy's does the same. For barbecue, the Trail Smokehouse is a recommended stop. For a bit more elegance, both wineries have restaurants offering gourmet specialties.

## MUST STAY

Parson's Bed and Breakfast is in a stately home built in 1842, which predates the establishment of the town. The three available rooms combine history and elegance. Along with gracious accommodations, Parson's offers a limo service, making this the perfect launching point for a wine tour.

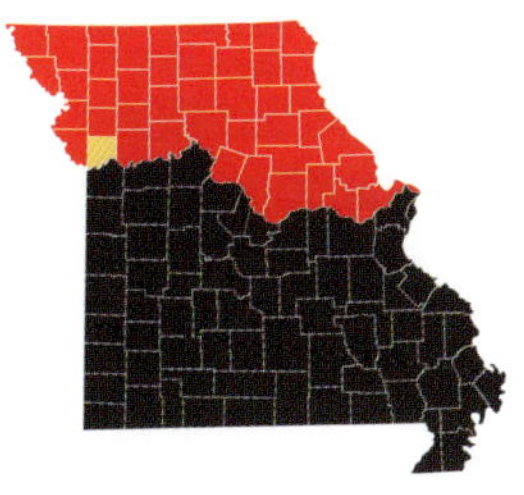

# 4

# Excelsior Springs

Stress causes a need to escape and relax. What do you envision as the most stressful situation you could face? Imagine becoming president. That alone would be pretty stressful, but what if it was due to the death of someone who had been president for twelve years, and your presidency began during the largest war the world had ever seen, you dropped atomic bombs to level two cities and end the war, and you trailed in every election poll in your attempt to win the presidency on your own terms. Yes, a bit stressful. That's why on the night of the 1948 election, President Harry S. Truman, a Missourian, was snuck out of the Democratic campaign headquarters in Kansas City by the Secret Service and into a historic, luxurious resort synonymous with therapeutic relaxation. And today you can travel the same thirty miles out of Kansas City and stay at the same resort.

To finish the story, President Truman didn't stay until checkout in what is today room 300 but was awakened during the night to hear that he was now ahead in the presidential race he had been counted out of, and he returned to Kansas City.

That historic and luxurious hotel was the Elms Hotel and Spa, a storied hotel in a storied town, Excelsior Springs, which at one time was a leading national tourist destination. It was known as "America's Haven of Health."

Excelsior Springs was first settled in the late 1800s, and within the first couple of years the town had grown faster than any other in Missouri.

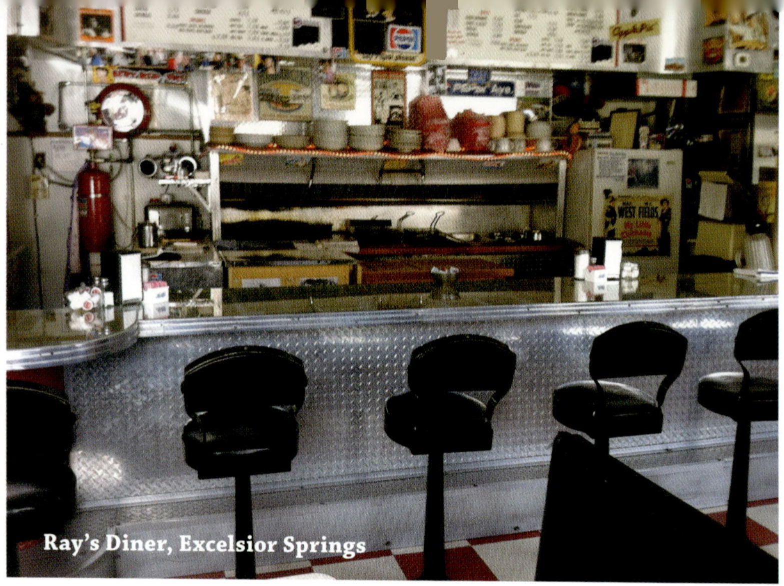
Ray's Diner, Excelsior Springs

By 1888, a company had been formed around the town's precious resource, its pure and reportedly healing spring water, and two hundred homes were built—many more people lived in camps. Parks were added, and the Elms Hotel went in.

The town's growth was fueled by the discovery of a natural spring that contained medicinal value. An early settler's daughter became sick with tuberculosis but was healed after bathing in and drinking from the spring. On hearing that news, another settler began to treat his old Civil War wound and was also cured. When word spread, people rushed to the city. In the following years, close to forty separate springs were discovered, and out of those springs, five different mineral mixtures were identified. The number of springs and their mineral combinations made it the greatest collection of mineral waters in the world. One researcher declared that one of the mineral combinations was present in only five locations in the world: four of these were in Europe, and Excelsior Springs was the fifth.

Unfortunately, the springs began to lose popularity in the 1960s. Because of major flooding and population decreases, things aren't what they were a hundred years ago, but one can still walk the streets that brought in celebrities, political leaders, and even gangsters. Yes, gangsters. Notorious Prohibition-era mobsters Al Capone, "Pretty Boy" Floyd, and Bugs Moran held less-than-legal events at the Elms. Unfortunately, very little remains of the wonder of those many springs. One pagoda exists, and visitors can taste the different mineral water combinations at the largest water bar in the world. And the Elms continues the tradition of relaxing waters with their spa.

## MUST DO

The Spa at the Elms is a destination unto itself. Their world-class spa features a full menu of treatments perfect for a relaxing weekend. The magical lore of the Elms makes for a romantic getaway—a couple's massage, walking through the gardens, dining in the multiple restaurants, and escaping for a walk downtown.

A trip to Excelsior Springs is perfect for the historian. One can relive Victorian America along with some glam from the 1920s. Any visit to town, regardless if for escape or history, needs to include the Hall of Waters. The name takes one back to the comic book home of the Justice League—the Hall of Justice. This 1930s Public Works Administration project was a masterful idea. The structure was built to bring all the different springs of the area into one place. For those who enjoy architecture, the Art Deco style is captivating. It's a real work of art, with craftsmanship rarely seen today. It's decorated with reliefs and imagery of Mayan Indians connecting with their water gods. At one time, this building held both men's and women's bath areas, each for up to three hundred people, a large pool, and a water bar for bottling and enjoying piped-in mineral water. Remnants of those activities can be seen today. The water bar is still in operation, and here you can sample different mineral waters.

After a refreshing drink at the Hall of Waters, you can continue downtown, hitting some of the antique and boutique shops. If you visit on the weekend, Willow Spring Mercantile has Live Music Weekends. Also, you can catch glimpses of buildings from the past like the Oaks Hotel that now serves as apartments.

**Hall of Waters, Excelsior Springs**

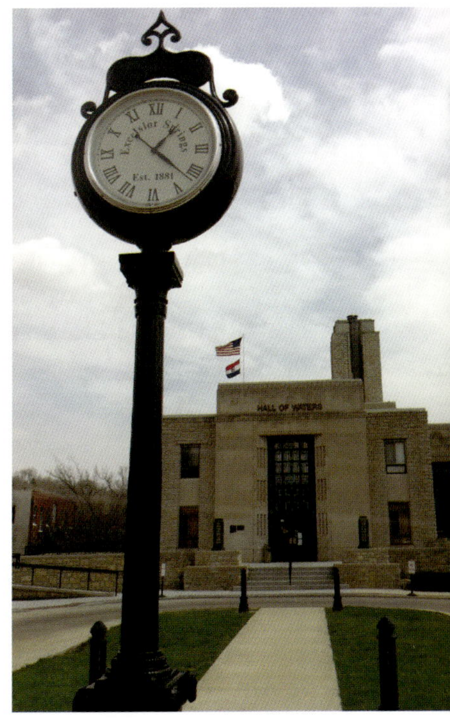

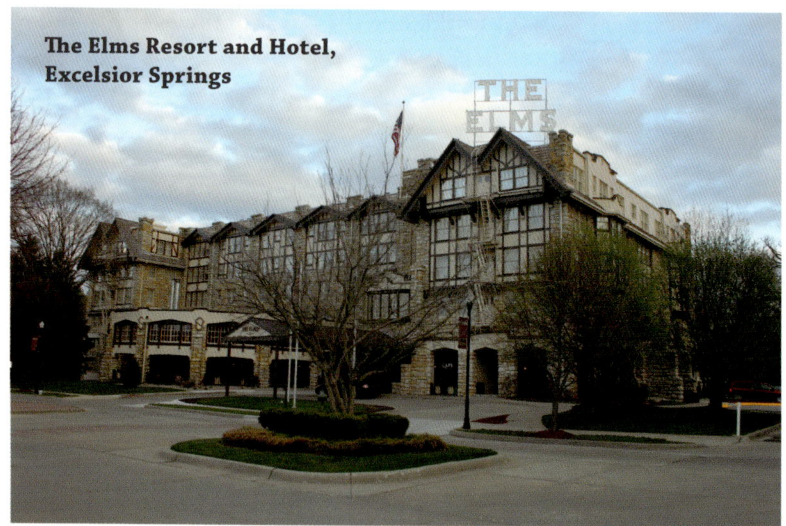


**The Elms Resort and Hotel, Excelsior Springs**

## MUST STAY

Obviously, the Elms is a destination itself, but there are other elegant and charming options. A bed-and-breakfast to check out is the Inn on Crescent Lake. Two others to consider are the Guest House and Payne Jailhouse Bed and Breakfast.

## MUST EAT

The Elms has the option of their own restaurant, 88 at the Elms. It has a luxury vibe and great dishes, but there are two less luxurious restaurants visitors must also seek out. It's hard to rank one over the other. Wabash BBQ, located in the remodeled railroad depot, offers well-respected smoked meat and ribs that make lists of the top ribs in Kansas City. That's a big honor, earned by must-try grub. The second is Ray's Diner. One can't visit Excelsior Springs and pass up ribs that Kansas City folks drive out to enjoy, but Ray's is one of the oldest restaurants around. It's been dishing out burgers since 1932. The small vintage diner is full of memorabilia from the past seventy-five years, and they're still cooking on the original grill. Surely it's perfectly seasoned by now.

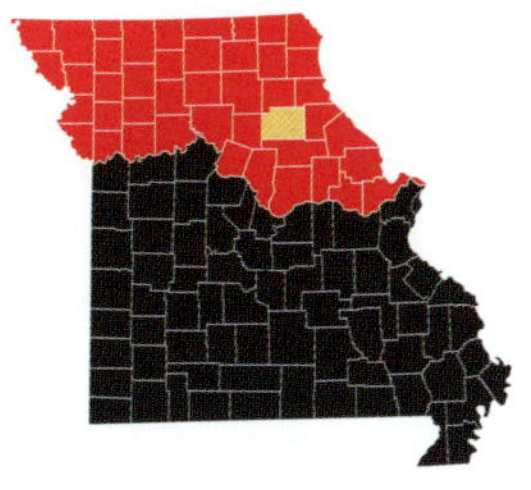

# 5

# *Florida*

Florida is the smallest town this book will cover. The 2010 census concluded that the town was uninhabited, but ten years earlier, census records showed nine residents. *Village* is probably more accurate than *town*, but the name is perfect for its geographical location. Florida is on a long peninsula that extends into the man-made Mark Twain Lake. The village long pre-dates the reservoir, which was completed in 1984. Interestingly, Johnny Cash performed during the dedication ceremony. Although the exact date of establishment is uncertain, there is evidence that the village existed on November 30, 1835, for Samuel Langhorne Clemens would later note its size. Of course, Samuel Clemens is the birth name of Mark Twain. Twain was born in Florida, and that is why it makes it into the book. Of the smallness of his birthplace, he once said, "The village contained a hundred people and I increased the population by 1 percent. It is more than many of the best men in history could have done for a town."

Close to two hundred years after his birth, Twain still keeps that small village on the map. His birth home has been preserved at the Mark Twain Birthplace State Historic Site. The small cabin has been placed inside a museum to protect it. Several first editions of his writings are stored at the museum. Most notable is a handwritten copy of *The Adventures of Tom Sawyer*. Twain's cabin was moved from its original location in town, which is now marked by a monument. His family lived in the village for only the first four years of his life and then moved twenty miles away to Hannibal.

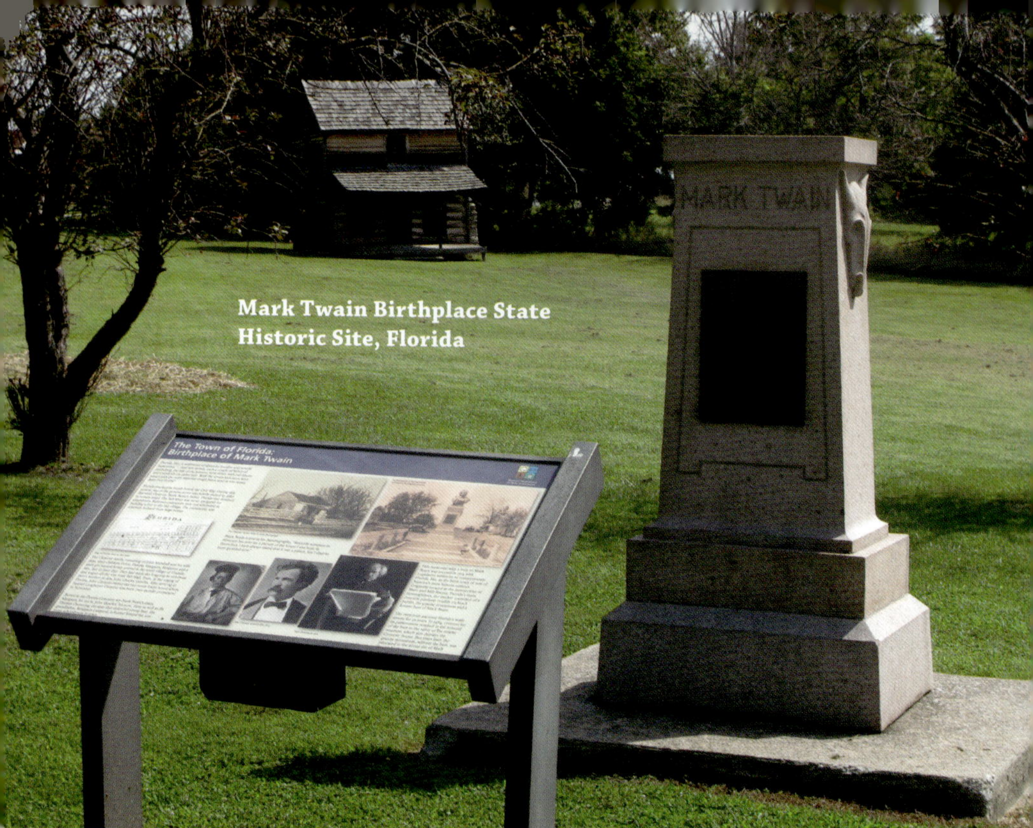

Mark Twain Birthplace State Historic Site, Florida

## MUST DO

Visit the Mark Twain Birthplace State Historic Site, perfect to tie in with a trip to nearby Hannibal.

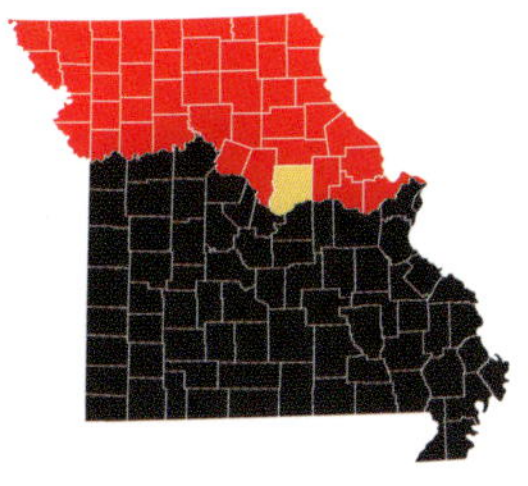

# 6

# Fulton

Would you believe that there was a Winston Churchill museum in America? And if there were a museum on American soil dedicated to a British leader, where might it be? New York? Washington? Boston? Philadelphia? Chicago?

And if Sir Winston Churchill gave a speech that some say marked the beginning of the Cold War, where would you expect it to have been given? The East Room of the White House? The Rose Garden? The Senate? Harvard? Princeton?

Remarkably, there is a Churchill museum on American soil, and one of the first speeches in which Churchill used the phrase "Iron Curtain" was given in the United States in 1946. But none of those expected places hosted the speech or became the site of the museum. It's incredible, but that famous "Sinews of Peace" and "Iron Curtain" speech was made in Fulton, Missouri, a town of 12,790 inhabitants. And in the 1960s, construction began on a museum in Fulton commemorating the leader and his speech.

Fulton was founded in 1825 and has always been a center of education. First came Synodical College in 1842, a Presbyterian college for women and one of the first women's colleges in the nation. Next came a school for the deaf in 1851. That same year, Westminster College began, which was originally a Presbyterian men's college. Westminster was the site of Churchill's speech and is today the location of the National Churchill Museum.

## MUST DO

The National Churchill Museum at Westminster College is worth a trip to Fulton. Guests are taken back to wartime Britain and see World War II through European eyes. But detailed and interactive exhibits are mere starters compared to the two main sights at the museum: To commemorate the twentieth anniversary of the famed speech, Westminster College purchased a London church that had been badly damaged by German bombs. St. Mary the Virgin Aldermanbury was a Christopher Wren–designed church originally built in 1677 and was moved stone by stone from London to the Westminster campus where it was rebuilt to its original state. The Churchill museum is beneath the church.

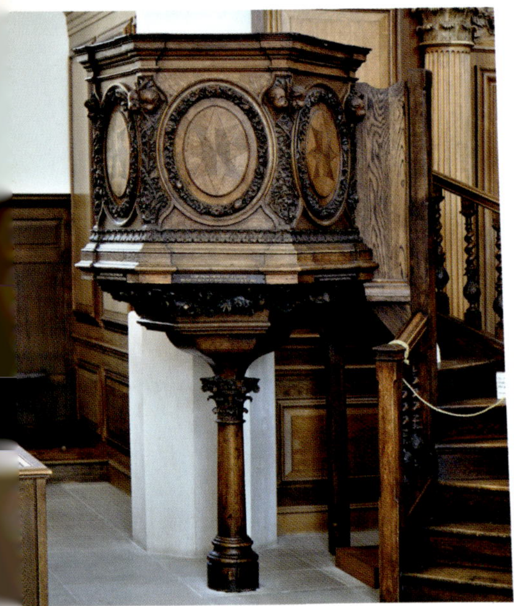

**National Winston Churchill Museum, Fulton**

As stunning as the church is to behold, with its remarkable raised pulpit, another import might be the greatest treasure. On campus are eight sections of the Berlin Wall. Those who remember President Reagan saying, "Tear down this wall!" will be thrilled to put their hands on actual pieces of that wall, the physical embodiment of the Iron Curtain.

In a small town like Fulton, you would think one awe-inspiring museum would be enough, but that is not the case. Also in town is the Auto World Museum, which displays over one hundred vehicles built between 1896 and 1997. They are arranged in chronological order, allowing the visitor to walk through history and see the evolution of motor vehicles. The museum began with the personal collection of former Backer Potato Chip Company owner William E. Backer. He felt that classic cars were not just vehicles to travel here and there but could also take us back to special memories. The collection is stunning and will be enjoyed by the car enthusiast, the historian, and even those not that interested in cars. It's about more than just cars—it's the history of America. And for kids of the eighties, there's even a 1982 DeLorean Coupe.

## MUST EAT

Fulton eateries match the extraordinary attractions in town. There are several unique restaurants in town, but three stand out. Starting with the most upscale, Bek's Restaurant is located downtown and offers fresh, high-quality meals. The classy atmosphere makes it perfect for a dinner date, but their lunches are top-notch. Everything is made from scratch with locally grown produce. A customer favorite is the grilled chicken chipotle sandwich, and meals must be topped off with Bek's carrot cake.

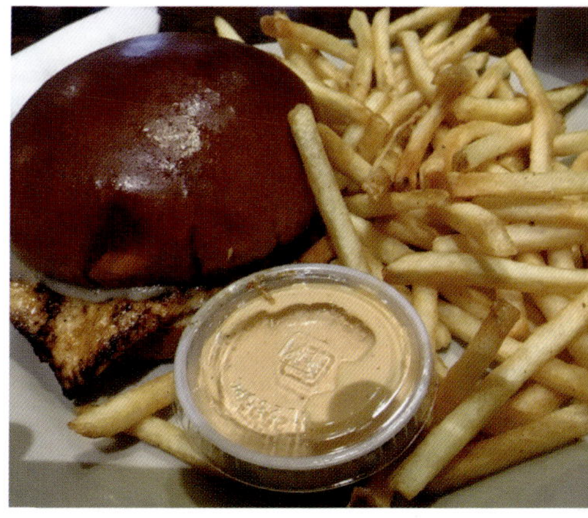

**Bek's Restaurant, Fulton**

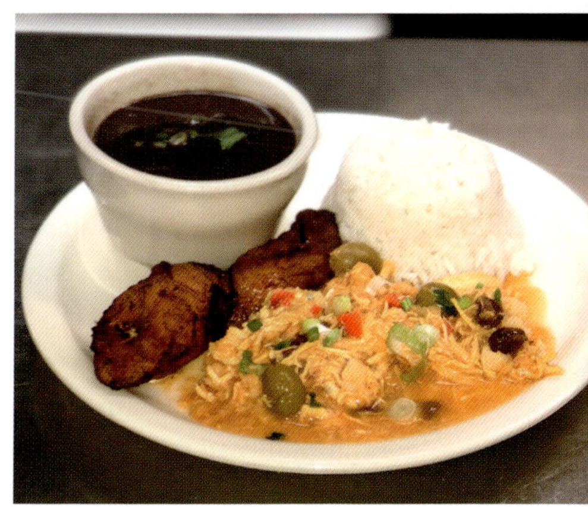

**Fulton Café, Fulton**

Downtown's Fulton Café is owned by John and Betty Atkinson. Betty is from Cuba and brings her native dishes to Missouri. Few Midwestern towns can boast a Cuban restaurant, but besides serving soup, sandwiches, and salads, Fulton's Café offers a menu of typical Cuban choices. Favorites include Cuban sandwiches and shrimp creole, and each dish is served with plantains. One more must-try downtown restaurant is Brooklyn Pizza. Owner Brian Atkins is originally from Brooklyn and brings authentic recipes to Fulton.

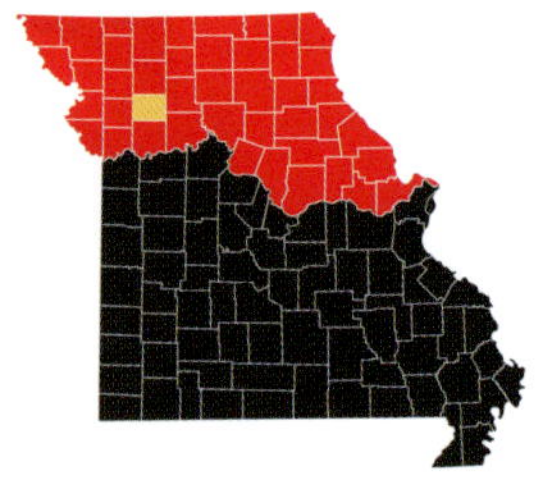

# 7

# *Hamilton*

What is found in small towns across America is amazing, especially in Missouri. A town of just eighteen hundred inhabitants has launched two major retail revolutions over the past hundred years, with results that rippled across the country. One is commemorated in a museum on Davis Street. The other is only in its eleventh year, but already owns twenty-six buildings in town.

This town is Hamilton, which dates back to 1855, shortly before the Civil War, and was named after Alexander Hamilton and his brother Joseph. Railroad traffic and eventually coal mining brought growth to this prairie-land location. Unlike most southern and central western Missouri settlements, Hamilton survived the Civil War mostly unscathed. A company from the 50th Illinois Infantry was sent to protect Union-supportive Hamilton from Confederate Bushwhackers.

In 1875, the town's most famous citizen was born: James Cash Penney, founder of the J. C. Penney retail stores. The first store was opened in 1902, though not in Hamilton, or even in Missouri, but in Wyoming. Hamilton did have the privilege of receiving the five-hundredth J. C. Penney location in 1924. At its height, the company had over two thousand stores across the United States and Puerto Rico. Today, Hamilton remembers James Cash Penney with a local museum and as the namesake of the local high school.

Penney's fame and impact will be difficult to eclipse, but Jenny Doan might be the Hamiltonian to do so. Doan is a founding member and public

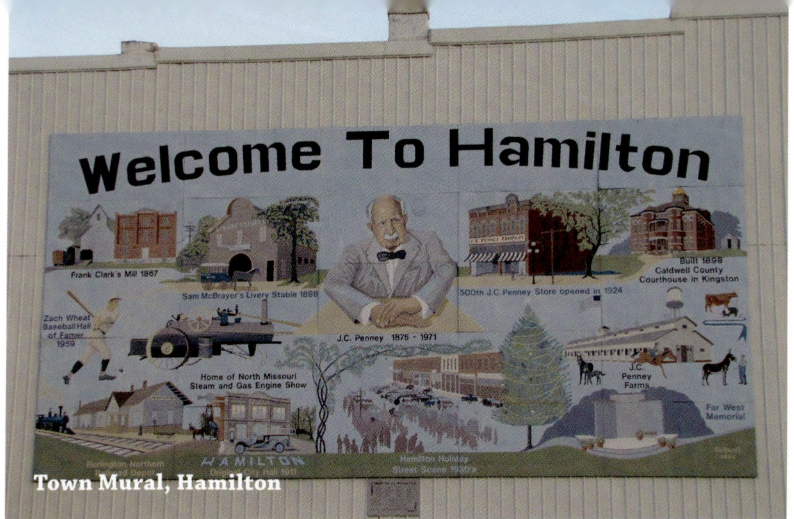

Town Mural, Hamilton

face of the growing quilting empire Missouri Star Quilt Company, owned by her children Sarah Galbraith and Alan Doan and their business partner David Mifsud. The company is an international phenomenon that grew out of Doan's children getting her started with a small quilting business in Hamilton. The kids purchased a dilapidated old building and a longarm quilting machine and encouraged Jenny to record tutorials on quilting and upload them to YouTube, where they became a hit. Her videos have been viewed over 138 million times as of 2018. Her engaging personality and the time-saving methods she uses to produce a quilt in days versus months resonated with quilters around the world. The popularity of those videos has led to the Missouri Star Quilt Company becoming a true quilting destination in Hamilton, bringing in millions of dollars in revenue for the company.

## MUST DO

The famed retailers are the main attractions. J. C. Penney's museum is a fascinating journey through American retail history. One interesting note is that Penney was always very hands-on in his stores, and in 1940 he happened into one of his stores in Des Moines where he advised a young man on how to package a purchase with less paper. That young man, Sam Walton, would later surpass Penney in retail stores and revenue with his Walmart stores.

Missouri Star Quilt is growing so fast, there is no telling what new attractions they will have in town in the coming years, but today they host five to ten thousand guests a month, earning Hamilton the nickname the "Disneyland of Quilting." In 2018, Forbes reported eight thousand visitors

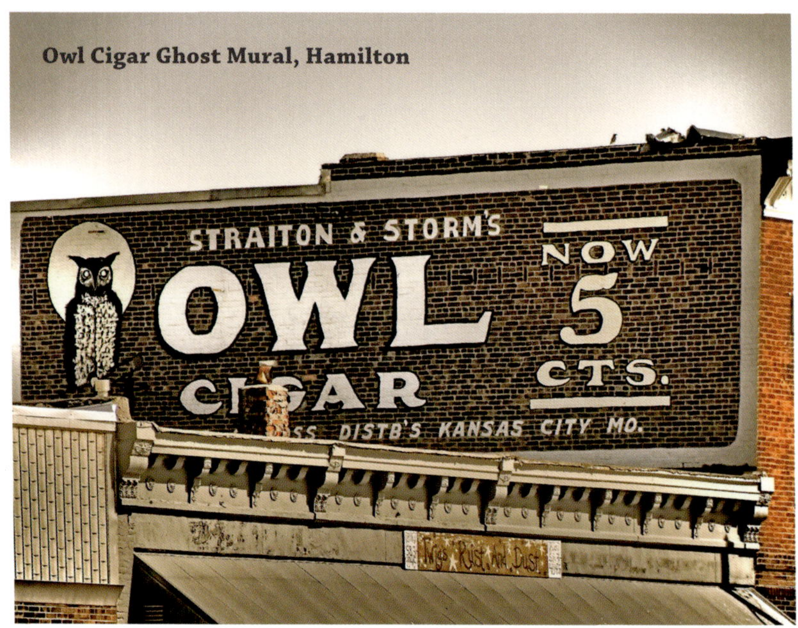

**Owl Cigar Ghost Mural, Hamilton**

a month. A sewing center has been built for quilting retreats and events. It sleeps thirty-seven people, has a large kitchen to feed the sewing parties, and hosts special events throughout the year.

Along with the sewing center, there are twelve quilting shops in Hamilton. There is even an excuse for husbands to accompany their quilting wives: "Man's Land" is full of recliners, televisions, and pool tables. Like other towns across Missouri, Hamilton has stunning murals painted on old downtown buildings.

## MUST SHOP

If you want to buy fabric, equipment, or quilts, this is Quilt Town, USA.

## MUST EAT

Missouri Star has worked with local restaurant owners to bring in new restaurants, and they are receiving grand reviews. If you're looking for a burger or milkshake, consider J's Burger Dive, owned by navy diver John Dawson—hence the play on words. If you are in the mood for barbecue, try Hank and Tank's BBQ. The ongoing growth of Missouri Star and Hamilton creates a continual increase in restaurants and treat shops.

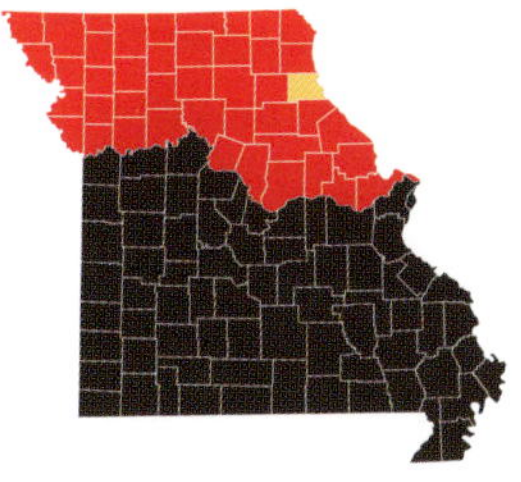

# 8

# Hannibal

For the Harry Potter fan, what would it mean to be able to walk the halls of Hogwarts? For the *Star Wars* fan, what would it mean to travel from planet to planet in a galaxy far, far away? For fans of *The Lord of the Rings* or *The Hobbit*, who wouldn't miss a chance to travel through Middle Earth?

Though none of those places exist, one famous author's fictional world is not so fictional. One can actually walk through the real-life locations featured in Mark Twain's *The Adventures of Tom Sawyer* and *The Adventures of Huckleberry Finn* and see the homes that inspired the characters and were described in the books, along with the real geographical landmarks. These landmarks took on different names in the books, but there's no mistaking the genuine articles when you visit Hannibal.

Mark Twain fans will want to make a pilgrimage to this northeastern Missouri river town, but the city is not just for Twain enthusiasts. Hannibal is slightly over the "small town" target size for this book, but its importance to the state, its incredible offerings, and its small-town feel prevent it from being left out. The city celebrated its bicentennial in 2019, as it traces its beginning back to 1819. It remained a sleepy town until Mark Twain's father and others organized the Hannibal and St. Joseph Railroad, which boosted Hannibal to third-largest city in Missouri at that time. It's far from that high ranking today.

The Mississippi River has been the lifeblood of the city, with its fixture as a port on the river north of St. Louis, and that lifeblood flowed through its most famous citizen, Samuel Langhorne Clemens, better known by his pen name, Mark Twain. Clemens moved in at age four and continued to live there until age eighteen. Though he traveled the world and lived most of his life in other places, it was those boyhood years that framed his most notable writings. Therefore, it's right that his boyhood home has been enshrined and is open to visitors today.

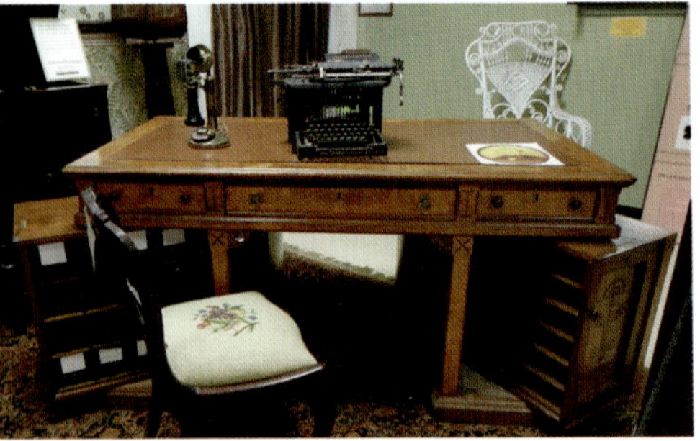

**Mark Twain Boyhood Home and Museum, Hannibal**

As mentioned, Hannibal is not just for Twain fans, but the aura that captivated audiences through his books can be felt as one walks along the banks of the Mississippi, or on the cobblestones lying between the restored buildings of his past, or through downtown. It's as if the nineteenth-century American river port life has been preserved for modern-day visitors.

## MUST DO

You would think that the Mark Twain Boyhood Home and Museum would be the main attraction of Hannibal, but review after review lists another stop as the number-one thing to do: a stay at and tour of Rockcliffe Mansion. Rockcliffe is now a bed-and-breakfast offering an elegant and historical experience. The home was completed in 1902 and served as the residence of John J. Cruikshank Jr., who had made a fortune in the lumber business and built the home to display his finest woods and furnishings. Following his death, the mansion was unoccupied for forty-three years, leaving it in bad shape, but since then it has been restored to its original grandeur and is a popular destination. It sits several blocks from the riverbank and rests on a limestone cliff (hence the name), offering stunning views of the river and town in between. Much of the recent attraction comes from the rumors of paranormal activity within the mansion, and numerous paranormal investigators have studied the bed-and-breakfast. The mansion also relates to Twain, as he visited the home on his last trip to Hannibal in 1902, and it captures the "high society" aspect of the town at the start of the twentieth century.

Mark Twain's Boyhood Home and Museum is a phenomenal experience. It's not just one stop, but multiple buildings. His actual boyhood home is the focal point and was the family home from 1843 to 1853. In 1912 it became the property of the City of Hannibal and was opened to the public. Since that time more buildings have been added. Tours are available in the two-story home, which features period furnishings along with Twain artifacts. The highlight for readers of Twain's novels is attached to the side of the home: a white wooden fence, a reminder of the fence Tom Sawyer was told to paint but tricked others into painting for him. In 1935 the WPA Stone Building was added. For years it served as the museum, but as the museum grew it became the Boyhood Home Gift Shop. Also on site is the Office of John Marshall Clemens, Twain's father. Warner Brothers bought the two-story office building and gave it to the city in 1943. In 1956, it was moved to its current location.

Also part of the museum properties is Grant's Drug Store, which is the oldest building and dates back to 1846. Twain writes in his autobiography that it was the place his father died. It is still under restoration, but the first floor has been recreated as a drug store of the era. Across from Twain's boyhood home was the home of Laura Hawkins. In his river novels, Twain modeled Tom Sawyer after himself. In *The Adventures of Tom Sawyer,* he is in love with Becky Thatcher, and Laura Hawkins was the real person Becky was based on. Laura's childhood home remains and is rightfully named the Becky Thatcher Home. Elsewhere stands the Huckleberry Finn House. Huck is Tom's best friend in the novels, and Tom Blankenship was the real-life inspiration for Huck. The Blankenships' family home was demolished, but eventually the land where it sat was given to the museum, and the home has been reconstructed using salvaged materials.

In addition to the homes, there is a museum downtown that offers numerous exhibits on Twain and his books. Other attractions are traced back to Twain, too, such as the Mark Twain Lighthouse. Originally built in 1935, it was wiped out by a windstorm and rebuilt in 1963. It sits on top of Cardiff Hill, which in the books was called Holiday Hill, and was a favorite play spot for Huck and Tom. South of town is the Mark Twain Cave, where the first organized guided tour was led in 1886, making this the oldest official cave tour in Missouri. As you might gather, the cave can be found in Twain's writings.

In keeping with the Twain theme, the Mark Twain Riverboat offers tours and dinner cruises on the Mississippi River. A riverboat cruise is not unique to Hannibal, but taking the cruise on the river made so famous by Twain and hearing the lore associated with him and the area make it special.

While you're in Hannibal, don't miss a visit to another historical home there: the Molly Brown Birthplace and Museum. Margaret Brown, better known as "The Unsinkable Molly Brown," was one of the few survivors of the sinking of the *Titanic* in 1912. After being rescued in a lifeboat, she helped lead continued efforts to look for other survivors. Her survivor status allowed her to rally support for many important causes throughout her life. Her birthplace home is available to be toured today, along with a museum of her life and her survival story.

Another attraction to check out in Hannibal is the high point of Lover's Leap, which has a fascinating history and offers striking views of the city and river. Also, the downtown area has many great shops to explore, and Big River Train Town is a spot for both children and children at heart. The shop is full of train memorabilia and features large toy train exhibits.

Several festivals and events are held in town annually, but the most popular is the Big River Steampunk Festival. Steampunk is a sci-fi genre that connects future technology with turn-of-the-century tech and lifestyle. The rich history of Hannibal at the turn of the century has made this festival very attractive to steampunkers around the country.

## MUST EAT

Several great restaurants are scattered around town. The overwhelming favorite is the Labinnah Bistro. It's small, and you will want to call ahead for a reservation, but it is a real treat that patrons travel to from miles away to enjoy. Familiar American cuisine is given international flair, transporting diners to the cafés of Europe. Much of the cuisine is Mediterranean influenced. This is a special place not just in flavor but in overall experience. They also serve up unique appetizers and breathtaking desserts. Other favorites in Hannibal are Fiddlesticks Food and Spirits and the Becky Thatcher Diner.

As good as each of these three restaurants is, the highlight in town is Java Jive. Jive is a coffeehouse that began in a downtown pottery shop.

The response to the coffeehouse has been so positive that the owners ended up closing the pottery business to expand the coffeehouse. Java Jive has become the hangout center in downtown Hannibal. Along with great coffee, it offers ice cream, bakery items, sandwiches, salads, and soups.

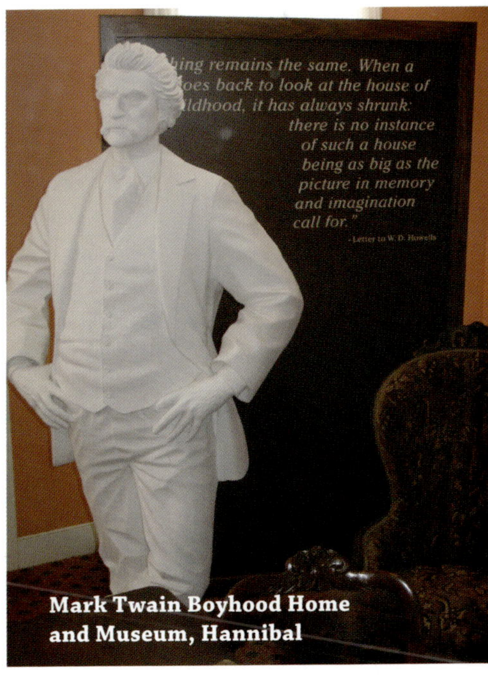

Mark Twain Boyhood Home and Museum, Hannibal

## MUST STAY

Although the Rockcliffe Mansion sets the bar high, there are several other great options for an overnight stay. One that may surpass even the Rockcliffe in elegance is the Garth Woodside Mansion bed-and-breakfast. The historic luxury and beauty of the rooms are breathtaking. Other choices are Main Street Bed and Breakfast and the Belvedere Inn. Modern hotels are available, but if you are seeking to immerse yourself in the history of the famous river town and truly capture the aura, you'll want to pay extra and pretend to be a turn-of-the-century lumber baron arriving to explore the gateway to the west.

## MUST SHOP

Historic attractions dominate the town, but specialty shops like Chocolaterie Stam, Hickory Stick Quilt Shop, Mississippi Marketplace, Native American Trading Co., and Puddin' Heads are mixed in too. Chocolaterie Stam will blow your mind and your taste buds. The European chocolate company has been in business since 1913. They feature fifty-five different flavors of chocolate. And although neighboring Hamilton is Quilt Town, USA, Hannibal's Hickory Stick Quilt Shop has long been one of the nation's top quilting stores. The shop has been in operation for close to forty years and has been ranked in the top ten quilting stores in North America.

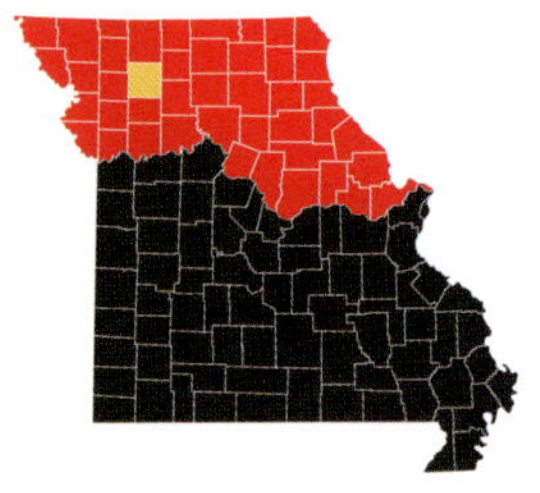

# 9

# Jamesport

The search is over. Here it is: "The best day trip in Missouri." Eighty-nine other day trips are mentioned in this book, but this is the slogan of Jamesport, and a trip to this town is right up there among the best day-long getaways.

Jamesport is home to the largest Old Order Amish settlement not only in Missouri but west of the Mississippi River. This Amish influence provides a step back in time. You will see and pass several horses and buggies while there. Numerous shops offer homemade, direct from the farm or shop, groceries and goods. Visitors enjoy leaving the quick pace of their towns and slowing down—to a consistent twenty-five miles per hour.

The town dates back to 1857, as does much of the Amish way of life practiced there, but the Amish citizens actually did not move into the area until 1950. You will find here a unique blend of small-town rural America and the old way of life.

## MUST DO

Drive around, take it in, let the kids see how life used to be. Let the history textbooks come to life. The working farms and shops associated with lots of countryside stores are fascinating to watch and admire. There's a good chance you will luck into some kind of special event because the area is not merely a tourist stop but rather an invitation to experience life as it was lived two centuries ago.

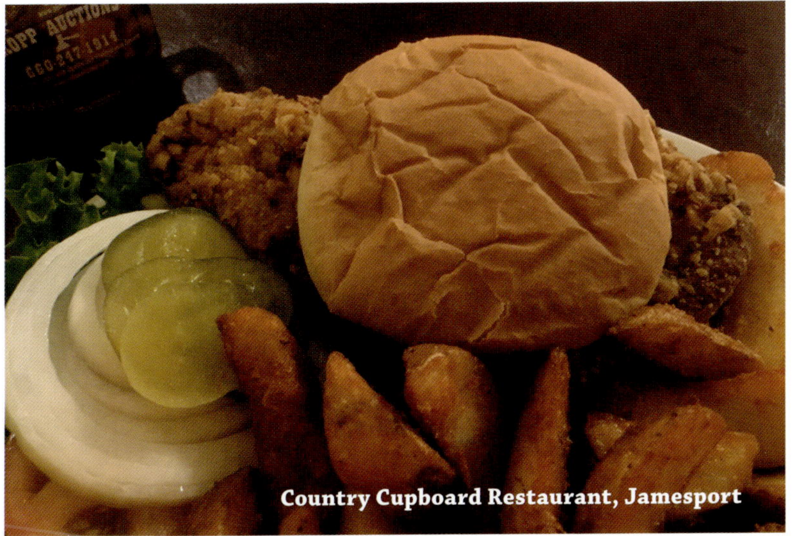
Country Cupboard Restaurant, Jamesport

For first-timers, tours by Step Back in Time Tours allow one to see how the community works and get an overview of all that's available to enjoy. In subsequent trips you can then know what you want to revisit or explore in more depth. If you admire woodworking or homemade crafts, there are several shops to view.

## MUST SHOP

The community has a lengthy list of country stores, specialty shops, and antique shops. Simply Primitive Antiques and Collectibles is one of the favorite antique stops. There is no telling what you can find, so you better come in a big vehicle. Another favorite stop is the H & M Country Store, which features locally made foods and bulk foods at low prices. You'll find a great selection of candy that will divert your attention as well. In visiting these stores, be prepared to pet a goat or some other livestock.

Furniture stores are a highlight. Stop into one of these stores and admire the fine, solid pieces. Second only to the furniture is the food, and several places sell homemade canned goods, preserves, and jellies. Countryside Bakery will have your mouth watering with all kinds of custom homemade treats. Definitely give the specialty loaves of bread a look, especially the jalapeño cheese bread. And don't buy just one loaf; that would be a mistake.

## MUST EAT

Among the restaurants in town, the overwhelming favorite is the Gingerich Dutch Pantry, where everything on the typical Midwestern menu is great, whether it's a sandwich or a dinner plate. Whatever you do, don't leave without trying their amazing mashed potatoes and unique Dutch pepper slaw. Also in town is the Country Cupboard Restaurant, which tempts hungry diners with a large tenderloin sandwich.

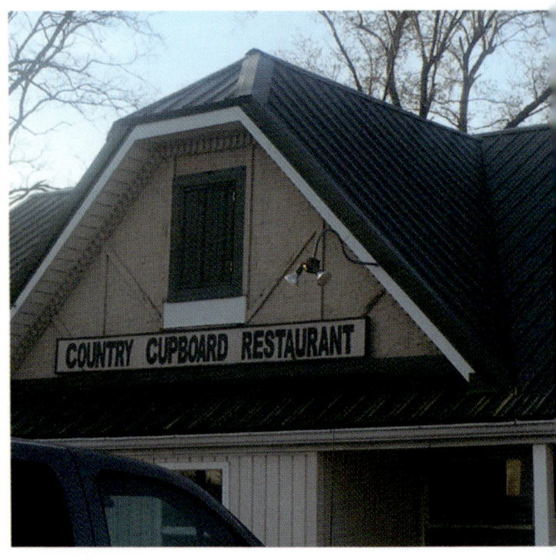


**Country Cupboard Restaurant, Jamesport**

## MUST STAY

The Arbor House Country Inn offers a stay that matches the timeless flavor of the town. They have several personalized rooms to pick from. You'll feel like you're on an Amish farm, but with the modern amenities that you enjoy.

## MUST NOTE

Although it's known for being home to one of the area's largest Amish communities, the town's history is more diverse. Jamesport is the birthplace and hometown of Dr. F. C. "Phog" Allen, a revered college basketball coach known as the "father of basketball coaching." He is the "Allen" of the famed Allen Fieldhouse in Lawrence, Kansas. He coached the University of Kansas Jayhawks for thirty-nine seasons, reaching nearly six hundred wins, twenty-four conference championships, and three national championships.

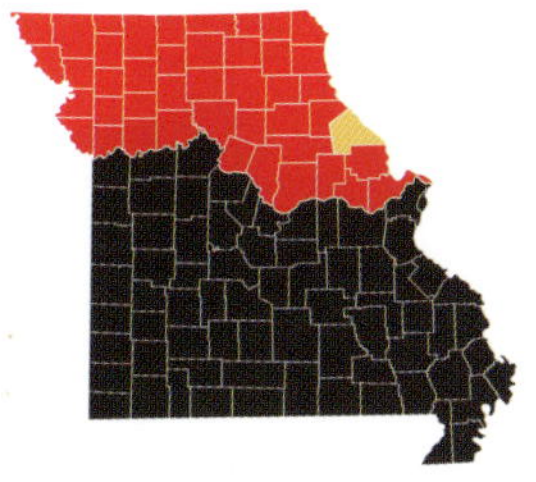

# 10

# *Louisiana*

Surprisingly, the name of this northeastern Missouri town has nothing to do with the state or the territory purchased in 1803 from the French. Rather it was named for Louisiana Basye, the daughter of the town's founder, John Walter Basye. Founded in 1816, Louisiana is between Hannibal and Clarksville on the Great River Road and offers a different take on northern port cities on the Mississippi. Like both Hannibal and Clarksville, Louisiana sits directly on the riverbank, and its history is deeply rooted in its role as a port city. But this middle river town reflects more of the industrial aspect of river traffic. As you drive into town, you pass mills, factories, and warehouses from the past and the present.

Although the most "working" town of these ports, it is not void of historic elements. The Missouri Department of Natural Resources notes that the town has "the most intact Victorian Streetscape in the state." A visitor who drives through is likely to say, "This must have once been a huge town." That's not necessarily the case, but there are a lot of old downtown buildings. The Georgia Street Historic District, for example, consists of fifty-five historic buildings built before 1935. The most striking of these is the Masonic Temple. Many of these historic buildings have been refurbished as restaurants, lodging, and other current businesses. The Eagle's Nest, which offers wine tasting, shopping, dining, and lodging, has repurposed several of the Georgia Street buildings.

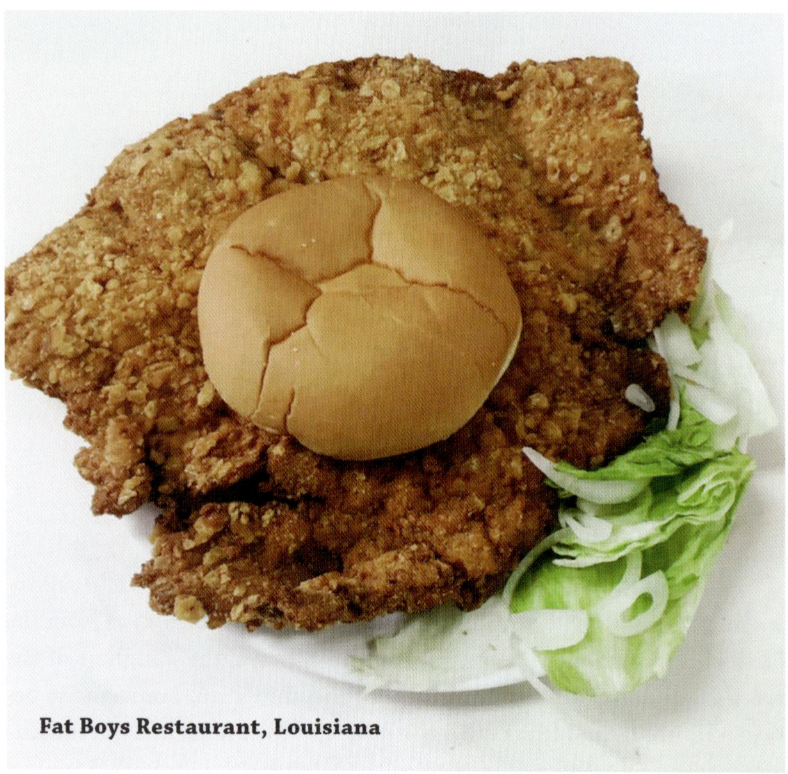

Fat Boys Restaurant, Louisiana

## MUST STAY

The Eagle's Nest Inn and bed-and-breakfast is an atmospheric getaway where nostalgia meets modern amenities. The historic downtown location just a few blocks from the riverbank makes this a fun stay.

## MUST EAT

Josephine's Bakery, which is connected to the Eagle's Nest, is a must-stop for dessert, especially for the cinnamon rolls or sticky buns. The bakery and winery both offer a quality lunch special. But the highlight of Louisiana restaurants is Fat Boys. Its name forewarns how you will feel when you leave. All of the comfort food choices are done well, especially the catfish. Though catfish is typically more common farther south, Fat Boys does it right. There's just something magical about eating fried catfish while feeling the breeze from the nearby Mississippi. Tenderloin sandwiches are a staple in this area, and Fat Boys knocks them out of the

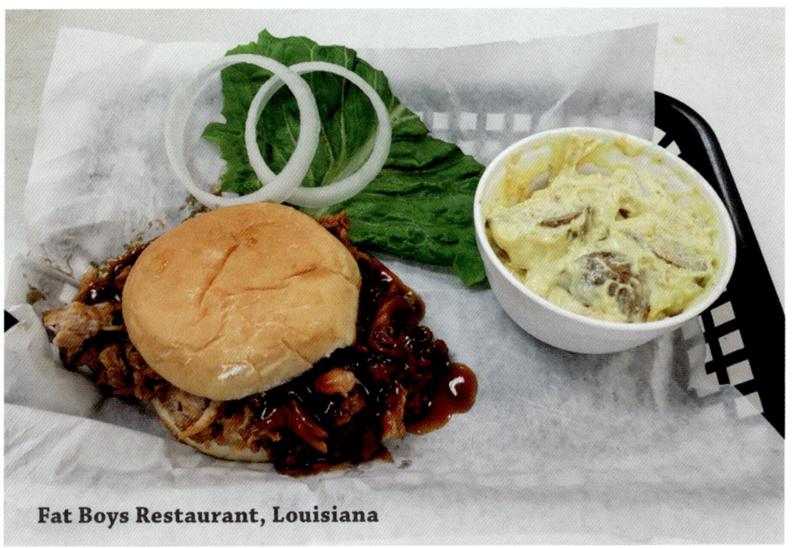
Fat Boys Restaurant, Louisiana

park with some of the biggest and tastiest around the Midwest. Often the side dish has to be placed on top of the tenderloin because it's so big. It's hard to believe that the bun really is normal sized because it looks so small compared to the meat.

## MUST DO

A stay and a wine tasting at the Eagle's Nest is an entire vacation on its own, but while in town, visitors should cruise down Georgia Street to see the historic buildings and walk along the river. The Louisiana History Museum is very nice as well. And if you like to catch regional events, each fall the town puts on Colorfest, which has entertainment, crafts, and food vendors.

## MUST NOTE

An interesting fact about Louisiana is that following World War II, scientists from Nazi Germany were brought in through Operation Paperclip to work at a plant to help produce liquid hydrocarbon fuels.

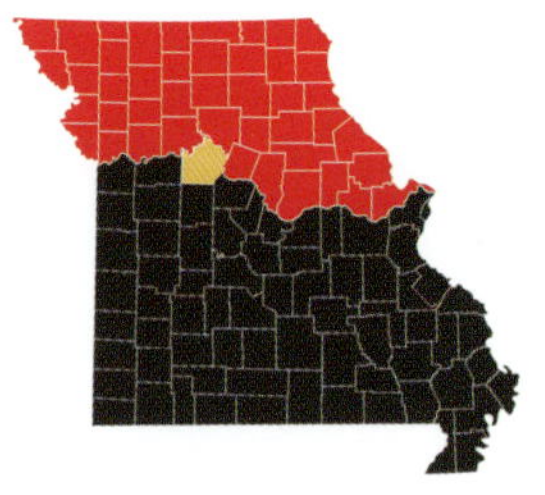

# 11

# Marshall

In this journey through small-town Missouri, two towns are home to famous dogs, or maybe more accurately, the dogs made the towns famous. One dog was commended for his loyalty, and the other for having special powers. Marshall is the final home of the one with special powers: Jim the Wonder Dog. The story seems too strange for real life, but it's true. Marshall has a statue memorializing Jim.

Marshall was established in 1839 and named after Supreme Court Justice John Marshall. It was a farming community. During the Civil War, it was occupied by Union soldiers, which subjected it to Confederate raids. After the war, it became home to Missouri Valley College, which is still a thriving liberal arts college today.

During the 1920s, the Nicholas-Beazley Airplane Company made the town a player in the airplane industry. The company did well until eventually closing in 1937. Its main aircraft, the NB-3, is on exhibit at the Nicholas-Beazley Aviation Museum at the Marshall Airport.

But the most intriguing saga from the city's past is Jim the Wonder Dog. Jim was a Llewellin setter from Louisiana that was bought by avid quail hunter Sam VanArsdale in 1925. Jim was such a good hunting dog that *Outdoor Life* magazine named him "The Hunting Dog of the Country." Mr. VanArsdale found that Jim could tell trees apart and would go to whatever tree he was asked to go to. If told to go to the hickory, he would go. If told to go to the walnut, cedar, and on down the line, he would go. On top of that, Jim was able to point out details on command, like picking

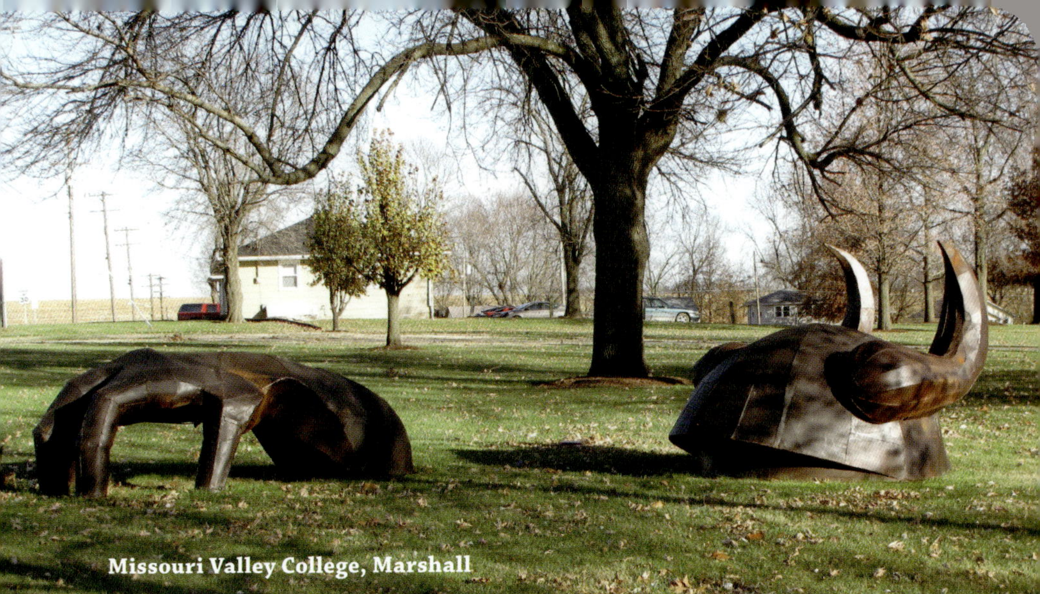
Missouri Valley College, Marshall

a certain car make, a person's profession, and much more. He could carry out commands in different languages—even Morse code. His most remarkable talent was predicting future events, like the sex of unborn babies. He even chose the winner of seven Kentucky Derbies and the World Series.

Jim was examined by veterinarians at the University of Missouri in Columbia and psychologists at Washington University in St. Louis. Dr. Durant from the University of Missouri concluded that the dog "possessed an occult power that might never come again to a dog in many generations," as the *Rural Missouri* reported. Jim passed away and was buried in Marshall. In 1999, a statue of Jim by Andy Davis was erected in town.

## MUST DO

The statue of Jim and a memorial park to him sits at the location where his owner, Sam VanArsdale, had a hotel. It's an interesting aspect of history to take in. Also, at the Marshall Airport is the Nicholas-Beazley Aviation Museum, which is especially fascinating for airplane enthusiasts.

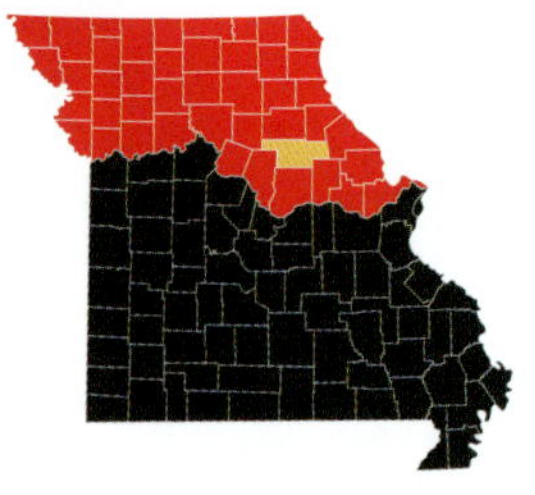

# 12

# Mexico

It's understandable that a state named New Mexico would border Mexico, but a town named New Mexico in northern Missouri? That's a different story. The town of New Mexico was a regular stopping point for settlers who were traveling to the country of Mexico, which at that time consisted of modern-day Texas. In 1836, Texas gained independence from Mexico, which led to the dropping of "New" from the town's name. As its name suggests, Mexico has had an international impact. Once it was known as the "Fire Brick Capital of the World," for it was one of the leading manufacturing sites of fire brick, a refractory brick used to line fireplaces and furnaces and used in the most heat-stressed industries. In 2002, the plant closed, and there is no longer any quarrying in the area.

But Mexico has had another international influence, as it was known as the "Saddle Horse Capital of the World." Saddlebreds are an American horse breed that was the top choice for officers of the Revolutionary War and Civil War. They are known for their impressive looks, intelligence, and comfortable ride. They also became the most popular riding horses in America. Mexico became the central location of this breed when in 1885 Cyrus F. Clark and Joseph A. Potts built the "The Big Barn on the Boulevard." In 1949, famed horseman Arthur Simmons took ownership of these famous stables and took them to new heights. The 254-foot stable ceased operation in 2001 and is being remodeled, but at one time it was the oldest and largest public US stable in continual use as a horse facility. During that time, other saddlebred stables popped up, and the most famous saddlebred trainers were drawn to work near Mexico.

One of these trainers was Tom Bass. He trained in the Mexico area and is buried in Mexico. At Bass's death, Will Rogers wrote in a syndicated column carried by *The New York Times*, "Tom Bass . . . died today. Don't mean much to you, does it? You have all seen society folk perform on a beautiful three- or five-gaited horse and said, 'My, what skill and patience they must have had to train that animal.' Well, all they did was ride him. All Tom Bass did was train him. He trained thousands of horses that others were applauded on." Some of those he trained for were Buffalo Bill Cody, Theodore Roosevelt, Will Rogers, and others. He trained many horses for Hollywood. Making Tom's story even more fascinating is that he was born into slavery.

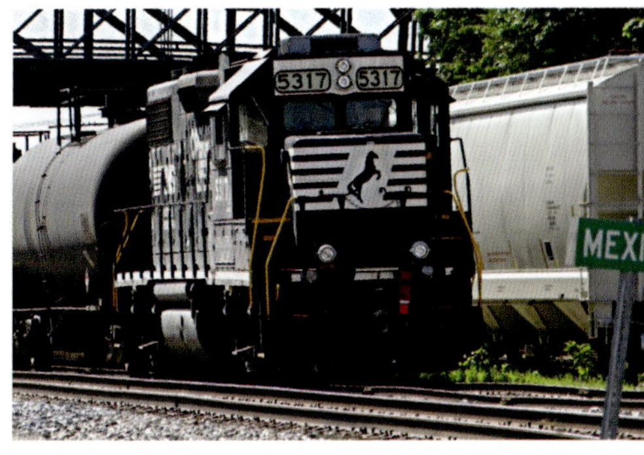

**Mexico Train Depot, Mexico**

In Mexico today you can catch a glimpse of this history through Simmons Stables, which is still standing, and other historic buildings related to the American saddlebred horse. Mexico is also home to the American Saddlebred Horse Museum, located at the Graceland Mansion, which is also the site of the Audrain County Historical Society Museum.

## MUST EAT

A trip back in time for early-twentieth-century horsemanship will leave you with a need for lunch, and Dagwood Jr. is the place to stop. Dagwood features sub sandwiches and salads, and the overwhelming favorite is the Reuben.

## MUST STAY

A. P. Green was also an American saddlebred owner in Mexico during its heyday, and his large home is still open as a bed-and-breakfast. The A. P. Green House Bed and Breakfast offers an enjoyable stay that mixes the past with modern amenities.

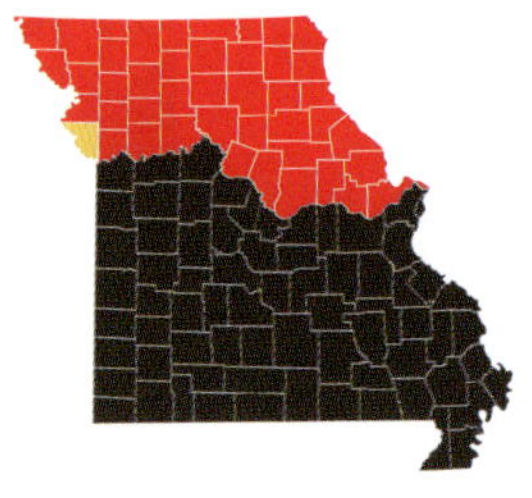

# 13

# Parkville

Parkville is a small-town treat that has been pulling folks the ten miles from Kansas City for a long time. The main draw is the laid-back atmosphere along with the quaint shops and restaurants of Main Street and the English Landing Center. In 2018, downtown Parkville received the Great Neighborhood Award from the American Planning Association Great Places in Missouri. Numerous publications have recognized the town for its cleanliness and beauty. A trip into town clearly verifies what all the fuss is about. If you park in the English Landing parking lot and walk up to the corner of English Landing Drive and Main Street, you're able to see the Missouri River to the south, look up Main Street at the line of shops, and then see the centerpiece of Park University, Mackay Hall, that stands like a castle on a hill above the town.

The town was named after its founder, George S. Park. Park lived an adventurous life. He was a hero of the Texas War of Independence, being one of the few survivors from the Goliad Massacre, where over four hundred captive Texas soldiers were killed and their bodies piled up and left to rot. After a short stint teaching school, Park traveled into the Platte Purchase to establish a steamboat landing at what is Parkville today. In 1844, the city was platted. A year later Park established the Parkville Presbyterian church. He is also credited with the founding of Manhattan, Kansas.

On leaving Parkville to move to Illinois in 1875, Park gave land to John A. McAfee to establish Park College, which in 2000 became

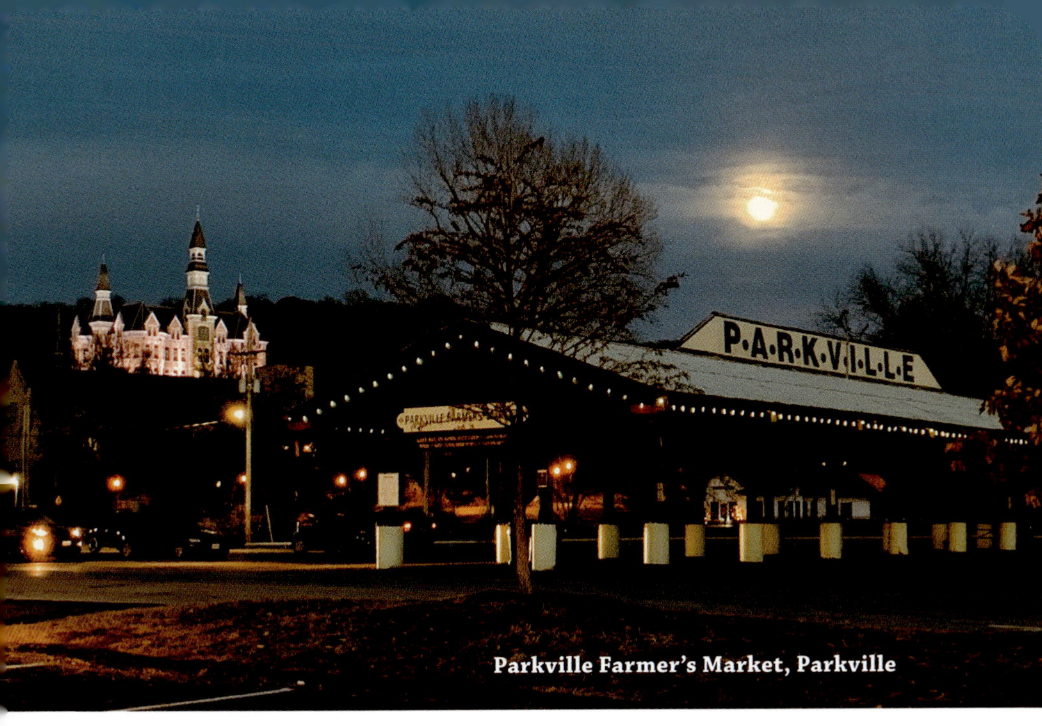

Parkville Farmer's Market, Parkville

Park University. McAfee commenced what he deemed the "Parkville Experiment" in which students would receive free tuition by doing work at businesses located at the college. It proved to be a success. In 1886, the trademark building of the university was built, Mackay Hall. Its three stories feature a tall clock tower and spire with other tall towers. All of the construction, even the quarrying of limestone, was done on campus by students. The college originally prepared Presbyterian missionaries, but the university is no longer affiliated with the church.

## MUST EAT

The draw for guests is to stroll down Main Street shopping and eating. There are many great restaurants on Main Street and throughout town. Overwhelmingly, the favorite of guests is Café des Amis, a bistro offering elegant dining and genuine, traditional French cuisine. It's considered one of the most romantic restaurants in the Kansas City area. Each dish is a work of art, and there's likely to be a beautiful flower garnishing it. During good weather, patio seating is a magical option.

Although the following three restaurants don't have the romantic mystique of Café des Amis, they do have great grub. Nick and Jake's is a hit restaurant with multiple locations around the Kansas City area. It serves a combination of gourmet meals with much-loved American bar food, along with top-end steakhouse meals. Stone Canyon Pizza Co. is the place to go for pizza. They have been recognized as one of the top one hundred independent pizzerias in the country. Though their pizza is fabulous, they have much more on the menu. White Horse Inn is more than just a horse, it's a bit of a unicorn: a British eatery in small-town Missouri. And if you're in need of coffee, Parkville Coffee offers a great atmosphere and on-site roasted coffee.

## MUST SHOP

The wonderful shopping choices are simply too numerous to cover comprehensively, but three stand out. First is Bentley Guitar Studios. If you're a musician, especially a guitarist, this place needs to be on your list. They sell top-end gear, both vintage and new. If you time it right, you can catch some live music. Second is a place that is fun to walk through even if you're not in the market for a new watch. Cool Vintage Watches was one of the first vintage watch stores on the internet, and this is their shop. They focus on men and women's watches, but in the store they have all kinds of hard-to-find vintage items. There's a huge selection of vinyl records, along with stereo equipment from the 1960s and 1970s. It's also the place to find antique radios, cameras, and typewriters. And last is the Farmhouse Collection. The main store is in Jamesport, but the Parkville location has a great selection of home décor, household items, and country cookware.

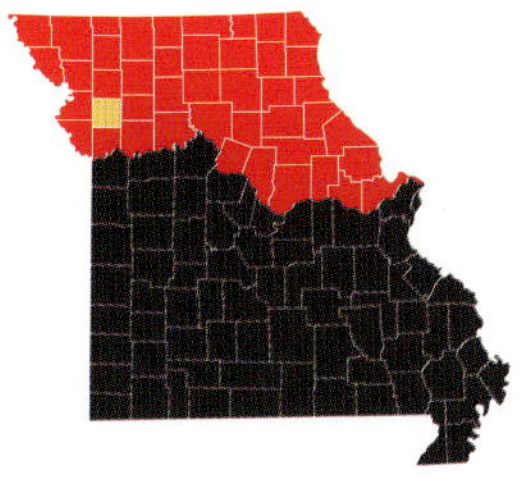

# 14

# Plattsburg

United States presidents have come from only forty different cities, and only one city has claim to a president who was president for only one day. That city is Plattsburg, the man was Senator David Rice Atchison, and the day was Sunday, March 4, 1849. In 1849, the March 4 Inauguration Day fell on a Sunday, so president-elect Zachary Tayler waited until the next day to be sworn in, as did vice president-elect Millard Fillmore. The previous president and vice president, James K. Polk and George M. Dallas, had left their positions. This left only Senator Atchison, who was third in line for succession. Scholars debate if he truly was president for that day, but his tombstone and monuments in town are sure he was.

Plattsburg has had an influential history. The area had long been the home of Native Americans. Once it was settled by European Americans, it was first called Concord and then Springfield. In the early 1830s, the town was the farthest-west non-military settlement of the United States. In 1835, it was named Plattsburg after Plattsburgh, New York, because the latter was the county seat of Clinton County, New York, and Plattsburg was in Clinton County, Missouri.

The area began to explode with settlers after the Platte Purchase of 1836, which expanded the northwest boundary of Missouri. Plattsburg served as a gateway to this new area and held the US land office for a while. Most settlers were from Kentucky and Virginia, leading it to be called "Little Dixie." Like the Bluegrass region of Kentucky, hemp and tobacco became the major crops and created the need for slaves. This led

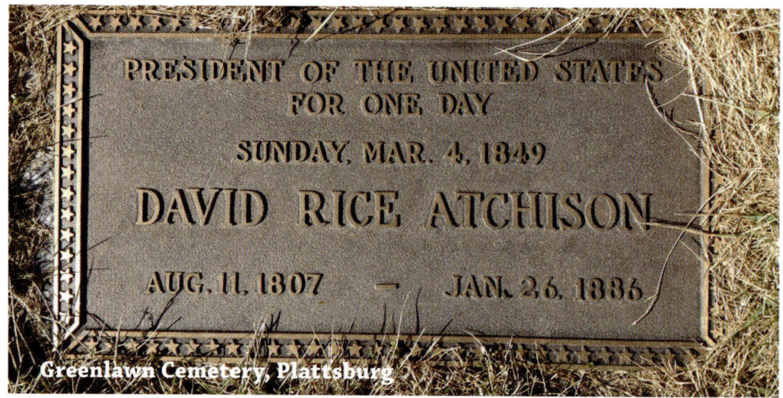

Greenlawn Cemetery, Plattsburg

to the area being sympathetic to the South during the Civil War. Two skirmishes happened here.

## MUST DO

The David Rice Atchison monuments are something to check out. Beyond the "president for a day" narrative, Atchison lived an extraordinary life as a US senator, major general of the Missouri State Militia during the Mormon War, and Confederate brigadier general under Major General Sterling Price.

A few miles down the road in Osborn is a unique opportunity perfect for families with young children. The Shatto Milk Company is a small, family-owned-and-operated dairy farm that is open for tours. Guests can bottle-feed a calf or even milk a cow.

## MUST EAT

If the home of the only-one-day president can't get you to Plattsburg, Sugar Whipped Bakery is a worthwhile drive from wherever you are in the state. The small, unassuming bakery is home to former New York City baker and pastry chef Melissa Fahlstrom. On a trip home to Kansas City, she fell in love with Plattsburg and found an empty bakery space. Each dessert has a big-city look and top-notch taste. The cupcakes and cookies look superb, but it's hard to pass up the s'more cake balls.

While in town for Sugar Whipped, if you want to grab a meal, check out James Kennedy Family Restaurant and have a prime melt and seasoned fries.

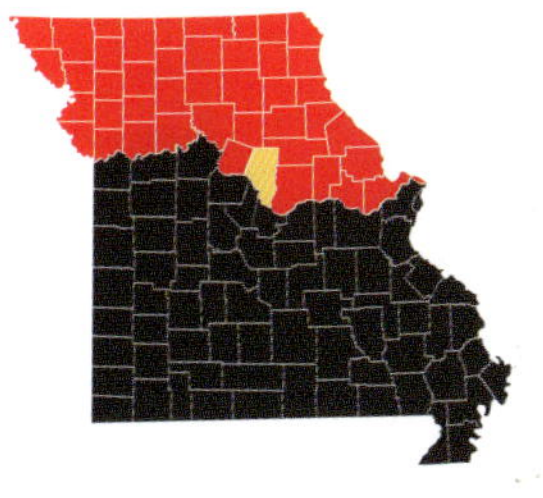

# 15

# Rocheport

There may be more bed-and-breakfasts in Rocheport than residents, and definitely more bikes to rent. A population of 239 has not kept Rocheport from being one of the most recognized and celebrated small-town destinations in Missouri. *Southern Living* magazine named it 2018's Best Tiny Town in Missouri and listed it as the tenth best tiny town in America. A stay in one of the area's delightful bed-and-breakfasts will help you understand its charm. Rocheport is one of Missouri's most romantic destinations and feels straight out of a Hallmark movie: small, quaint, charming, away from the busyness of life, and a place to realign your priorities.

*Southern Living* and other travel magazines aren't the first to find many things to report. In 1804, when the Lewis and Clark expedition came through, William Clark noted many things about the location. The bluffs along the Missouri River were the most striking. In fact, it's where the town's name comes from: Rocheport means "rocky port" in French. In 1806, more notes were recorded by Zebulon Pike, who led another expedition through the area. He wrote that at that time there was a combined village of Sauk, Meskwaki, and Ioway tribes. Soon after those expeditions, European-Americans settled the area, and it became a well-used trading post for settlers and Native Americans.

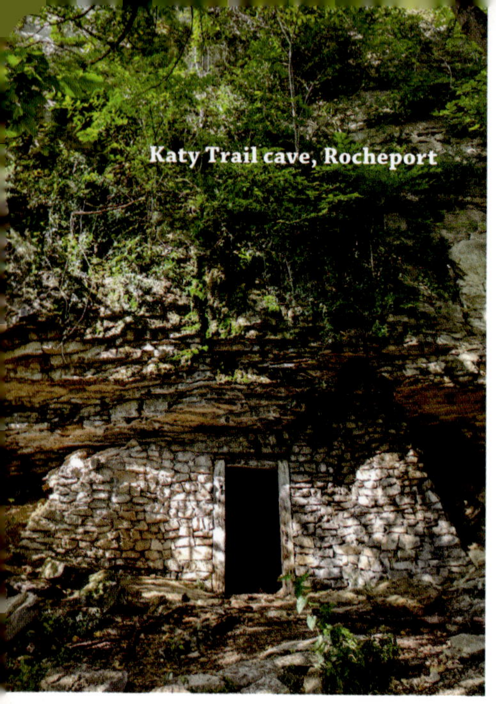
Katy Trail cave, Rocheport

## MUST DO

Rocheport sits near the center of the two-hundred-forty mile Katy Trail. The trail is a converted railway that has been made into a park for bicycling, hiking, and, in some areas, horseback riding. Launching onto the trail from Rocheport allows one to go east or west. Bicycles are available for rent near the trailhead.

Guests have to check out the trail, but the unique find in town is the bed-and-breakfasts. All offer a combination of historical context, modern amenities, and a friendly atmosphere.

## MUST STAY

Two inns to point out are located in town: the Yates House and the School House Bed and Breakfast. The Yates House has been recognized as the "Best Breakfast in the Midwest" and "One of Missouri's Top Destinations." It's a renovated 1840s home owned and operated by Dixie and Conrad Yates. The Yates House is a Select Registry property, which recognizes the house as a Distinguished Inn of North America.

The School House Bed and Breakfast is located in an elegantly converted 1914 school building. It has consistently been voted "Best B&B" in the *Rural Missouri* magazine Readers' Choice competition and was recently voted "One of the Top 3 B&Bs in the Midwest" by readers of *AAA Midwest Traveler* magazine. Four of the rooms have two-person whirlpool tubs.

Along with these bed-and-breakfasts and others, the area is full of Airbnb options. Lodging along the bluffs of the Missouri River offers great scenic views.

## MUST SHOP

In the tiny town you'll find both antique and specialty shops. The standout of these shops is the Shirahaze Gallery. It's an artisan workshop and store where ceramic artist Yukari Kashihara creates wheel-thrown, one-of-a-kind porcelain items. Each piece is hand-painted with slip, decorated with colors of underglaze, and high fired. Most of the designs feature nature. It's the type of shop you have to visit over and over, and you'll have a difficult time deciding what you are going to purchase. Whatever masterpiece you choose will become a treasure to you for years to come.

Another artisan shop to check out is Art and Antiques and Blacksmith Shop. It's a unique blend of artistic creations, but you'll enjoy seeing the creativity and craftsmanship.

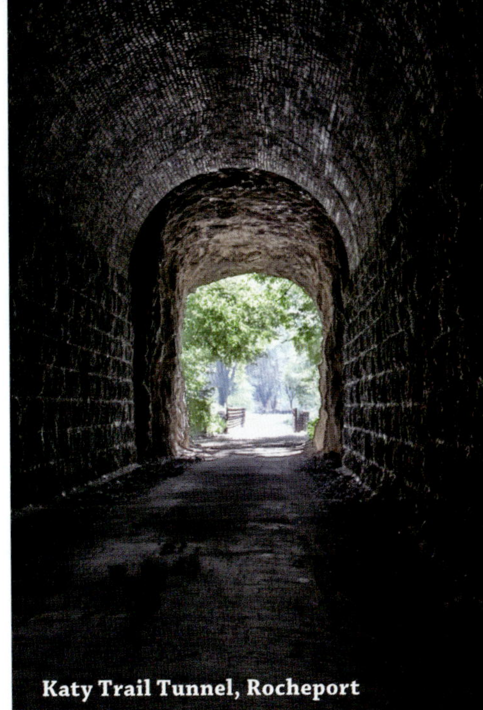

**Katy Trail Tunnel, Rocheport**

## MUST EAT

Breakfasts are covered by the chefs in the Rocheport bed-and-breakfasts, but if you go looking for a meal later in the day, Abigail's is everyone's favorite recommendation. Also, the Blufftop Bistro at Les Bourgeois Vineyard offers distinguished meals and a breathtaking view from the bluffs overlooking the river.

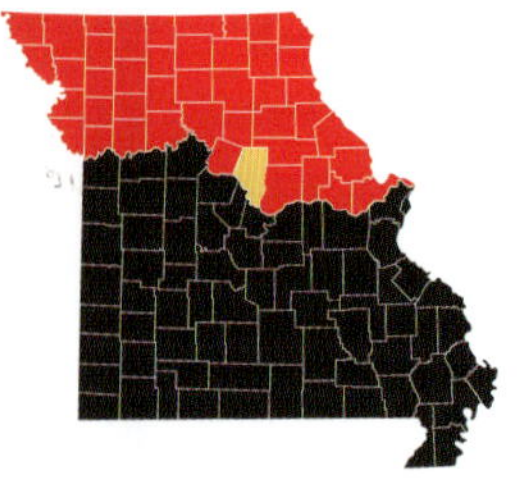

# 16

# Sturgeon

Sturgeon was platted in 1856 and grew rapidly due to completion of the North Missouri Railroad (now the Norfolk Southern). The town was so committed to the railroad that the name came from the superintendent of that railroad, Isaac H. Sturgeon. A trip through town reveals the railroad still plays a prominent role in the landscape.

Though rail commerce gave Sturgeon a rapid boost, a tornado and several fires plagued growth. An increase of a different group of settlers began in 1953, as the first Amish family moved in. Now many Amish families call the area home and operate multiple home-based businesses.

## MUST DO

This railroad town is now known for a natural area that's operated unlike almost any other park in the country and is home to one of the most unusual geological formations around. Pinnacles Youth Park is a 27-acre nature park that is privately owned but open to the public each day from 8:00 a.m. to sunset. The land was deeded to the youth of Boone County in 1965 and is overseen by the Boone County Pinnacles Youth Foundation.

It's the perfect outing for families, with a mix of difficult and mild hiking and lots to explore. The focal point of the property is the Pinnacles, a tall, thin, rocky ridge of stylolite that stretches between two creeks. Large holes pierce the rocky structure, giving it a stone skull look. While

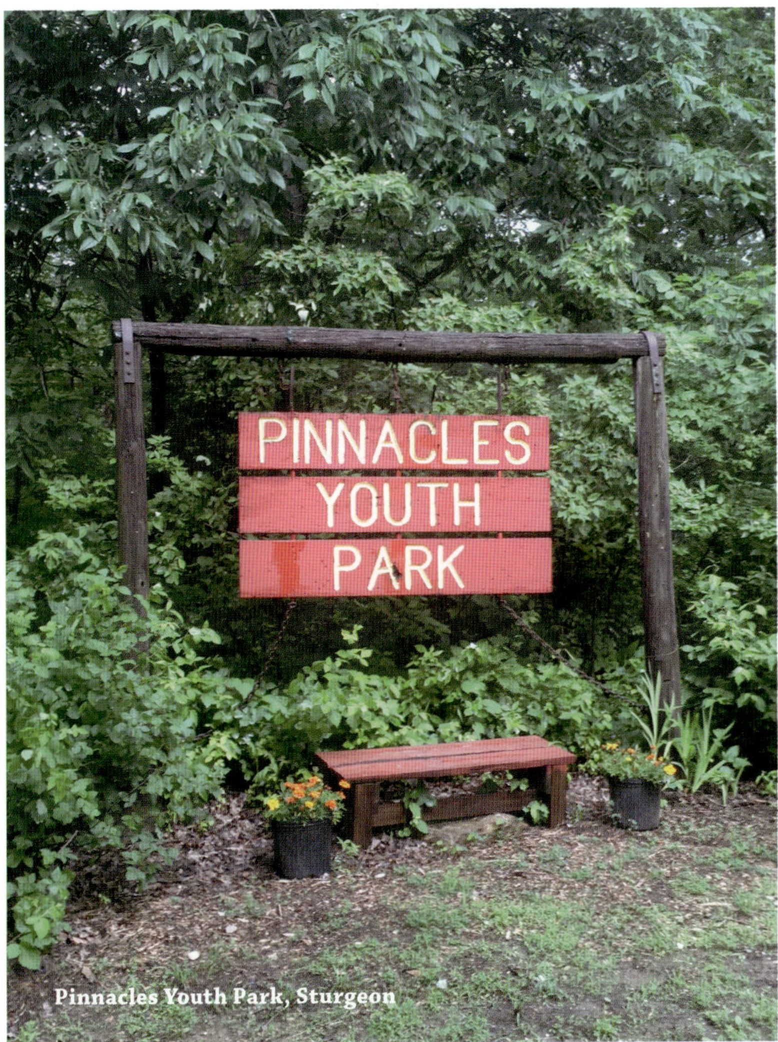

Pinnacles Youth Park, Sturgeon

you're exploring the rocky crags, keep an eye out for crinoids embedded in the limestone. These fossils of sea creatures point to an ancient time when the area was covered by water.

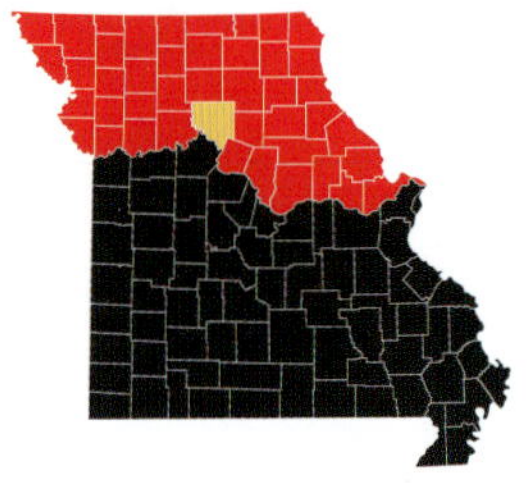

# 17

## Sumner

Where would you expect to find over one hundred thousand Canada geese or the "Wild Goose Capital of the World"? And where would you expect to find the world's largest Canada goose?

You probably would expect Canada, but that would be incorrect. The answer is Sumner, Missouri. Sumner bears the title "Wild Goose Capital of the World." And as you enter town from the west on Highway 139 after passing over Stanley Lake on your left you'll spot the World's Largest Goose: Maxie. Maxie is the perfect sculpture and landmark for Sumner; she stands forty feet tall with a wingspan of sixty-one feet and weighs in at four thousand pounds. She was sculpted by David C. Jackson in Kansas City and was flown into town by helicopter.

Long before being recognized for its geese, Sumner was a trading post established by Thomas Stanley. Stanley was one of the first European American settlers to explore the area before Missouri's statehood in 1821 and traveled the Grand River with two sons of the legendary Daniel Boone. The town remained a trading post for several years before being platted in 1882.

Disaster led to what brings visitors to this small town of barely over a hundred. The Dust Bowl of the 1930s prompted the US government to restore wetlands that had been drained for farming. One of the conservation refuges built in 1937 was the Swan Lake National Wildlife Refuge near Sumner. It was already a flyway, but the new wetlands created an attractive stop for geese and waterfowl. By the fourth year, eight hundred

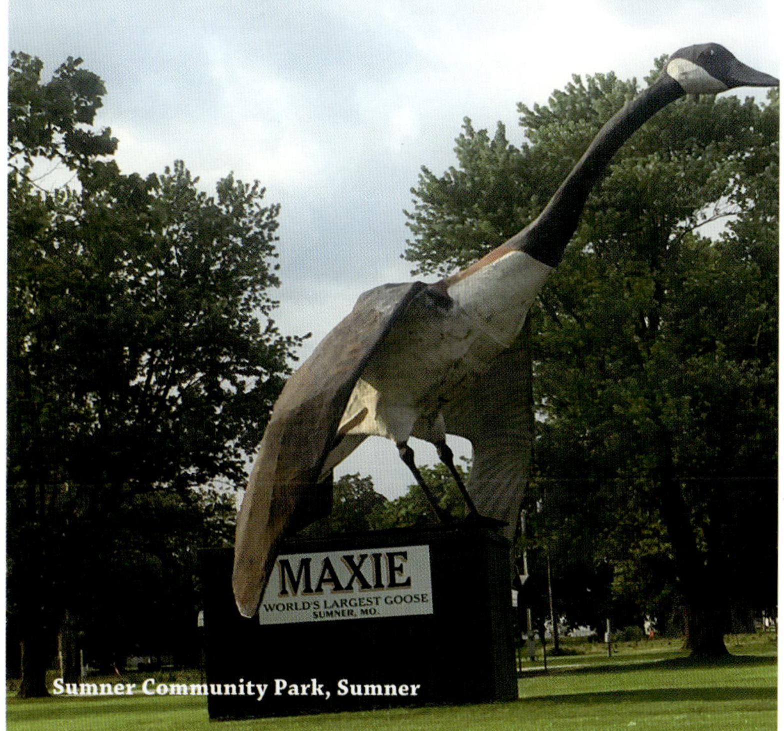

Sumner Community Park, Sumner

geese were wintering there, and by the 1980s the number had grown to over one hundred thousand.

## MUST DO

Maxie, the World's Largest Goose, is a sight to be seen. Also consider a drive to Sumner to catch a glimpse of the thousands of geese. A great time to do so is in October at the annual Goosefest, which began in 1955. If you're looking for a place to hunt geese, this is it. Habitat Flats, one of several outfitters in the area, offers comfortable lodging, great meals during the hunt, and well-managed wetlands. In late October they see tens of thousands of waterfowl on their private farms. An incredible experience is catching the spring snow goose season.

## MUST NOTE

Longtime US senator J. William Fulbright was born in Sumner. He represented Arkansas for close to thirty years in Washington and was influential in many important decisions. His name lives on through the Fulbright scholarship program, which he sponsored in 1944 and which now has close to three hundred thousand recipients worldwide.

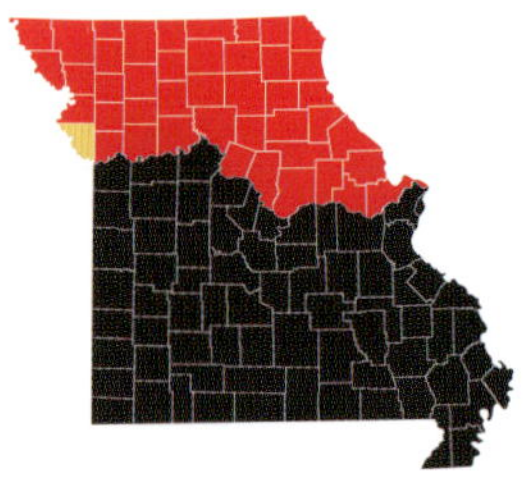

# 18

# *Weston*

Weston is the town that almost was, but today is clearly the destination that is. Before the Civil War, Weston was one of the largest cities in the West, the second largest in Missouri, and the second largest port on the Missouri River. Kansas City and St. Joseph paled in importance to Weston, which, from its founding in 1836 until Texas's statehood in 1845, was the farthest western city in the United States. Hence the name, which is short for "West Town." In 1850, two hundred and sixty-five steamboats were docked there. The town was the major launching point for the Santa Fe Trail, the Oregon Trail, and travel to California during the Gold Rush. Factories, mills, and craftsmen worked around the clock to supply the settlers heading west. This important town was the home of William "Buffalo Bill" Cody. Now the town is home to fewer than two thousand residents.

The Civil War did not cause the decline; rather, a large flood in 1881 caused the Missouri River to move two miles away. The port dried up, making it the town that almost was. If that had not happened, it's possible Weston would be what Kansas City or St. Joseph are today.

Yet residents and visitors aren't complaining. The change in the river may have left the town behind, but now travelers can find what time preserved. As a slogan on a Weston travel website said, "Weston, Just a Short Drive but a Million Miles Away." The town is just thirty miles from Kansas City but carries you back in time. Visitors are not only transported to the

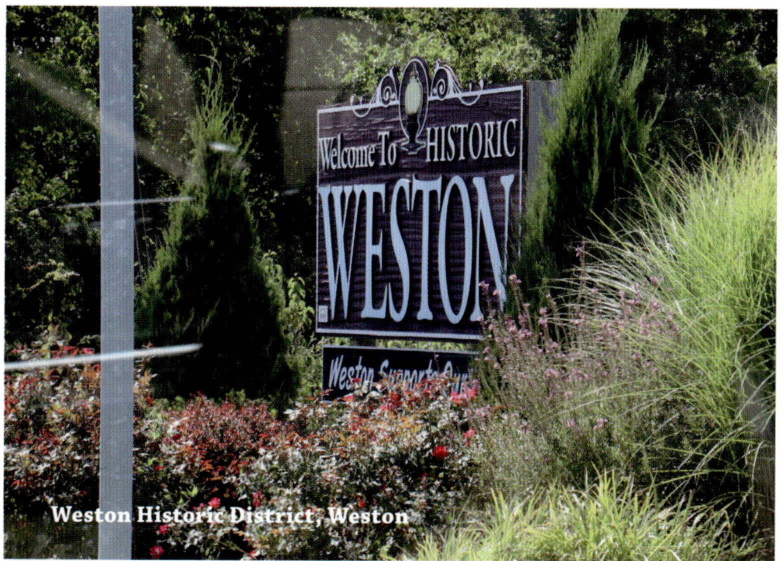

Weston Historic District, Weston

past but can take advantage of the isolated escape and change of pace found in Weston.

That same travel site lists a few of the recognitions the town has received: voted #1 Best Day Trip fifteen years running by *Ingram's* magazine, voted Best Overnight Destination by VisitKC.com, called Best Day Trip & Beautiful Town by *Rural Missouri* magazine, voted Best Small Town in Missouri by *AAA Midwest Traveler* magazine, and voted Most Beautiful Town in Missouri by Expedia Viewfinder Travel Blog. These are only a few of the honors Weston has received. The accolades are justified with the historic buildings and the many area attractions.

## MUST DO

Weston's historic district includes twenty-two blocks in the city and more than one hundred antebellum and Victorian buildings. Nearly all the antebellum homes have been restored. It's easy to enjoy many of the buildings on foot or on a quick drive. Maps and recommended walking tours are available from the Weston Historical Museum, which is one of five museums.

Connecting with its history, Weston is home to one of the oldest breweries in the United States: Weston Brewing Company. The brewery was built underground, and, after being closed for several years, it has reopened. It's available for tours, and it houses O'Malley's Pub. Also, the oldest distillery continuing to work in the same location, the McCormick Distilling Company, operates in the area. It's no longer open for tours, but you can check out their store, McCormick on Main. Several wineries are also in the area.

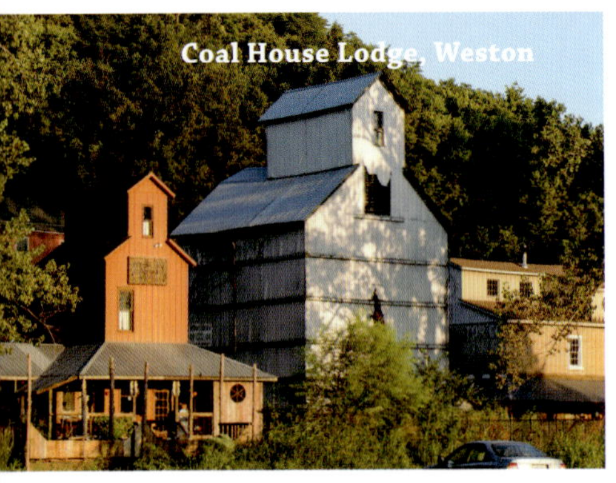
Coal House Lodge, Weston

Along with all the history, Weston is home of one of Missouri's two ski resorts: Snow Creek. The three-hundred-foot drop has twelve trails. Beyond skiing and snowboarding, they also offer snow tubing, which is a blast!

## MUST STAY

Take your pick of several great bed-and-breakfasts in Weston, a few of which are distinctive. The Coal House Lodge provides the most unusual stay. It's a beautiful lodging space and places its guest in the midst of the historic vibe. The lodge has only one guestroom, so you need to plan ahead. The Inn at Weston offers the most historical experience of the bed-and-breakfasts. A great lodging choice for families, along with being a destination itself, is Basswood Resort. Basswood's Country Suites are nice and spacious. With multiple well-stocked lakes on-site, the scenery is beautiful and the fishing plentiful. Other amenities and activities include paddleboats, hiking, indoor activities, and a pool with kids' play area.

If you're on just a weekend trip, the Saint George Hotel should be the choice. The historic 1845 hotel sits on a corner in the historic district and is like stepping into a time capsule.

## MUST EAT

A list of great restaurants in town could fill this book, but if you could pick only one, don't miss The Tin Kitchen. It serves up great barbecue that can compete with the standards in Kansas City, but with a gourmet twist. Beef brisket has to be on your plate, whether by itself, on a sandwich, or with another meat. The sauce matches perfectly with the brisket. But you

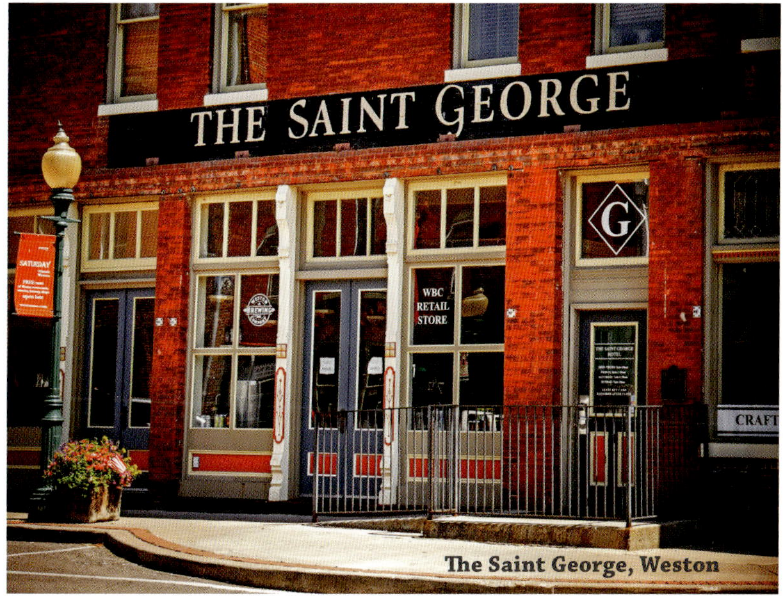

The Saint George, Weston

can't go wrong with any of the pecan-wood-smoked meats. They have two outstanding main dishes to keep from being outshined by the sides. You'll have to order both the hand-cut fries and twenty-four-hour slaw.

If you are able to eat a couple of meals in town, check out O'Malley's Pub, which is located underground in the Weston Brewing Company. You're likely to catch some live music while you're there. For unique cuisine, American Bowman's has traditional Irish food. And for a more elegant meal, there's Avalon Café, which not only serves beautiful presentations of high-end meals but offers a scenic overlook of downtown.

## MUST SHOP

The town is host to lots of shops that you'll want to check out, but here are the ones that you can't find just anywhere. McCormick on Main is a great experience. Celtic Ranch keeps the Irish flair going with all things Irish and the largest selection of Irish whiskey around. Renditions is one of the few dealers of Manufaktura Polish pottery in the Midwest. Weston Tobacco is an experience all of its own, and at certain times visitors can watch cigars being made.

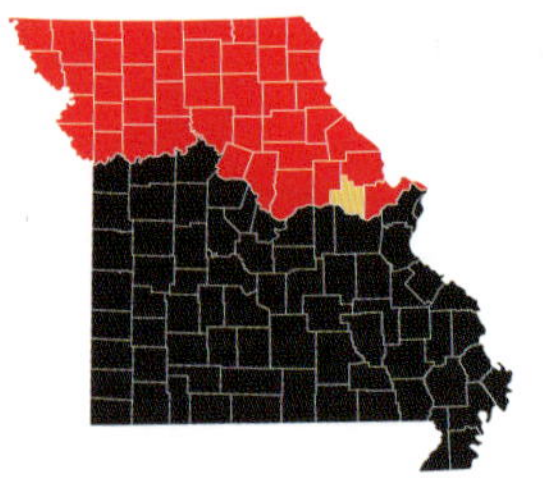

# 19

# *Wright City*

Wright City is less than an hour's drive from downtown St. Louis and is home to just over three thousand residents. It was named after its first settler, Dr. Henry C. Wright, and was platted in 1857. The attraction that was the town's claim to fame—and one that residents may actually want to forget—left town in 2007. From 1992 to 2007, Wright City was home to the Elvis Is Alive Museum, which was run by controversial minister Bill Beeny. The museum was intended to spread Beeny's theory that Elvis Presley was still alive.

Beeny had amassed a collection that was interesting and sizable, if a bit comical, which caught the attention of mainstream media when it was sold on eBay. It was purchased by an individual in Hattiesburg, Mississippi, who opened a museum there briefly.

Fortunately, a new attraction is keeping Wright City on the map, and this attraction is the perfect activity for families.

## MUST DO

In 2012, Wright City became home to Big Joel's Safari Petting Zoo and Educational Park. The safari is a walk-through petting zoo with a large number of animals both domestic and exotic. Guests get to interact with the animals in a much more personal way than at a zoo. You're able to pet, feed, and occasionally hold exotic species like kangaroos, camels, zebras, lemurs, water buffalo, ostriches, emus, yaks, monkeys, and more.

The same for barnyard critters and North American animals like deer, porcupines, pheasants, buffalo, and more. Owner Joel Clinger said of the park's goal, "The idea was to get you closer. When you go to the zoo, you're far away. And we work with all the animals all the time, so it's not like they really freak out when people are around."

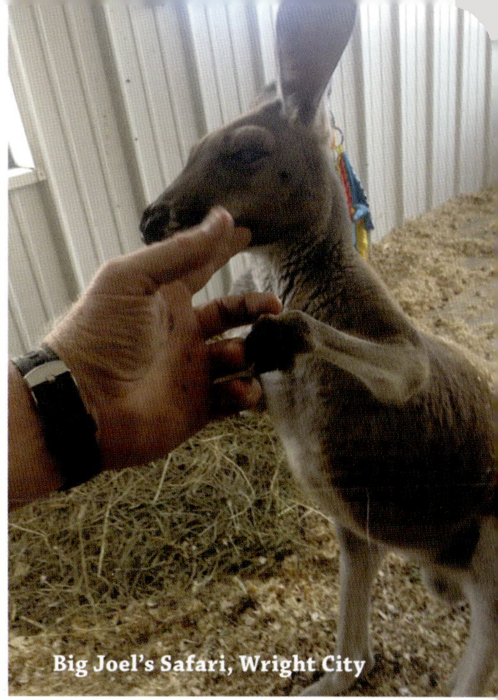

Big Joel's Safari, Wright City

The staff takes extra measures to allow for such personal experiences between animals and guests. They acquire animals as babies and hand-feed them so that the animal is conditioned to be comfortable around people. Many guests purchase season passes and check in weekly to watch babies grow or see how their favorite is doing. The park offers pony rides and camel rides, and there is an indoor reptile exhibit. The park also provides livestock for Six Flags over St. Louis's Holiday in the Park, which points to the quality of animals within the safari.

The story behind the park is as good as the park itself. Joel Clinger is "Big Joel." He was a local football standout who went on to play at the University of Missouri, where he received All–Big 12 honors. After initially signing with the Giants, he played arena football for several seasons. While playing for the Tigers, he got a degree in animal science. Rather than take a job in a larger city, he came back home and put his training to work. Joel and his wife, Mimi, opened the park to share their passion for animals with the public.

# *The Osage Plain in the Southwest*

Stretching from Springfield to Kansas City along the western border, this reprieve from the hilly Ozarks is host to great stops along the I-49 corridor.

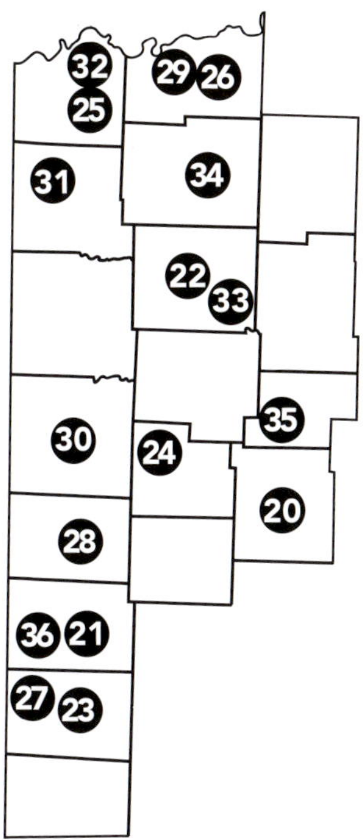


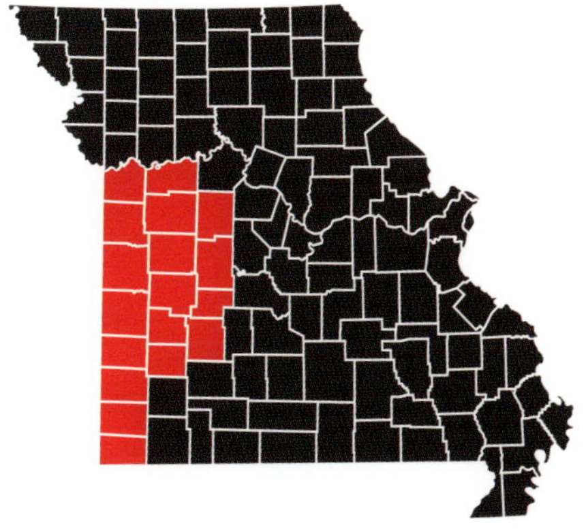

## The Osage Plain in the Southwest

20. Bolivar
21. Carthage
22. Clinton
23. Diamond
24. El Dorado Springs
25. Grain Valley
26. Higginsville
27. Hornet
28. Lamar
29. Lexington
30. Nevada
31. Peculiar
32. Sibley
33. Tightwad
34. Warrensburg
35. Weaubleau
36. Webb City

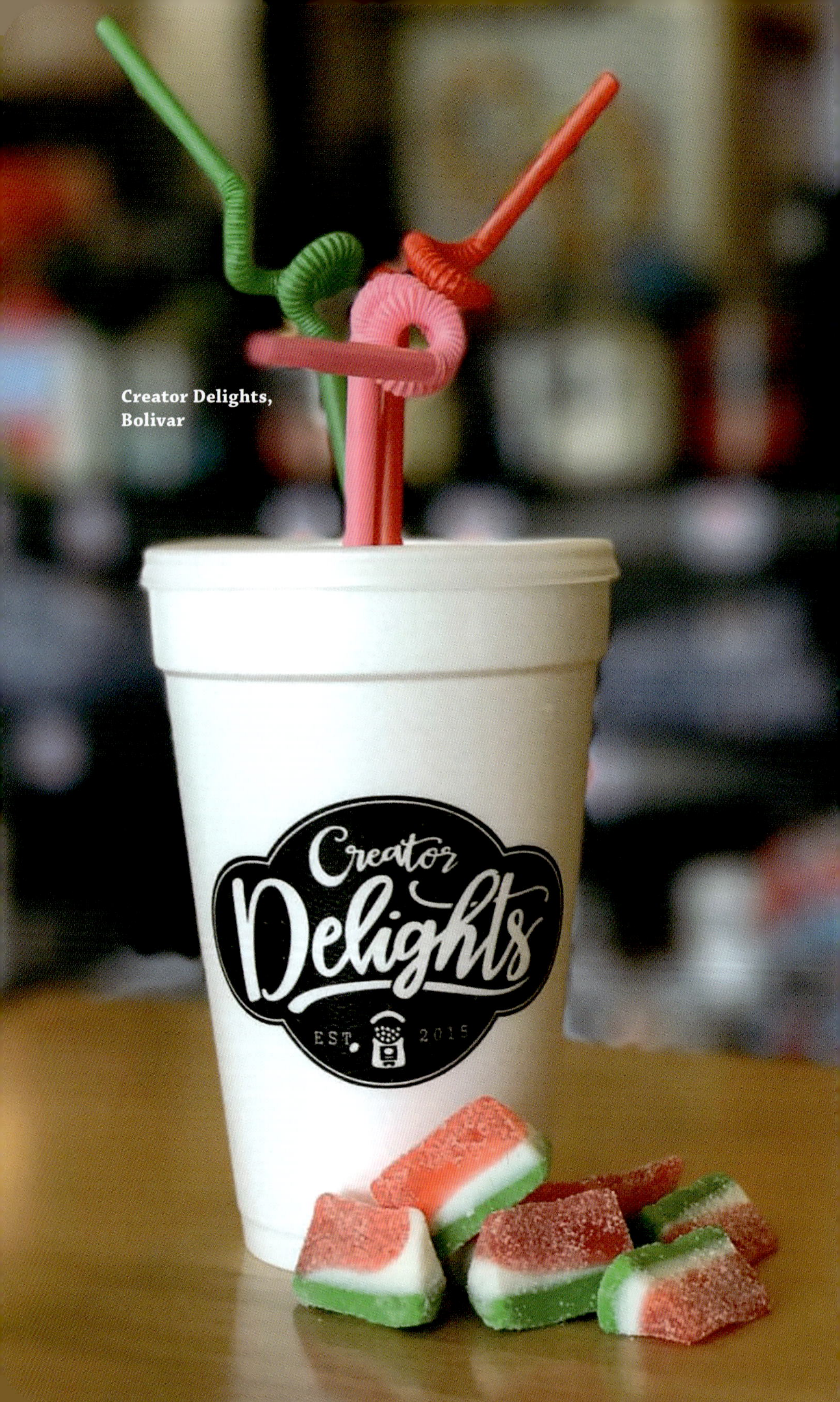


Creator Delights,
Bolivar

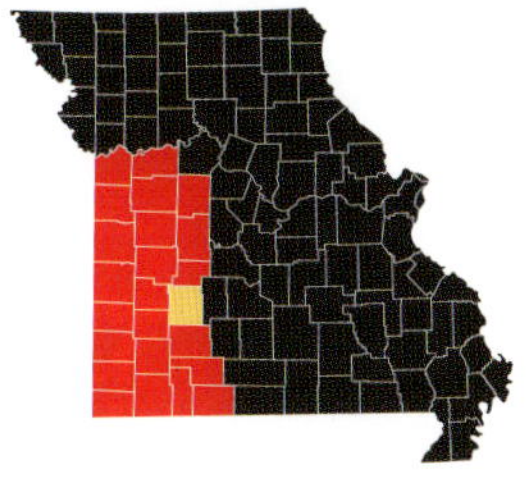

# 20

# *Bolivar*

With the name Bolivar, one would suspect a town to have roots in South America, but the roots of this southwest Missouri town are in Tennessee. Originally, settlers put down roots around Keeling Spring, which today is a park in Bolivar . The town was established and named the Polk county seat in 1835. The name comes from Bolivar, Tennessee, where Colonel Ezekiel Polk lived, whom the county was named after. Yet Bolivar, Tennessee, was named after the great liberator of Venezuela, Bolivia, Colombia, Ecuador, Peru, and Panama, Simon Bolivar. Therefore, there's an indirect tie to South America. Bolivar's high school continues this tradition, as they are the Liberators. From early on, the town has been home to Southwest Baptist University, which began in 1879. It's a private university belonging to the Southern Baptist Convention.

With the mention of South America and the Liberators, a name meant to conjure images of Spanish Conquistadors, the idea of treasure and gold could come to mind. And there is a treasure in Bolivar that is worth the drive: Creator Delights.

## MUST EAT/MUST SHOP

Creator Delights owner Trina Banner's vision is to inspire happy hearts and cheerful faces through sweets, soda, and shirts. The family is accomplishing that goal—one step into their sweets and soda shop and they'll accomplish it in your life. The Banner family has operated a large

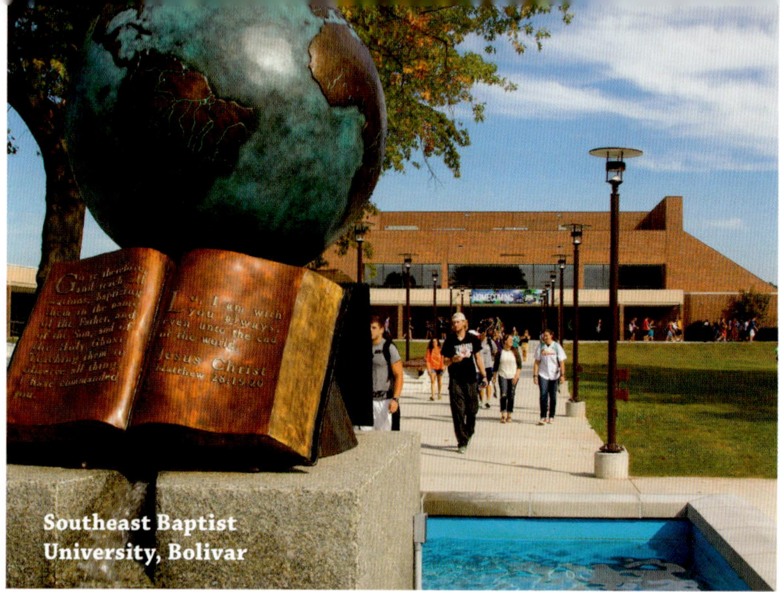

Southeast Baptist University, Bolivar

screen-printing business in town since 1991. In 2015, they began to look into taking their work into a retail shop, and that's when Creator Delights was born. They have a wide selection of candy, sodas, and specialty coffee drinks. The favorite is their marshmallow sodas. Yes, marshmallow. Dr. Mallo is the most popular, which is marshmallow and Dr. Pepper. Next is the Strawberrysicle with strawberry, marshmallow, and Sprite. An honorable mention is the Dreamsicle, made with marshmallow, orange, and Sprite.

You really have to leave with a drink in each hand because they also offer gourmet coffee drinks like the Liquid Pecan Pie and S'mores Hot Chocolate. During each holiday you will find a specialty drink and custom holiday T-shirt.

With the drinks, muffins, and over three hundred varieties of candy, you'd think local dentists had their work cut out for them, but each candy bag comes with a disposable toothbrush.

## MUST EAT

There's plenty to get full on at Creator Delights. The advice from your mom about not letting a lot of sweets ruin dinner should be ignored on a trip to Bolivar, but if you feel the need to get real food, here are two recommendations. El Rodeo Mexican is a local favorite that stays packed. It's basic Mexican food, and done well. Another local favorite is Brenda's Café. It's located downtown on the square and is small, but it serves up great food, especially breakfast.

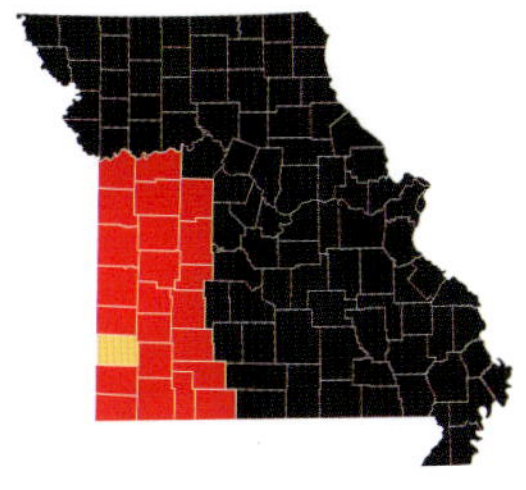

# 21

# Carthage

Missouri has been a state since 1821, which is close to 200 years ago, and it was inhabited long before that by Native Americans. That's a lot of history. In many of the small towns covered in this book there's one focal point of their history, and together they represent the stratigraphy of Missouri history. But in some places, all of the layers are present. Carthage is one with multiple layers of history that can be experienced today.

The town was platted in 1842 and was named after Carthage, an ancient city in northern Africa. The land was purchased from the Osage tribe. Carthage remained small up until the Civil War. Two Civil War battles took place in the area. The battle on July 5, 1861, was one of the first engagements of troops in the Civil War. Confederate guerrillas burned the town in 1864, destroying much of it. Following the war, the arrival of the railroad and local mining led to an economic and population boom. Most noteworthy about that mining was a type of limestone that could be polished into "Carthage marble," which was used in the construction of Missouri's state capitol building.

Route 66 also passed through Carthage, continuing growth and leading the town to be called "The Open Gate to the Ozarks." Multiple remnants of that time period remain around town. Many nationally recognized artists have come through Carthage, making it a place of cultural impact.

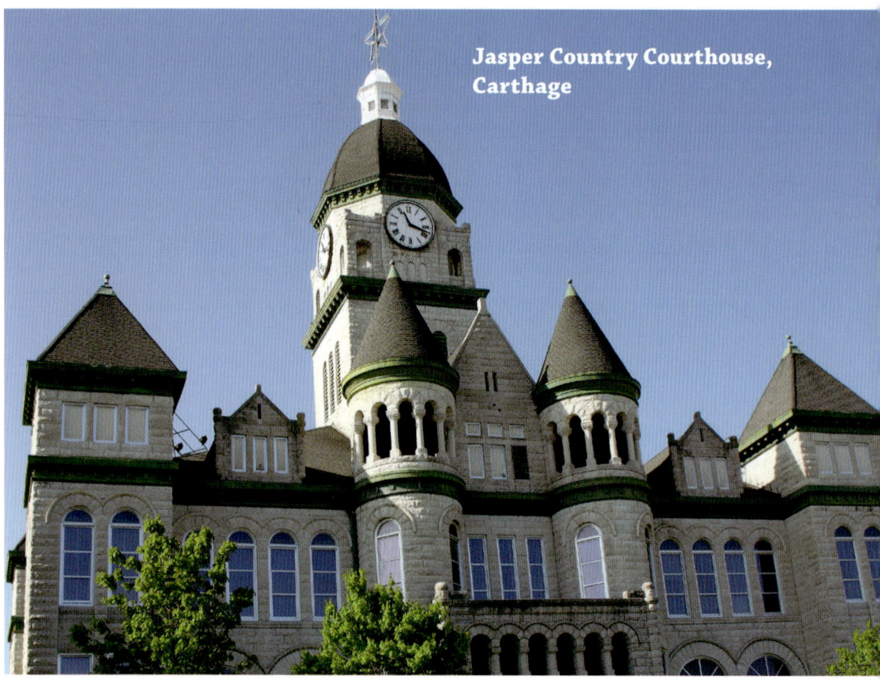

Jasper Country Courthouse, Carthage

## MUST DO

Carthage's history offers much to do. A museum and state park share the history of the Battle of Carthage. The Civil War led to a temporary demise of the city, but fortunately, nearby mining brought prosperity, evident in the beautiful Jasper County Courthouse located downtown. It's one of the more beautiful courthouses in the country, resembling a castle with its Carthage marble construction, arched windows, spires, and tall clock tower. It's unverified, but locals say it was the inspiration for the iconic Hill Valley clock tower in *Back to the Future*.

The city has kept its roots from the heyday of Route 66. Boots Court, a vintage motel, has been restored to the style of 1949. If you're into 1950s nostalgia, AM radio station KMDO has been on the air since 1947 with its slogan, "Too cool for FM." And there's a fully operational drive-in movie theater, 66 Drive-In. It opened in 1949 and continued until 1985. In 1998, it was remodeled and reopened and shows movies every weekend.

Keeping with mid-twentieth-century nostalgia, the highlight of a trip to Carthage is Red Oak II, a "town" that's a combination of painting and sculpture by internationally known artist Lowell Davis. Red Oak II is a life-size tribute to Davis's real hometown of Red Oak, Missouri, and is a living embodiment of his "rural Norman Rockwell" painting style.

After traveling as a well-known artist, Davis returned to find his hometown a ghost town. So in 1987, he began to rebuild it—on his own farm. Over time, this ghost town would take on its own life: there's a general store, blacksmith shop, Phillips 66 station, schoolhouse, feed store, diner, town hall, jail, and several homes. There are also sculptures and old vehicles. Today this unusual work of art is open to visitors to roam and take pictures. It's a fun place to reminisce and learn.

Continuing with art attractions, Carthage is home to the Precious Moments Chapel and Park. Samuel J. Butcher was the artist behind the popular Precious Moments figurines, which were extremely popular in the late 1980s and early 1990s. At the height of their popularity, this beautifully articulated property was a theme park based on those characters. The centerpiece was a chapel painted like the Sistine Chapel in Rome, but done with the Precious Moments characters.

Having two locations of physical expressions from famous artists is unheard of for a small town, but Carthage is also home to one of the finest art galleries in the area: Cherry's Art Emporium, which is privately owned and is located in the downtown square. The gallery has an overwhelming collection—it houses pieces from well-known artists, high-quality paintings, and many sculptures. It serves as a sales outlet for artists like Andy Thomas, Bob Graham, Paul Dykman, Larry Clingman, John Lasater, Don Goin, Greg Kelsy, Todd Williams, Kira Fercho, and more. And not just one work per artist, but volumes. The mix of artists and their works captures the culture of southwest Missouri: frontier west, Texas cowboys, rural life, Midwest agriculture, and sophistication. The western art in Cherry's rivals collections like the Remington and Russell collection in the Amon Carter Museum of American Art in Fort Worth.

Cherry's Emporium is not just a gallery, it's an eclectic mall of attractions. There's the art, a wine room, a gift shop, a coffee shop, a restaurant, and often live music—all connected.

A couple more items to add to that Carthage to-do list are a fall tour and downtown bowling at Star Lanes. The city is known as America's Maple Leaf City because of the high number of maple trees, which make for a beautiful drive in the fall.

## MUST EAT

Carthage boasts lots of good places to eat, and here are a few of the most notable. If it's breakfast you seek, try the Pancake Hut. If you're staying at the Boots Court, the Hut is right next door. There's also a long-running staple, Whistler's Hamburgers. But the most entertaining is Lucky J Steakhouse and Arena. The food is excellent, but the environment and entertainment are available in only a few places around the country. Lucky J is a high-quality steakhouse built alongside an indoor rodeo arena. Customers can dine while watching rodeo events, and the arena's schedule is loaded. The menu is loaded as well. From salads to steaks to pork chops to seafood to sandwiches and burgers. It would be hard to pass up one of their steaks, especially the Lucky J House Steak or Ribeye. But the specialty burgers make for tempting choices. If you like some kick, the Crossfire Burger with buffalo sauce is hot, but a great mix of flavors. And on the Hawaiian Burger, the mix of Swiss and pineapple complement each other.

And if it's pizza you crave, Cave Gang Pizza and Pub is one of the best pizza places in the state. Their mix of a unique, flavorsome sauce, the wood-fired crust, and fresh meats make their pizzas masterpieces. But

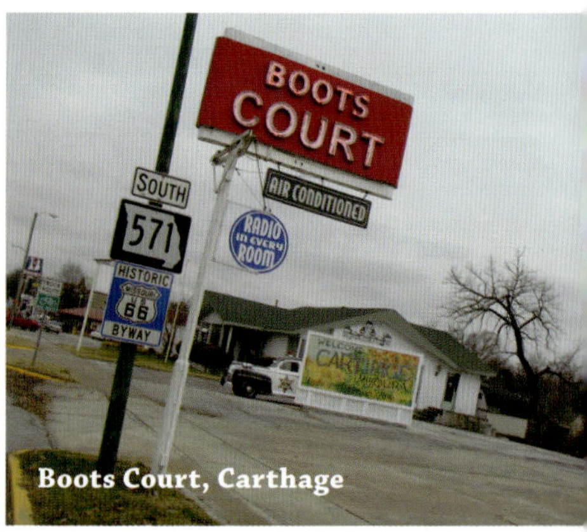

Boots Court, Carthage

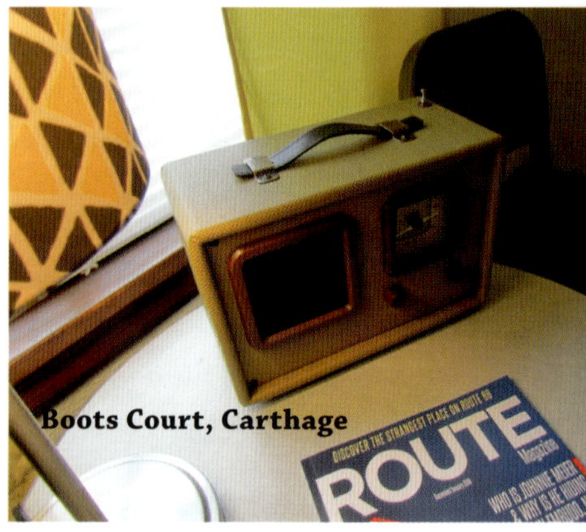

Boots Court, Carthage

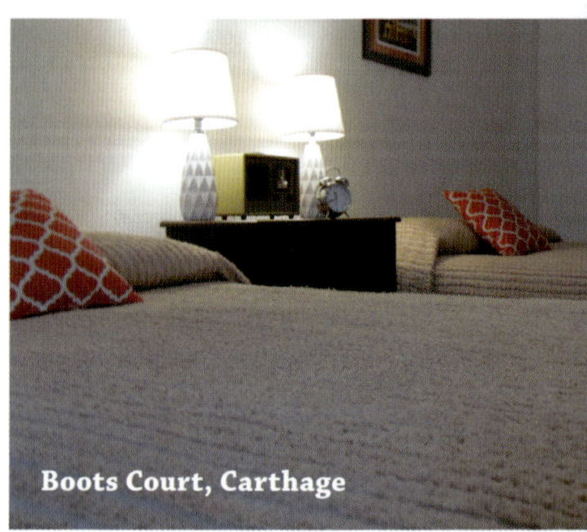
Boots Court, Carthage

their wings may even be better than their pizza. Viewing and tasting their wings leaves customers feeling that Cave Gang spends more time on wings than anyone else in the wings business. They aren't thrown together or quickly tossed, they're works of art.

## MUST STAY

Located along Route 66, the Boots Court Motel is one of the most special places in town. It's easy to pass by this outdated, streamlined, art-deco motel and think it's just some old place, but when you dig into the history and, even more important, the renovation efforts, the Boots becomes magical, as it has for so many Route 66 enthusiasts.

It was built by Arthur Boots in 1939 and persevered as a motel well beyond its years. In 2011 it was on the edge of demolition, but two sisters, Deborah Harvey and Priscilla Bledsaw, saved it and have poured themselves into renovating the Boots and remaking it as it was in 1949. They've completed much of the work, and along with on-site operator Deborah Real they have made the Boots come alive once more. They have worked hard to make it nice, but have kept the original period furnishings and even bedding. The rooms are comfortable and vintage, and each room's radio is set to KMDO and plays 1950s music. Guests can even stay in the room where Clark Gable stayed. A night's stay is reasonably priced, the rooms are in great shape, and it's a perfect place to relive the past or even do some time traveling with the kids.

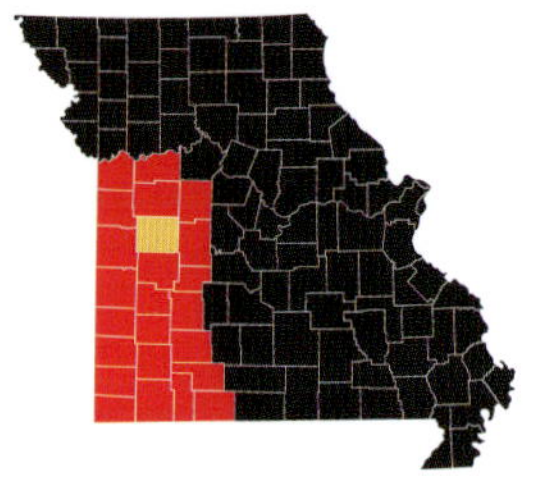

# 22

# *Clinton*

Many of the towns in this book have great downtown town squares. Some are preserving history while others are focused on renovation. Of all of them, Clinton may have the cleanest, most beautiful downtown square. It includes over sixty historic buildings and is still central to the town's lifeblood.

Clinton was platted in 1836 and was named after New York governor DeWitt Clinton. The Clinton Square Historic District is the largest historic square in the state. Though places like Weston may have more historic buildings, it's the old downtown square around the courthouse that sets Clinton apart. Those buildings date from 1885 to 1957 and include the Anheuser-Busch Brewing Association Building, which was used from 1886 to 1920 and now houses the Henry County Museum. It's a small museum but provides a taste of history.

The historic downtown is the focal point of the town and is on display during the Olde Glory Days festival over Independence Day. The festival began in 1994 and has become the largest Fourth of July celebration in Missouri. That's quite the achievement. Downtown visitors can also catch the Soldier Memorial, which commemorates three Civil War skirmishes in the area. There's a historic granite fountain, which was a gift to the city in 1911, as well as a memorial bandstand that was built in 1921 in memory and honor of World War I soldiers from the county.

**Katy Trail, Clinton**

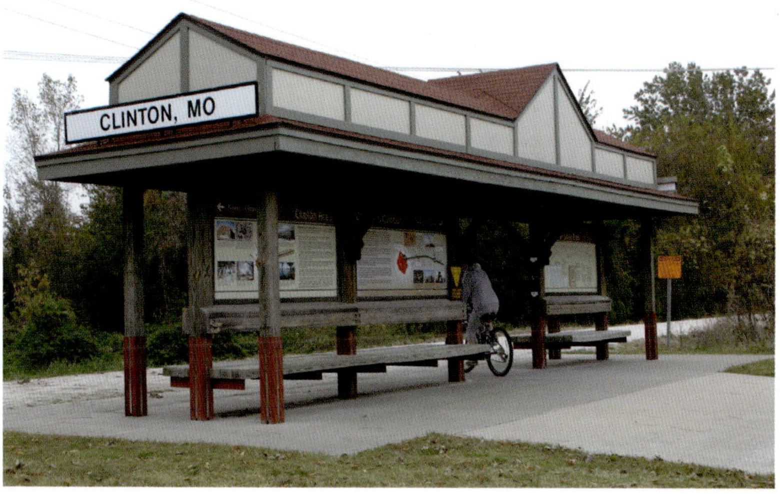


## MUST DO

A stroll downtown is a must-do in Clinton. You will be transported to a time when life was much slower. And the best time to do so is around Olde Glory Days. Along other historical lines—gas lines, that is—there's a D-X fuel station in Clinton that is the envy of most D-X collectors. D-X stations began in 1922 and were popular across the middle parts of the nation. The company was purchased by Sunoco and eventually became Sunoco stations. If you're a collector, you need to see it, but you don't have to be a collector to enjoy the station.

Clinton features lots of outdoor adventures to enjoy in and around town. Truman Lake is nearby, and there's a trailhead to Katy Trail. The portion of the 240-mile former railway near Clinton includes horseback riding. Bicycles are available for rental at the Katy Trail Depot. And for the more daring, Glidersports, a skydiving outfitter, is in town.

## MUST EAT

Clinton is home to a restaurant with a following that would make one think it's been around for decades, but Mallard's Roadhouse has only been in business since 2013. Mallard's pulls in patrons from seventy-five miles away in Kansas City and has regulars who work it into their route

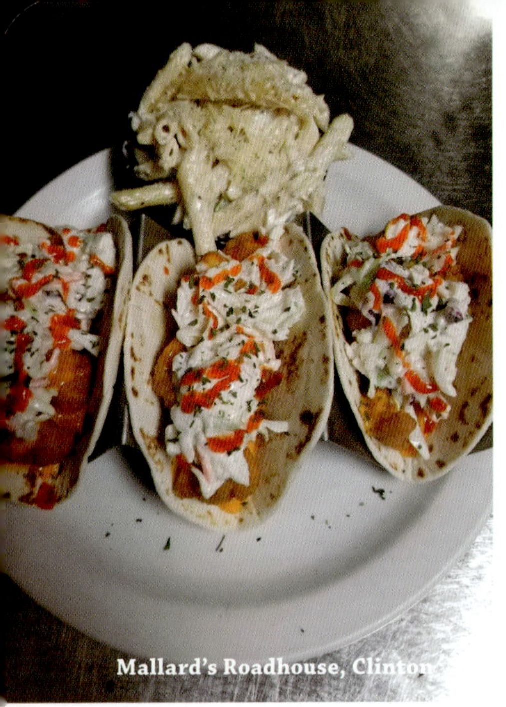
Mallard's Roadhouse, Clinton

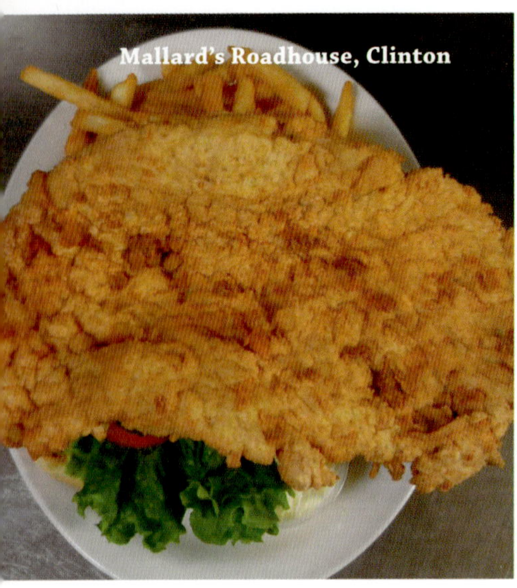
Mallard's Roadhouse, Clinton

to Truman Lake or Branson. The building was formerly the home of Graffiti's Restaurant, a staple in the area, but owners Chad Beaty and Creston Peck have taken Mallard's to another stratosphere. The area is home to quite a bit of duck hunting, hence the name. It's like walking into a Bass Pro Shop when you enter the restaurant with its rustic décor and taxidermy mounts. The typical Midwestern fare is led by an outstanding pork tenderloin. Not far behind are their barbecue and steaks. But in the midst of the Missouri standards, there is a surprise.

Peck and Beaty are originally from the area, but before opening Mallard's they ran a restaurant in the US Virgin Islands and have brought back dishes from the islands. Boom Boom Shrimp Tacos is the runaway favorite with its mix of sweet slaw and spicy sauce. And they're followed up by the mahi-mahi.

It was not meant to be a slight to call the food "typical Midwestern." Though the menu may include regular favorites, Mallard's takes each item up a notch. Everything is of the highest quality, presentation, and taste. Another highlight of this place is the effort to have side dishes that pair perfectly with the main dish. On top of the outstanding food, there's a steady schedule of live music.

Mallard's presents a high bar for tasty grub, but there are a couple other worthwhile stops. Smith's Restaurant does a solid job on Midwestern staples. And if you're in the mood for pizza, Pizza Glen is great whether you're getting a pizza, sandwich, or salad.

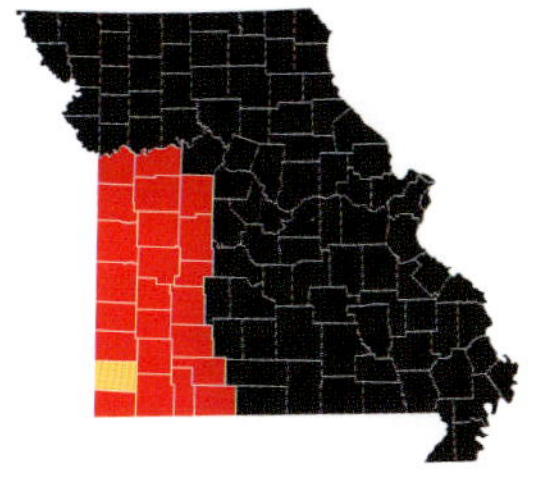

# 23

# Diamond

Diamond is a town that's easy to overlook. Actually, it was left off the first selection of small towns for this book, and then when it was added to the list it was driven by twice when visited. Like several towns in this book, from the outside it can seem like it doesn't have much to offer, but this town of 902 produced a young man who saved the South and therefore this country.

George Washington Carver was born in Diamond in 1864. His birthplace and the land that made him the man he was have been preserved as a national monument. Though born into slavery and then kidnapped as a slave, he would go on to become one of the most prominent botanists in the world and one of the most famous African Americans of his day. He advised US presidents and had the chance to advise Mahatma Gandhi.

At a time when cotton production was severely declining in the South and its overproduction had wreaked havoc on the land, Carver educated farmers to grow crops like peanuts, soybeans, and sweet potatoes to regenerate the soil. He also, through a miraculous story of prayer, found three hundred uses for peanuts, which included over a hundred ways peanuts could be eaten. He also came up with over a hundred uses for the sweet potato when he headed the agriculture department at Tuskegee University.

Carver's birth predates Diamond. Records show a post office began operation there in 1883. Though the area around Diamond was a major mining area, the town's name was not due to diamonds being mined. A

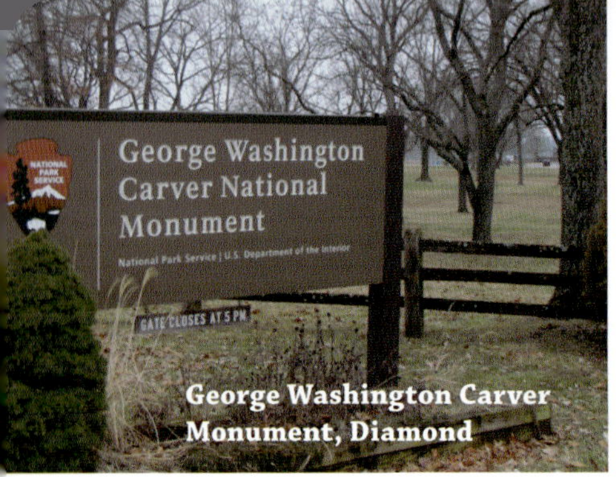

George Washington Carver Monument, Diamond

tract of land near the original townsite was shaped like a diamond, and that gave the town its name.

## MUST DO

If you are near Diamond, you need to drive out to the George Washington Carver National Monument. It was the first national monument to an African American and the first to a nonpresident. Birthplace monument parks usually consist of a marker, a renovated home, and a museum, but there is a lot more here. The park is spread out, giving a view of rolling hills, woodlands, and tallgrass prairie. Also on the property are his boyhood home and the home of the slave owners. It was there he learned to read and was propelled to the academic accomplishments he would achieve.

The park has been designed to put visitors in Carver's footsteps. It's an inspirational experience. In the visitor center is a classroom modeled after his lab at Tuskegee Institute, which shows that he was not just a man of great achievement but also an educator.

In a small town like Diamond, you might think the national monument would be the only main attraction, but the town is also home to the World's Largest Small Electric Appliance Museum. Touring the museum may seem odd, as it is in the back of JR's Western Store, but it's a big place with an epic collection. A tour is free, and it's a private collection of seven thousand small appliances like toasters, coffee pots, mixers, hair dryers, blenders, and on and on. The collection contains seven hundred toasters. It's truly fascinating. For older guests, it's a walk down memory lane, and for younger guests, it's educational.

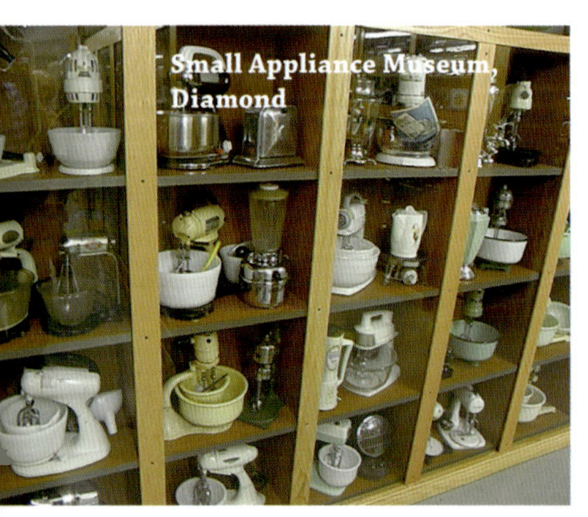
Small Appliance Museum, Diamond

A few miles from Diamond is Grandby. As mentioned, the early industry of the area was mining. Grandby has a mining museum that is extremely well done and worth a stop.

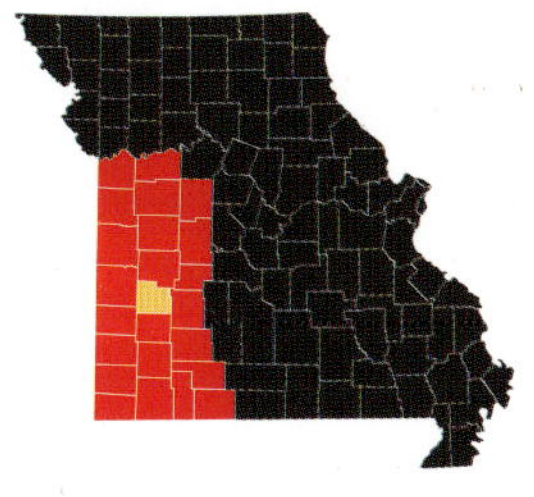

# 24

# El Dorado Springs

There's no gold in El Dorado Springs, as the legendary name would seem to suggest. Town founders Nathaniel and Waldo Cruce had hoped the healing spring around which they built the town would bring riches. For a few decades, the spring did bring prosperity.

In the late 1800s, a farmer in the area, Joshua Hightower, set off to take his wife to the healing waters of Eureka Springs, Arkansas. Her health would not allow the travel, so they stopped at a spring that the Osage claimed had healing powers. Mrs. Hightower improved, and the fame of the spring spread. Watching hundreds flock to the spring, the Cruce brothers laid out a town with the spring in the middle. This town became El Dorado Springs in 1881. By 1900, the population was close to what it is today. At the same time, the water was tested by the University of Missouri and proved to be medicinal. The city grew, and water from the spring was shipped around the world. But as advancements in medicine were made, the need for mineral water waned, and so did El Dorado Springs.

The town's history is still alive and well. The city park established in 1881 to house the spring remains open. It's home to the oldest continual bandstand in Missouri, and the park hosts the annual Founder's Day, a tradition begun not long after the town's founding.

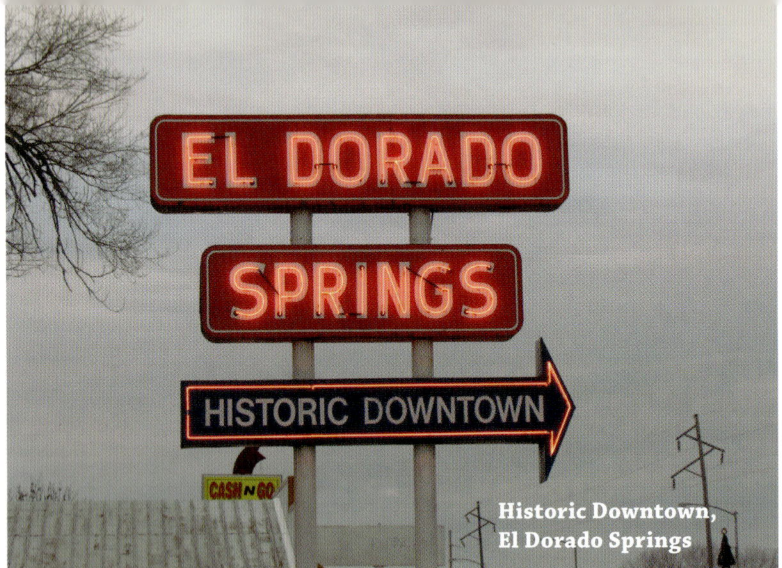


Historic Downtown, El Dorado Springs

## MUST DO

If you visit this historic spot, you need to travel downtown and walk through the park that was the center of all the action. Stand on the bandstand that has cycled through multiple generations of music during its nearly one hundred and forty years.

Two prairie conservation areas preserve the grasslands that once covered a fourth of the state. The largest is Wah'Kon-Tah Prairie.

One place in El Dorado Springs is unique for small towns. Bear Arms is a firearms and tactical gear dealer that also has a shooting range. The range not only features the typical indoor handgun lanes with paper targets, but they have the Milo Training System, an interactive simulation often used to train military personnel and police officers. At Bear Arms, this technology is available for training and recreation. Almost any shooting scenario is possible.

## MUST EAT

On a trip through time at El Dorado Springs, visitors need to stop for a specialty coffee drink at the Bulldog Brew, named after the local high school's mascot. Although the list of drinks is long, don't pass up The Happy Camper: just imagine s'mores, coffee, and a campfire in a drink. They don't just serve coffee, they also have a large breakfast menu as well as sandwiches, soups, and a burger that you wouldn't expect to find at a coffee shop.

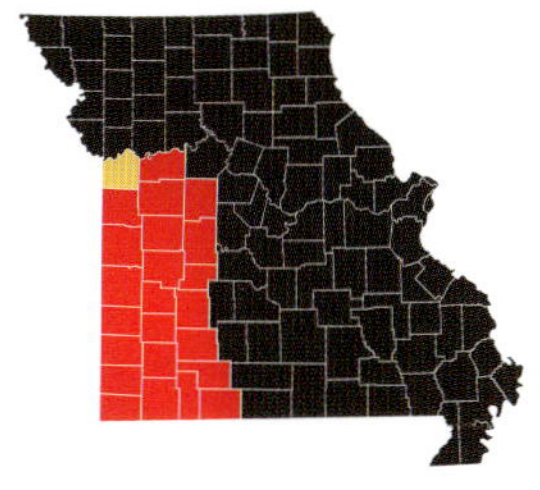

# 25

# Grain Valley

Grain Valley is only twenty-three miles from downtown Kansas City and sits on Interstate 70. So there's much to do within a short drive, but there is also an antique mall that is considered one of the best in the state and in the country: the forty-two-thousand-square-foot Brass Armadillo. With all there is to do in Kansas City, this massive treasure horde brings visitors in from all over the United States.

The town has an interesting history and has played a large role in the American cattle industry. Maybe it should have been called Cattle Valley instead of Grain Valley.

In 1878, Grain Valley was established by merging two smaller towns, Pink Hill and Stoney Point. Both towns were declining and needed to connect to the railroad. When a rail line came through, the two towns met in the middle and created one town to benefit all, an opposite approach to that of Northern Prairie towns Defiance and Matson (see the Defiance chapter).

The raiding and chaos of the Civil War wreaked havoc on the two towns, but they were able to rebuild and resettle. A large amount of grain in the area led to the name. After the consolidation, the town grew. In 1904, Kansas City's William Rockhill Nelson made a move that had lasting impacts on the cattle industry and Grain Valley. Rockhill was a cofounder of the *Kansas City Star*. He purchased twenty-four hundred acres in Grain Valley for Sni-A-Bar Farm, a nonprofit with the mission to develop

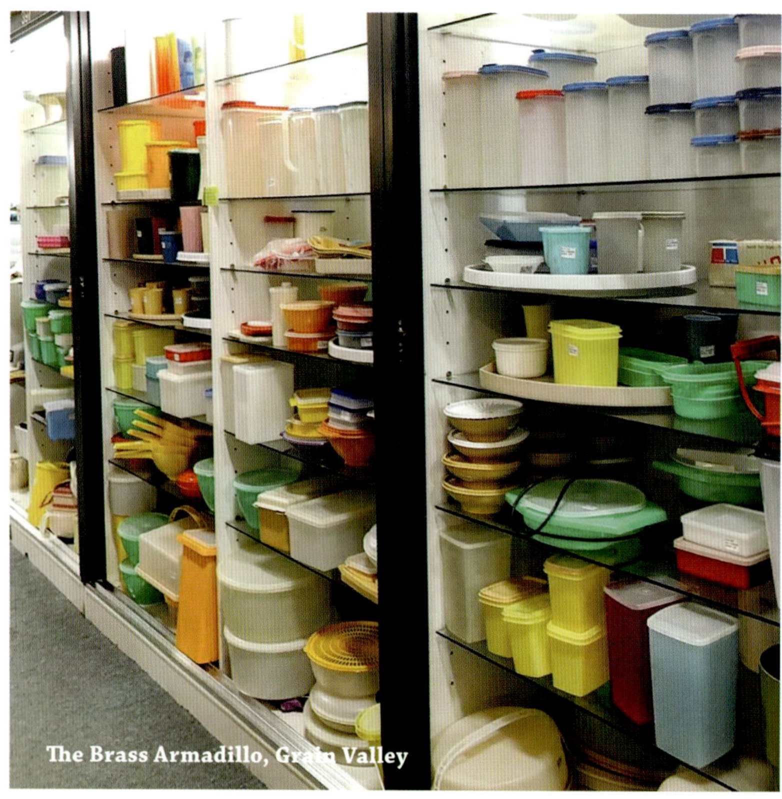
The Brass Armadillo, Grain Valley

improved breeding methods and livestock. After Nelson's death, the farm was left to trustees of the University of Missouri, University of Kansas, and the University of Oklahoma. It has been called "the greatest gift of any man to the beef cattle industry." It's said to have improved conditions of cattle farms across the Corn Belt, with more information gathered on that farm than at any other government research area. Eventually, the trust expired and the farm was sold to private owners.

## MUST SHOP

With the famous Sni-A-Bar Farm gone, the Brass Armadillo is the draw of Grain Valley. It's part of a chain of six antique malls across the Midwest and Southwest. The Grain Valley mall is forty-two-thousand square feet and features over five hundred dealers. It's open every day except for Christmas.

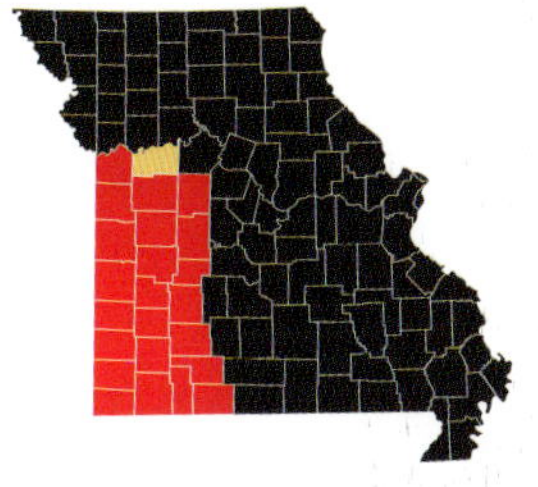

# 26

# *Higginsville*

Chasing one of the most popular barbecue restaurants in Missouri (which is saying a lot) leads to a fascinating historical park along with an elegant restaurant serving up dishes from Belarus, all of this in the farming community of Higginsville, fifty miles from downtown Kansas City on Interstate 70.

Higginsville was founded in 1869 and named after the original owner of the site on which the town sits, Harvey Higgins. In 1893, a center was opened that has since made the town the hub of Missouri's Confederate history. The Confederate Soldiers Home of Missouri was opened in Higginsville and continued operation until the final Confederate veteran passed away at the age of 108 in 1950. As a soldiers' home, it served much like a retirement home for veterans and their wives. During those fifty-seven years, sixteen hundred veterans and their families lived in the home. Historian Dr. Amy Fluker wrote about the home at its height of operation: "The Home grew into a campus of thirty buildings, including dormitories, a chapel, and at least fourteen private cottages. There was also a cemetery and manicured parkland. For the most part, however, the grounds remained open farmland, where the veterans raised crops and livestock. Not only did the residents produce their own food, but they also generated their own electricity and steam heat. In effect, the Home was an entirely self-sufficient community."

Without this endeavor, these Confederate soldiers and their families would have been in dire situations. Because they fought for the South,

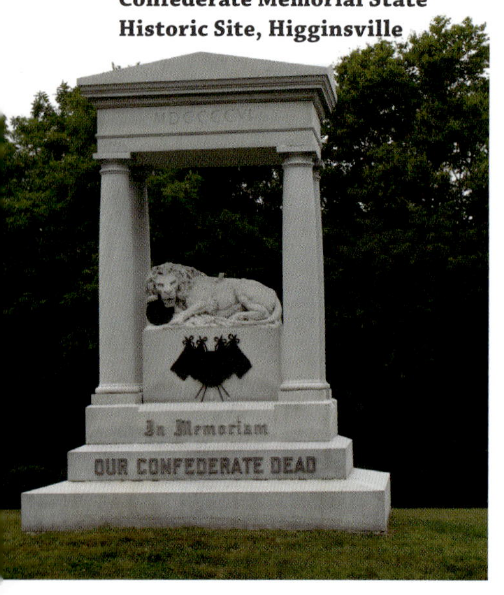


**Confederate Memorial State Historic Site, Higginsville**

they had been stripped of their right to vote, deprived of financial benefits, and denied medical treatment. Though many in Missouri look at the role of Southern sympathizers as a stain, this home and now its memorial represent a great effort put forth toward recovery. Following the death of that final veteran, the home and the grounds were transitioned to a memorial park, the Confederate Memorial State Historic Site, which can be visited today. It consists of three historic buildings and a cemetery with over seven hundred graves, including the grave of William Quantrill. One of the buildings is a renovated chapel. In the cemetery is a granite monument modeled after the famous Lion of Lucerne in Lucerne, Switzerland. The lion has been wounded and rests its head upon the shield of the Confederate States of America. There's one like this in Georgia, "The Lion of Atlanta" in the Oakland Cemetery, but the one in Missouri is a closer replica of the one in Lucerne.

## MUST DO

If you're a Civil War buff, this place is a jewel to visit. It's not a battlefield but a memorial of the aftermath. Even if you aren't much of a history buff, the place features a great park with stocked ponds to fish and places to picnic.

## MUST EAT

Although the Civil War memorial park is fascinating, the greater treasure in town is the Red Shanty BBQ and Roadside Café. From the outside, it doesn't look like much. An old pickup truck is the café sign, and the building is a liquor store and bait shop. But there is a lot more barbecue being sold than bait. Kenton and Annette Dittmer owned the liquor store and bait shop but later put the restaurant in the back. Word spread of the great grub, and the place has garnered a strong reputation for some of the best barbecue in the state. They call it home-style food in a casual atmosphere. Home-style is appropriate, but each menu item is taken a degree better with a gourmet-chef touch, not that you'd expect to see a chef in a white coat in this place.

Their signature barbecue sauce is something special, especially combined with their smoked meats. They have a full barbecue menu and often have a special smoked meat of the day. But they're far from a one-trick pony—they have a wide menu with sandwiches, burgers, dinner plates, large salads, and especially desserts. One dish that will make you chuckle is the "Man's Salad," which is a smoked hamburger steak, sautéed onions, chopped tomatoes, bacon, jalapenos, and a hot and spicy BBQ glaze all served over a bed of deep-fried potato rounds. And if that's not "man" enough for you, you can double that order. Enough can't be said about this little joint. Their sides are phenomenal as well, starting with their fresh fried home-style chips, which can be ordered plain or with different seasonings. And who can pass up trying deep-fried brussels sprouts?

There's a contrast of dining styles in town. There's the bait shop experience, and then there's the Belarussian Baker Tea Room, a Victorian house with white-linen table clothes and elegant place settings and plate presentations. It's a special experience that mixes fine American dining with Eastern European specialties.

## MUST STAY

The Red Shanty owners aren't just serving up mouthwatering barbecue or selling bait and liquor. They have also created some very interesting guest houses and RV sites. There's the Lake Mizzou Guest House, which sits on a seventeen-acre fishing lake. There's the Red Brick Farmhouse Bed & Breakfast, a 1920s prairie-style home surrounded by trees and fields. Don't let the vintage bathtub sign turn you away. And if you really want to have a romantic redneck getaway, there's the Ain't She Cute vintage travel trailer, which has been nicely renovated.

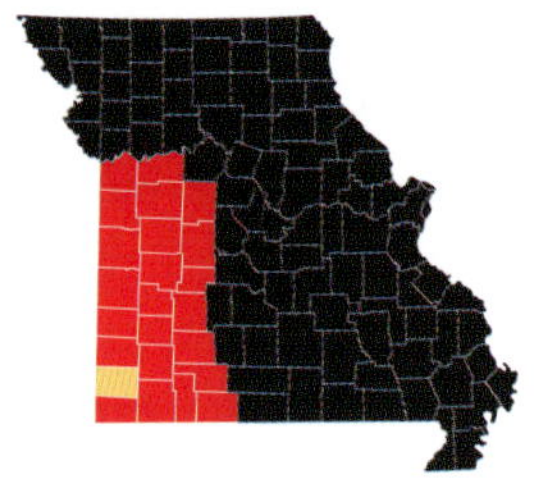

# 27

# *Hornet*

Hornet is not necessarily even a town today, as its post office closed in 1902, but a gas station and some homes line this stretch between Seneca and Joplin along the Oklahoma line. However, this "small town" is home to one of the most enduring Missouri attractions and certainly the most unexplainable. On a lonely stretch of county road is a phenomenon that has been deemed the "Hornet Spooklight." The first documented sighting occurred in 1881, but reports have come forward indicating that it was seen in 1866 and maybe even during the time of the Trail of Tears in the 1830s.

On this stretch of rural road, a light will appear. It's a bright orb that seems to dance above the center of the road. It has been spotted regularly since the late 1800s. It's considered one of the longest appearing light phenomena in America. There have been multiple theories to explain this light, ranging from underground crystals to ghosts, but the jury is still out. The Army Corps of Engineers concluded it was a "mysterious light of unknown origin." The location of the fireball has been called the "Devil's Promenade."

## MUST DO

If you're interested in unsolved mysteries or the paranormal, the Hornet Spooklight needs to be on your list. From Interstate 44 west of Joplin, take Route 43 and head south. Turn right onto Coyote Road from Route

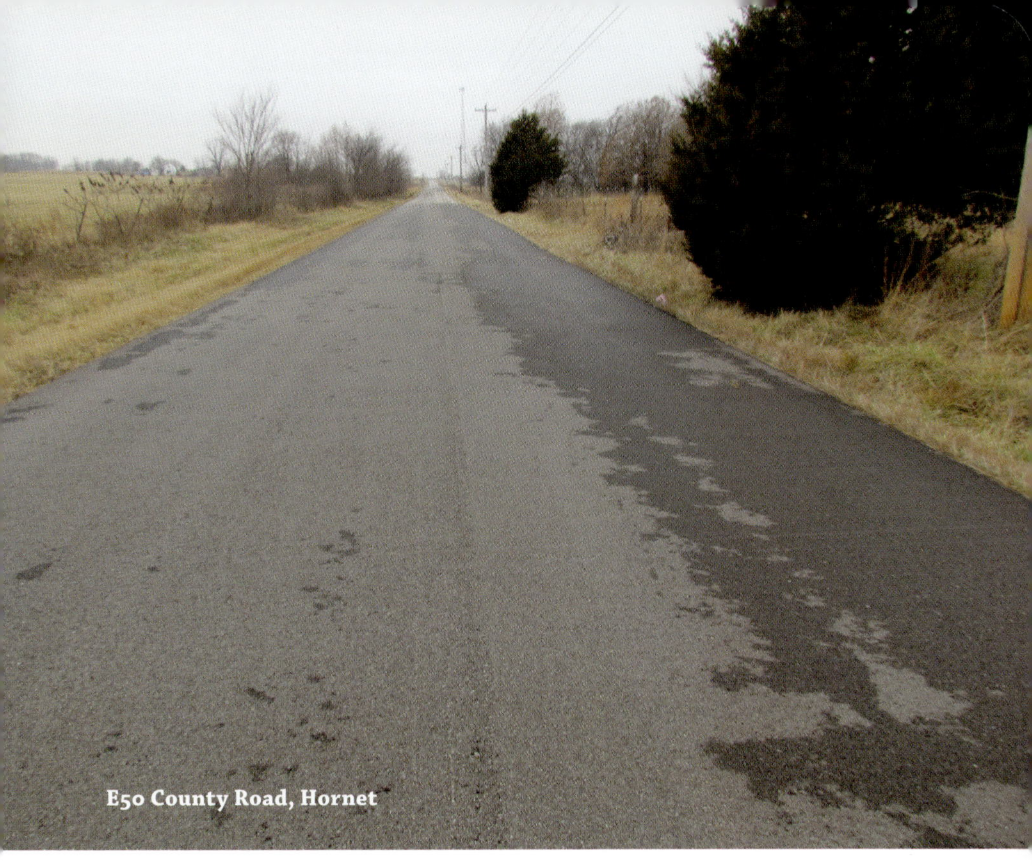
E50 County Road, Hornet

43. Then turn right on Gum Road. Then left on State Line Road. Take the first right and turn onto E50 County Road. You'll actually be driving into Oklahoma. After dropping down a big hill, park in the dip to look up the next hill. Chances are you'll catch a glimpse of the light.

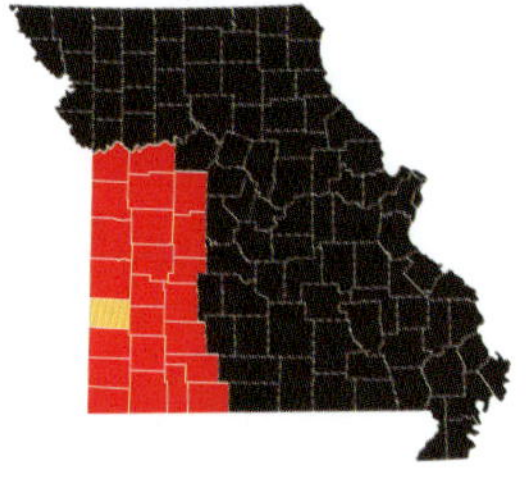

# 28

## *Lamar*

Lamar took a while to get started as a town. It was first laid out in 1856, the result of a pit stop that never ended. Two families were traveling from Louisiana to California. Some of the party became ill and had to stop. They fell in love with the area and formed a town—named after the second president of the Republic of Texas, Mirabeau B. Lamar. Not long after the start of this town, the Civil War brought difficulty. In 1862, William Quantrill and his raiders burned the town because of its Union occupation. Then it was burned again in 1864. By the end of the war, Lamar and the county were mostly empty. People began to return and it was incorporated in 1870. That year is one of the town's most famous for more reasons than one.

President Harry S. Truman put Lamar on the map because it was his birthplace. The home in which he was born in 1884 has been preserved and is now a state historic site. President Truman would not be the town's only well-known citizen.

As mentioned, 1870 may be the most famous year for the town for that was the first full year of Wyatt Earp's term as constable. The famed frontiersman from the shootout at the OK Corral began his storied law-enforcement (and law-breaking) career at age twenty-one. While in Lamar, he married. Shortly after that marriage, his wife passed away along with their unborn child. By 1872, after being accused of embezzlement and horse theft, he left for Peoria, Illinois. Each October, Lamar remembers Earp's time during the annual Wyatt Earp's Fall Fest.

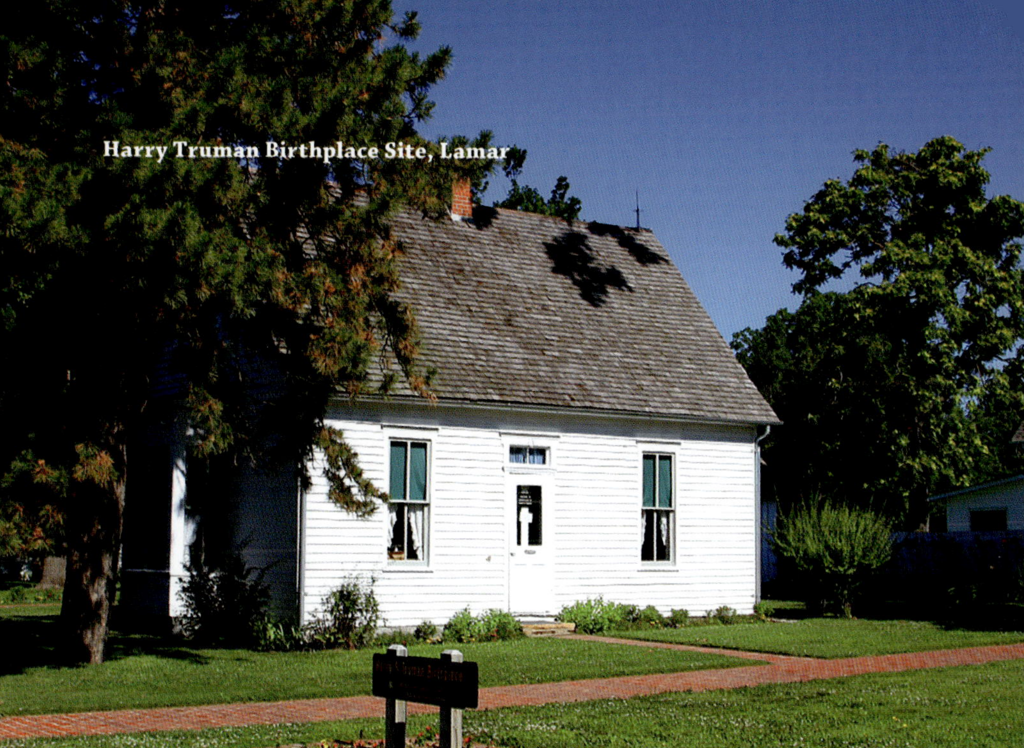
Harry Truman Birthplace Site, Lamar

## MUST DO

You can visit the Harry S. Truman Birthplace State Historic Site and see where President Truman was born. Lamar is also the place to catch a movie—vintage style. There's the Barco Drive-In, which opened in 1950 and still shows movies today. Then there is the downtown jewel, the Plaza, which opened in 1934. It was built to rival the Fox Theater in Joplin and the Gillois Theater in Springfield. The Plaza did this. Over the years the building went through different hands and was even used for storage. In 1998, it reopened after being closed since 1986. Today, movies can still be seen in this beautiful vintage theater.

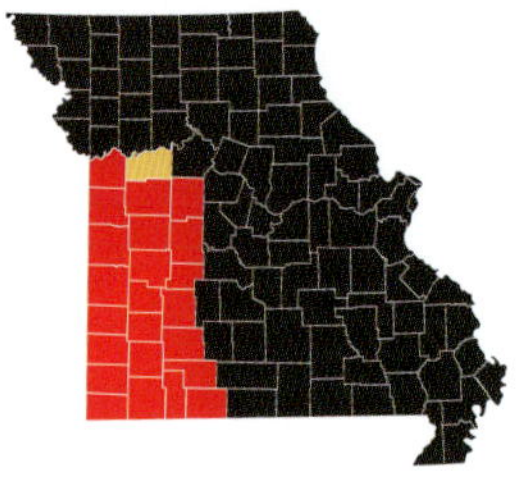

# 29

## *Lexington*

Civil War monuments and experiences can be found throughout Missouri, but no town offers quite the opportunity to travel back in history, especially Civil War history, as Lexington. It was the site of two Civil War battles, one of which was the largest in the western theater of war, the Battle of Lexington. Remnants of the battle can be seen at the battlefield historic site, throughout town, and in museums.

Lexington began as a ferry site in 1819 and was platted in 1822. It was named after the Battle of Lexington during the Revolutionary War. The naming was an eerie prophecy. Throughout the 1830s and 1840s, it was the largest city west of St. Louis because of the fur trade and westward travel. The success of the city in those early days was marred by the largest steamboat accident in Missouri, which took the lives of 150 people in 1852. Forever aligned with Civil War history, Lexington never returned to its prewar prominence. The increase in transporting goods via rail replaced the steamboat traffic to the town.

Wentworth Military Academy and College, located in town, was the second oldest military school west of the Mississippi and remained operational until 2017. The school can be visited today.

But it is Civil War history that engulfs Lexington. The most iconic piece of that history is the cannonball lodged in a pillar of the Lafayette County Courthouse. It can still be seen today. Among the most fascinating aspects of the Lexington battlefield are the trenches dug by Union soldiers. Union troops were fortified in a defunct college and dug

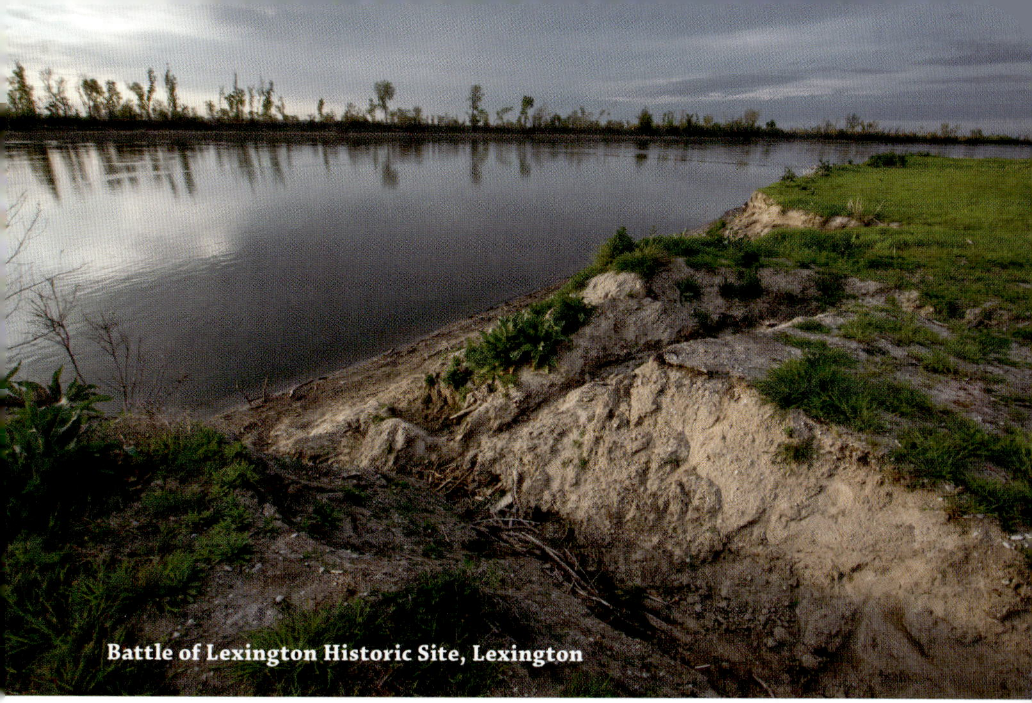
Battle of Lexington Historic Site, Lexington

defensive trenches around it. The Confederate force was five times larger, but the Federal Army had the high ground. In the final stand of the battle, Confederate forces soaked bales of hemp overnight in the river, turning them into a moving, if very heavy, fortification that allowed the soldiers to progress up the river bluff to within striking distance of the makeshift Union fort.

## MUST DO

The cannonball lodged in the courthouse is a fascinating sight. But to further explore the Civil War roots of town, visit the Battle of Lexington Historic Site, where guests can sit in actual trenches from the battle. Also visit Anderson House, used as a hospital during the battle. A museum is there, with great pieces from the battle.

Lexington is a walk into the past. Four historic districts can be toured, one of which is the Highland Avenue Historic District. These large homes are on a ridge overlooking the Missouri River and were originally built on the Santa Fe Trail by area merchants. The Visit Lexington, MO, website offers free maps and self-guided audio tours. They've done a tremendous job creating an enjoyable and informative experience.

The Lexington Historical Museum also has great historic pieces, especially those from the Civil War period. One of the features is the sword of Colonel James A. Mulligan from the surrender of Federal forces in the Battle.

Another Civil War period experience is a tour of the Linwood Lawn home. It's known as "the finest antebellum mansion in the Midwest." At the time of its completion in 1859, it was the first home west of the Mississippi to have hot and cold running water, and the first to have a central heating and cooling system. It's a breathtaking tour.

## MUST STAY

Not only can you see the history but you can sleep in it. Lexington has several great bed-and-breakfasts, but two older hotels are recommended. The Inn on Main is a few suites in a renovated 1840s building in the downtown historic district. Yet the Wentworth Hotel receives the number-one-choice nod. It's a perfect mix of history and luxury.

## MUST EAT

At Big Muddy Ice Cream Company, you'll have to decide if you want dessert before lunch. It's a hard choice. They have great ice cream treats, but their sandwiches are no slouches either.

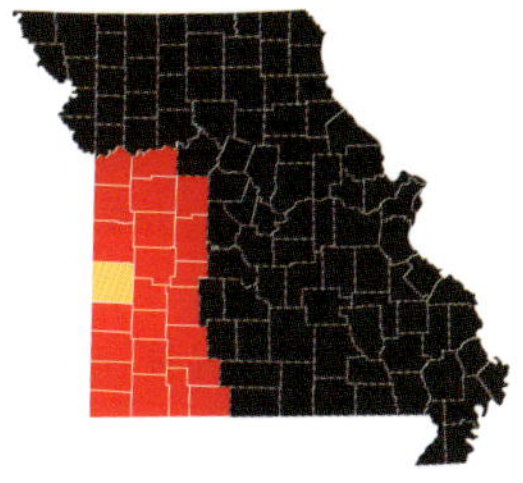

# 30

# *Nevada*

Nevada is a must-visit for onion rings and Suzie Qs—burgers, too—at the iconic White Grill. And you will be in the company of presidents if you make the small diner a destination. Harry S. Truman is said to have stopped in many times during his presidency. A couple other restaurants in Nevada need to be on that list as well.

The town's original name, Hog Eye, may have been more appropriate for the role food plays in its appeal. Hog Eye was platted in 1855, but fortunately, the name was changed to Nevada City, after Nevada City, California, where the county clerk at the time had mined during the Gold Rush. Over time, "City" was dropped from the name. Like much of southwestern Missouri, Nevada was greatly influenced by the Civil War. It was considered the Bushwhacker Capital, and therefore pro-Union soldiers burned the city in 1863. Little remained after that fire. One lasting building is an old jail, preserved as "The Bushwhacker Jail."

After the town rebuilt from the war, a strange industry moved in that put it on the map. Nevada became home to the Weltmer Institute of Suggestive Therapeutics. This was a form of healing using telepathy and hypnosis pioneered by Sidney Abram Weltmer. At the height of the institute's success, it treated four hundred people a day. The institute closed in 1933.

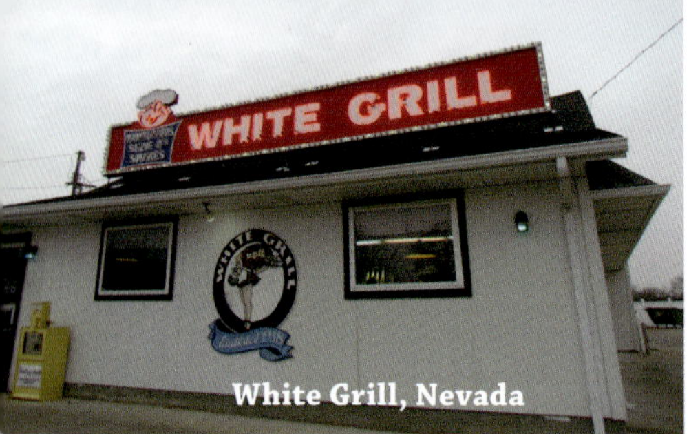

White Grill, Nevada

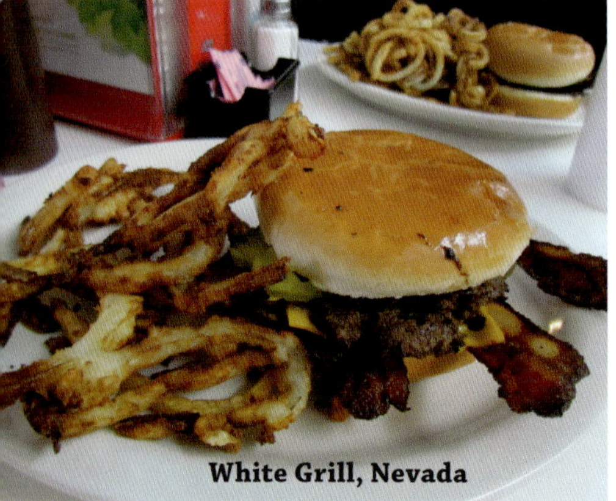
White Grill, Nevada

## MUST EAT

The Weltmer Institute had recently closed when the White Grill opened in 1938. It was part of a local chain in Kansas and Missouri. Nevada's restaurant is the only one still open. It's a small, classic diner with counter stools and limited table seating. The menu is small and low priced. Their burgers are excellent, but it's the onion rings and Suzie Qs that are worth a long drive. Original owner Red McLaughlin is credited with inventing Suzie Qs, what many call "curly fries" today. Each day since 1938, whole potatoes have been hand twisted and then fried to provide each patron a massive pile of potato joy. But it's the onion rings that may be even better. Some critics have listed them among the best in the state, and they are on to something. Even though you're given a massive pile, you'll want more. And it's fitting to end the meal with an old-fashioned milkshake.

It's rare for a small town to have multiple nostalgic burger joints, but Nevada does. Del Way Drive-In also serves fresh Suzie Qs and has a burger to rival White Grill's.

Beyond the burgers is a unique dining experience at the Gobblers Roost. The Roost is out of town a bit, but the drive into the country is well worth it for a five-course meal of down-home classics done in an elegant way. Add a laid-back atmosphere and barnyard décor, and you'll be left with a memorable experience.

## MUST DO

Long before European settlers filled southwestern Missouri, the Osage possessed the land. Nevada is home to the Osage Village State Historic Site, an archaeological site on a hilltop above the Osage River. The village is believed to have been made up of over two hundred lodges and three thousand Osage at one time. The site can be toured today.

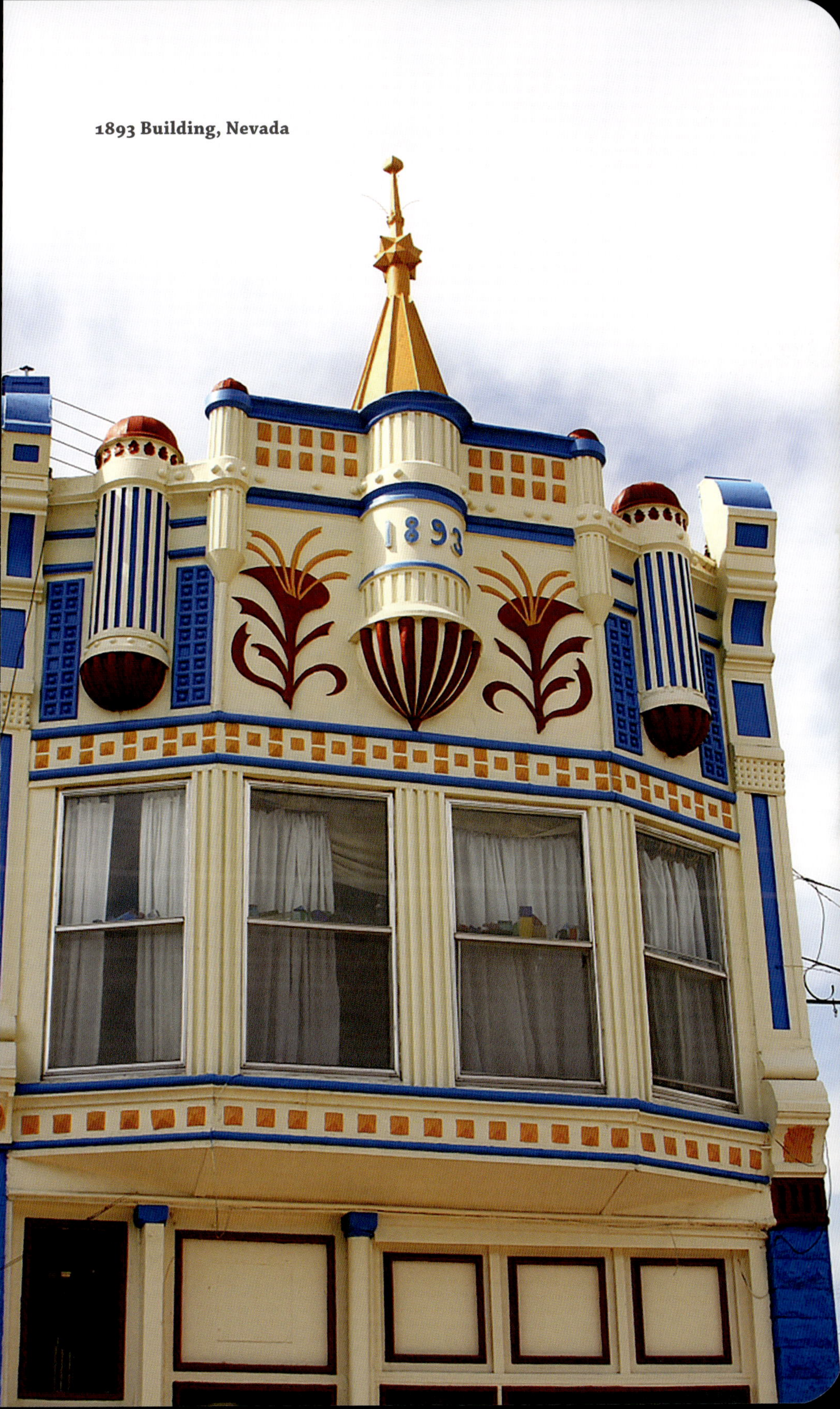

1893 Building, Nevada

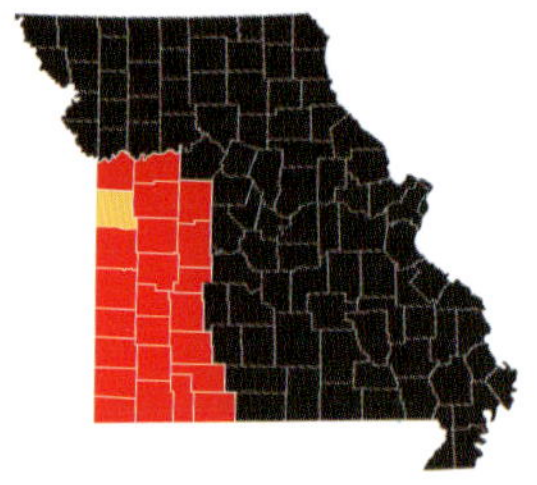

# 31

# Peculiar

Yes, Peculiar is the name of this peculiar small town. It has a population of over four thousand and was platted in 1868. So, what makes Peculiar so peculiar? Well, nothing in particular, but it makes the list because who doesn't want to say they have been to Peculiar? Is there a cooler name?

There are multiple stories of the name's roots. According to author Tori Wiseman, the name came from the postmaster general. The townspeople submitted three choices, but all were already Missouri town names, so as the story goes, they allowed the postmaster general to make the final decision. They told him, "We don't care what name you give us so long as it is sort of peculiar." Thus he decided on the name Peculiar and wrote, "My conclusion is that in all the land it would be difficult to image a more distinctive, a more peculiar name than Peculiar." This might be a sign that townspeople need to create their own names.

Another story comes from author Margot Ford McMillen, who wrote that a settler said, "Well, that's peculiar! It's the very place I saw in a vision back in Connecticut."

Either way, it's a great name, and the town has an equally great motto: "Peculiar, where the 'odds' are with you."

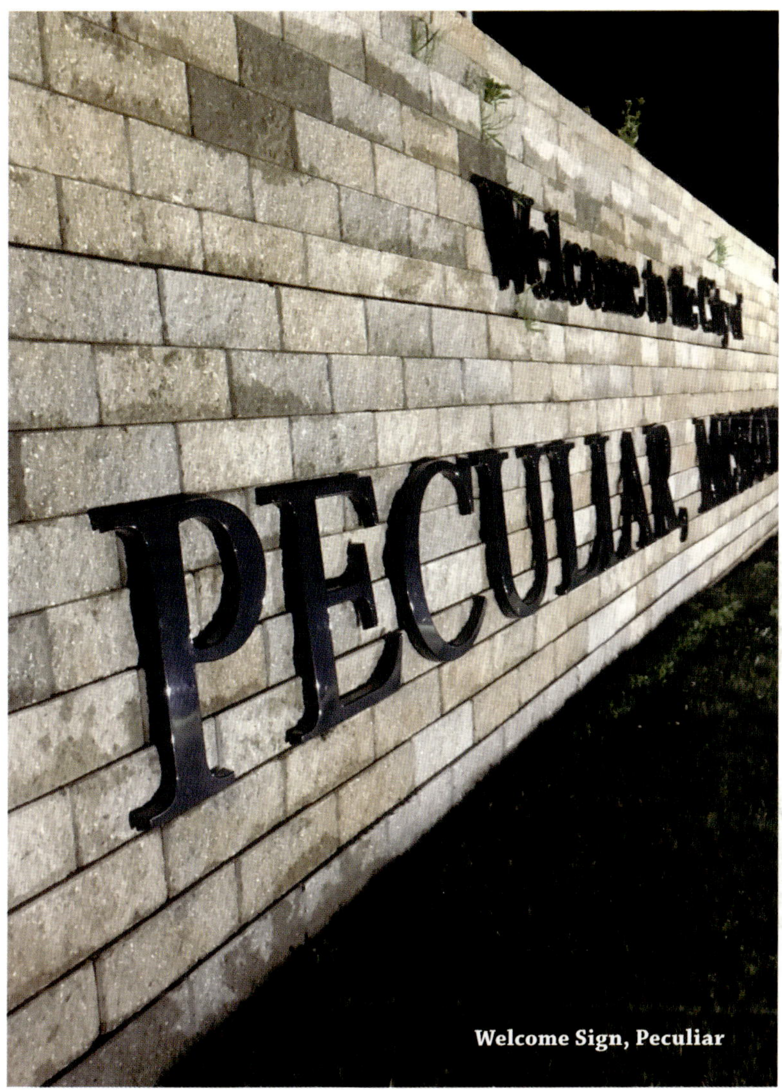

Welcome Sign, Peculiar

## MUST DO

You need to find a town sign or business sign and get a Peculiar selfie. And there's plenty of Peculiar apparel and gear to purchase.

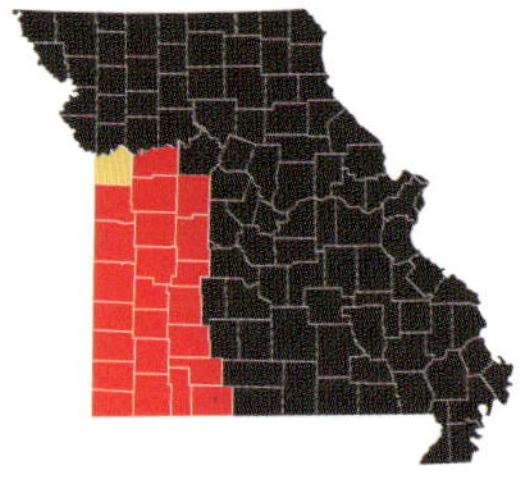

# 32

# Sibley

With a population of 350, there's not much to see in Sibley, but there is a piece of history that is fun to explore. This historical landmark had already closed by the time Sibley was platted in 1836.

That notable landmark is Fort Osage, a wooden log stockade and cowboy and Indian fort resting high above the Missouri River. Lewis and

**Fort Osage, Sibley**

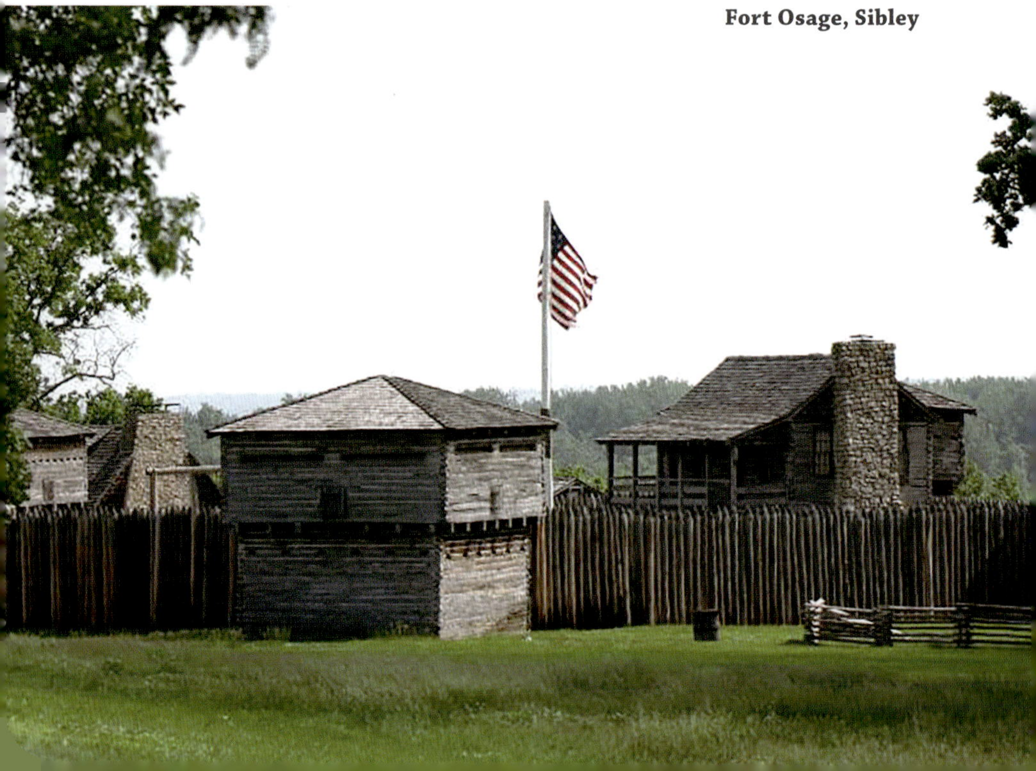

Clark traveled through the area in 1804, and Clark noted this was a key spot for a fort because of its strategic vantage point. Clark would later become the militia commander and chief Indian agent for the Louisiana Territory. Remembering his notes, he built Fort Osage in 1808. It remained operational until 1827 when Fort Leavenworth was opened.

Fort Osage was a "factory system" fort meant to serve the interest of Native Americans in the fur trade. George Sibley, for whom the town was named, was the lead Indian agent stationed there.

The original fort is long gone, but in 1951 a replica was built to the original specifications. It's a fascinating site. There's history to learn and relive. Many will find that the fort seems like something from their childhood imagination.

## MUST DO

Visit and tour the Fort Osage National Historic Landmark.

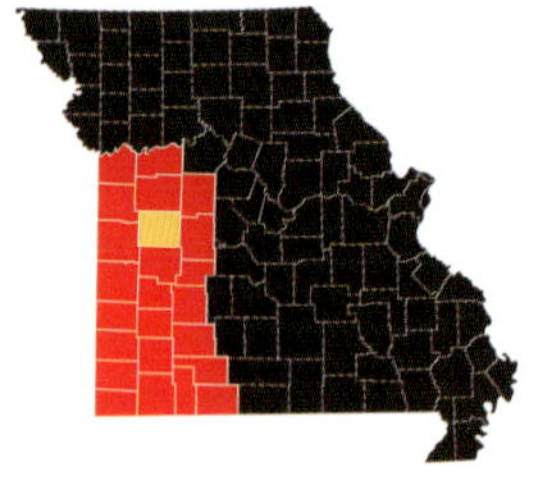

# 33

# *Tightwad*

A few pages earlier was the town Peculiar, chosen to be covered in this book because the name was so, well, peculiar. If there is a town sign that may make a funnier picture, it's Tightwad. Yes, Tightwad. But what makes a visit even more enticing is that a visitor can take a picture in front of Tightwad Bank

And technically, "town" is not the right term for Tightwad—it's actually a village with a population of sixty-four. There seem to be multiple

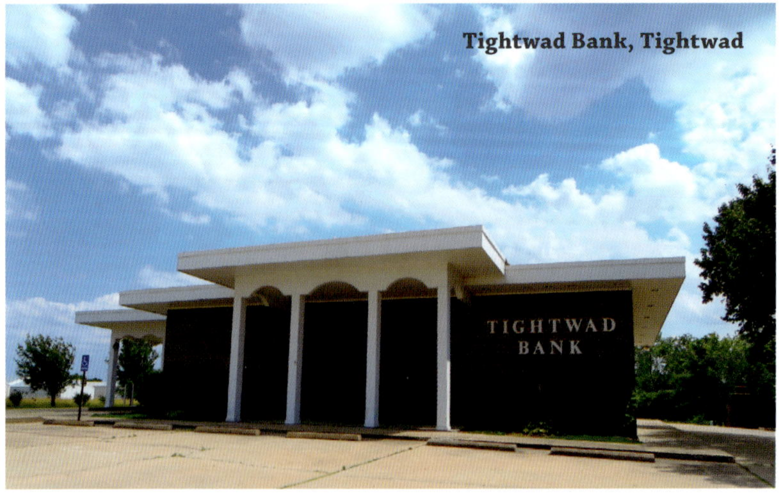

**Tightwad Bank, Tightwad**

stories behind the village's name, but between them all is a common thread and, you guessed it, a tightwad.

The story is not so much about the village, but rather its bank. In 1984, a branch of Citizens Bank of Windsor opened but was closed in 2006. In 2008, the bank opened under the name Tightwad Bank, but by 2018 this bank too had closed. The bank took its name from its location, but the humor of such a name in the financial sector has drawn much attention. Today that bank and sign sit ready for a fun road trip and selfie.

## MUST DO

Visit Tightwad Bank, take a picture, and get a good laugh.

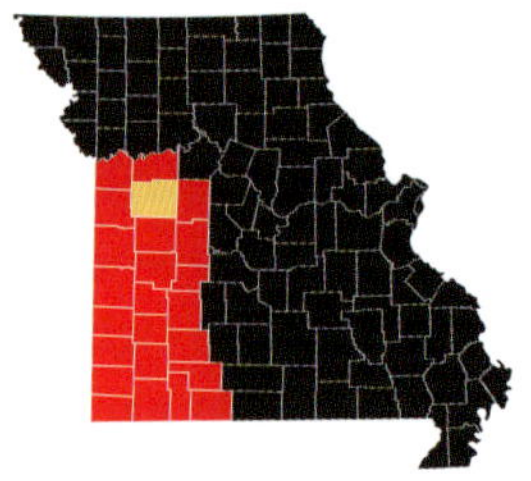

# 34

# Warrensburg

Warrensburg is a bit over the target population for this project at nearly nineteen thousand, but that includes the University of Central Missouri with over twelve thousand students. A visit here proves Warrensburg to be a quintessential American small town. There are great things going on that are fun to do and beneficial to others, as well as fascinating history. But above all that could be mentioned about this town is the origin of a phrase likely assumed to have always existed. It's surprising that a small Missouri town would be where this term was coined.

Here in 1837, as documented by court records, a dog was first called "man's best friend." Surprising, isn't it? Now it's no doubt possible it was said before, but the coining of the phrase is traced back to a famous court case originating in Warrensburg and making it to the Missouri Supreme Court. Burden v. Hornsby came about when Charles Burden's black-and-tan hound, Old Drum, was shot for wandering onto Hornsby's property. Burden then sued Hornsby and won the case. Much of the victory came from the powerful closing arguments of Burden's lawyer, George Vest. In these closing words he stated that a dog is man's best friend. The case is commemorated by a statue of Old Drum in front of the Warrensburg Courthouse.

Warrensburg traces its establishment back to 1833, when Martin Warren settled in the location from Kentucky, hence the name Warrensburg. Beyond Old Drum, there's more four-legged history to this town, for it was once called the Missouri Mule Capital. Mules belonging to

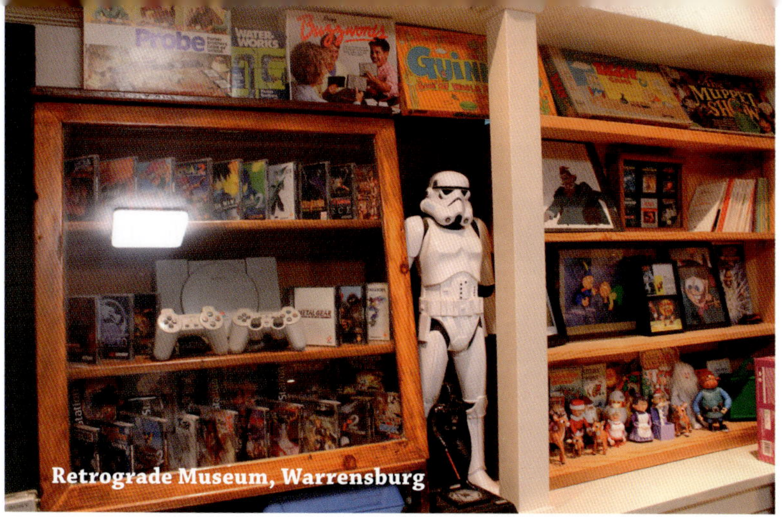

Retrograde Museum, Warrensburg

the local Jones Brothers Horse and Mule Barn won awards at the Missouri State Fair and the St. Louis World's Fair. They also provided mules for the army during World War I. Though no longer in operation, the barn is still there.

## MUST DO

It's worth the drive to the historic sites around Warrensburg—Old Drum, the Mule Barn, and the famous Pertle Springs. But there are also recent attractions to visit, like the Retrograde Charitable Toy and Video Game Museum, which is the type of place many have to pinch themselves to believe is real. It's a shocking experience when you walk into the first floor of this old Victorian house. Definitely not what you would expect. It's a layered experience—there's the entertainment end of the museum and the arcade, but there's also the tangible community difference being achieved.

If something has been played within the last forty or fifty years, this museum has it—vintage Fisher-Price, GI Joe, Strawberry Shortcake, Teddy Ruxpin, He-Man, Lite-Brite, Star Wars, handheld electronics, and much more. They also have a prized collection of authentic animated movie cels along with vintage board games. And the collection grows daily. On the arcade side are several vintage arcade games and nearly every game console from the past decades. The museum often hosts game tournaments.

Retrograde is a perfect affordable activity for families, kids, and kids at heart or for a fun date night. Along with the trip back in time, the museum and arcade are making a difference in the community: Retrograde is

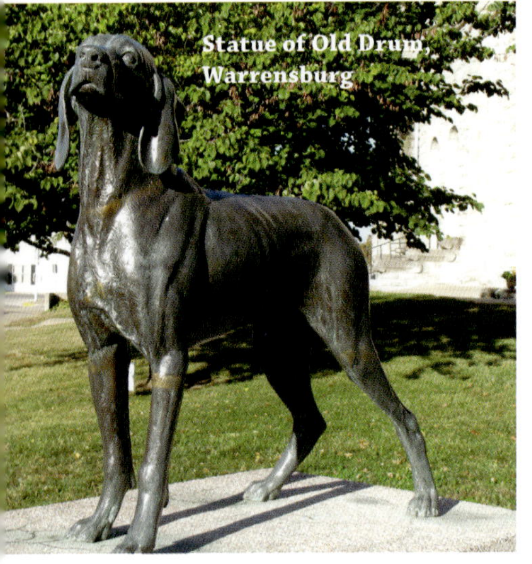
Statue of Old Drum, Warrensburg

a nonprofit benefiting the Children's Community Charity, which in return works with other local nonprofits to meet the basic needs of children and families. To have a more direct effect, Retrograde president Brian Chamberlin says the museum is meant to be a safe space for kids and families. Along with regular hours, they open the arcade for children's groups for free. Chamberlin says that tapping into the joy of one's childhood breaks down many of the barriers we have in society. One look back at that favorite toy or game quickly sparks a smile.

Another must-do in town dealing with more recent history is Those Were the Days Antique Mall, which, at fifty-five thousand square feet, is one of the largest in Missouri. With three stories, chances are you'll find what you are looking for, and you'll definitely be transported back in time.

## MUST EAT

Another business that is producing a great product and making a difference in town is Rise Café. The café is part of Rise Community Services, which helps individuals with developmental disabilities and their families. There's a two-fold benefit to the café as it provides work for those in the program and supports the organization financially. Don't let the charitable aspect of the café make you think the quality is subpar. The down-home cooking is great. There's not a dish you won't like. The tenderloin sandwich is one of the best around.

## MUST NOTE

Warrensburg was home to Dale Carnegie, the author and speaker who wrote famous self-improvement books like *How to Win Friends and Influence People* during his teenage years. He also attended what is now the University of Central Missouri.

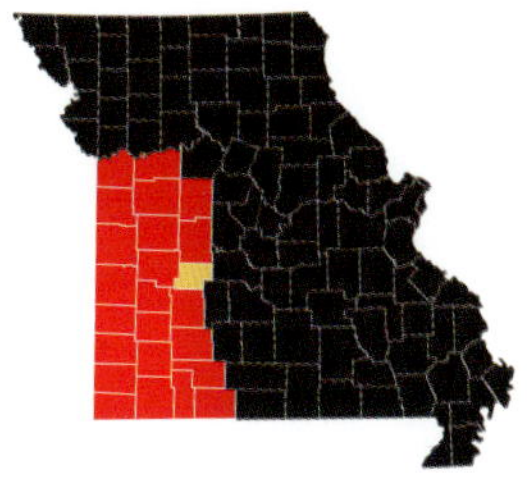

# 35

# *Weaubleau*

There's not much to see and do in Weaubleau with its population of 418, but there is a type of rock found only in the area near town. And the town sits in the fourth-largest meteorite impact crater in the United States. It's a must-visit for geology enthusiasts, but for everyone else, the lore of the rocks and their possible cosmic roots is fascinating.

Weaubleau was first called Haran and was later given the name of a nearby stream. Weaubleau came from the Native American name of the creek, meaning "blue water." The town was founded in 1867, and what growth it had was due to Weaubleau Christian College, which closed in 1914.

It's the geological phenomenon that has kept this town on the radar. The Weaubleau structure is a twelve-mile-wide probable meteorite impact site. It's located along the thirty-eighth parallel, which places it in line with other impact sites around the globe. The meteorite is estimated at 1,200 feet in diameter and is believed to have struck the area in ancient times. Scientists have been very interested in the site because it's the largest exposed site in the United States.

More tangible are the unique rocks found only here. These perfectly round stones are fondly called Weaubleau eggs not only because of their shape but because of a yolk-like appearance within the stone when split open. They also are called Round Rocks, Missouri Round Rocks, or Missouri Cannonballs.

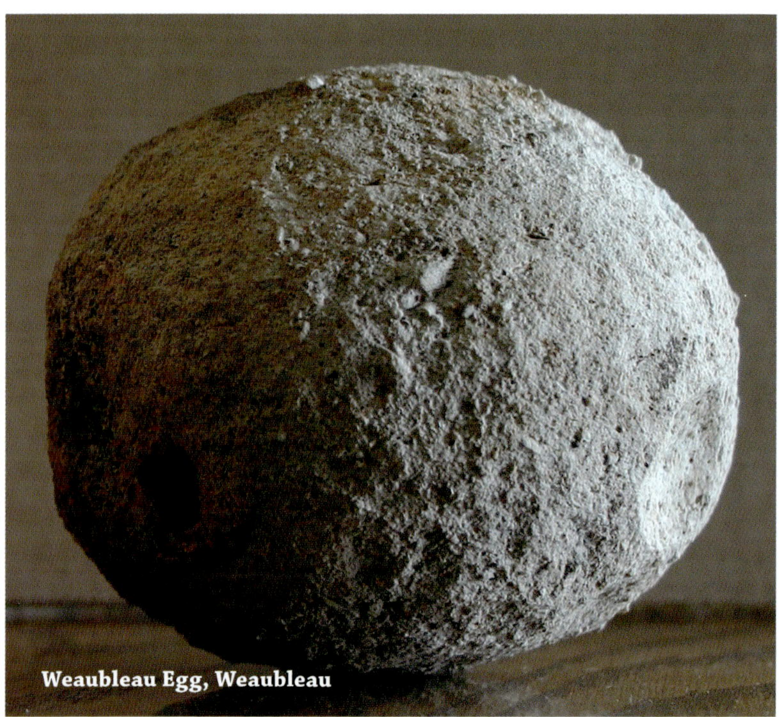

Weaubleau Egg, Weaubleau

## MUST DO

Plenty of Weaubleau eggs can be found without much effort. Try walking creek beds, especially in hot summer months when they are drier. Certain locations along the Osage River leading into Truman Lake can also produce some.

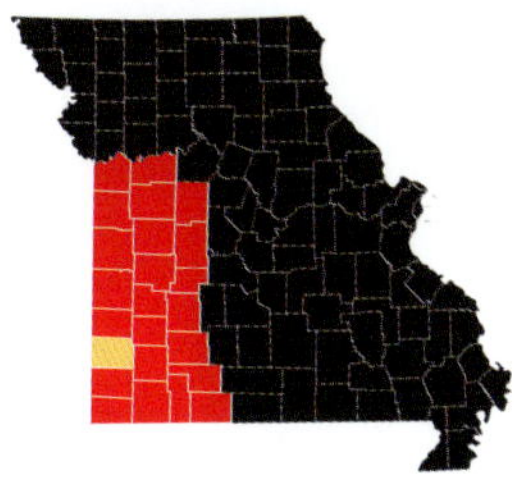

# 36

# Webb City

A quick drive through Webb City and it becomes clear that high school football is a big deal. You see "Cardinal" appear on almost all business signs, and there's a nice stadium with the Cardinal Dome next to it. No town in Missouri could be prouder of their high school football than Webb City, where, as of 2018, the team had made fourteen state championship game appearances and had won the title eleven times, ten since 2000. The Cardinals won five in a row from 2010 through 2014. The *Joplin Globe* wrote, "Since 2000, Webb City has either won a state championship or lost to the eventual state champ in every year except for 2007." Head coach John Roderique, in a Time Warner Kansas City interview, credited the hardworking mindset of the town as one of the major reasons for success.

Webb City has a history built on hard work. It was platted by John C. Webb in 1875, hence the name. A couple of years prior, he found lead while plowing. This led to a mining boom. Within twenty years, there were seven hundred mines in town and the area became a leader in zinc ore. The town boomed to a population of 15,000, which is more than today's 10,996. In the area (including Joplin) there were over 100,000 people. Prosperity continued throughout World War I, but following the war, there was a lead boom in Oklahoma, and companies were prompted to move their operations.

The city quickly brought in new industries, which stopped depopulation, but it never returned to the turn-of-the-century glory. Route

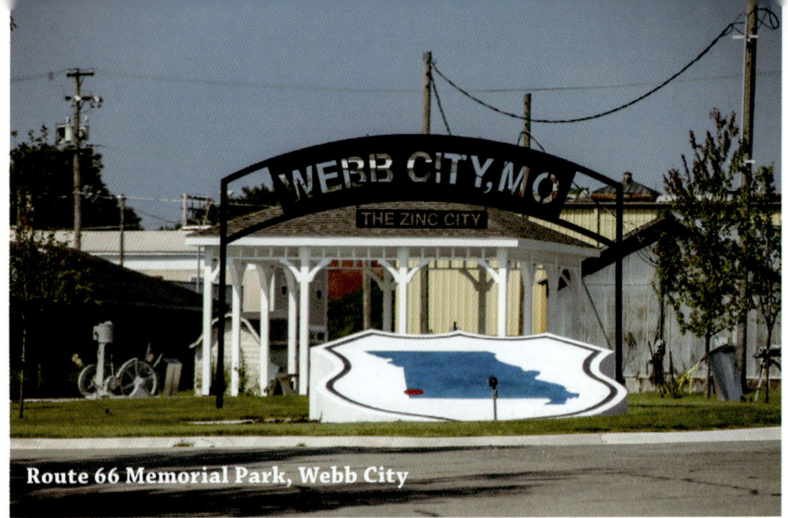

Route 66 Memorial Park, Webb City

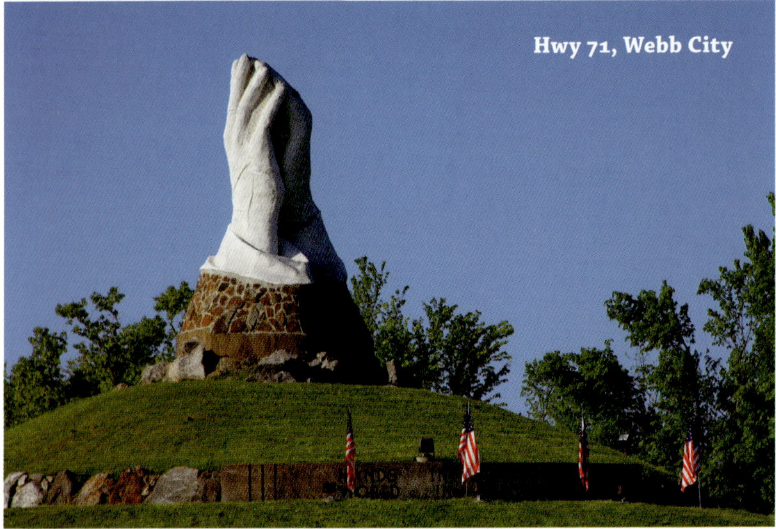
Hwy 71, Webb City

44 also passes through Webb City, and visitors come to see the historic downtown district.

## MUST DO

Since 1972, Webb City has been identified by a giant sculpture of hands in prayer. The statue created by J. E. "Jack" Dawson is thirty-two feet tall, but a forty-foot hill at the base brings the fingertips to over seventy feet. Webb City sits only a few miles from Carthage and Joplin.

# *The Ozarks across the South*

Stretching nearly across the entire state is this hilly, tradition-deep region.

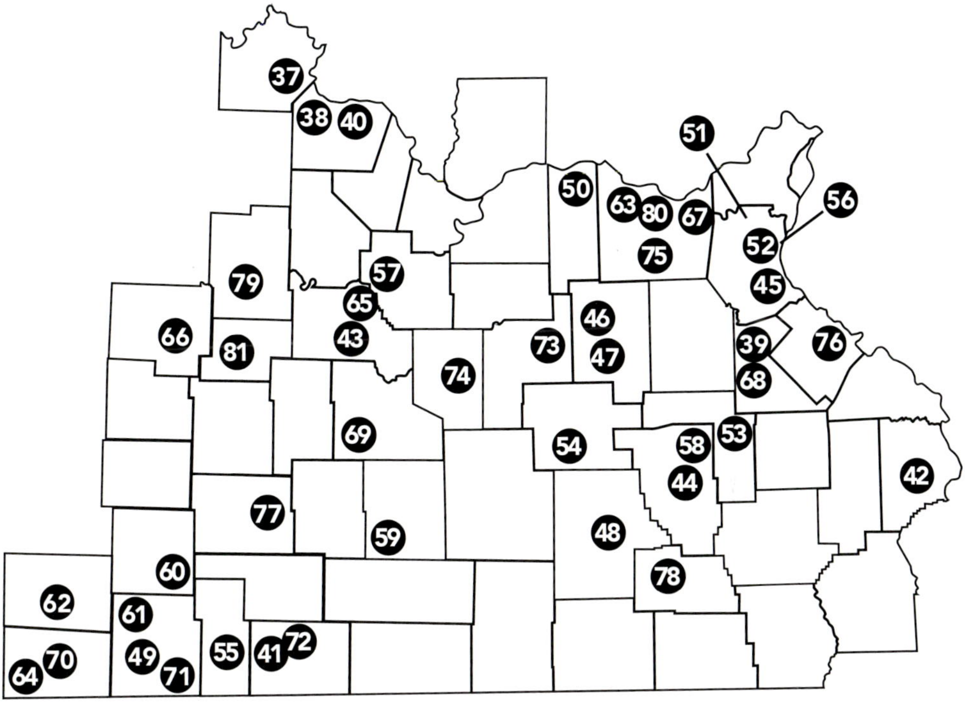

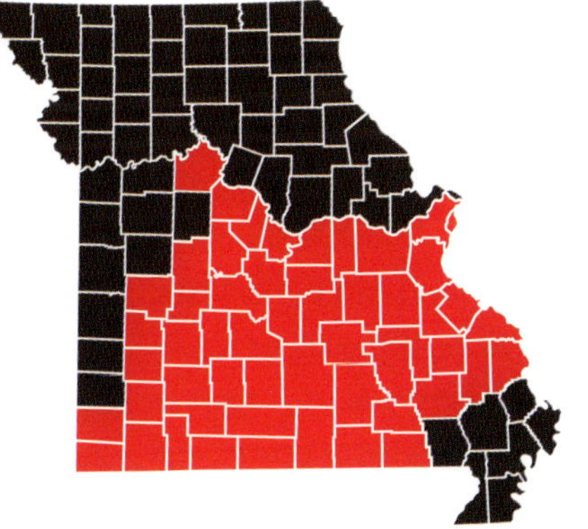

## The Ozarks across the South

37. Arrow Rock
38. Blackwater
39. Bonne Terre
40. Boonville
41. Branson
42. Burfordville
43. Camdenton
44. Centerville
45. Crystal City
46. Cuba
47. Davisville
48. Eminence
49. Exeter
50. Hermann
51. High Ridge
52. Imperial
53. Ironton
54. Jadwin
55. Kimberling City
56. Kimmswick
57. Lake Ozark
58. Lesterville
59. Mansfield
60. Marionville
61. Monett
62. Neosho
63. New Haven
64. Noel
65. Osage Beach
66. Osceola
67. Pacific
68. Park Hills
69. Phillipsburg
70. Pineville
71. Roaring River
72. Rockaway Beach
73. St. James
74. St. Robert
75. Stanton
76. Ste. Genevieve
77. Strafford
78. Van Buren
79. Warsaw
80. Washington
81. Wheatland

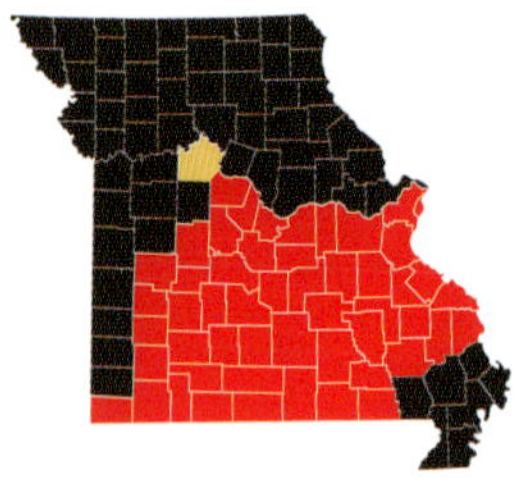

# 37

# *Arrow Rock*

Visiting Arrow Rock means you must visit a historical site and state park, for the whole town is a national historic landmark: the Arrow Rock Historic District. It was the first Missouri state park when it was acquired in 1923, which was rightfully so because Arrow Rock is full of history.

Founded in 1829 with the name Philadelphia, or New Philadelphia, in 1833 the state legislature changed the name to Arrow Rock. The name for the area has been traced back to a 1732 French map noting the identifiable bluff along the Missouri River that contained flint that native tribes would use for arrowheads. The 1804 Lewis and Clark expedition also called the bluff Arrow Rock. The name seems to have been ingrained in the Native American tribes and early European settlers, and this identifiable location became noteworthy to travelers who came through on the Santa Fe Trail. Much of this history has been preserved in the park, like the J. Hustin Tavern, the oldest continuously serving restaurant west of the Mississippi River, which traces its establishment back to 1834.

## MUST DO

Arrow Rock is one of the most popular small-town locations in the state. Entering the town is like stepping into the past. Everything about it connects to history, from where you might stay to where you might eat or shop. There are shops to check out, the museum at the visitor center, and other historical sites to see.

Since 1961, the town has also been home to the Lyceum Theatre, which is one of Missouri's oldest professional theatres. This theatre, their performances, and its tenure are "eighth wonder of the world" material. In this little town of fifty-six people, there has been a professional theatre that has put on Broadway-caliber productions for almost sixty years, with professional actors, actresses, and dancers who audition in New York. They regularly fill up their 416-seat theatre and have over 33,000 guests come through each summer. It has to be seen to be believed. The venue itself is also unique: originally, the theatre began in an old Baptist church. Though the auditorium has been upgraded they have maintained this historic, folksy facility which provides an intimate experience for high-level shows.

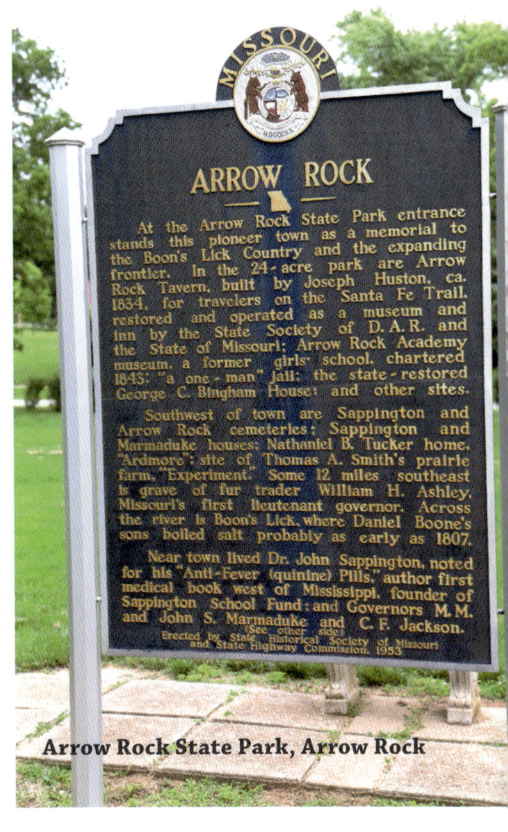

**Arrow Rock State Park, Arrow Rock**

The middle of Missouri has some of the deepest historical roots of European settlers in the state. During the early 1800s, Arrow Rock and its environs were known as Boone's Lick Country. At that time there were large numbers of saltwater springs in the area. Nathan and Daniel Morgan, sons of the famous frontiersman Daniel Boone, produced salt from the springs, which they would then transport to St. Louis. Their work brought notoriety to the area through the famous Boone name and the hard work in building this salt business. Nearby is the Boone's Lick State Historic Site where visitors can see the remnants of that business.

## MUST EAT

In this journey through ninety of the most special small towns in the state, there are stellar restaurants. There are two that have left this author with a one-word description—"perfect," and Catalpa in Arrow Rock is one of them. And truth be told it's the most perfect one. The best in the state.

Catalpa could possibly be the smallest restaurant you've ever seen, but inside an experience awaits that you will not forget. The list of accolades that this restaurant and its chef have amassed is unreal. They have earned Restaurant or Chef of the Year by *Feast* magazine for four years as of 2018 and have won Best Restaurant by *Rural Missouri* magazine for six consecutive years.

As stated, it's small, with only eight tables in the dining room and a chef's table in the kitchen. Reservations are a must! The food is presented so beautifully that you almost (notice almost) don't want to disturb it. But the taste—oh my! Each item is masterfully made and seasoned. The menu is selective: there are only five main dishes, but they are diverse enough that it's still hard to decide. The appetizers are works of art themselves. The meals are higher in price than what is typically found in small towns, but the overall experience makes the price worth it. It's a mix of elegant, casual, and just plain fun. It's a very interactive experience. They also have special Christmas meals.

J. Huston Tavern is one of the oldest operating restaurants. The environment is special— you feel like you've just deboarded from a riverboat and are hitting the local tavern. The food is fabulous, especially the all-you-can-eat family-style Sunday lunches.

## MUST STAY

Arrow Rock and its surroundings are bed-and-breakfast galore—there are numerous choices and a B and B is the best way to enjoy the town. There are several in town and some nearby in Rocheport as well. The Iron Horse Hotel in Blackwater is a popular choice. Also keep in mind vacation rentals. Check on Airbnb.

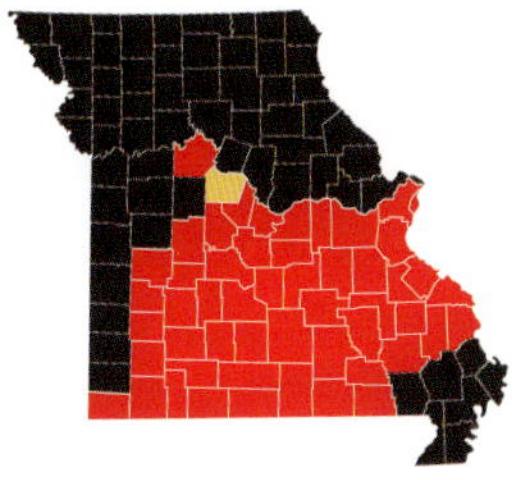

# 38

# Blackwater

Driving south on K Highway from the previously mentioned Arrow Rock, you first spot the Blackwater River with its muddy water and dark-stained banks, a brief strip of farmland, a railroad crossing, and then the quaint town comes into view. Draped on the left is an elevated late-1800s train depot, and on the right, an old boardwalk traces the edge of an old brick building, both landmarks warning that it's about to be a trip back in time—a quick trip, but a good trip.

The historic downtown strip of Blackwater is short but has an allure about it. Almost like a movie set. It's just a few buildings with distinct parking in the middle rather than at the curb. And deep center is an endearing windmill.

Blackwater is another Missouri town seemingly made for a Hallmark movie. If it was the location for one of those movies, the Iron Horse Restaurant and Hotel would be the centerpiece. It's a place for a romantic weekend or a family road trip to relive the late 1800s.

Blackwater was platted in 1887 and became the only coal refuel stop for the Missouri Pacific Railroad running from Jefferson City to Kansas City. The name has roots in Native American tribes from the area. They had named the river Blackwater due to its dark mud banks, and the town took on that name.

The town has always been small, now with a population of just 162, and the loss of a rock quarry in the 1980s caused the town to fall into

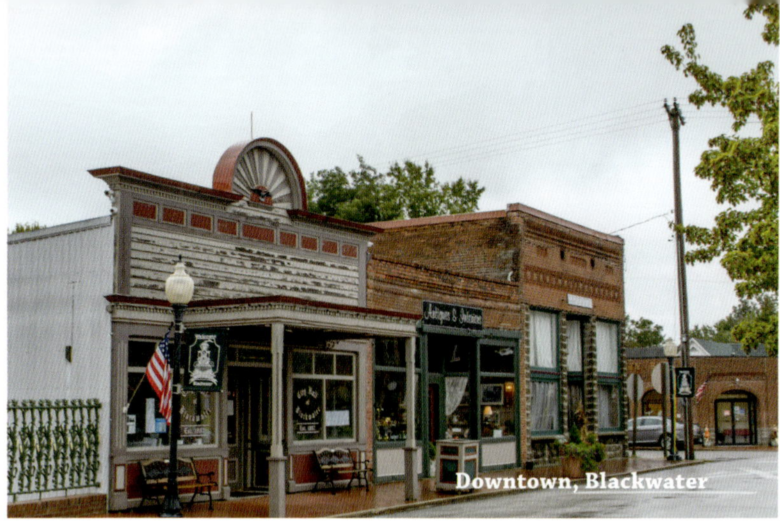
Downtown, Blackwater

disrepair. But a revival led by twenty-six-year-old mayor Bobby Danner turned the town around and made it an attractive destination.

## MUST STAY

In that one block of downtown sits the Iron Horse Hotel, known as the City Hotel in the late 1800s and early 1900s, and it was the place the wealthy railroad barons would stay. The hotel has been restored and now has ten rooms that take guests into the past. It's a magical stay, as guests can easily walk down the steps and within a block visit the sights.

## MUST EAT

The Iron Horse boasts an elegant restaurant where owner and chef Tracy Russell serves specialty dishes with a beautiful presentation. Chef Russell was born in New Orleans and trained in Italy. He brings a varied experience to create a unique dining experience but will usually have some New Orleans twist. Another choice is Kimberly Place, which offers a more casual experience and where one can find a large tenderloin sandwich.

## MUST DO

When visitors begin planning their itinerary, they're likely to be surprised by all there is to do in town. You can stroll through downtown and down the boardwalk to the 1890s jail. There's an 1800s-era vault to crack and a jail cell with fold-down bunks to try out. Also in town is the Mid-Missouri Museum of Independent Telephone Pioneers, which

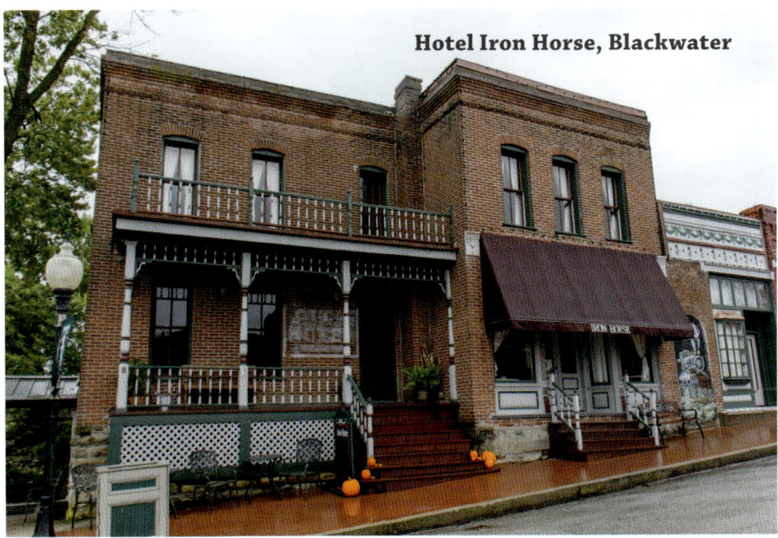
Hotel Iron Horse, Blackwater

houses telephone memorabilia. The old switchboards are fascinating to see in person.

In particular parts of the year, the West End Theater is open. This local production company brings entertainment to the evenings. Along with the sights in Blackwater, Arrow Rock is nearby, and the two could be combined in a trip, with the recommendation to stay at the Iron Horse.

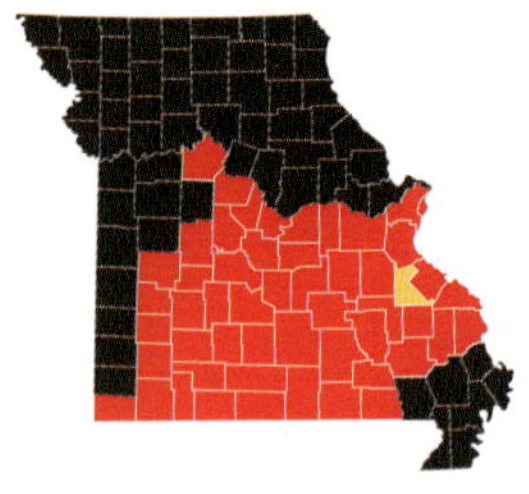

# 39

# Bonne Terre

Only sixty miles south of St. Louis is a town with an attraction that National Geographic Adventure called one of America's top ten greatest adventures: the world's largest freshwater dive resort. And this one-billion-gallon lake is located in downtown Bonne Terre. Hard to imagine how such a large lake could be downtown, especially when on a drive or stroll there, you cannot see this wonder. But you would be there. You'd be on top of it. For the Billion Gallon Lake is underground in the Bonne Terre Mine. A mine tour, and especially a dive, will be an unforgettable adventure in your life.

Bonne Terre is a remnant of when the territory belonged to the French. French settlers discovered lead in 1720 and called the city La Terre Bonne, which means "good earth" or "good soil." The actual town was not established until 1864 when the St. Joseph Lead Company bought land to begin operations in the area. They were initially set back because of General Sterling Price's Raid, the Confederacy's last campaign in the west, which intended to recapture Missouri and secure supplies for the Confederate Army.

Following the initial setbacks in mining, Bonne Terre was platted in 1880. The St. Joseph Company's mine proved productive and was the world's largest producer of iron until its closing in 1962. During much of that time, St. Joseph's mines produced 70 percent of US lead. In the 1970s, Doug and Cathy Goergens bought the mine and transformed it into the great experience it is today.

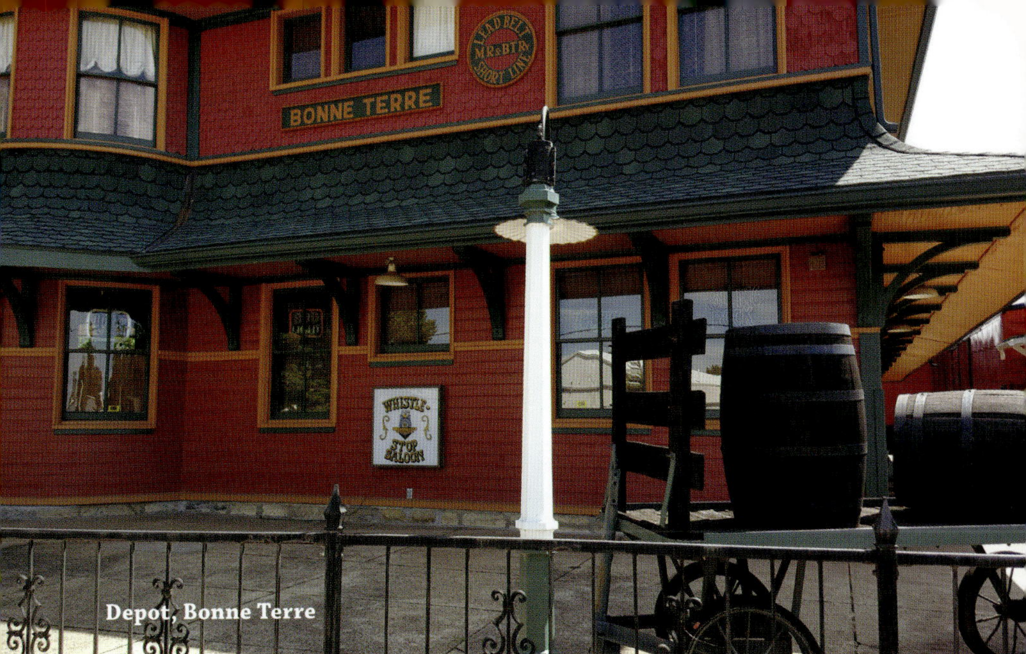

Depot, Bonne Terre

## MUST DO

There's no doubt why you need to visit Bonne Terre—the Bonne Terre Mine. In 2016, the mine was named America's best underwater attraction by *USA Today* readers. From May to September it's open seven days a week. During the winter months it's only open on weekends. It's a fascinating tour. The mine has five layers, and part of the tour is an hour walk through the top two layers. Guests are able to see abandoned mine equipment. The work in this area dates back to the 1860s. The tour then moves to a boat ride on the seventeen-mile lake, illuminated by stadium lights to allow the viewing of abandoned mine shafts and mining equipment. Be warned that it is impossible to stay dry on the tour.

The walking and boat tour is worth the drive, wherever you might be road-tripping from. But if you're a diver, how have you not been here already? It has eighty-eight miles of passageways, taking divers through archways and past shafts and pillars in crystal-clear water lit by stadium lights. The bottom remains a ghost town, as mining equipment has been left throughout the lake.

There's more than the mine in town. Another fun stop is the Space Museum, which exhibits the personal space collection of Earl Mullins along with space-travel gear on loan from NASA. It's strange to find this in an old building of the mining company, but it's a fascinating museum that takes visitors back to when they thought about being an astronaut.

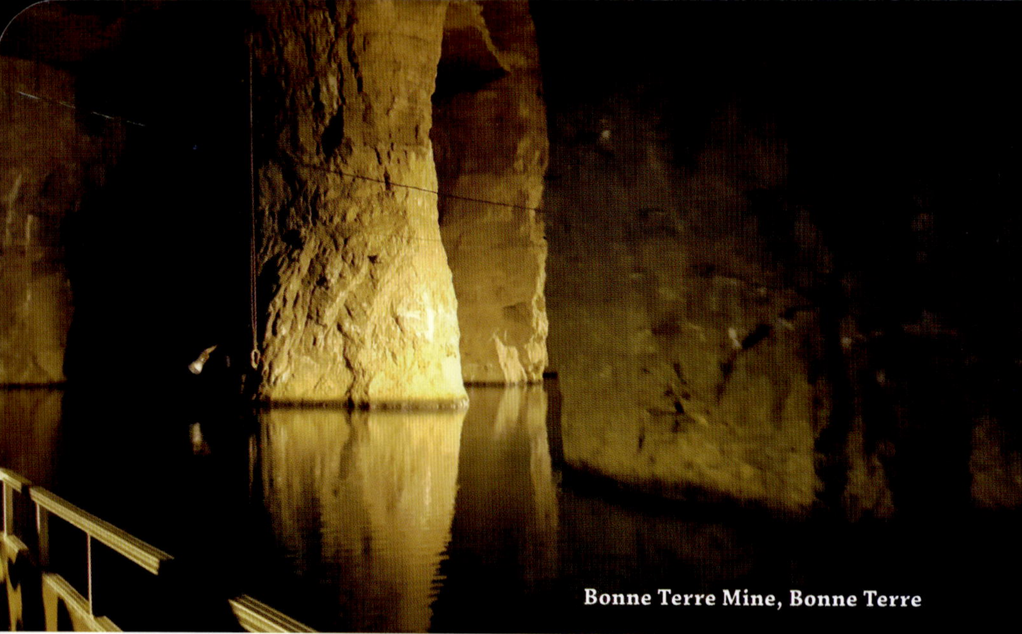
Bonne Terre Mine, Bonne Terre

Maybe these aren't worth the drive by themselves, but while in town go meet Sam, the 1920s-era lead miner sculpture. This 1981 statue was created by local artist Samuel Forrest Wright, whose family were miners in this mine. And then there's the local car lot, Blackwell Motors, with giant animals standing watch over the inventory.

## MUST STAY

The owners of the Bonne Terre Mine have also renovated the historic 1909 railroad depot into a bed-and-breakfast. Historic depots all convey a transportive, nostalgic vibe, but this product of the St. Joseph Lead Company is a remarkable building historically. It's unique among most dotting the state. The decorative staging done by the Goergens take this inn to a whole new level. Staying at the depot feels like you are preparing to catch a train the next morning. The inn has four guest rooms in the depot and two train car suites that make this an incredible stay.

## MUST NOTE

A haunting, intriguing, or infuriating element of town (that's up to you) is the Eastern Reception, Diagnostic and Correctional Center, where all the state's criminal executions have been carried out since 2005.

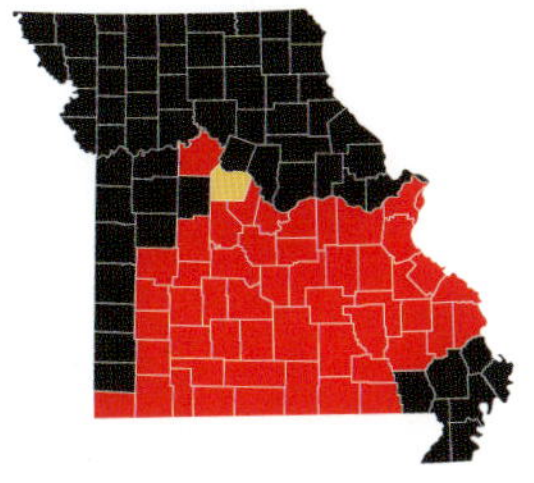

# 40

# Boonville

A rail town that's now a trail town, Boonville is one of the best weekend getaways because of four hundred historic sites, beautiful outdoor adventures, and a town that exudes relaxation and smiles.

Boonville was platted in 1817 but can trace settlement back even further. The names have famous roots, for it was named after Nathan and Daniel Morgan Boone, who were sons of Daniel Boone. They made the area famous with their salt business, which earned it the name Boone's Lick Country.

The Civil War found Boonville. There were two battles there, and the town was captured during Price's Raid. Following the war, Boonville maintained prominence as a river and railroad town, and most of all it was on the Santa Fe Trail. That history has been preserved. As mentioned, there are four hundred buildings that comprise fourteen historic districts in town. The oldest is the Cooper County Jail and Hanging Barn. The jail was built in 1846, operated until 1978, and at that time was the longest continually serving jail in Missouri history. Its most notable inmate was Frank James, brother of Jesse James, and the barn was the site of the last Missouri hanging in 1930.

Another of those long-operating historic buildings is Thespian Hall, which was built in 1855 and continues to host events. Also, the 1912 Spanish Mission–style Katy Depot remains in use as a home to bike rentals for the Katy Trail.

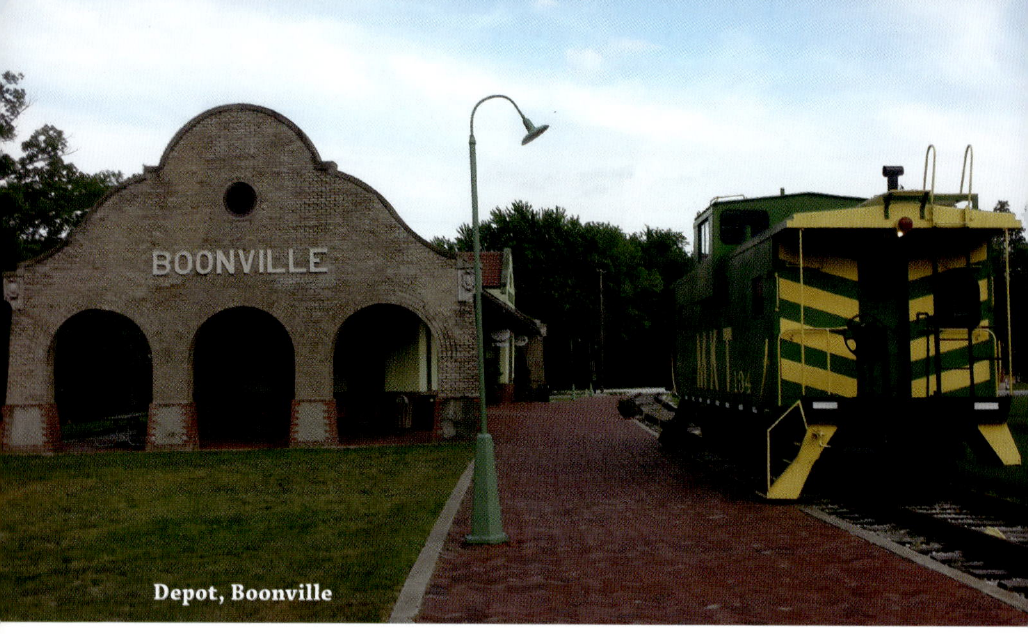


Depot, Boonville

## MUST DO

It seems like there's no end to Boonville's history-related activities. Take a self-guided tour of the historic buildings. Maps are available at the River, Rails, and Trails Museum and Visitor Center. The museum provides a look into the formative years of the town. To top off a historical trip, stay in one of the many bed-and-breakfasts, which are mostly in historic buildings or homes themselves. Hotel Frederick is also a great historic choice.

Keeping with history aspects of the city, there's the Lewis Miller's Mitchell Collection. It's the finest and most extensive collection of Mitchell wagons, bicycles, motorcycles, and automobiles in the world. Miller himself is a member of the Mitchell and Lewis family. The Mitchell family made some of the most popular wagons during the mid-to-late 1800s. They would expand into motorized bicycles and automobiles but would not survive past the early 1920s. Reservations are needed to tour this collection.

Another site to see is Warm Springs Ranch, the primary breeding farm for the Budweiser Clydesdales. The farm is open for visitors. Its sheer size and immaculate grounds make this a beautiful stop.

Boonville is also one of the most popular stops on the Katy Trail, the over two-hundred-mile bike trail created from the former Katy Railroad. The trail weaves in and out from the Missouri River banks, traveling under a shady canopy of trees, along with diving through tunnels and over former rail bridges. Boonville is where the trail crosses to the northern bank of the river. Bicycles and gear are available for rental in town.

And if you're feeling lucky, there's the Isle of Capri Casino in town.

## MUST STAY

Boonville is home to many bed-and-breakfasts. Most continue the historic trappings of town. The High Street Victorian is one to consider. Don't plan a stay without first shopping Airbnb and vacation rentals. The landscape is covered with treasures to stay in.

If an Airbnb is not available, Hotel Frederick needs to make your list. This is a treasure and a distinguished stay. It dates back to 1905—can you imagine all the stories of those who have stayed there? It has a stately, historic feel, but the décor provides a degree of warmth, comfort, and regality that makes it a hip place for those who aren't interested in the history. Each room has its own character. Some even have fully glass-walled bathrooms, so decide how much privacy you want to have during your stay.

## MUST EAT

WJ's has the best mix of quality food and presentation in town. They serve up fine cuisine with a homemade taste. It's located in a historic building, but it doesn't have the nostalgic ambiance that other historically located restaurants have. If it's a burger you're after, then Maggie's Bar and Grill is a great option.

## MUST NOTE

Boonville is the birthplace of Joseph Franklin Rutherford, who was a founder of the Jehovah's Witnesses. It's also the hometown of country music artist Sara Evans.

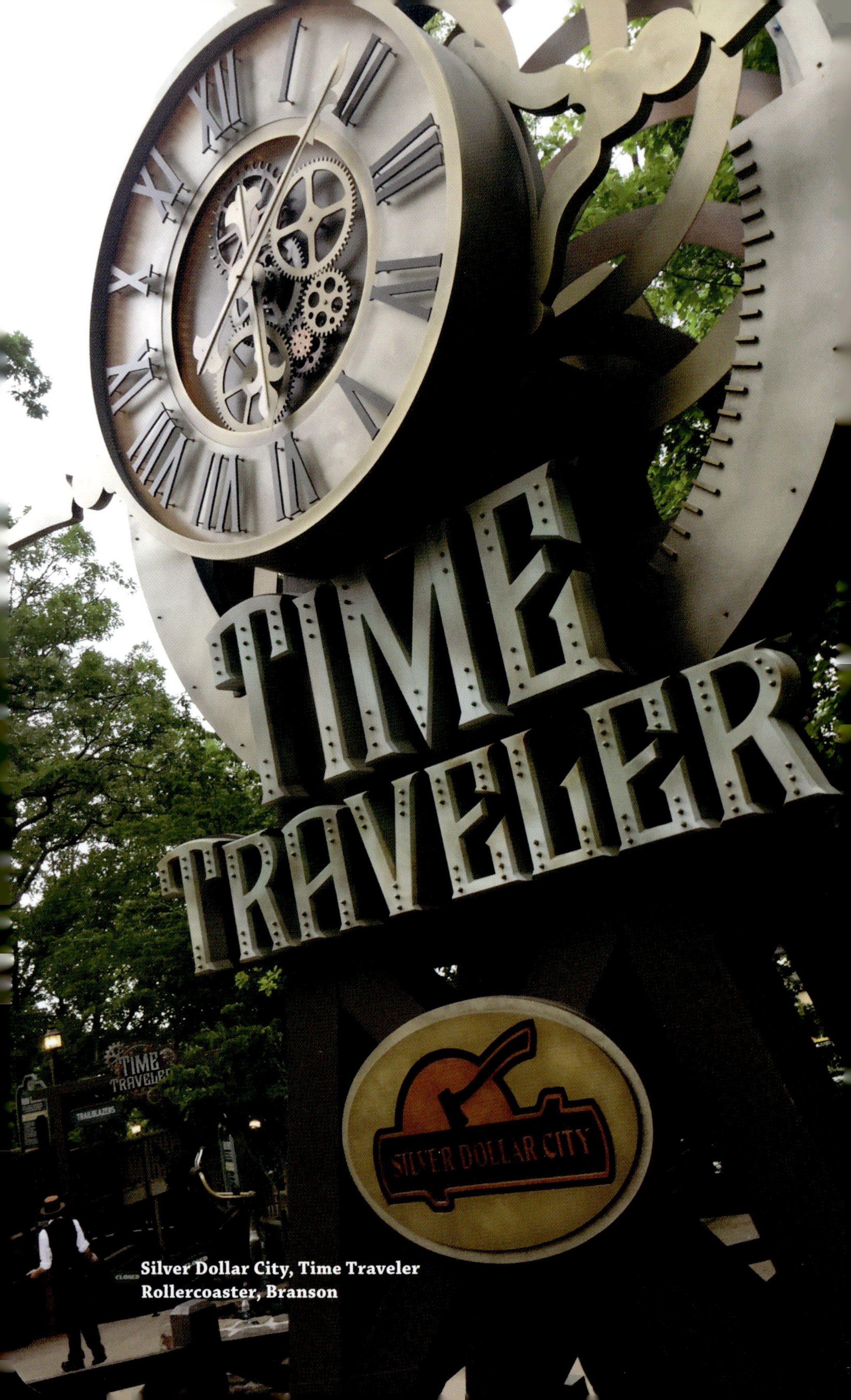


Silver Dollar City, Time Traveler Rollercoaster, Branson

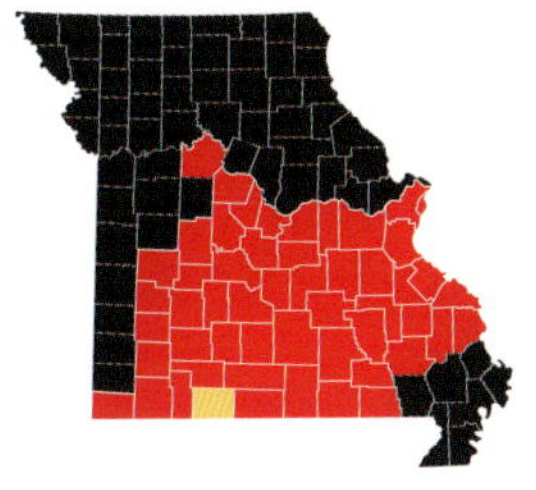

# 41

# Branson

It might be a shock to read that one of the leading tourist destinations in Missouri, and in the country, is a town of less than fifteen thousand people. This town of eleven thousand has over seven million visitors a year, which is not far off destinations in Chicago and San Francisco. A charter bus driver stationed in New England shared that this town, Branson, was the second most frequented place on his bus tours and second only to Disney World.

The story of Branson is incredible. It was established by 1882 and was named after Rueben Branson, who opened the first general store there. Tourism started in 1894, when William Henry Lynch opened Marvel Cave and began charging visitors. In 1960, the theme park Silver Dollar City was opened at the site of the cave.

Also in 1960, *The Shepherd of the Hills Outdoor Drama* began, which was a live reenactment of the famous Ozark novel, *The Shepherd of the Hills*. Table Rock Lake was created by a dam in 1959, and that same year the first live music show opened in Branson—the Baldknobbers Jamboree. During the 1980s and 1990s this small Ozark town became filled with theaters and attractions. A visitor from Australia said, "It's Vegas for families."

There's no shortage of comprehensive travel information or books on Branson, so rather than repeat the top must-do, must-eat, must-stay, must-shop, and must-see things in town, what follows are some of this author's personal favorite spots.

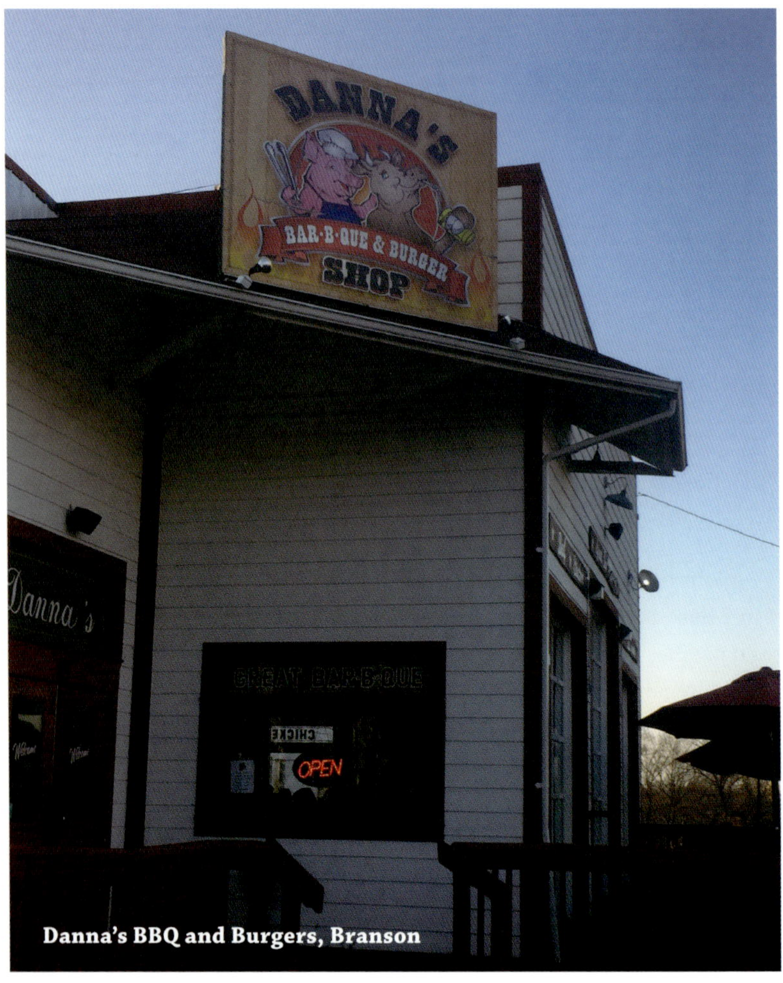


**Danna's BBQ and Burgers, Branson**

## MUST DO

This first must-do attraction is no surprise, for it's the biggest one in town—Silver Dollar City. It became the main attraction for a reason. Initially, Silver Dollar City lacked the number of major thrill rides that parks like Six Flags had, but in the last decade it's become filled with rides. The latest roller coaster, Time Traveler, spins while going upside down and through loops, but for all its chaos it's one of the most enjoyable rides out there. Classic rides like Fire in the Hole and The Lost River are still found at the park. The park is excellent even for younger kids, and there are three separate areas for them. Families have to work hard to do it all.

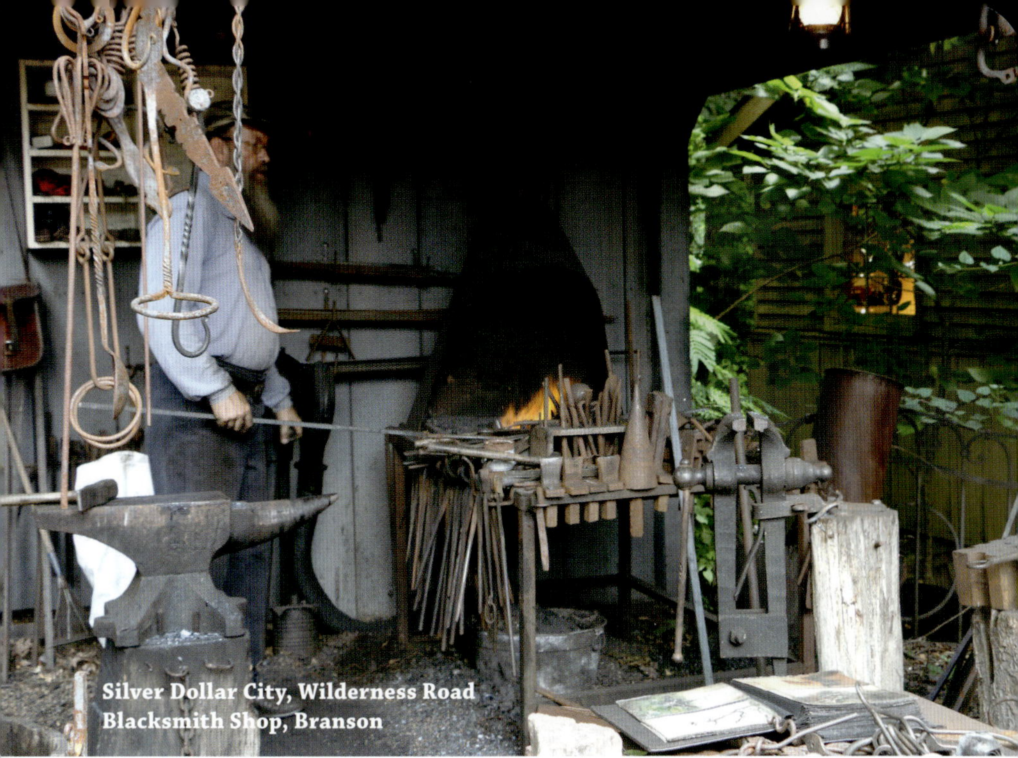

Silver Dollar City, Wilderness Road Blacksmith Shop, Branson

The nostalgia theme is something special, though, because it's downplayed more than it was in the past. If you've never been there, it may be hard to get excited when you hear it's like Disney World but instead of princesses and movie characters there are talented frontier craftsmen like candlemakers, blacksmiths, and others, but the theme works.

The next favorite attraction is the cornerstone for understanding the theme of Silver Dollar City and the culture that runs through and beneath all of Branson's attractions. It's *The Shepherd of the Hills Outdoor Drama*, which features the core story from the famous, 1907 novel *The Shepherd of the Hills*. It was the popularity of this book that initially brought people on a pilgrimage to the Ozarks. The show takes place outside and characters ride in and out on horseback and wagon. It introduces guests to the vigilantes gone bad, Baldknobbers. Expressing the change of the times, much of the Shepherd of the Hills property has been turned into an adventure park with ziplines and UTVs. Dolly Parton's Stampede is a lot of fun and is worth checking out on a family vacation. Also the Branson Landing shopping center along Lake Taneycomo should make the list. The shops may not necessarily be unique, but it's very pleasant to stroll along the lake with the coolness rising from it. There are tons of live shows in Branson, but one theater sits as high above the rest in altitude as it does in its production—the Sight and Sound Theater. It's a huge production with a large cast and remarkable effects.

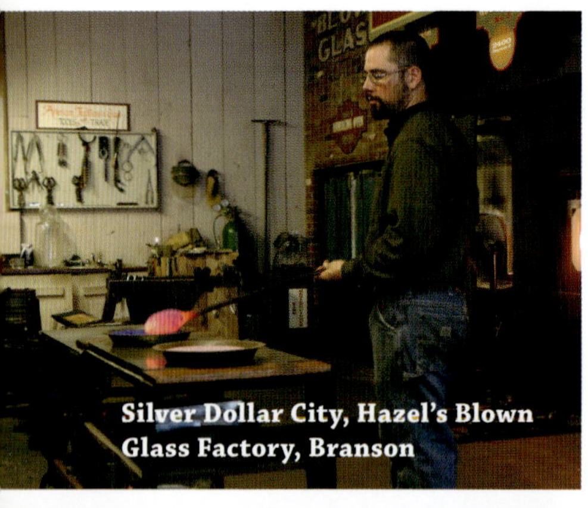
Silver Dollar City, Hazel's Blown Glass Factory, Branson

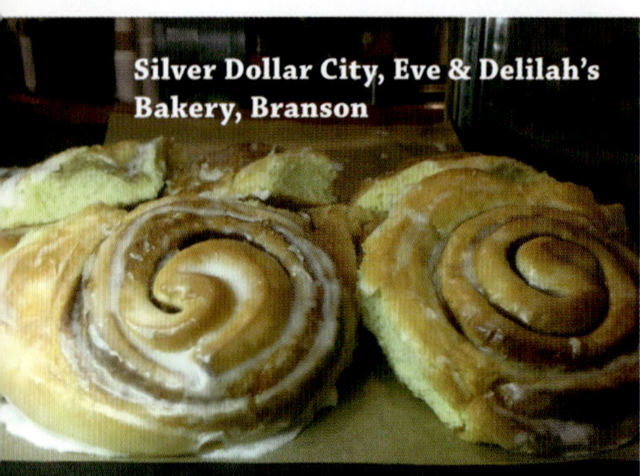
Silver Dollar City, Eve & Delilah's Bakery, Branson

## MUST EAT

Starting with breakfast, there's little competition to Grandma Ruth's cinnamon rolls. These large, life-changing treats must be on your list. Grandma Ruth began making these cinnamon rolls for her church, family, and friends. They were so good she was pushed to open a bakery. Get a cinnamon roll or any of the other breakfast rolls.

If there were competition for best cinnamon roll, it would come from Eva & Delilah's Bakery, close to Silver Dollar City's front gate, but if you plan to eat breakfast at Silver Dollar City, go early and eat the buffet at Molly's Mine. Then be the first in line for Outlaw Run.

As there was no competition for breakfast, there is none for lunch or supper. Anything else you eat should come from Danna's Barbecue. It's the hands-down best place to go. The BBQ is phenomenal, but the highlight is Mimi's Burger, a mix of blue cheese and candied jalapeños that melts with the mayo, making just the perfect combination of sweet, funky, and spicy. After three or four or seven trips to Danna's on your vacation, you might be interested in trying something else, and if you do, then it needs to be Cantina Laredo at the Landing. It's about the only chain restaurant to make the list, but you don't find it just anywhere and it's great Tex-Mex.

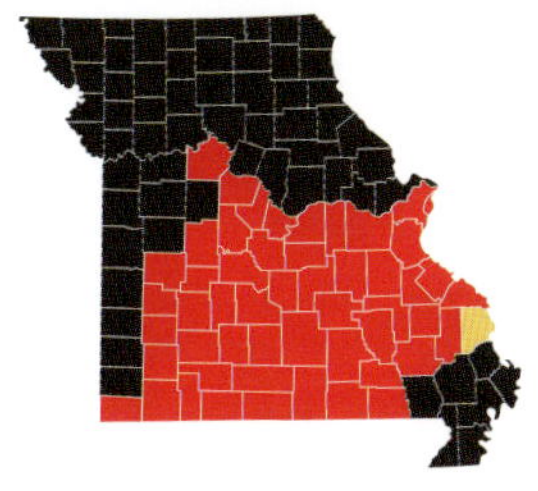

# 42

# Burfordville

The small community of Burfordville allows visitors the chance to step into a postcard or a painting. Side by side are the four-story Bollinger Mill, built in 1867, and the Burfordville Covered Bridge, built in 1868, with the Whitewater River cascading over the mill's dam. It's truly a magical scene—the type of scene that draws you back each of the four seasons to see how the picture looks during those times.

Burfordville is currently an unincorporated community, but its roots go back to 1797 when George Frederick Bollinger built the mill at the edge of the river on land granted to him by the Spanish. After building the mill, he traveled to North Carolina and brought back twenty Swiss and German immigrant families. The mill has always been a centerpiece. Bollinger later rebuilt the log dam and mill with limestone, but during the Civil War, it was burned down by Federal troops to keep the mill from supplying Confederate soldiers. Burfordville's centerpiece did not remain out of commission long. Solomon R. Burford built the current mill in 1867 on the existing limestone foundation from 1825.

The Burfordville Covered Bridge is the oldest surviving covered bridge in Missouri and one of four that remain today. Construction on it began in 1858 but was halted by the war. It was completed in 1868 and operated as a toll booth. A flood in 1986 caused damage to the bridge and ended vehicle traffic, but in 1998 it opened to foot traffic.

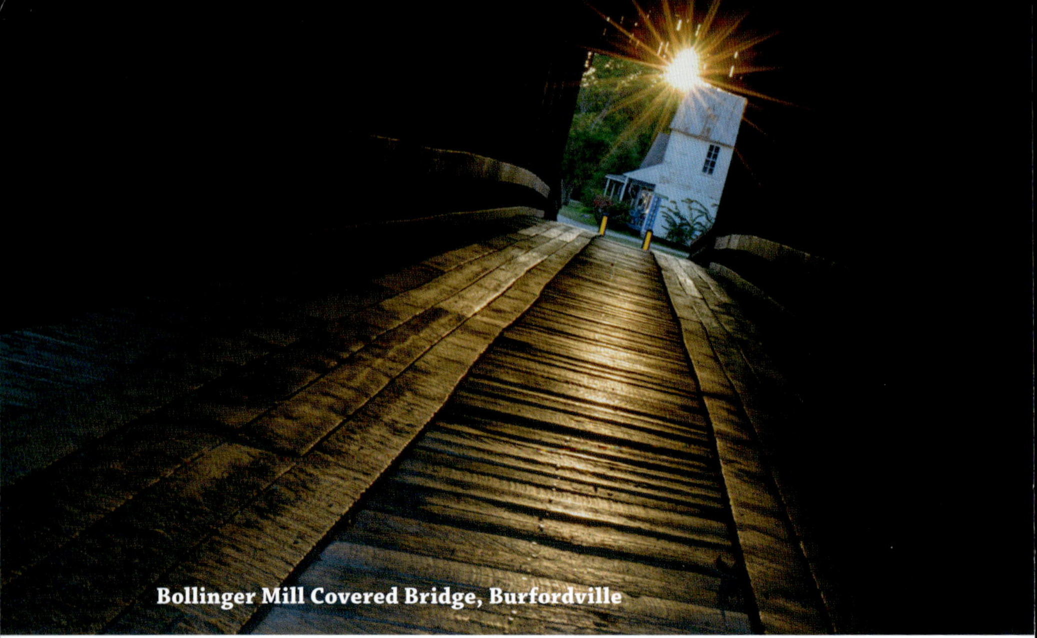

Bollinger Mill Covered Bridge, Burfordville

## MUST DO

A drive out to Burfordville will be rewarded with the sights that await. The bridge is open year round, and the mill offers tours. There are also picnic areas for this nostalgic trip. Most guests wonder why the bridges were covered. The main reason appears to have been to protect the inner structure from the elements.

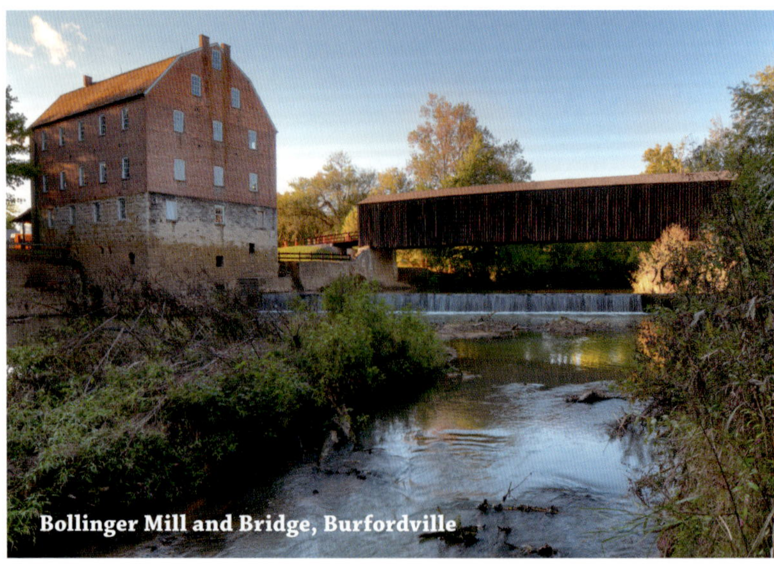

Bollinger Mill and Bridge, Burfordville

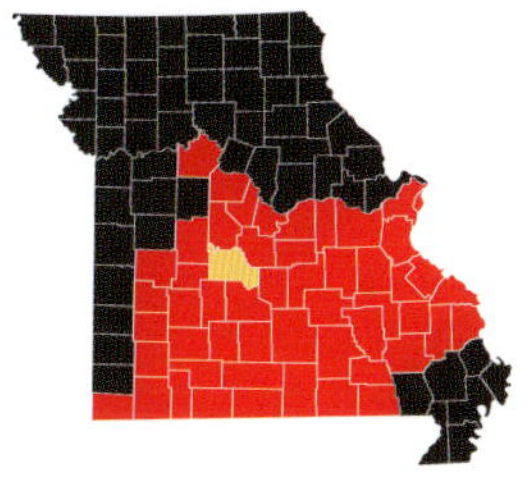

# 43

# Camdenton

Camdenton sits near the Lake of the Ozarks, which is a happening place in the summer. Between Memorial Day and Labor Day, the area receives an estimated five million visitors. With many activities and things to do along the lake, Camdenton has become one of those great places. It has the feel of a mini Gatlinburg: lots to do, a vacation atmosphere, and mountains all around.

There are several things to do, but one in particular makes the town unique: the Ha Ha Tonka Castle Ruins. Castle ruins aren't a typical American landmark.

The town is fairly new. It was established in 1930 to be the new county seat of Camden County when the Lake of the Ozarks was created and covered the existing county seat of Linn Creek. Therefore, the name has its root in Camden County. The courthouse and its unique position are strikingly different than most Missouri small towns where the courthouse sits in the middle of a traditional square. It was also the first modern-style courthouse in Missouri.

## MUST DO

Sitting high above Lake of the Ozarks and the Ha Ha Tonka Spring is the ruins of a European style castle. It's a delight to visit, as are the beautiful scenes around the state park housing the ruins. But this enjoyment was built on tragedy and broken dreams. The castle was the dream of a Kansas

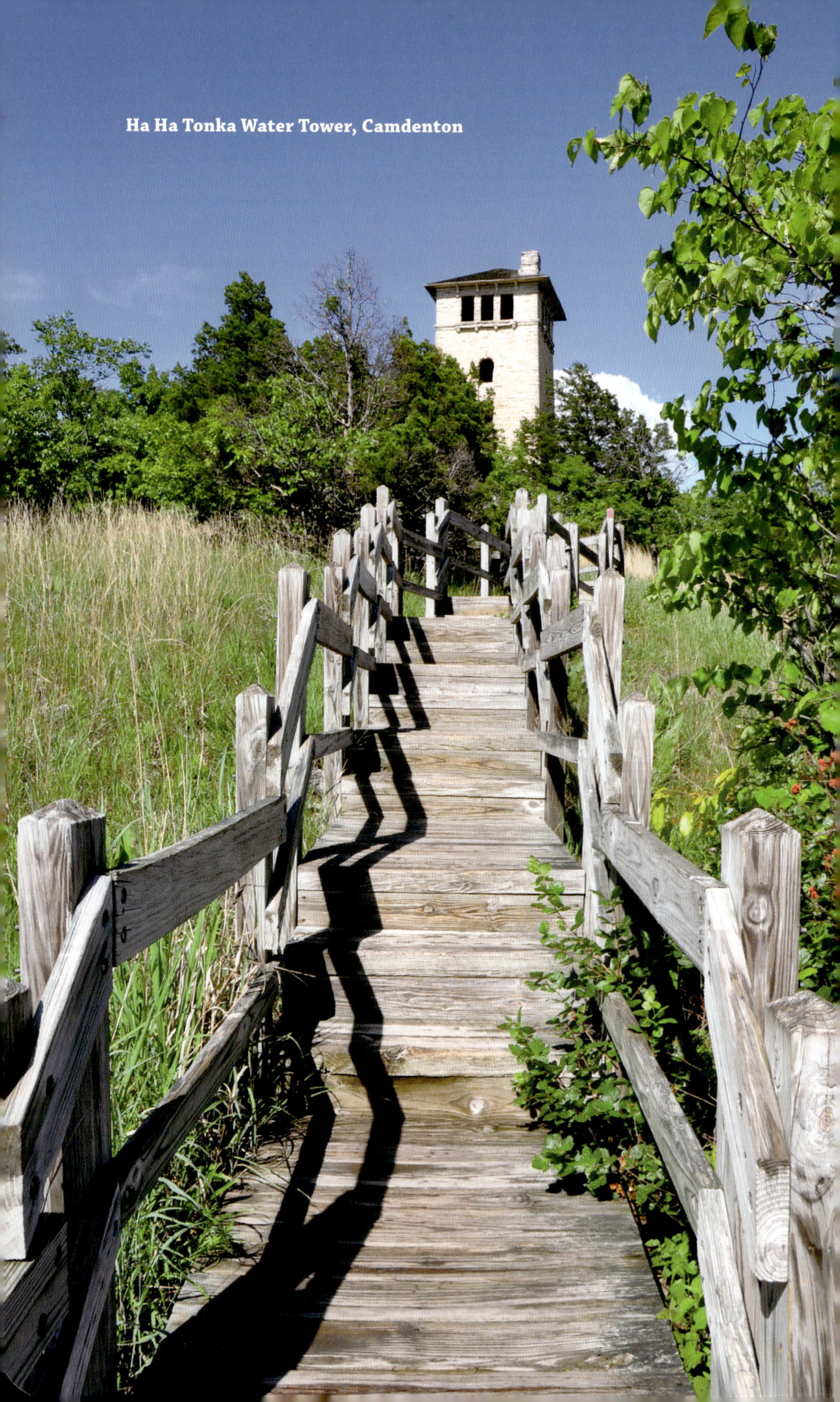

Ha Ha Tonka Water Tower, Camdenton

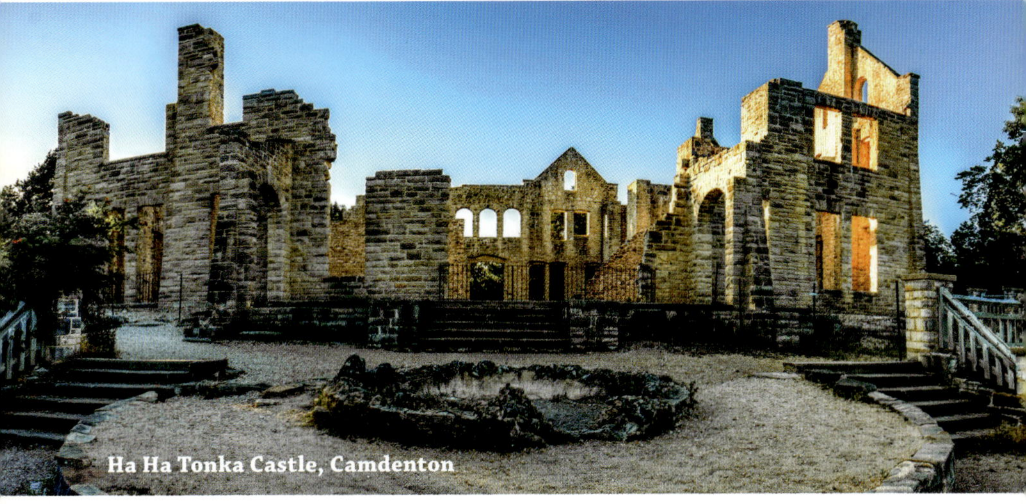
Ha Ha Tonka Castle, Camdenton

City businessman, but a year after starting construction he was killed in an automobile wreck. His sons picked up the work and finished in 1920, but their stay was short after running out of money. It then became a hotel, but in 1942 was destroyed in a fire. Today the stone ruins of the castle and the carriage house still stand.

In 1978, the house and much of its property became a state park. Hiking trails intersect with fascinating geological features like sinkholes, caves, and a natural bridge.

Bridal Cave is nearby, recognized as one of the most beautiful caves to tour in the country. It's full of spectacular mineral formations like columns, soda straws, and draperies. Guided tours are available, even a lantern tour, which allows you to explore the cave as it would have been in times past. The cave is a very popular wedding venue. There's a Bridal Chapel adorned with beautiful formations.

Camdenton is home to the Ozark Amphitheater, one of the best outdoor concert venues in the country and certainly in Missouri. The 10,000-seat concert venue is tucked into the midst of the Ozarks. The Ozark offers a full lineup of big acts. Attending a concert there is a surreal experience, as you look around and feel you are one with the mountains.

There are other fun activities like the Big Surf Water Park and Splatz Paintball. The Ozark Distillery can be toured, along with nearby wineries. And for the golfer, there's the top-notch Old Kinderhook Golf Course, which has been regularly ranked as the second best course in Missouri by *Golf* magazine. It offers a spectacular view.

In September, the Lake of the Ozarks Air Show takes place at the Camdenton airport and is a great treat.

## MUST STAY

The area around the lake and in Camdenton is chock-full of great vacation rentals. There are many hotels, but the Old Kinderhook Resort offers an exquisite stay in the lodge or its cottages and villas. There's great dining on-site along with the championship golf course and spa.

## MUST EAT

Again, the Old Kinderhook Resort is highlighted, but this time it's for the resort's Trophy Room. It's quite the change from the typical lake scene and offers elegant dining. There's great food, presented beautifully, and guests are treated like royalty. Every dish is good, but whatever you order, add jalapeno cheddar grits.

If a more casual meal is in the plan, then it needs to be Pepperoni Bill's Pizzeria, which provides some of the best pizza in the state. Every one of their pizzas is going to taste amazing, and their from-scratch crust is fabulous. The repeat favorite is Guy on a Buffalo, a strange name and one of the hands-down best buffalo chicken pizzas on the planet. But it's hard to turn down the Chicken Alfredo with Bacon or, if you're feeling daring, the Rockin' Reuben. On par with the pizza is the selection of craft beer, sandwiches, and calzones. Also, check out the decorated pizza boxes that fill the dining room.

And if it's hearty food you seek, RJ's Family Restaurant is a solid bet for hearty American cuisine. It's especially the stop for breakfast.

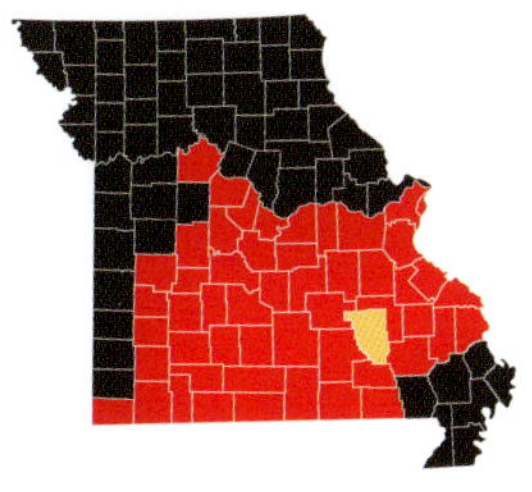

# 44

# Centerville

For Tolkien fans, here's a chance to visit the Shire in Missouri. And for those who care less about *The Hobbit* or *The Lord of the Rings*, it's a chance to see an old mill that looks like it came straight out of a fairy tale. A half mile from the Reynolds County Courthouse in Centerville is the Reed Spring Mill, a small log gristmill.

Centerville is a town of less than two hundred, but it serves as the county seat of Reynolds County. The town was established in 1846 as Centreville, but the "r" and "e" were switched in 1892. A lot of creativity went into the name, as it derives from being in the center of the county. Growth came early on from the timber industry, but both ended in the 1920s.

The draw to the area is this picturesque mill, which was built in 1881. A sawmill was built nearby soon after. In 1915, Centerville's electricity was generated by the mill; the lights were bright at the mill but dim in town. This continued until 1929. In 1939, the mill was used at the World's Fair in San Francisco. All of it was taken down and shipped across the country. That original mill is at the Smithsonian. The current mill is a replica of the original.

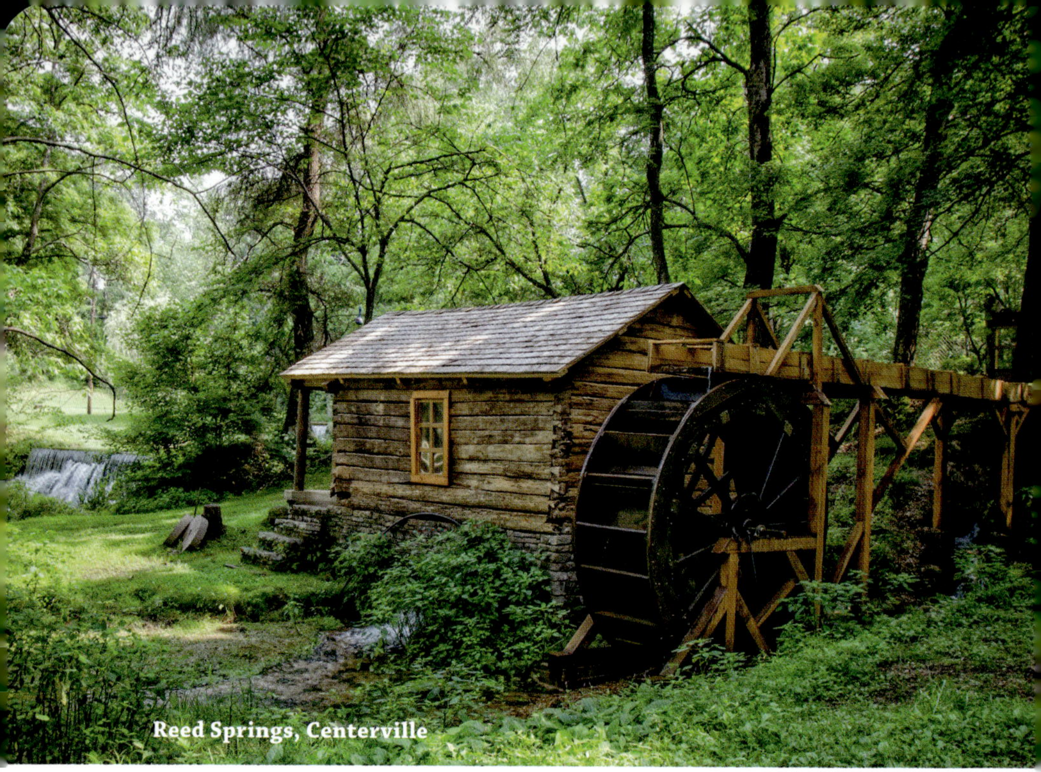
Reed Springs, Centerville

## MUST SEE

Reed Spring Mill is a magical sight. The mill is privately owned, but a caretaker lives there and greets visitors.

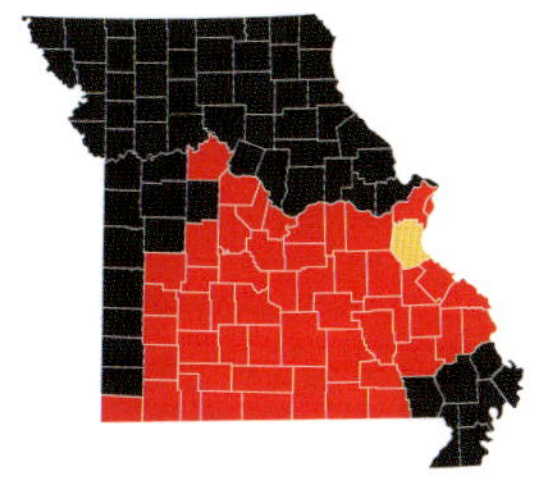

# 45

# Crystal City

The thirty-five-mile drive south from St. Louis is not too far to keep regulars away from a seventy-year-old burger joint in Crystal City. In addition to iconic burgers, there's an underground entertainment venue in town that captures the imagination.

Crystal City is a town of nearly five thousand. It's often referred to as part of the Twin Cities because of its proximity to nearby Festus. A drive downtown and it's hard to tell where one ends and the other starts.

Originally it was called New Detroit, and in the 1860s Pittsburgh Plate Glass Company opened a large manufacturing plant, which is unfortunately no longer in use. It was from the glass company that the town derived the name Crystal City, possibly as far back as 1872.

## MUST EAT

The PPG factory is no longer the iconic business of the city. Rather it's a restaurant that began in 1948. Gordon's Stoplight Drive-In has been using the same recipes for their smash burgers, Coney islands, chili, and shakes for all those years. They've become a staple for the Twin Cities, and for former residents, a trip back to their hometown must include a visit to Gordon's.

The Stoplight has a fascinating story. It was originally opened by Gordon Heddell. He retired and sold the restaurant in 1997. It was purchased by Chris Grass and his family. Chris's mother had been the

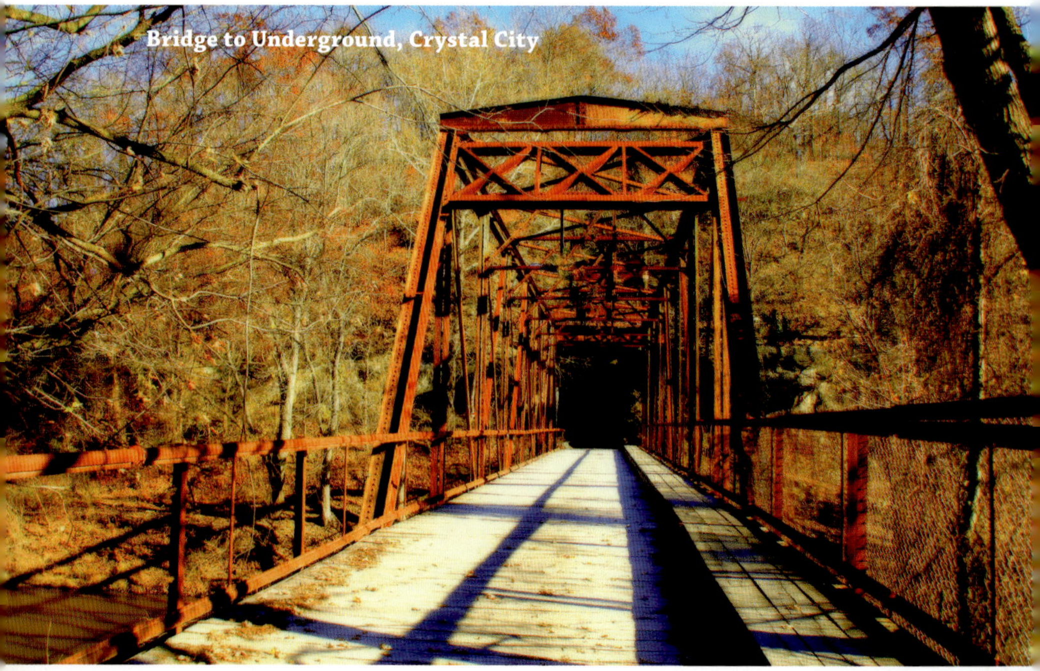

Bridge to Underground, Crystal City

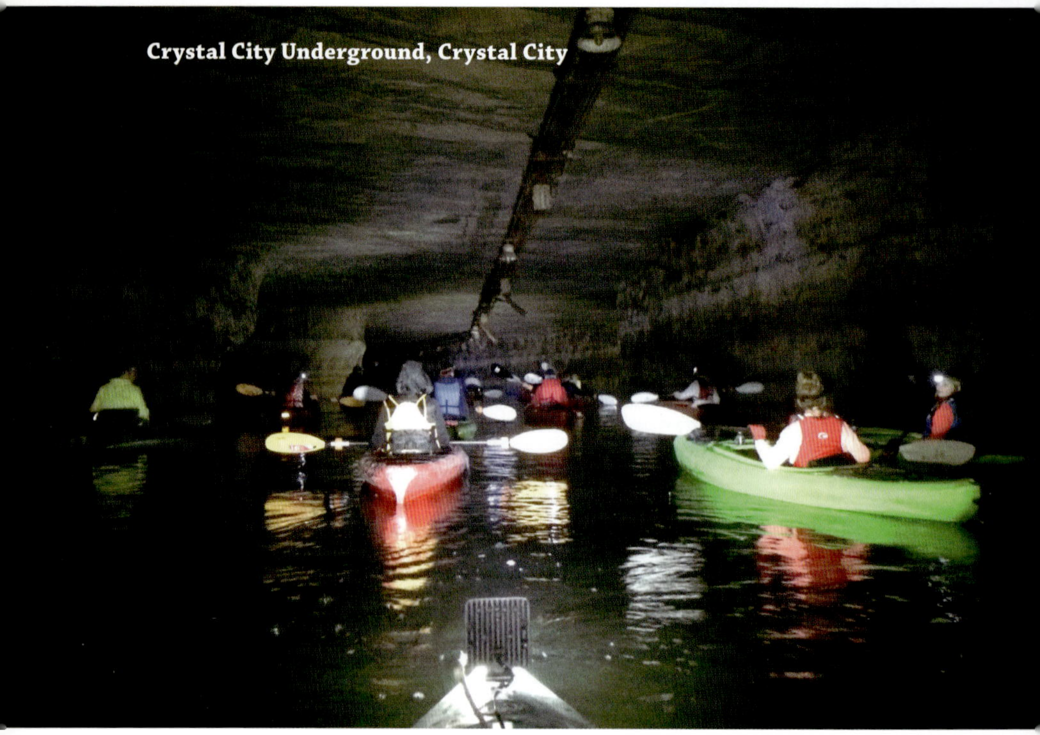

Crystal City Underground, Crystal City

original owner's neighbor. They kept the same recipes. They pride themselves on a consistent, great product. Even with a limited menu, it's hard to decide between a burger, a Coney island, or chili, for they are all good. They're known for the monstrous Quadzilla Burger, which has four patties. But a favorite is the Famous Jumbo Burger made with slaw, chopped onions, and BBQ sauce. On the Jumbo, customers are able to add as many patties as they want. The record is sixteen. There's also breakfast served at the Stoplight. The favorite is the Stoplight Slinger, a choice of meat, two eggs, two cheese slices, hash browns, and chili served on toast.

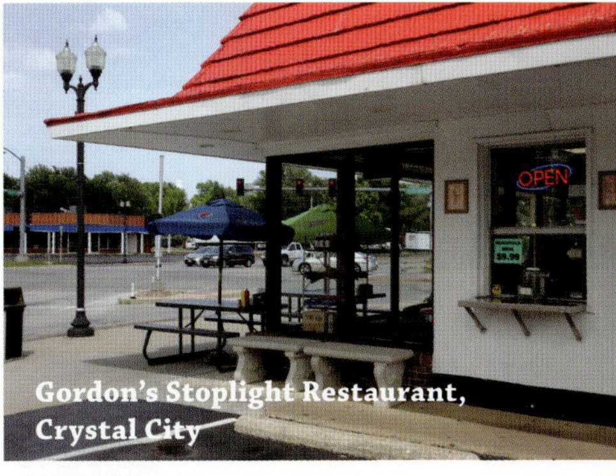

Gordon's Stoplight Restaurant, Crystal City

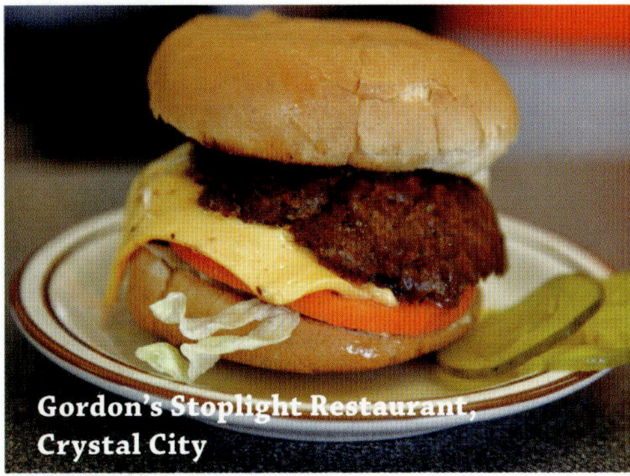
Gordon's Stoplight Restaurant, Crystal City

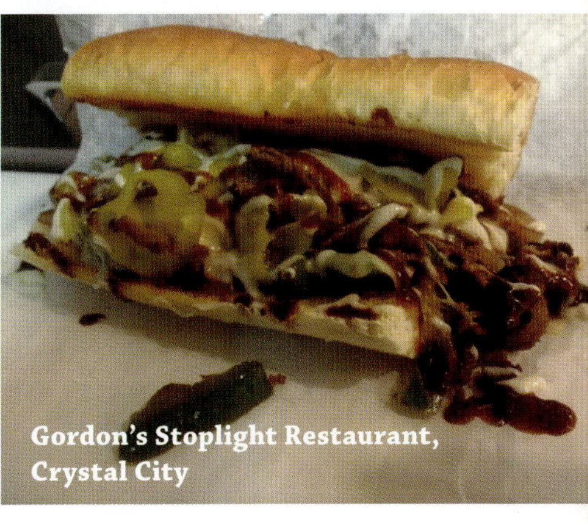
Gordon's Stoplight Restaurant, Crystal City

The Stoplight's sister restaurant is just a little farther down the street: Gordon's Cheesesteaks. The attention to detail and consistency is continued here. They use choice fresh bread from a local bakery, and the cheesesteaks are made just like in Philadelphia.

## MUST DO

Crystal City is home to the Crystal City Underground, an unusual attraction that just has to be seen. An old iron bridge leads into a cave of a former salt mine. This large cavern is home to kayaking, boat tours, a disc golf course, and other activities. Unfortunately, regular flooding impacts which activities will be available, but the kayak tours are usually open.

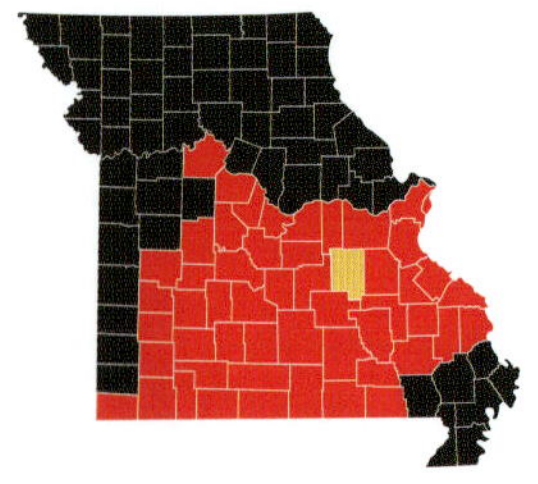

# 46

# *Cuba*

Cuba is a popular stop in Missouri, in large part because of its history on Route 66. It seems odd there would be a "Cuba" landlocked in the center of America. But early settlers named their town out of sympathy for the people of Cuba, who at that time were dealt with harshly by the Spanish who ruled the country.

Those early settlers laid out the town in 1857 in expectation of the Union Pacific Railroad stopping there. Settlers were already mining iron ore in the area. In 1860 the railroad did come. The town grew much because of the apple industry. From 1895 to 1920, Cuba was the leading producer of apples and earned the nickname "The Land of the Big Red Apple." Also, it was known for wooden barrel production. The apple industry waned, but Cuba is now a world leader in wooden whiskey and bourbon barrels. McGinnis Wood Products is the manufacturer of some of the most popular white-oak barrels in the world.

All of this history can be gathered on a walk through town to view the remarkable murals detailing that history. Among stories of the Osage, settlers, apple industry, Civil War, and barrel making, there's the commemoration of significant historical events like the time Amelia Earhart had to make an emergency landing here or when Bette Davis came to town. Also commemorated is the role Route 66 has played in the life of Cuba.

Some of the town's landmarks are remnants of those early days of Route 66, like the Wagon Wheel Motel, which opened in 1938 and is one

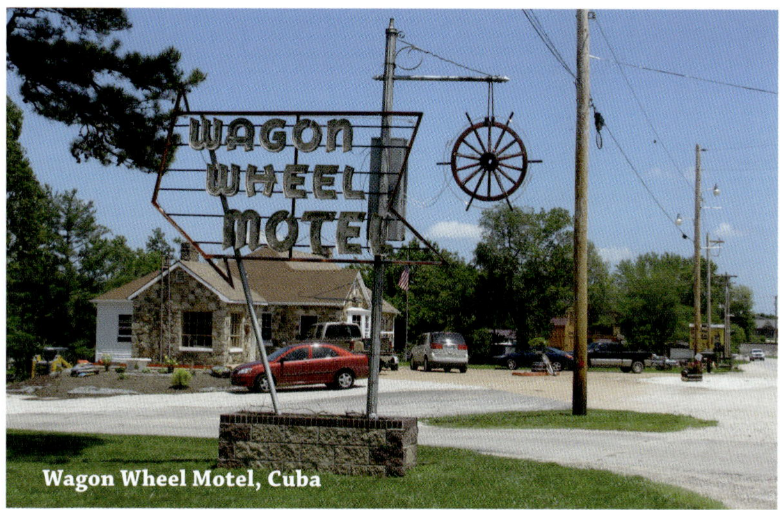

Wagon Wheel Motel, Cuba

of the oldest motels on the route. Then there's the giant rocking chair that once reigned as the largest one in the world. Remnants of the past like these have helped revitalize the town.

## MUST DO

The large rocking chair is a sight to behold. It looks big, but just wait until you stand beside it. Unfortunately, it's no longer the largest in the world, but it's still huge. The town has many other quirky things to see, like the shoes from the world's tallest man at Hayes Shoe Store. Customers can hold a size thirty-five or thirty-seven. Maybe the rocking chair was built for that guy? Then there is Bob's Gasoline Alley, a private collection of over three hundred vintage gas station signs. Many are outside, but more are inside. Chances are visitors will meet owner Bob Mullen as they explore the collection.

Cuba's murals are a sight to behold. They have earned the city the name "Route 66 Mural City." They can be viewed by foot or by taking a private trolley car tour.

## MUST EAT

Missouri Hick barbecue has become a destination for fun and food for those traveling near Cuba. The two-story rustic cabin plays the part of an Ozark hick joint. Wood and stone décor weave throughout the restaurant.

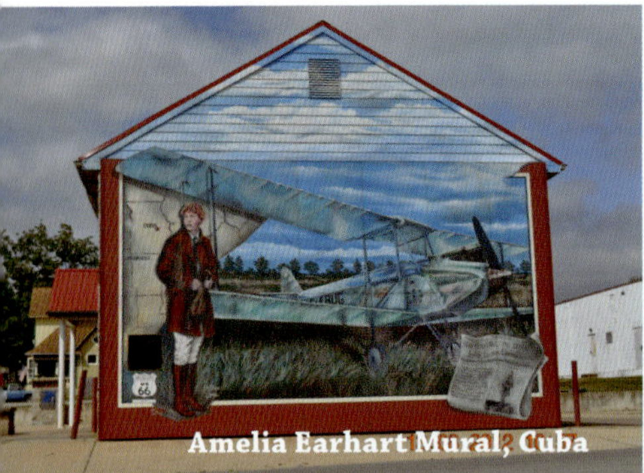

Amelia Earhart Mural, Cuba

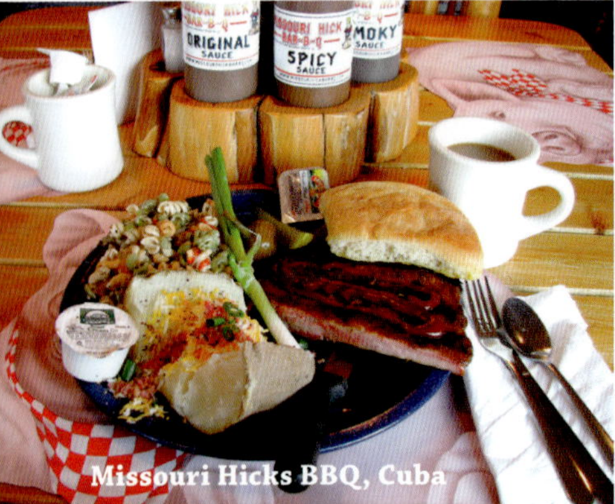


Missouri Hicks BBQ, Cuba

If customers weren't thinking about barbecue when they arrived, the scene around them directs their taste buds to it. All of the smoked meats, whether pulled pork, brisket, or ribs, are good. They offer several of their own sauces. But the prize may be Ory's Spud, a gigantic baked potato stuffed and topped with baked beans, barbecue-sauced pork, cheddar and Monterey jack cheese, bacon, chives, and their special seasoned sour cream. The eclectically decorated cabin offers great grub.

There's also the Fourway, which offers a strange but tasty mix of Mediterranean and American food. Even with the European flair, the burger and steak fries are to be recommended. On top of the great food is that the restaurant is located in a renovated Route 66 icon: a 1931 Phillips 66 Station.

## MUST STAY

The Wagon Wheel Motel, which opened in 1938, is still open today and offers a chance to stay, as many have over the decades. A renovation was begun in 2009 and the motel now offers a mix of new and old.

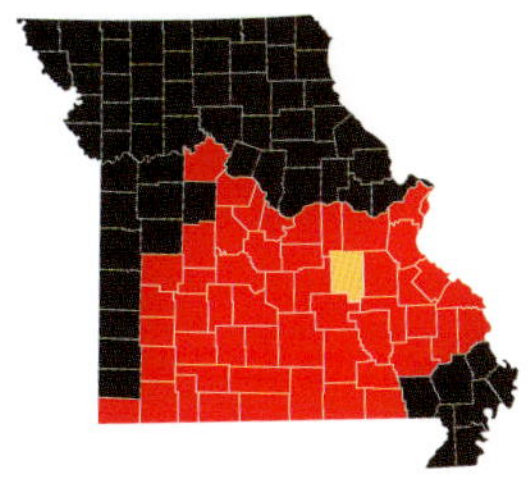

# 47

# *Davisville*

Keeping up with the name of the town that is home to one of the most picturesque mills in the country is a bit difficult. Once it was Pucky Hollow. The mill bears the name Dillard, but the mill's address is Davisville.

Nestled in the Mark Twain Forest is Davisville, which was named after the family that was instrumental in establishing a post office there in 1880. History of settlement dates back further. In 1853, a mill was built on Huzzah Creek, but it was destroyed in a fire in 1895. A new owner came and built a mill in 1908, and this mill used updated technology like an underwater turbine rather than the waterwheel. It remained operational until 1956, and then in 1975 the state of Missouri began managing the property and renamed the mill Dillard Mill for the town of Dillard a mile away.

## MUST DO

The mills around the state are awe-inspiring, but the Dillard Mill might be the most spectacular scenery. It's as if it was built to be a photography backdrop. At the historic site are hiking trails and picnic areas. Tours are offered of the mill, which features the most intact machinery in the state. Also nearby is the Pucky Hollow General Store, which is fun to check out.

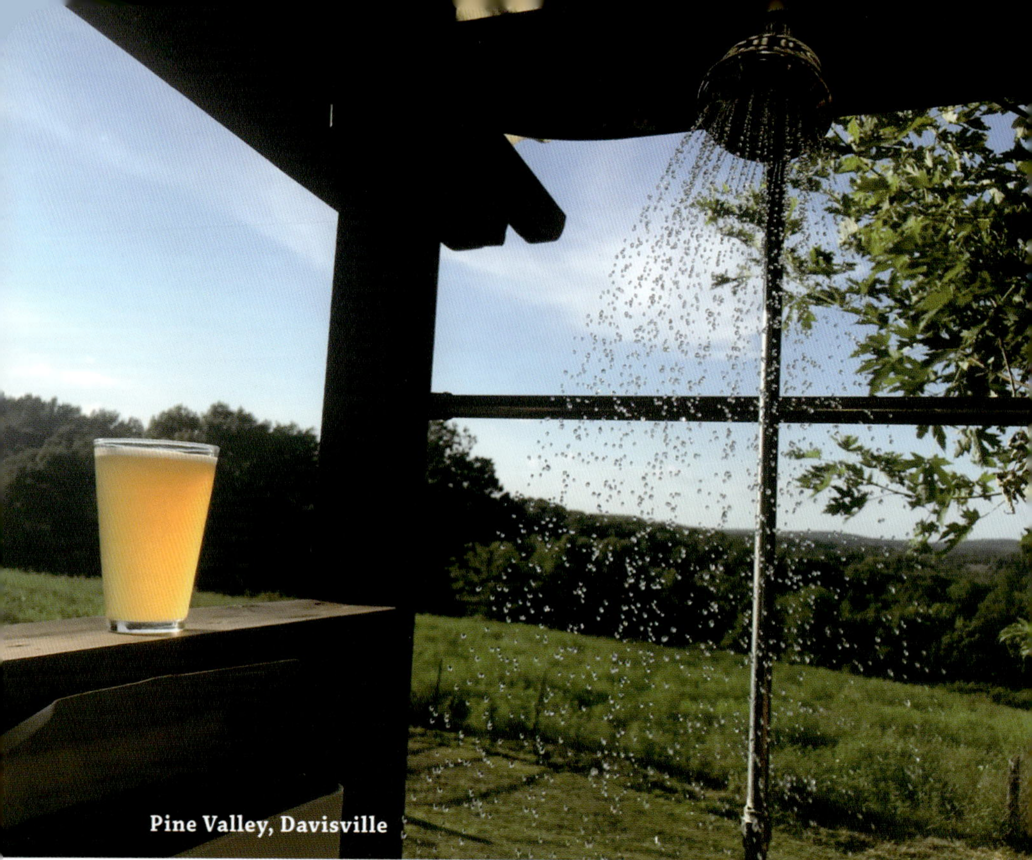
Pine Valley, Davisville

## MUST STAY

Near the mill is Pine Valley at Dillard Mill. They offer lodging for guests to stay close as they explore the area. There's a cottage attached to the main house. Or choose from two more eclectic choices—the Airstream and Avion. Both are vintage travel trailers set up for lodging. The Airstream has a large deck, as well as an outdoor tub and shower.

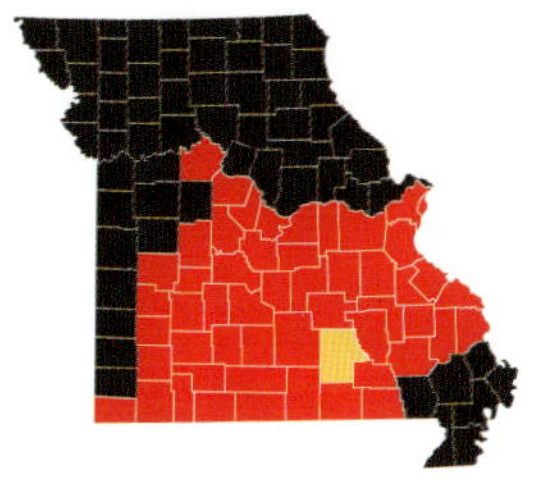

# 48

# Eminence

Don't let the small town and population of six hundred fool you; during the summer months, Eminence is a bustling hub of outdoor adventure. There could be up to three thousand people on horseback at a time in town since it's home to America's largest trail-riding establishment. There will probably be more than that on the water in a canoe or kayak, as it sits in the middle of Ozark National Scenic Riverways, with one hundred and twenty miles of navigable waters, making the area the "Canoe Capital of the World."

Eminence was established in 1844, and the nearby landmark, Alley Mill, was built in 1868. The original mill was replaced in 1894. Alley Mill is also called the "Old Red Mill," but it was not always painted the iconic red. It first was white, then green, and finally red. The mill became the centerpiece of the Alley community in 1902. The one-room schoolhouse from that time period remains today and can be toured, as can the mill. Apart from the picturesque image of the mill and its Ozark forest backdrop, the spring water that pours through the mill's dam is a beautiful turquoise.

That's not the only beautiful spring in the area. Nearby is the Blue Spring, which is a magnificent blue; the Osage called it "Spring of the Summer Sky." It's one of the largest in the state and is the deepest at three hundred feet.

Ozark stream scenes, like these springs and others, draw visitors to Eminence, and they find plenty of adventure, whether it's hiking,

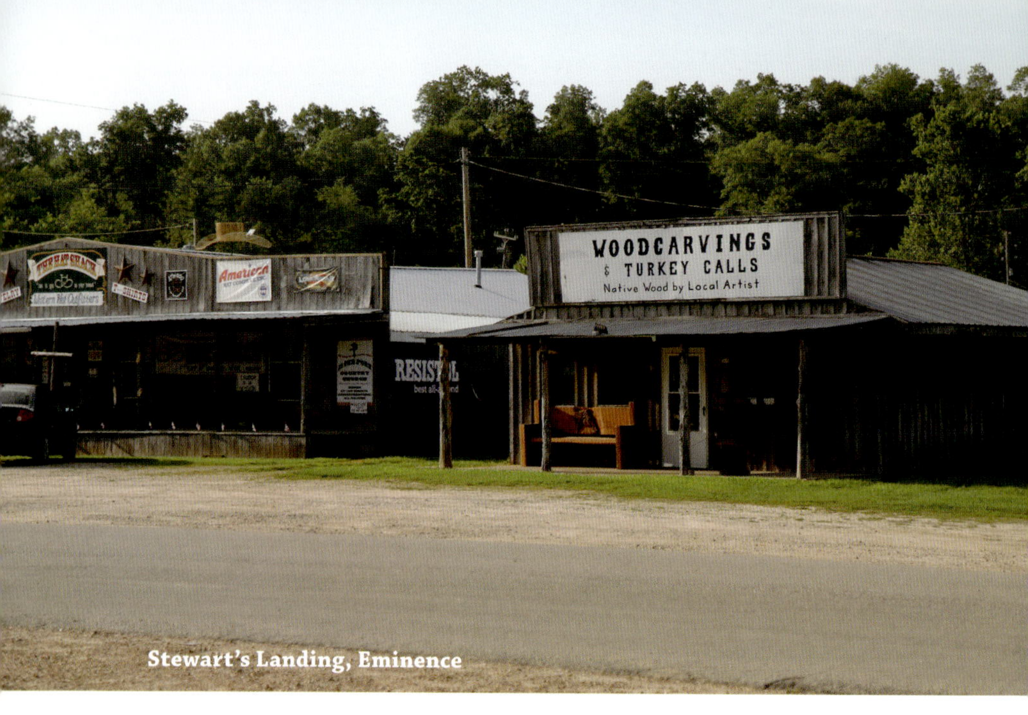

Stewart's Landing, Eminence

horseback riding, bicycling, fishing, hunting, kayaking, canoeing, zip lining, or riding ATVs.

## MUST DO

The Alley Spring Grist Mill Historic Site and the nearby Story Creek Schoolhouse are sites of interest. Also, Blue Spring is a beautiful site. Not far away is Rocky Falls Shut-In. This waterfall is a fun place whether you are hiking to the top of the falls, scrambling down the falls, or swimming in the swimming hole.

Ozark Riverways is the spot to canoe and kayak, and the area has many outfitters to help you. If watercraft is not appealing, many places rent horses or give tours.

Located in Eminence is Cross Country Trail Rides, the largest trail-riding establishment in the nation. They offer seven all-inclusive events a year. These multiday events offer guided trail rides, great grub, horseshoes, concerts, access to an indoor arena, and much more. Up to two thousand participants may attend these events. They have stable space for nearly three thousand horses.

With so much to do on the water, the ATV/UTV guided tours at places like Eagle Falls Ranch get lost, but these are lots of fun.

## MUST STAY

The area is covered with bed-and-breakfasts, cabins, lodges, hotels, and vacation rentals. Visitors are encouraged to look through all the options. Missouri State Parks has a lodge and cabin that provide very nice accommodations and breathtaking scenes from the balconies at Echo Bluff State Park. If uncertain where to stay, the Betty Lea Lodge at the state park is a safe bet you'll be pleased with. Eagles Landing River Resort is an honorable mention. It's situated above the river and offers sensational views and comfortable rooms. Both places have restaurants on-site. As far as bed-and-breakfasts go, the Hawkins Bed and Breakfast is a favorite.

## MUST EAT

At Echo Bluff State Park is the Creekside Grill. It's inside the lodge and offers spectacular views of Echo Bluff and the river. There is both inside and outside seating. Great food matches the view.

## MUST NOTE

As one explores Eminence and the Ozark National Scenic Riverways, it's as if it can't get any better. The views and opportunities are fun and beautiful. In the midst of a forest, mountains, overlooks, bluffs, shoals, and clear waters there is a band of wild horses that will make appearances in fields along the rivers. This small herd has wandered the national forest for decades. In 1991, the National Park Service sought to remove them, but the Missouri Wild Horse League campaigned to allow the horses to stay. In 1997 they were successful. Currently, thirty-five horses can be seen here and there. Recommended areas are the Broadfoot fields north of Eminence, the Shawnee fields east of Eminence, or in the fields above Two Rivers on Highway V east of Eminence. The Missouri Wild Horse League is happy to receive calls and advise where these horses can be spotted.

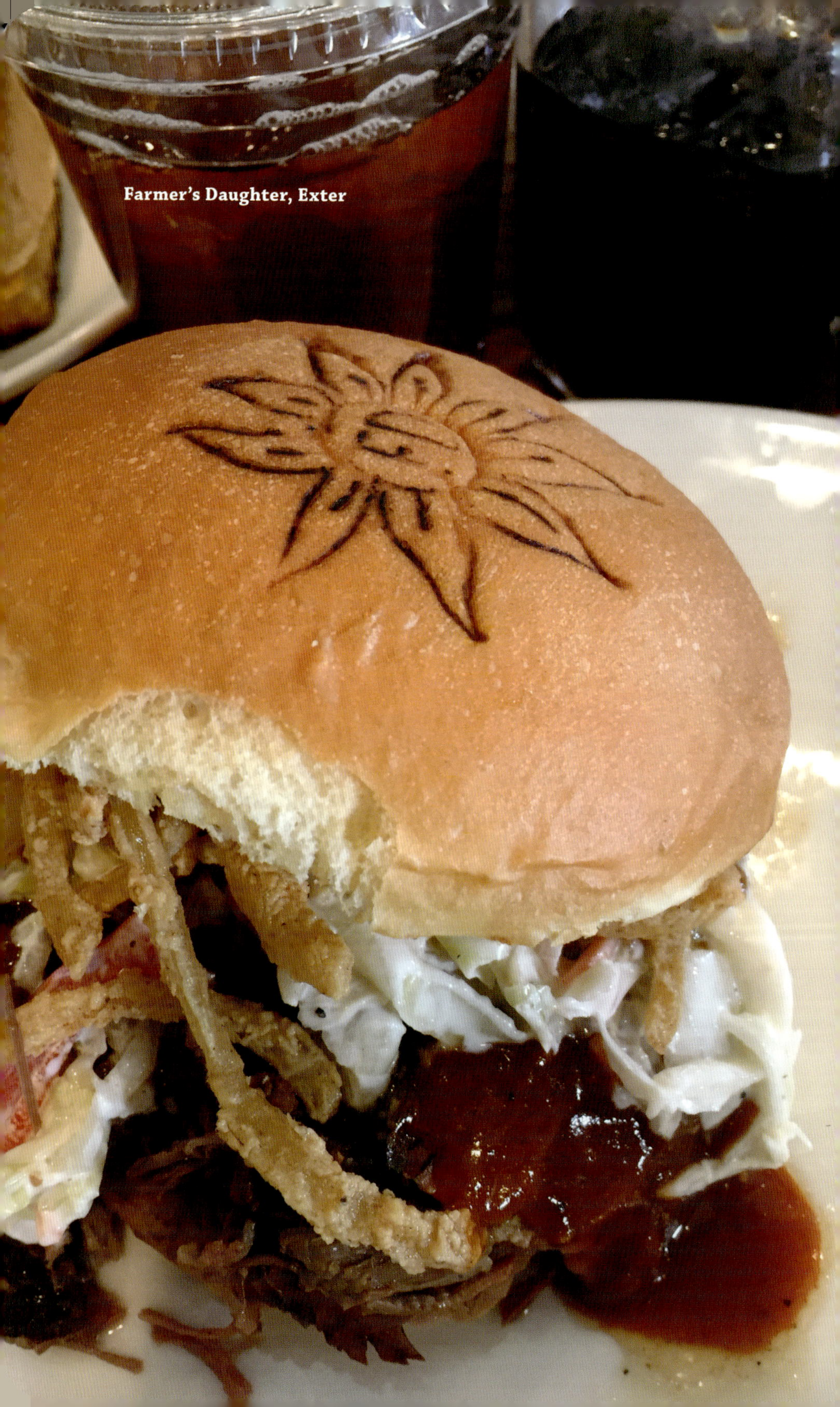

Farmer's Daughter, Exter

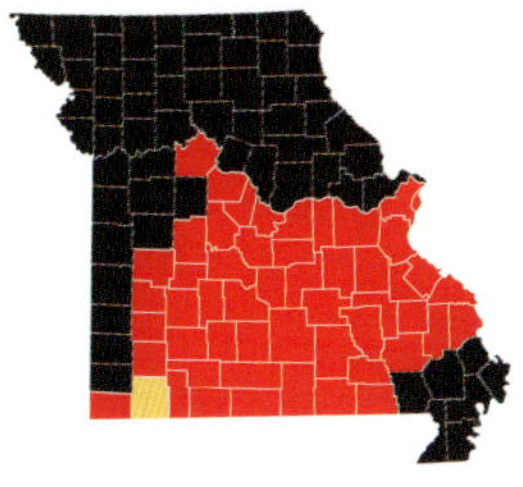

# 49

# *Exeter*

Exeter is a sleepy town in southwest Missouri with a population of 772, but in the fall it becomes home to one of the best corn mazes and pumpkin patches around. The maze is outstanding, but what sets this fall attraction apart from others is the sheer volume of things to do. It's more of a fall theme park than a pumpkin patch. The name Exeter comes from a city in England where the original settlers of this town were from. In 1880 it was first platted.

## MUST DO

When fall rolls around, schedule a family trip to the Exeter Corn Maze. There's so much to do. Of course, there is a large corn maze and a pumpkin patch, but recently, a haunted corn maze has been added. This "after dark" feature has the maze coming alive with terror. Then there's the popular haunted barn, a two-story fright fest that's been voted one of the scariest in the state. And if the haunted maze or barn didn't scare you enough, try Zombie Paintball, a combination of hayride, the walking dead, and paintballs that equals lots of fun. At the maze are two giant jump pads, wagon rides, combat archery, indoor paintball, indoor barn swings, giant corn pits, pedal cars, a zip line, a "cow" train for little ones, and lots more. At the far end is a pumpkin cannon that launches pumpkins seemingly to the next county. If the heavy artillery is too much, there are the smaller

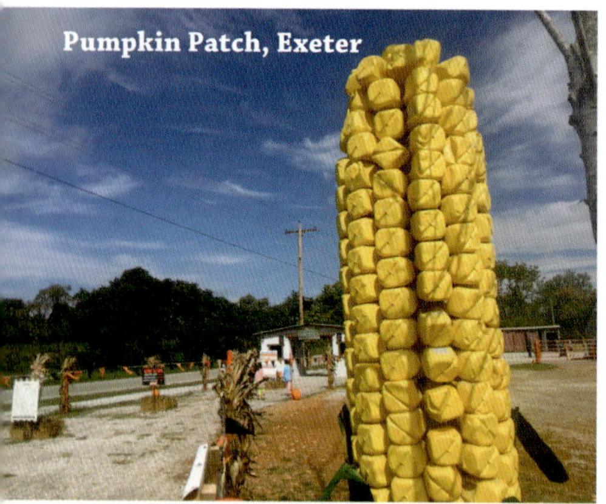

Pumpkin Patch, Exeter

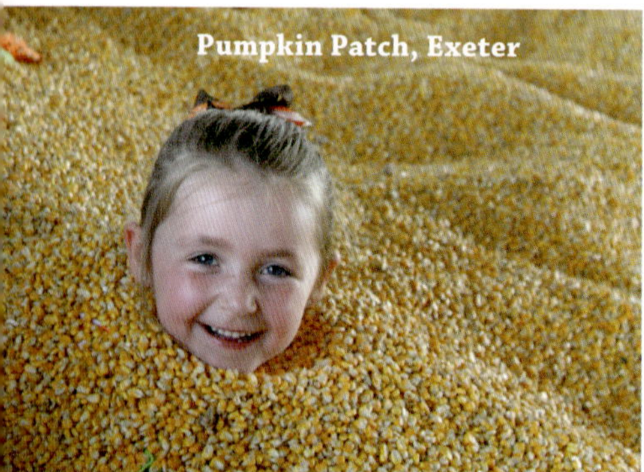

Pumpkin Patch, Exeter

potato guns. On top of all those activities, there is a full-fledged paved go-cart track.

All around the park are great photo opportunities. Another feature that is useful for families and groups is the opportunity to rent covered picnic tables and fire pits, which allows for a home base during a full day of play.

## MUST EAT

Exeter does not have a lot of food options, but the much larger Cassville is only four miles away. It offers quite a few restaurants, but the gem to remember is the Farmer's Daughter. This is not a restaurant one expects to see in a small town. It's very clean with a shabby-chic farmhouse look, which is an inviting vibe. But the quality and presentation of the food surpasses even the stylish look.

The Farmer's Daughter is the vision of Abby Carr, a Cassville native, and Matt Lowman, who has been a chef in high-end restaurants in Little Rock and northwest Arkansas. Everything is made from scratch using locally sourced products. Choosing what to order can take a while because everything looks good, from salad to sandwich to burger to steak. They serve high-stacked burgers full of flavor. Whatever you order, make sure to have some of their fresh-baked bread products. The attention to detail and flavor is the real charm of this place, like the to-die-for grilled sweet corn tossed in house-made Caesar dressing and shaved Parmesan, the homemade remoulade sauce on their fried catfish sandwich, or any of their desserts.

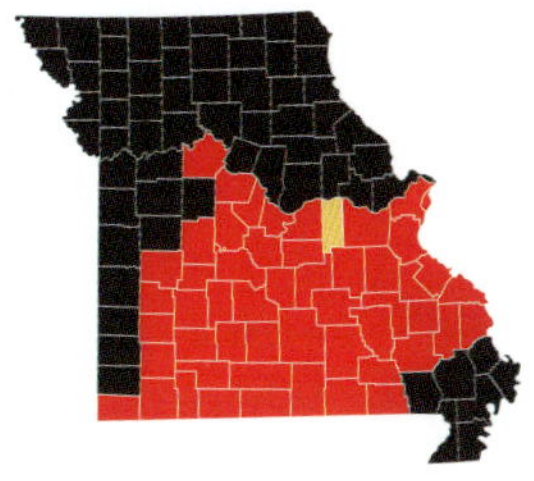

# 50

# Hermann

If you would like a taste of Germany on American soil, Hermann is the place. German immigrants founded the town, and their history and culture remain even today, in particular, the culture of Rhineland. Not only does Hermann keep the vibe of its roots, but it's the hub of Missouri's own Rhineland, its wine country.

The German Settlement Society of Philadelphia, led by George Bayer and Edward Hermann, founded the town. Their goal was to create a settlement that would continue German culture in America, and though they did not live to see it, they were successful, as the town of Hermann has continued to carry the torch. Bayer named the town after the German leader who defeated three Roman legions in 9 AD, Hermann der Cherusker, and a statue of him is in Hermann Park.

Hermann is the hub of Missouri's wine country, which runs along the Missouri River for its last hundred miles. The first winery to open in the area was Stone Hill in 1847, while the first wine in Napa Valley was not produced until 1857. Stone Hill grew to be the second-largest vineyard in the United States and the third in the world. Their wine became world-renowned, and they won gold medals in eight world's fairs. Other wineries soon dotted the landscape of Hermann. Hermannhof opened in 1952.

Prohibition took a toll on these Missouri vineyards, and they were shut down. Stone Hill resorted to growing mushrooms, but in 1965, Jim and Betty Held purchased the winery and made it the first to be

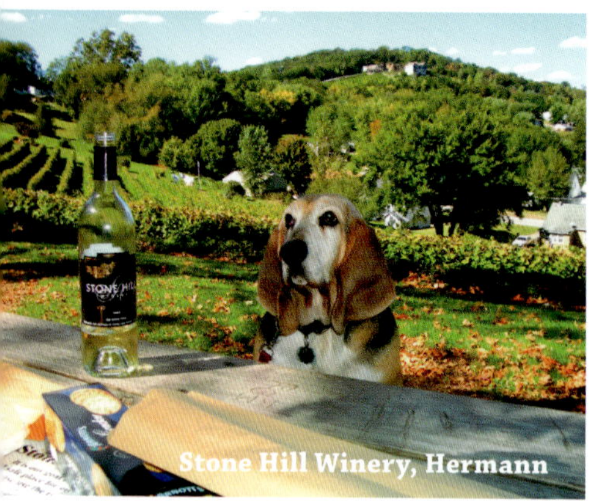
Stone Hill Winery, Hermann

Inn at Hermannhof, Hermann

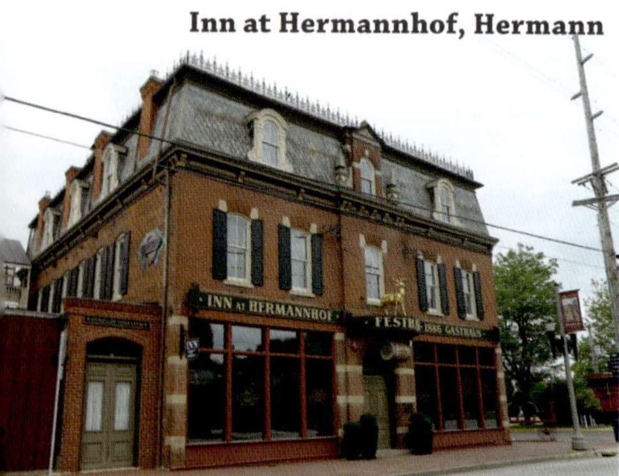


reestablished in the state. Others followed, but today there is only half the acreage of vineyards that there was in the late 1800s. Today this German-influenced town is a busy tourist hub. Beautiful bed-and-breakfasts cover the area, and there's much to do.

## MUST DO

Take in the historic architecture of the area. There are several historic districts and landmarks, like the Deutschheim State Historic Site, which has preserved houses and other structures, such as a barn and winery, built and used by German immigrants in the nineteenth century. The Gasconade County Courthouse is a magnificent sight to behold. It sits perched high on a ridge overlooking the Missouri River and the older parts of town.

Check out the wineries, the most notable being Stone Hill and Hermannhof. Also, check out Adam Puchta Winery, or take the Hermann Wine Tour. Throughout the year are special wine-tasting events like the Farmer's Table Wine Trail in April, which features meeting local farmers, tasting their produce, and pairing it with local wine.

## MUST STAY

Hermann is perfect for a romantic weekend getaway. Take a wine tour, stroll the historic downtown, then stay in one of the many charming bed-and-breakfasts. Numerous vacation rentals are also available. The gold standard for a perfect stay in town is the Inn at Hermannhof. Throughout the state, many inns have sought to honor the past but combine it with the best of modern luxuries. Hermannhof has blended the two perfectly—it retains historic, old-world charm, but the rooms are so elegant and distinguished that guests will feel like VIPs of the late 1800s. The Hermannhof's mix of an inn and cottages places the guest in the middle of the second oldest winery in Missouri and in the midst of all the downtown sites. The original construction ranges from the 1840s to the 1880s.

Another lodging option that stands above others is Hermann Hill, where several inns and cottages await. The River Bluff Cottages offer the most stunning view of the Missouri River. Breakfast is brought to the room, and a picnic lunch is provided for those staying two nights. The view makes it a tempting choice. Their luxury vineyard suites offer almost as compelling a view of the Missouri River and of the whole town as well. The elegance factor is turned up a bit higher in the vineyard suites.

If a quirky stay is more your style, check out Murphy's Bed and Breakfast Wine Cellar Room. It's literally a wine cellar: a mix of elegance and romance in a basement. This customized cellar is not for everyone, but many get a kick out of staying there.

## MUST EAT

There's so much great food in town. The recommendations start with Stone Hill Winery's Vintage Restaurant. The former carriage house and horse barn has been converted into an upscale gourmet restaurant, resulting in a casual atmosphere but with much more formal food. They have German dishes and modern favorites and are considered one of the best German restaurants in America.

Sticking with the German theme is Hermann Wurst Haus. This German market and deli is a mecca for sausage and bratwurst lovers. Their Wurstmeister, Mike Sloan, has won more than 350 awards for his sausages and brats. At the shop, guests can purchase specialty meats and dine in.

If you need a break from German dishes, consider 4th St. Pizza or Tin Mill Brewery. Both have great food and their own unique atmospheres. If somehow, after enjoying all these great eateries, you're still in need of something sweet, there's Sugar Momma's, a candy, homemade pie, and frozen treat paradise.

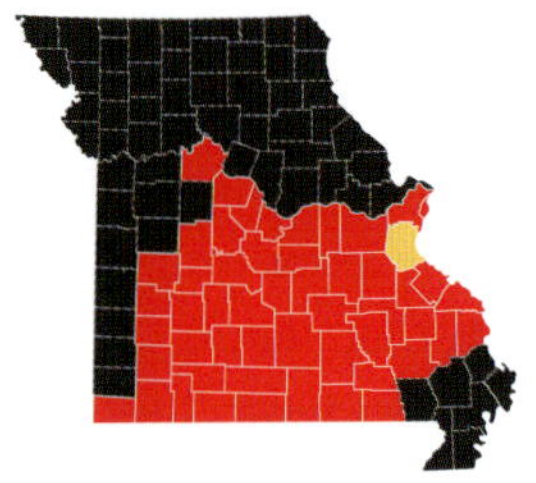

# 51

# High Ridge

High Ridge can be traced back to 1856. Its name comes from its high elevation. Though this town only twenty-five miles from St. Louis has been a destination for awhile, a new restaurant has put it even more on the map. Iron Barley's High Hog Ridge opened in 2017. Iron Barley has been around since 2003 in St. Louis. While there, it racked up numerous awards and accolades. It was featured on two Food Network shows—*Diners, Drive-Ins, and Dives* and *Man v. Food*.

On *Man v. Food*, the Oak Roasted Pork Chops and the Monte Cristo Hog Dog were featured. These dishes represent the two avenues of chef and owner Tom Coghill's menu. It's been summarized as "traditional but unusual." Choose from hearty classic entrees like Oak Roasted Pork Loin or Prime Rib, with home-style sides like corn, green beans, and smashed potatoes. Then there are the unusual concoctions like the Monte Cristo dog, which is two large franks grilled and topped with Swiss cheese then placed on a bun with strawberry jam, or the Hot Ridge, which is a potato pancake topped with house-cured ham, turkey, and gravy with white cheddar. Chef Coghill is a master of finding just the right pairing. Regulars have learned to trust him. Another unique feature is the number of dishes made with barley.

### MUST EAT

Visit one of the most recognized Missouri restaurants—Iron Barley's High Hog Ridge.

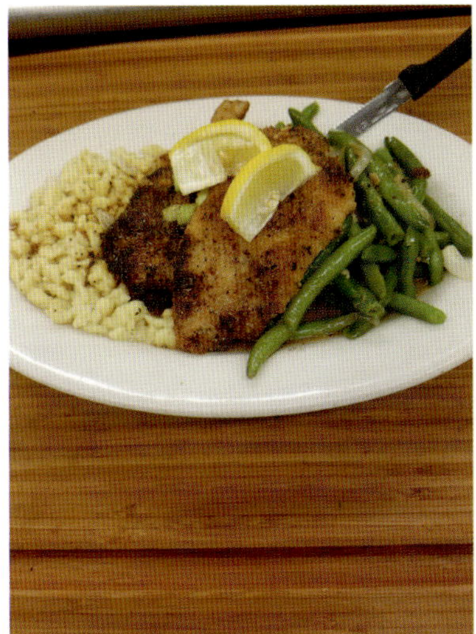

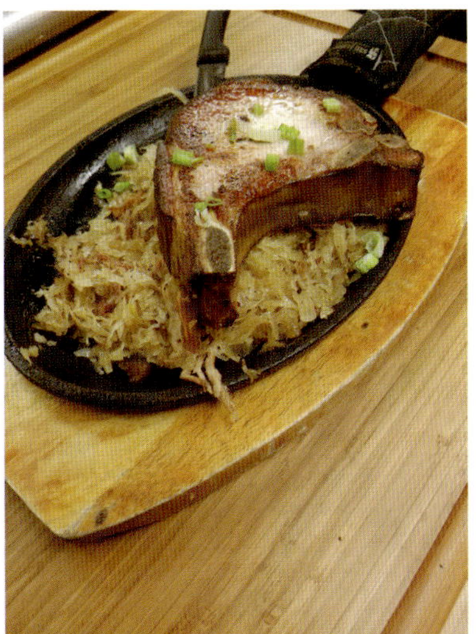

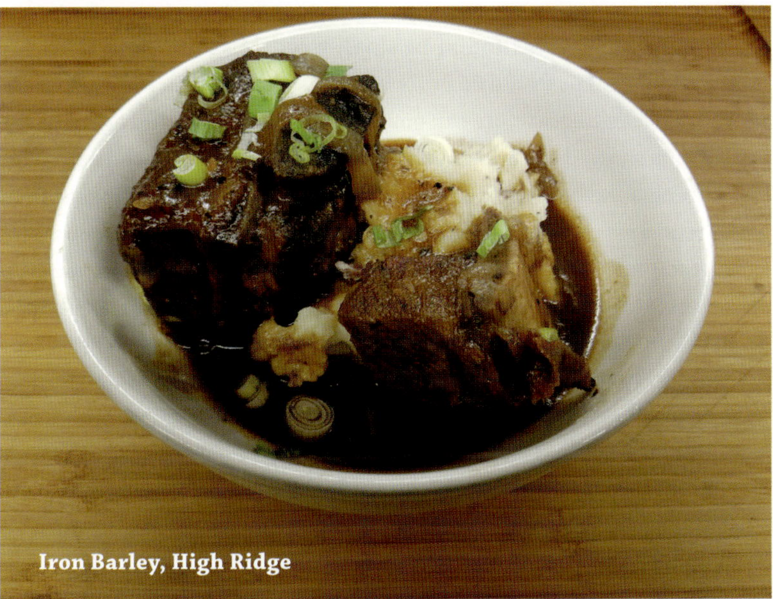

Iron Barley, High Ridge

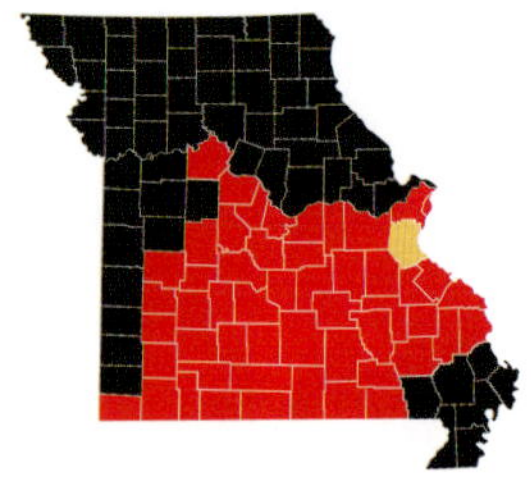

# 52

# *Imperial*

Most historic sites found in small-town Missouri date from the 1800s and or Route 66 era. Imperial's site goes back almost as far as an American historic site can go. Excavations in 1839 and again in the early 1900s showed the area to have one of the most intact and extensive Pleistocene bone beds in the country. The clearest of the extinct animal bones found was of the mastodon. Bones from over sixty mastodons were excavated here. The mastodon is an ancient mammal similar to modern elephants. Mastodons were shorter than both mammoths and elephants. Archaeologists believe the site to be extremely important in that it was the first to show signs of people and mastodons living at the same time. These scientists believe that the area was once swampy, containing salt and mineral springs, and that the salt and minerals drew both creatures and people to the area. In the process, some mastodons may have become stuck in the mud.

Even before the 1839 excavation, there were European-American settlers in Imperial. The town was founded in the early 1800s. Originally it was called Rock Township, then West Kimmswick, Liberty, and Rockport. Finally, it was named Imperial after a clock company in the area during World War I. Businesses began to arrive in 1904, and a rail stop on the Frisco Rail Road brought more growth. But presently the area is growing faster than it ever has, as it offers small-town life only twenty-two miles from St. Louis.

## MUST DO

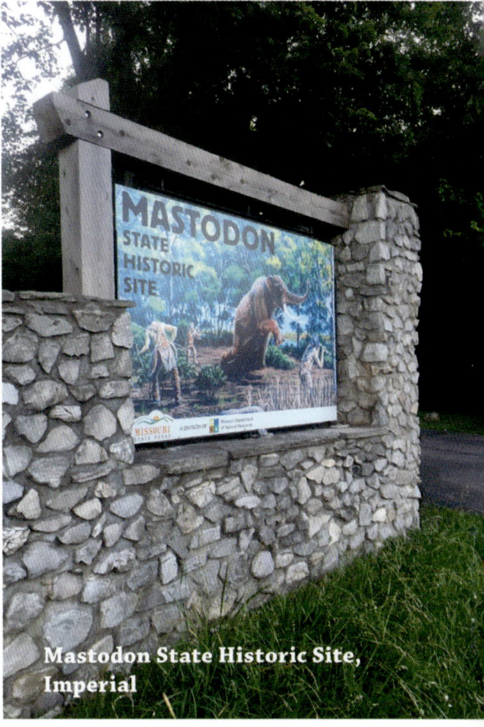

Mastodon State Historic Site, Imperial

The Kimmswick Bone Bed has been preserved and is now the Mastodon Historic Site. There's a great museum that tells about the archaeology that has been done at the site and about the time period. There's a full-scale mastodon skeleton on display as well. Hiking trails and picnic areas are found around the park.

## MUST EAT

Nearly straddling the line between Imperial and Arnold is a classic burger joint that has been in operation since 1959, Bob's Drive-In. They serve the classic drive-in staples: burgers, fries, onion rings, chili dogs, corn dogs, sandwiches, shakes, sundaes, and slushes. Customers can also find a few surprises on the menu like shrimp and toasted ravioli. Unique sides like fried mushrooms, cauliflower, zucchini sticks, and okra are favorites among patrons, especially the okra. The S'mores Sundae is a must-try. Unlike many of the preserved 1940s and 1950s diners across the state, Bob's doesn't have smash burgers, rather they offer up large patties much like one would at home. The burgers are a greasy miracle of near-liquefied cheese, a swirl of sauces, and giant slabs of meat.

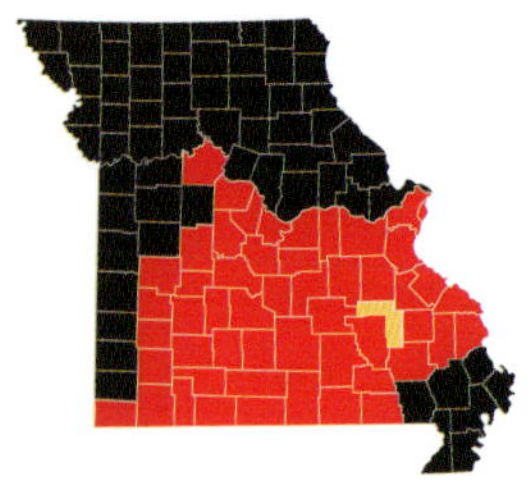

# 53

## *Ironton*

Ironton is home to one of the most naturally fun state parks around. Whether children or adults, visitors will leave as if someone was there handing out smiles. Settlers to Ironton have been traced back to 1805. Early on, it was a sleepy town. The few that were drawn there came for the abundant buffalo and deer. In 1836, iron ore was found and the place grew. The town was established in 1857 and was named after the iron ore mined nearby. That same year, the St. Louis and Iron Mountain Railroad came through, which helped the transporting of the ore.

The Civil War wrecked this forward progress. The two sides fought over the area to prevent the iron ore going to the other army. Early in the war, Colonel Ulysses S. Grant was sent to Ironton to protect the ore for the Union. While there, he received orders that he had been promoted to brigadier general. A marker in town commemorates this pivotal moment in history. Later in the war, a battle took place nearby at Fort Davidson in Pilot Knob. A Confederate force of twelve thousand took on the Union force of twelve hundred that was entrenched in the fort. After three days of fighting, the Union army snuck out of the fort at night. The Confederate losses in this battle possibly prevented a march on St. Louis. After the war, people began to move back into the area, but mining eventually waned.

## MUST DO

Ironton is nearby the Elephant Rocks State Park. This is one of the most fun parks in the state. It's peculiar, but the sights and availability of exploring make it fun for all ages. The mountainous park is full of giant boulders that look like elephants. These rocks are scattered throughout the area. Trails have been created to travel in and out of the large rocks. The rocks and formations of rocks are climbable. As you weave in and out of these strange stones, you can enjoy breathtaking overlooks. The Fort Davidson Historic Site is also nearby and features a museum and the battlefield. Earthworks from the former fort can be still seen.

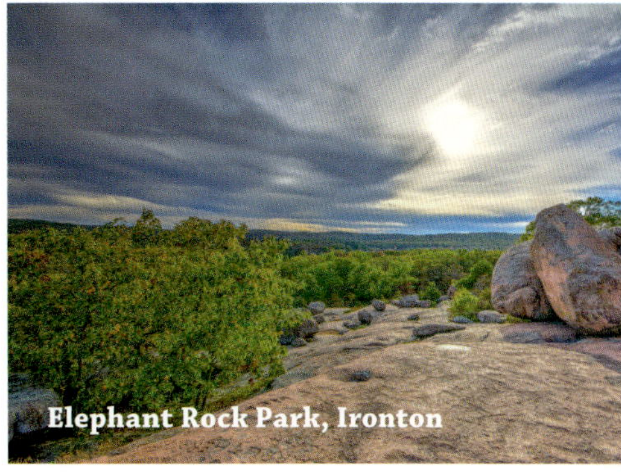

Elephant Rock Park, Ironton

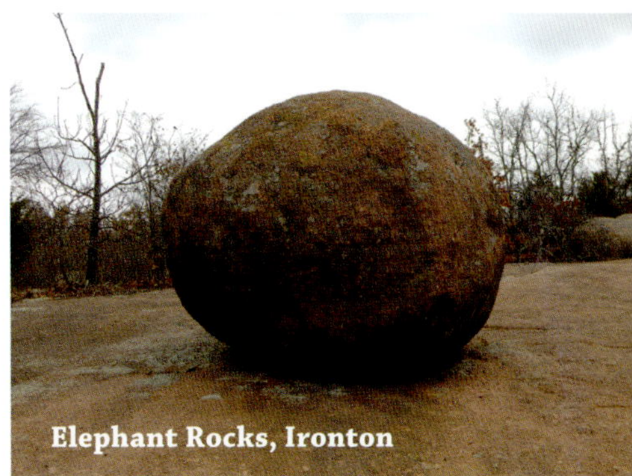

Elephant Rocks, Ironton

## MUST STAY

The area offers numerous bed-and-breakfasts and vacation rentals. One of the nicest and likely the most unusual is the Arcadia Academy Bed and Breakfast. In 1847, the Arcadia Valley Academy was started as a Methodist high school. The school did well, but the Civil War led it to be closed. It was also used as a Union hospital during the war.

In 1877 the building was purchased by the Ursuline Order of Nuns, and they operated the academy. It continued until 1971. Now it's a bed-and-breakfast with on-site restaurant and bakery.

Another bed-and-breakfast to consider is the Plain and Fancy Bed and Breakfast, which also offers horseback riding.

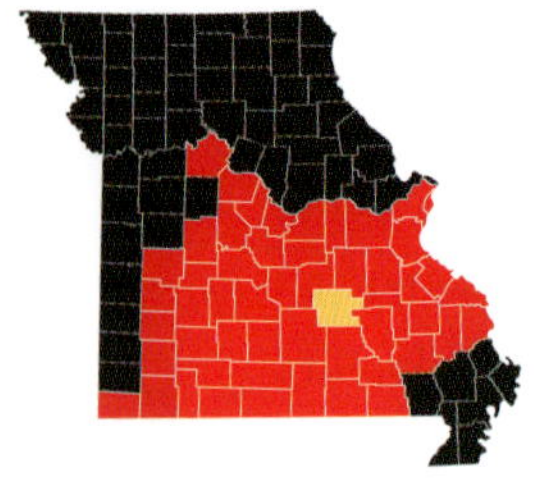

# 54

# Jadwin

That expression "If you blink, you'll miss it" more than applies to the Ozark town of Jadwin. If you blink at the right time, you'll miss the canoe-rental place and the grocery/liquor store. But don't be fooled by this community that traces back to 1875 and was named after one of its earliest settlers. Near the town is this author's favorite stop from the *Show Me Small-Town Missouri* journeys. It's the Welch Spring Hospital ruins. There's no fanfare, it's more something that one stumbles across while hiking in the Ozark National Scenic Riverways, but it's spectacular.

In 1913, C. H. Diehl, a doctor from Illinois, bought the spring and built a hospital to treat respiratory illnesses. His hospital was built over the mouth of the cave from which the spring flowed, with the goal of pushing the fresh spring air into the hospital. There was no treatment done other than breathing the air. Due to its remote location, the business was a flop. Following Diehl's death in 1940, his family did not keep the facility up.

Though it seems Dr. Diehl failed, he was onto something—today just hiking around the place is refreshing. There really is little to do in the area, but it's a favorite of this author because it's the perfect mix of nature's beauty, refreshing spring water, and the mysterious, almost haunting presence of the old hospital.

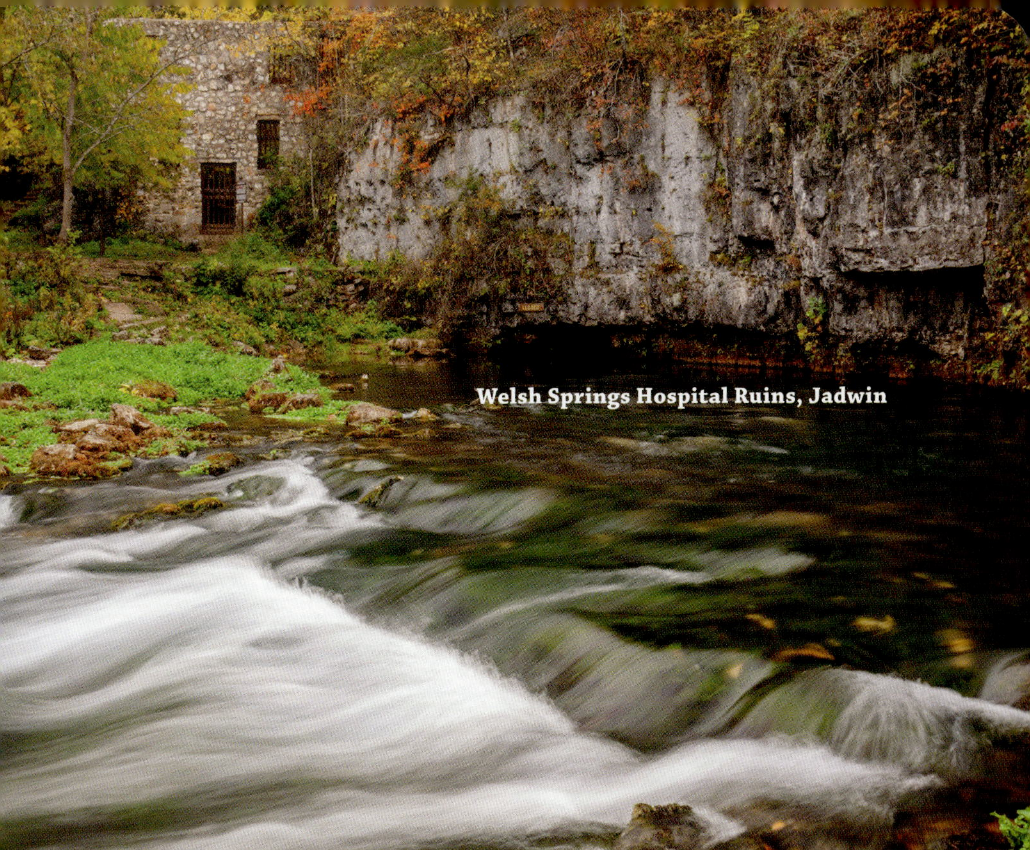
Welsh Springs Hospital Ruins, Jadwin

## MUST SEE

There's no exact address to the Welch Spring Hospital ruins, but the journey is worth it. It's located between Jadwin and Akers and may best be explored via canoe off the Current River. If driving to hike to it, turn west from Highway K on a dirt road, north of Akers Campground and south of K-A. That road goes to the Welch landing. Then a short hike north along the river will lead you to this secret historic treasure.

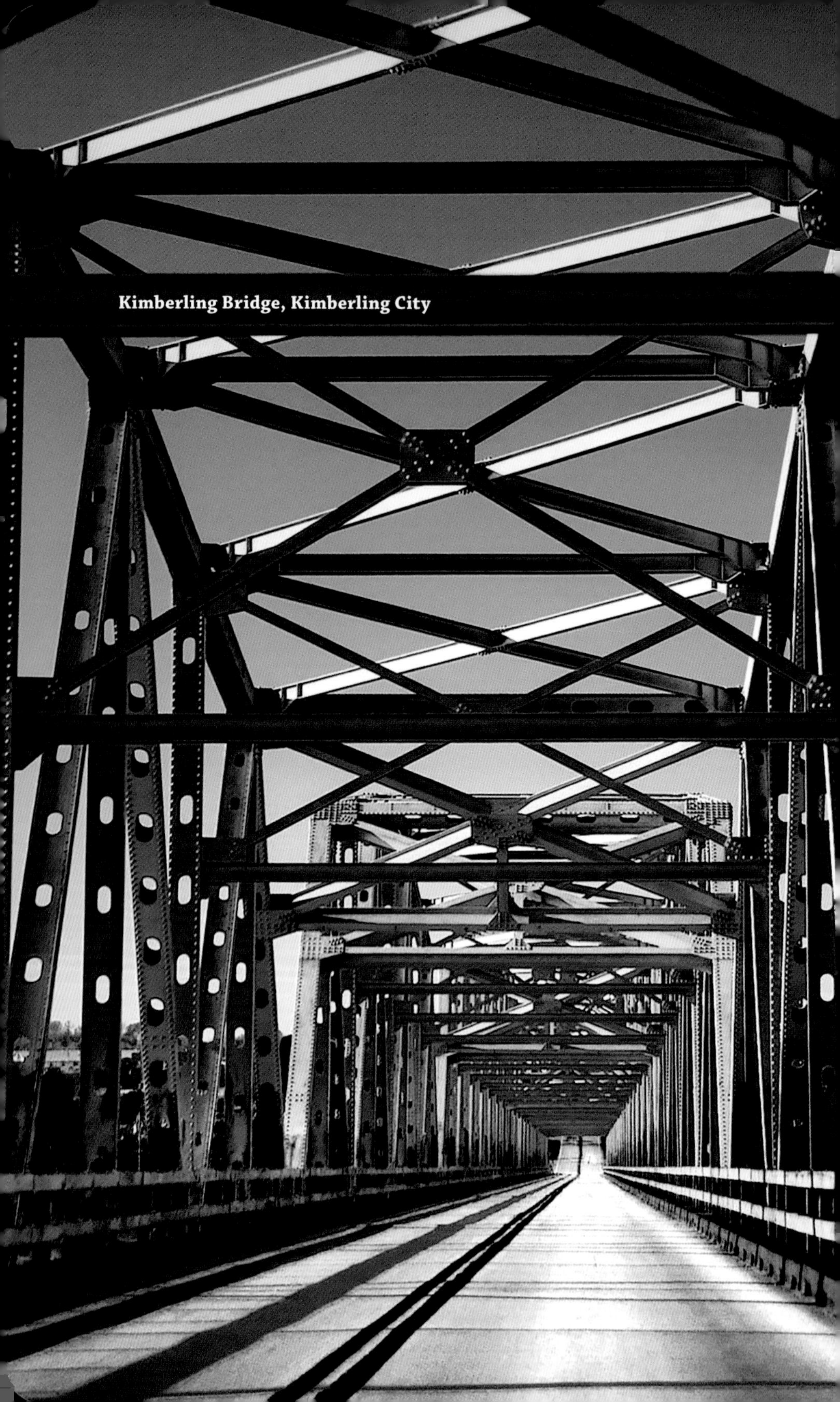

Kimberling Bridge, Kimberling City

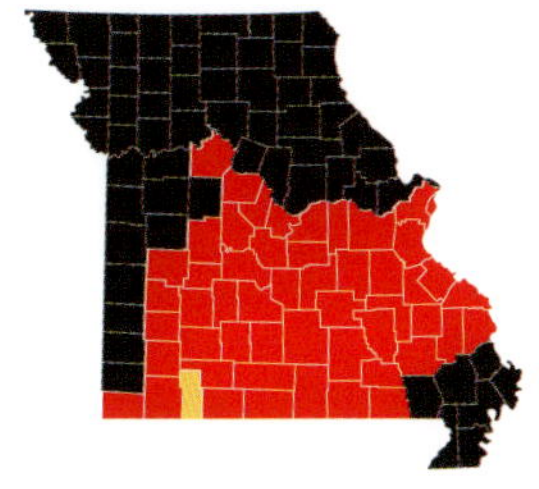

# 55

# Kimberling City

Kimberling City is one of the main hubs of activity on Table Rock Lake and is the location of one of the most iconic emblems of the lake, the Highway 13 bridge. The town's location had long been a crossing over the White River. Early on, it was the site of a ferry operated by the Kimberling family, which is how the city got its name. A bridge was later built, but after 1957 that bridge sat more than one hundred feet below water and a massive new bridge was in its place. This new bridge is a through-truss bridge that kept the look of the previous one. It spans close to two thousand feet and it's narrow, which adds to the vintage flair. It's a treat to cross Table Rock Lake on the Highway 13 bridge and take the opportunity to travel back in time and enjoy the scenic beauty of the lake and its crested Ozark boundaries.

The second Highway 13 bridge is older than the city itself, which is a baby by Missouri standards. It was incorporated in 1973 following the building of Table Rock Lake. Being a hub on Table Rock means boating activity and resorts all around. The town would be a larger and a more noted tourist destination if not for its very popular neighbor just over five miles away—Branson.

## MUST DO

If you enjoy lake life—boating, Jet Skiing, or pontooning—Kimberling City is a place to check out. The many watercraft rentals, boat charters, and resorts with boat slips for your own boat make for a fun time on the

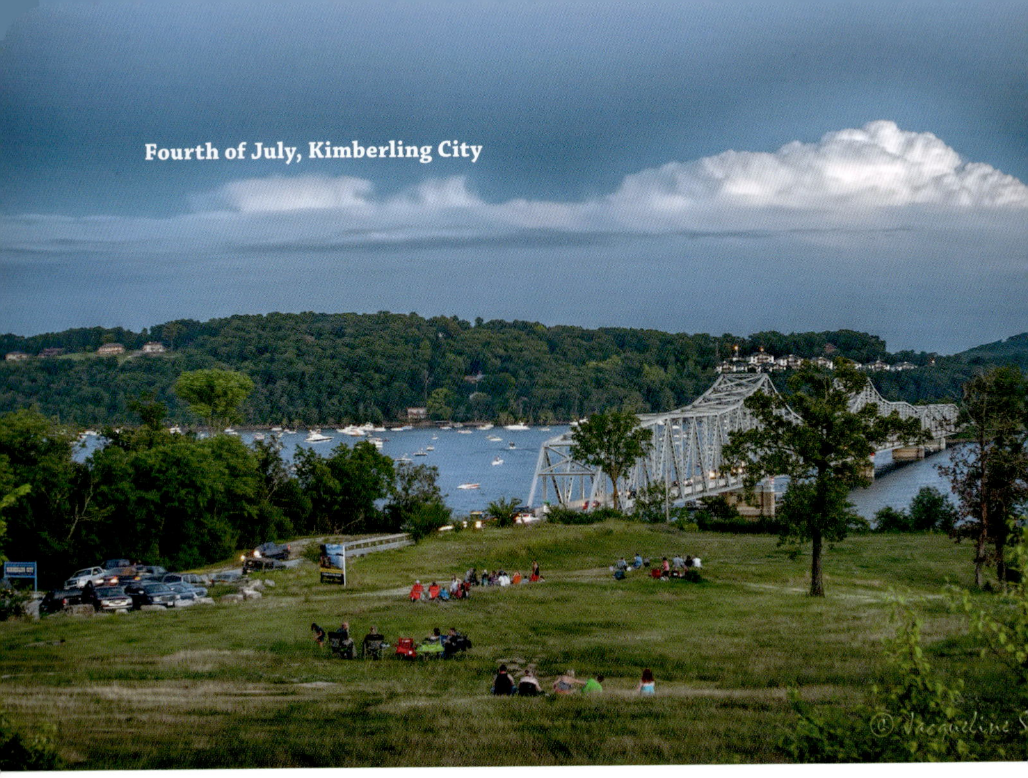
Fourth of July, Kimberling City

lake. And a short drive gets you to Branson. It's the best of two worlds. Because of its place on the lake, Kimberling City calls itself the bass fishing capital of Missouri, and numerous guides can help you cover all the lakes.

Although the lake activities are fun, the town is included in this book because of its holiday celebrations. During Christmas, the city puts on the Port of Lights display, a drive-through display with three miles of lights along the lake. This is one of the most celebrated light displays in the Branson area, with favorites like the long tunnels, the animated hillbilly fisherman, and the large animated paddle boat.

Then on the Fourth of July, Kimberling City hosts Fireburst, one of the most enjoyable firework displays in Branson. Spectators can watch from a boat or from the bank as fireworks explode over the lake.

## MUST EAT

Kimberling City and nearby Branson are full of great restaurants. The lake area has many catfish stops, but the Catfish Hole may be the best. The Catfish Hole is an icon in northwest Arkansas, with its Fayetteville location being featured on ESPN's *College GameDay*'s tour of top restaurants in Southestern Conference towns. Their clean, tasty fish are perfectly filleted and fried. Paired with endless hush puppies, tomato relish, and home-style fries, there's no wonder the place has received so much recognition. The Kimberling City outlet is the third location for the restaurant and adds a twist to the vibe with its lake location and live music venue.

Another restaurant to check out is Coyote's Dockside Café and Pub, which is actually out on the water and offers the opportunity to dine outside or inside.

The favorite restaurant from the Branson section has a location just a mile or two away in West Branson. Danna's BBQ offers extraordinary barbeque and some of the best burgers around.

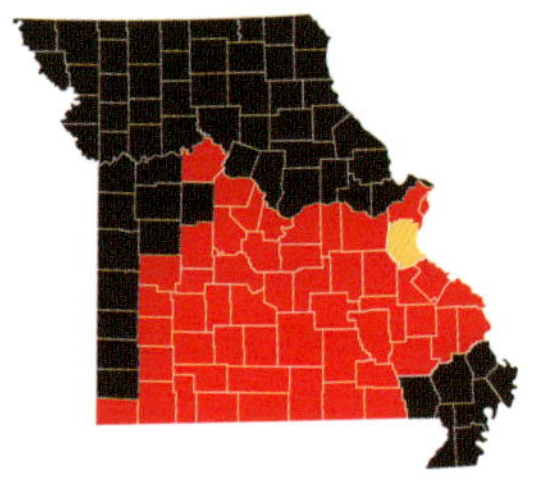

# 56

# Kimmswick

Kimmswick has a deep, rich history that is evident in the town today. It is practically a living museum, with many shops and restaurants operating in original buildings dating back to the start of the town in 1859. The town was platted by Theodore Kimm, and he named it, taking his last name and combining it with the "wick" from his native home of Brunswick, Germany. He was one of the early German immigrants to settle in the area.

The town's history goes much further back than Theodore Kimm, however, with revelations from nearby Imperial's Mastodon Historic Site showing signs of human habitation in the area as early as the Pleistocene. Early French and Spanish settlers had also been in the area. Kimmswick was on the *El Camino Real*, Spanish for "The King's Road." This brought traffic into town, and the town was ultimately further boosted by the railroad.

The proximity to St. Louis and other major Mississippi River ports kept the town's growth at bay. In 2010, the population was only 157, but a resurgence has been in motion for several years that has revitalized Kimmswick and made it a tourist destination.

Kimmswick is now a thriving community that has brought its historical roots to life. More than twenty-five specialty shops are open for business with more on the way, plus several restaurants. Many of these new businesses occupy buildings from the late 1800s. A forty-four-building historical district covers most of the town. Some of the highlights of these historical landmarks are the Historic Anheuser Estate Museum, built in 1867. This was the summer home of the Anheuser family and has spectacular views of the Mississippi River. There's also the Old House, a traditional log home dating back to 1770. The town's largest attraction is the famous Delta Queen steamboat, which was built as an overnight passenger vessel in 1927. It's estimated the boat has over two million miles on it. It has now made Kimmswick its home port as it prepares to offer overnight river cruises.

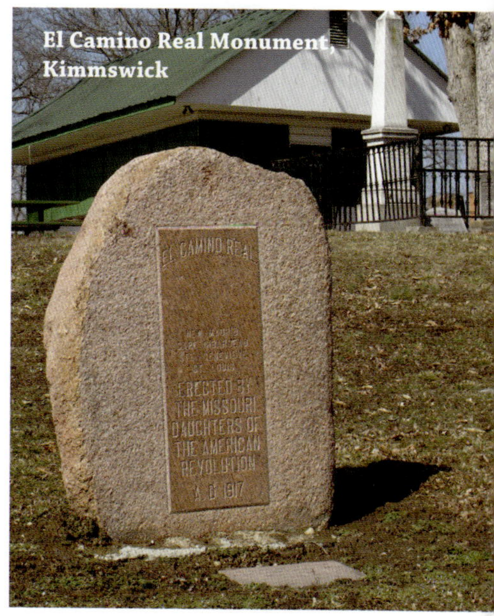

El Camino Real Monument, Kimmswick

## MUST DO

Whether you're a history enthusiast, a shopper, or someone who just wants a fun trip, visit Kimmswick. Stroll among the historic buildings and new specialty shops. It's fun to do and relaxing being along the river. Just don't plan a trip on Monday because all the shops and restaurants are closed. Make a weekend of the trip. Several bed-and-breakfasts are in the area.

## MUST EAT

Every restaurant that's opened in the revitalization initiative is great, and they aim to provide a special product both in food and atmosphere. The leader in this is the Blue Owl Restaurant and Bakery. This charming restaurant has been featured on both the Food Network and the Travel Channel and in many, many major magazines and newspapers. Just how good are their pies? Besides their Levee High Caramel Apple Pecan Pie being selected as one of Oprah's "Top 100 Favorite Things for the Holidays," owner and pie maker extraordinaire Mary Hostetter was invited to be a guest on Paula Deen's cooking show to teach Paula to make that renowned pie.

The Blue Owl is more than worth the drive, even though their famous desserts can be ordered online from all over the world. The restaurant

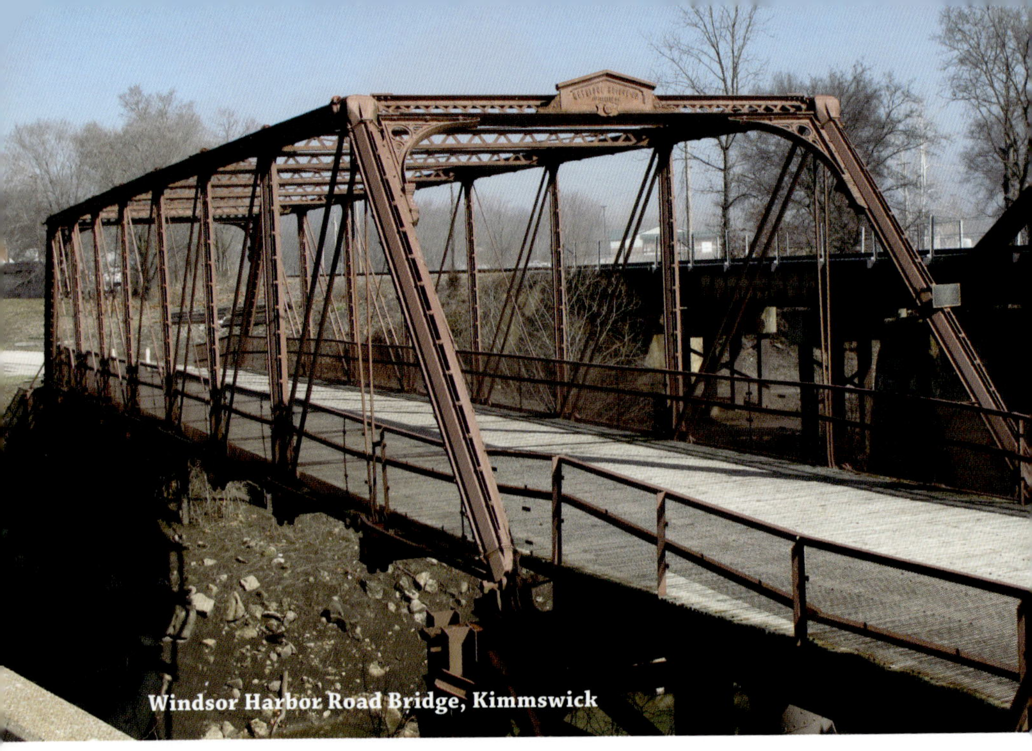
Windsor Harbor Road Bridge, Kimmswick

is charming, with the feel you're eating in a farmhouse. Every pie is an astonishing work of art, and it is challenging to pick one, but many are so rich you can't sample much of them. Though the main dishes are second to the pies, do try one of them because everything has a down-home feel and a perfected taste.

For smoked meats, keep in mind Smokee Robinson's Cajun Smokehouse. Smokee's serves up great cuts of meat with great smoke flavor.

## MUST SHOP

Kimmswick has a list of shops that are treasures to explore, but two jump out. First, Mississippi Mud Gallery and Gifts is a cross between an art gallery and retail store without appearing like an art gallery. The pieces are just awe-inspiring. Mississippi Mud has found some of the most amazing artists in all mediums and brought them together in one place. You'll find things here you won't find anywhere else.

If it adds flavor and spices up a meal, then it's sold at the Spicery. They have a huge selection of spices, herbs, extracts, and salts, as well as flavors of coffee and tea.

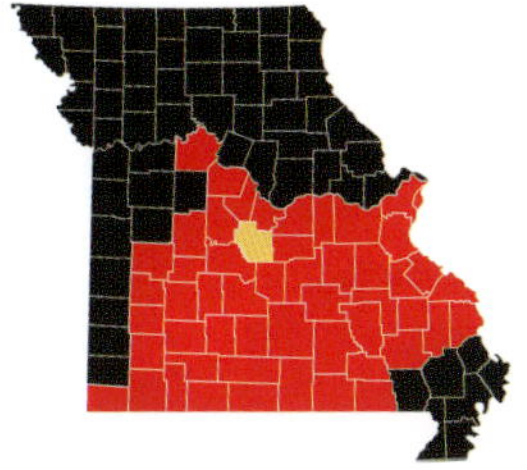

# 57

# Lake Ozark

Lake of the Ozarks is one of the most popular lake destinations in the country and is a favorite in Missouri. Three towns serve as the main hubs of activity at the lake: Lake Ozark, Camdenton, and Osage Beach. All three are covered in this book because they are some of the most exciting small towns in the state. The lake brings in an estimated five million visitors each year, and there are seventy thousand vacation homes. It's a happening place.

The lake offers such varied ways of enjoying it. There's the complete lake-life trip spent on a houseboat or at a vacation rental with a dock, where everything centers on boating, waterskiing, Jet Skiing, and so on. Then there's the boating party trip to Party Cove. There's the rustic camping trip in the state park or one of the many campsites around spent fishing, swimming, and hiking. There's the family trip to a hotel and seeing sights, with activities like water parks, bumper boats, go-carts, and paintball. Then there's the upscale getaway to one of the nice resorts on the lake with golf and spas, along with fine dining and wineries. It's all available, which is one of the reasons the area is so popular.

Each of the three hub cities has a different vibe. Camdenton is like Gatlinburg with activities for families. Osage Beach is like Gulf Shores—there's so much to do. Lake Ozark is home to some of the nicest resorts on the lake. Of course, there's overlap of activities with each town.

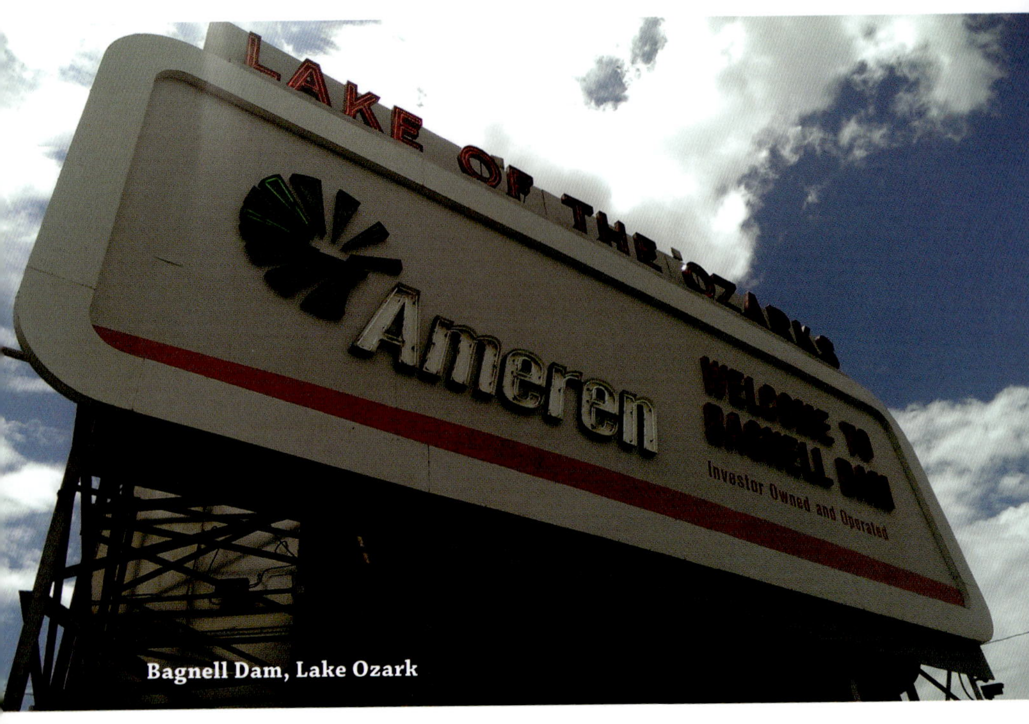

Bagnell Dam, Lake Ozark

Lake Ozark came into being following construction of the lake in 1931 and takes its name from the lake. It's home to only 1,586 residents, but during tourist season the population is much larger.

## MUST DO

Of course, there are all the lake activities, but in addition there is Shawnee Bluff Winery, which offers the best view out of all Missouri's wineries. It sits high on a bluff overlooking the lake. They have created a relaxing oasis that is the perfect place for an afternoon of wine tasting. They also have great-tasting food served in a very casual atmosphere.

If it's family fun you're after, try Leman's Family Fun Park for go-karts, bumper boats, miniature golf, and more.

## MUST STAY

Lake Ozark is home to three of the four top resorts on the lake—Camden on the Lake Resort, Lodge of Four Seasons, and the Lodge of Port Arrowhead. If an upscale resort is what you're looking for, these are what you want to consider. Remember also that the area is covered with vacation rentals.

The Lodge of Four Seasons is the home of two championship golf courses, the Cove and the Ridge. Both are recognized among the top five courses in Missouri.

## MUST EAT

Along with the nice resorts are nice restaurants like JB Hook. Sitting high above the lake on a tall bluff is this extremely popular restaurant. There's the patio to fully take in the view, but windows also allow panoramic views of the lake. It's fine dining in a casual atmosphere, with a classy ambiance. It's hard to choose between seafood or steak.

With similar location, views, and popularity is Tucker's Shuckers Oysters and Tap. Though there are similarities, the atmosphere is radically different, Tucker's is a party with live music, televisions, and a much more causal menu. The freshness of the oysters brought in daily is one of the big draws.

Baxter's Lakeside Grille is much like JB Hook. A breathtaking view of the lake and fine dining. The food also is extremely well done.

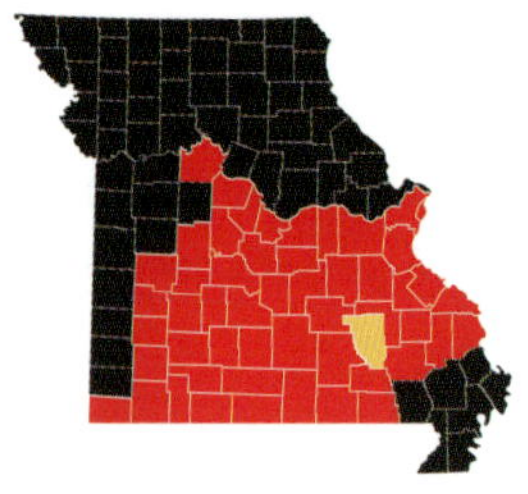

# 58

# *Lesterville*

Lesterville is another Ozark destination for outdoor adventure, with much canoeing, kayaking, and floating on the nearby Black River. Several outfitters are in the area, but the unique highlight of the town is its natural waterpark.

The settlement of Lesterville can be traced back to 1816 when the town's namesake, Jesse Lester, left Kentucky with his family for Missouri. He settled in the area that now bears his name. A trading post was established for commerce with Native Americans. As with almost all of Missouri, the Civil War set back progress. A nearby mountain pass, known as the Devil's Tollgate, led Union supply lines through town, which resulted in farms and homes being raided.

Following the war, the timber industry flourished, many mills were opened, and the town prospered. But soon the market was flooded and forests were depleted. That setback allowed the start of what now drives the area—tourism. Rarely is it easy to trace the roots of how a place becomes a tourist destination. But Red Hunt gets the credit for first inviting "city people" to his farm, where they would pay to tour the area and enjoy the sights. Hunt's farm continues to receive guests today, but now it is known as Black River Lodge.

## MUST DO

The Black River offers great canoeing, kayaking, or floating, and there are many outfitters in the area. But again the highlight is the natural

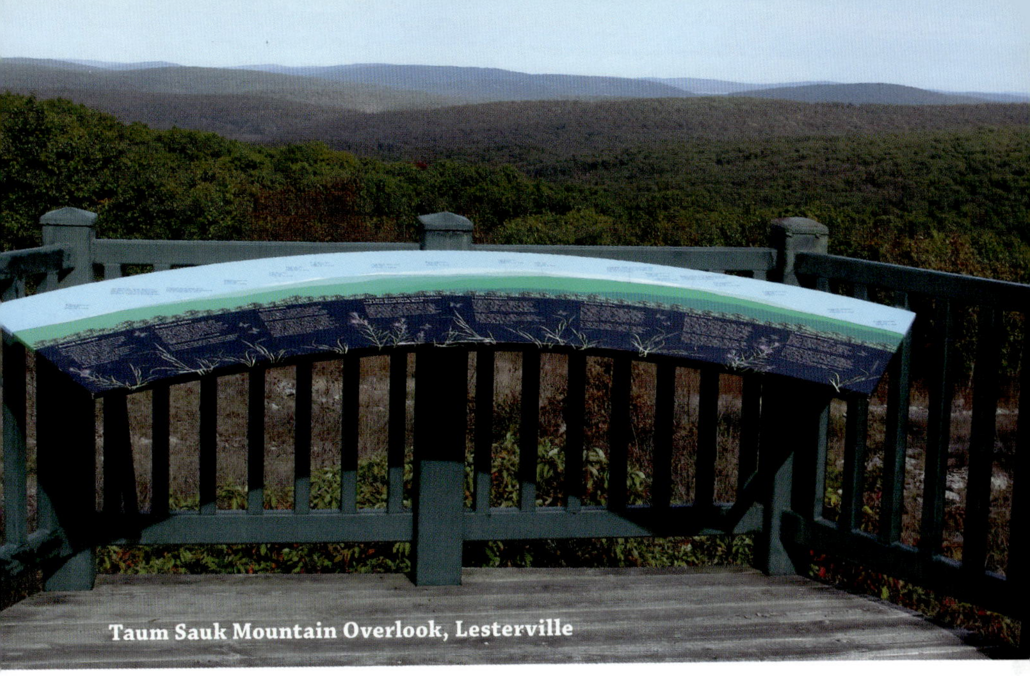
Taum Sauk Mountain Overlook, Lesterville

waterpark—Johnson's Shut-Ins. Of the multiple shut-ins throughout the state, this is the most recognizable and has by far the nicest park facilities. Shut-ins are areas on the river where the river bedrock resists erosion, causing them to turn into jagged waterfalls and pools. Small pools and crevices throughout the shut-ins hold water. These natural structures create different features much like a water park, and they become the perfect place to play and explore. A nice state park has been built around the shut-ins and was recently redone after the Taum Sauk reservoir breached, and millions of gallons of water inundated the park in 2005.

## MUST STAY

Mentioned earlier, the Black River Lodge has a long history, and now it not only offers a place to stay and float the river but has several amenities that make it fun for families.

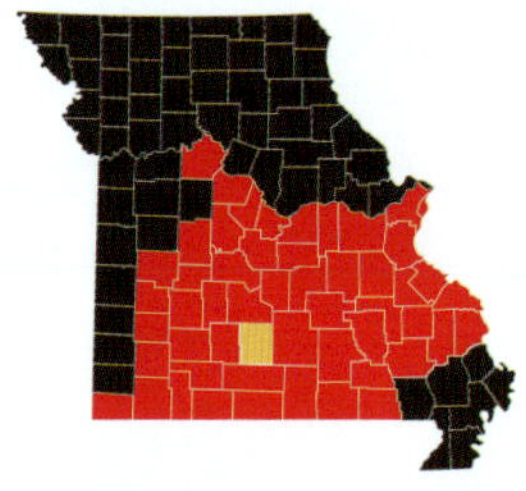

# 59

# Mansfield

For fans of author Laura Ingalls Wilder and her *Little House on the Prairie* books, Mansfield needs no introduction. It was the home of Rocky Ridge Farm, where Laura lived most of her life (1894–1957) and where she wrote her classic books. It's here in Mansfield that her body is laid to rest.

Mansfield's history does not predate its most famous citizen by much. It was platted in 1882 by F. M. Mansfield and was named after him. Wilder's life is intertwined with the history of the town, and her legacy would provide it a future with the Laura Ingalls Wilder Historic Home and Museum. In the same vein as Wilder's writing on the pioneer life, Mansfield is also home to Baker Creek Heirloom Seeds, which carries a large selection of seeds from the nineteenth century, many of them rare. Interest in Baker Creek's seeds has grown so much that the owners were able to create Bakersville Pioneer Village, a homesteader's mecca. They also host festivals annually.

## MUST DO

Through school, most every American has some connection with the *Little House on the Prairie* books, which makes the Wilder Home and Museum a fascinating stop. Wilder tied her books to her own life and to the lives of children everywhere, which makes this site even more important. Visitors to the Laura Ingalls Wilder Historic Home and Museum are able to tour the homes Laura and her family lived in. A focal point tends to be Pa's fiddle, which is on display with many other real-life objects that were parts of her books. There's the large farmhouse that the Wilder couple first lived in, and then there is a rock house that was purchased for them by their daughter, Rose Wilder Lane, who became a famous author before her mother. The Mansfield Cemetery is the burial place for Laura, and her grave can be visited today.

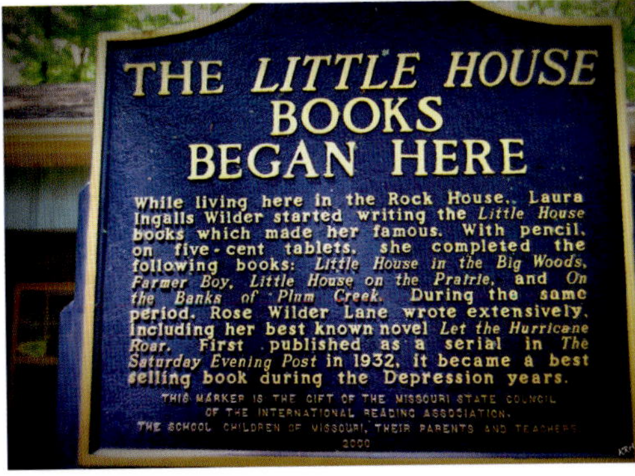


**Laura Ingalls Wilder Historic Home and Museum, Mansfield**

As the visit to the home and museum stirs up romanticized ideas of pioneer days, nearby Bakersville Pioneer Village allows you to live those out. There is the Baker Creek Seed Store, which is an epicenter of the heirloom gardening and homesteading life. The village includes a restaurant, speaker barn, mercantile, herbal apothecary, bakery, museum of gardening, blacksmith shop, music barns, old jail, farm animals, and more. In addition to the buildings are test gardens where the seeds have been planted. It's a refreshing oasis and one of the best ways to experience life in the 1800s and embrace the current organic gardening and homesteading culture.

## MUST EAT

Continuing the pioneer spirit of a visit to the Wilder home and especially Baker's Creek, the Bakersville Ozark Hotel Restaurant is a must-try dining experience. It's located in the pioneer village and offers guests the chance to try some of the produce grown from their seeds. There's no menu or set price. Each day the chef's special is posted, and all are invited to eat. There is no cost but donations are accepted.

## MUST STAY

In Mansfield, there's the opportunity to stay at the Weaver Inn Bed and Breakfast, which continues the 1800s theme. The Main Street two-story storefront building has been repurposed into a bed-and-breakfast. Downstairs is a coffee house. It's an endearing experience to stay in the very town where Laura Ingalls Wilder lived and worked.

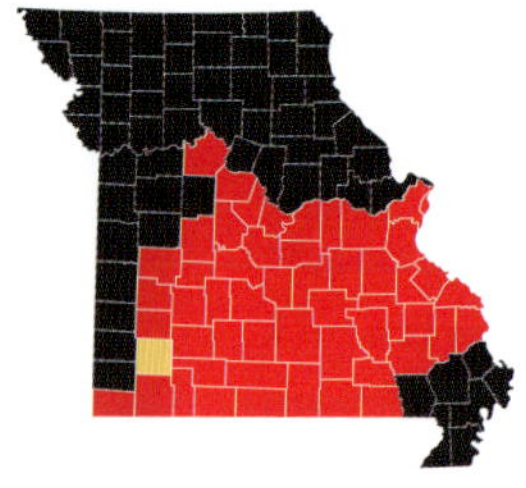

# 60

# *Marionville*

Much of this small-town journey is a unicorn hunt. It's looking for rare sights, tastes, and experiences that can only be had in these towns. Marionville presents two kinds of these, and one is closer to a real unicorn (as much as unicorns are real) than most other attractions, except this unicorn doesn't have a horn and is much smaller. But it is white and rare like a unicorn.

Marionville was platted in 1854 and named after Francis Marion, the Revolutionary War hero known as the Swamp Fox. He is also referred to as the Father of Guerilla Warfare. He led the Continental Army's campaign in South Carolina and used irregular tactics to defeat the much larger British army. He was also the inspiration behind the movie *The Patriot*.

The most intriguing aspect of Marionville's history is one that is alive and well today. That is those small, hornless unicorns, because the pride and calling card of Marionville is its population of white squirrels. It's one of four places in the country where white squirrels can be seen in large numbers. They have been spotted here since the late 1800s, and a picture proves their southwest Missouri existence as far back as 1913.

No one knows how they got here, but there are plenty of theories. The three main ones are that they came from a traveling circus, were created by a local scientist, or were stolen from Illinois. Also in question is which of the four places had the squirrels first. Regardless of where they came from or which town had them first, they are fascinating to see, and the

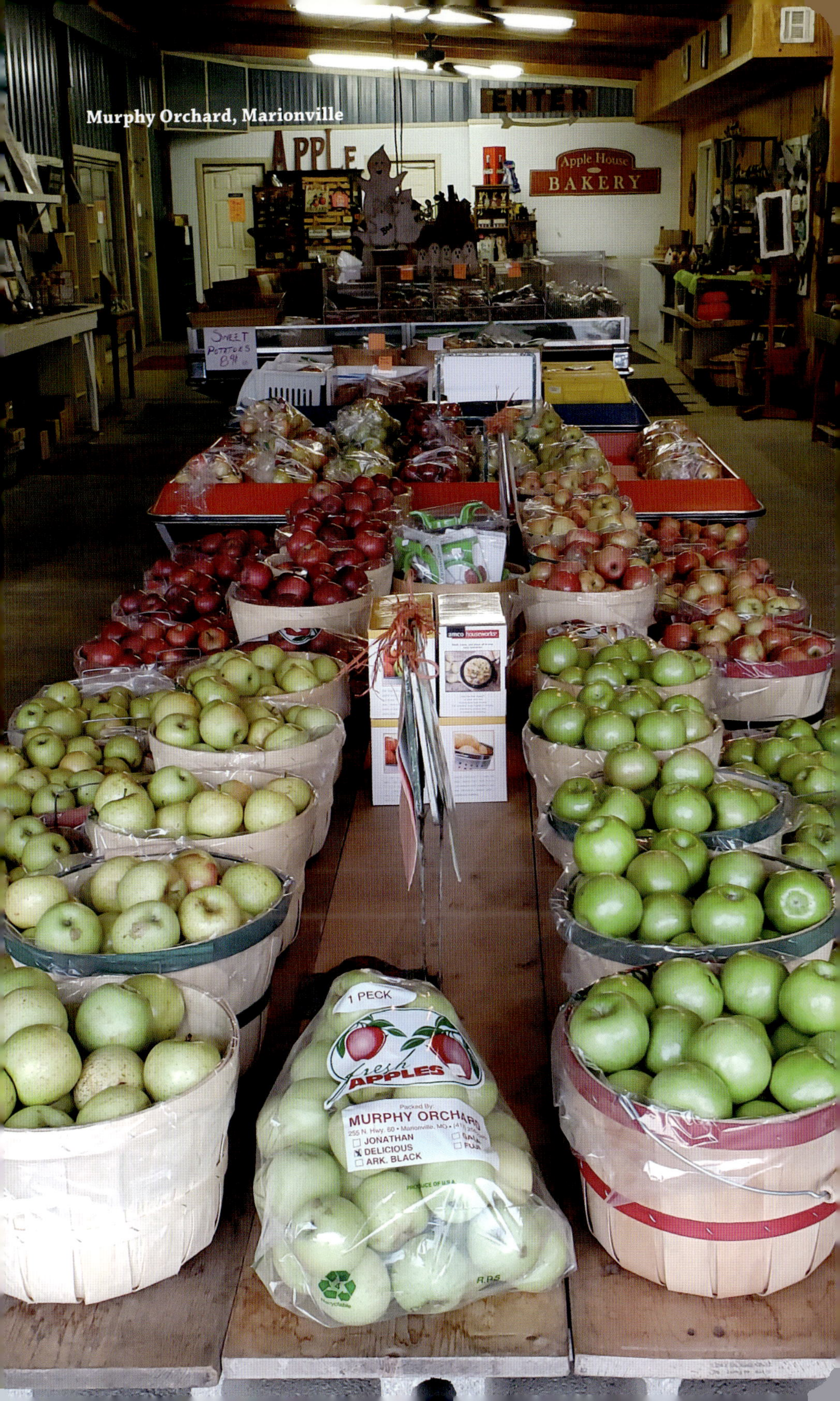

Murphy Orchard, Marionville

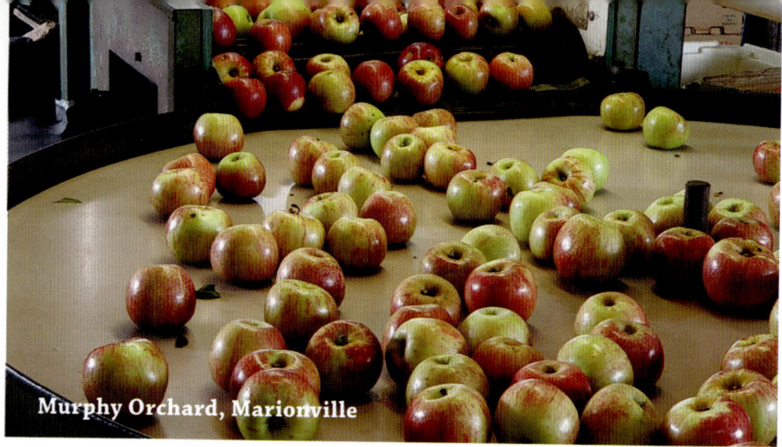
Murphy Orchard, Marionville

population is so high that they're easy to spot. Be careful not to harm one, or you could be fined $500 to $1,000.

As rare and surprising as those squirrels are in this small town of just over two thousand, they pale in comparison to a much greater treasure. This treasure is the fresh apple cider slush from Murphy's Orchard. It's a treat that gets customers hooked on the first sip.

Murphy's is a large orchard in Marionville that grows all types of fruits and vegetables, with the main focus being apples, peaches, strawberries, and blueberries. They have over twenty different varieties and provide an online schedule so that customers know when they will be harvested. At the orchard is a store where these fresh products and their signature apple cider slush can be purchased. Their cider tastes much different than store-bought varieties because of its freshness. Springfield's *417 Magazine* said it best in a feature on these slushes: "It's a drink that proves the only thing better than freshly picked apples is an addictive, sippable treat that's made with those perfect little fruits."

## MUST DO

Catching a glimpse of the white squirrels is a fun outing. They are most active in the early morning and can be seen anywhere in town, but the hot spot for a stakeout is Ozarks Methodist Manor Retirement Home. And before, during, and after the squirrel stakeout, you'll want to be slowly (due to brain freeze) sipping on a Murphy's Orchard apple cider slush.

## MUST EAT

Don't miss an apple cider slush from Murphy's Orchard. By the number of times this treat is mentioned, you can tell it's worth the drive.

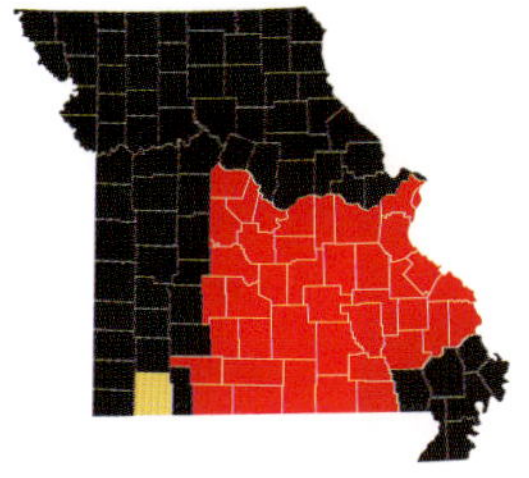

# 61

# *Monett*

Residents and visitors would be surprised to know the influence Monett wielded in southwest Missouri as a leading rail stop on the St. Louis–San Francisco Railroad. It was established as a railroad town in 1870 when the Frisco line came through, and later a line spurred off in Monett to Paris, Texas. This second line brought all rail traffic of western Arkansas, eastern Texas, and northern Louisiana through Monett.

There were several names for the town until finally Monett was chosen. It was the name of a popular railroad agent of the time. The town was platted in 1887. Railroad access opened doors for industry in the area. Monett also was a leader in fruit production. In the early 1900s it was known as the "Strawberry Capital of the Midwest."

Today Monett has a population of nearly nine thousand, and it has been included in this listing because it is home to the "Best Christmas Light Display in Southwest Missouri" and because it's home to one of the best Cajun restaurants in the state.

## MUST DO

Annually Monett hosts the Festival of Lights, a spectacular drive-through Christmas light display at the city's South Park. There are more than a half-million dollars' worth of custom light displays on the drive-through route. Best of all, the attraction is free. It's worth the journey to drive through the fun light designs.

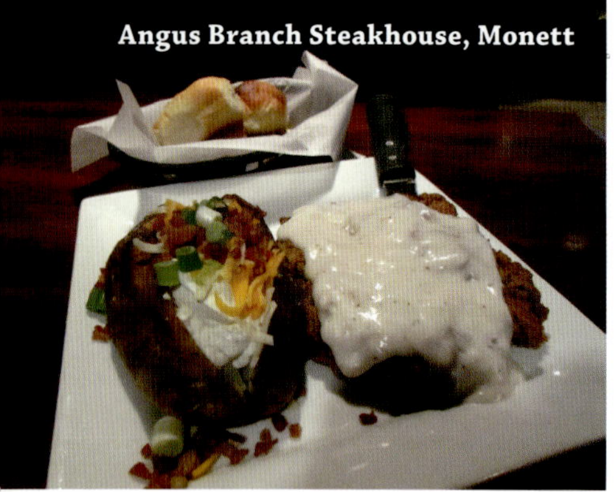
Angus Branch Steakhouse, Monett

## MUST EAT

With so much loss and destruction from Hurricane Katrina in New Orleans, Monett actually gained a gem. Darren Indovina lost everything in that hurricane. His wife got a job in Monett, and he decided the town needed a Cajun restaurant. From that uncertainty, the Bayou was born. The Bayou is one of the best Cajun restaurants in the state. It's been self-described as, "Down-home Cajun and Creole food offered in a laid-back atmosphere." All the traditional Cajun fare is served, like gumbo, jambalaya, étouffée, red beans and rice, oysters, shrimp, catfish, crawfish, and even alligator. Also keeping with the New Orleans tradition, the Bayou severs up a giant muffuletta, a meat and cheese sandwich with a generous layer of olive salad. They also have a huge selection of another Cajun staple sandwich, the Po Boy. The fried shrimp and the fried crawfish are the definite favorites, but it's the fresh bread that sets these apart. And if you're looking for fried seafood, the Fried Seafood Barge will cover your table. Although it's a Cajun joint, the burgers are insanely good. There's a large selection of standard Americana fare, too.

Though the Bayou may be the standout restaurant, the Angus Branch Steakhouse is a great stop as well. It's a typical steakhouse, but the cooking staff does very well in providing great-looking and great-tasting steaks.

## MUST NOTE

Monett was once the home of a farm team for the St. Louis Cardinals. The Monett Red Birds played from 1936 to 1939.

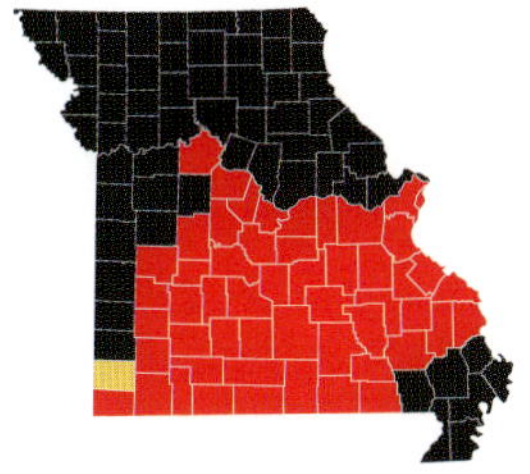

# 62

## Neosho

People all over the world have been to Neosho, a southwest Missouri small town with twelve thousand residents. And many of those came to Neosho weekly. Chances are you've been to Neosho.

No, they didn't know they were there, but each time they read the latest *Beetle Bailey* comic strip they were in Neosho. And that would be a lot of people, because the comic strip has been in circulation since 1950 and is syndicated in eighteen hundred papers. The setting of this army-influenced comic is Camp Swampy, inspired by Camp Crowder, where comic creator Mort Walker was stationed. And Camp Crowder was located in Neosho. So in a sense, when Bailey and Killer took their dates out on the town, they would have been in Neosho.

Neosho's history goes much further back than the World War II–era Camp Crowder. More than a dozen nearby springs (nine within city limits) made the area inviting to the Osage tribes, who gave the town its name, which means clear, cold water. No doubt this was because of the multitude of springs. In the early days of European-American settlement, it would be nicknamed "The City of Springs."

Settlers began to enter the area in the 1820s, and the city was founded in 1839. Soon after, lead and zinc were discovered, which created a mining boom. In 1888, Neosho became the home of the first national fish hatchery because of the bountiful spring water. Even today, as the hatchery continues operation, it is supplied with water from the springs, with two million gallons pumped in daily.

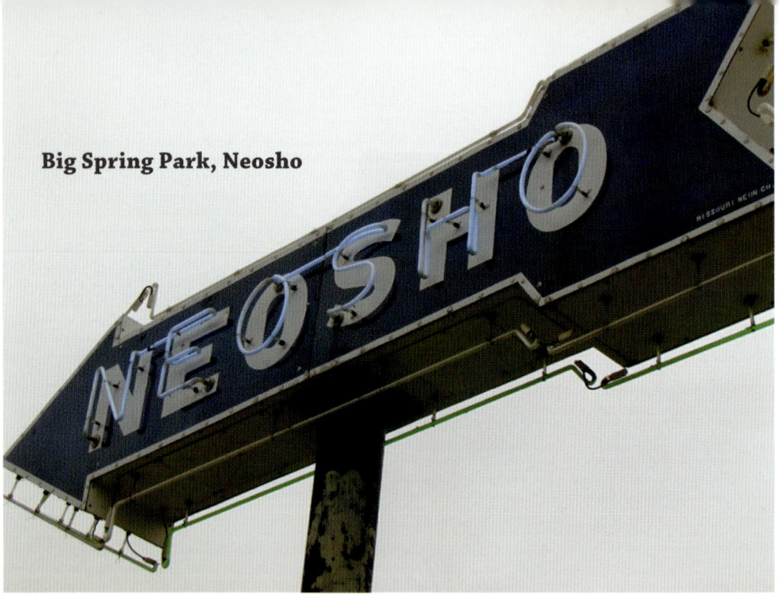


Big Spring Park, Neosho

The railroad was also a reason for the hatchery landing in town and for the city's growth. There were three rail lines that came through town. Sadly, in 1914, a tragic head-on collision of two passenger trains resulted in forty-three passengers dying. Many were burned beyond recognition and are buried in a mass grave in town.

During the Civil War, Neosho was the location of the first vote of the Southern supporters in Missouri's General Assembly to secede from the Union. There was not a quorum, but the vote took place in town. In 1863, much of the downtown was burned.

At the beginning of World War II, Fort Crowder was established, and it became the training center for the US Army Signal Corps. Some of the soldiers to pass through the camp were actor Dick Van Dyke, country music legend Jean Shepard, and Beetle Bailey's creator Mort Walker.

In the 1950s, the city became known as the Flower Box City because of a campaign that created hundreds of flower boxes in town.

Today Neosho is home to several manufacturers and diversified industries, but its claim to fame is being the host of Missouri's largest garage sale. The annual two-day Neosho City-Wide Garage Sale celebrated its thirtieth anniversary in April 2018. Over four hundred simultaneous garage sales across town bring in thousands of visitors.

## MUST DO

If you are a garage-sale shopper or flea-market frequenter, you have to come in April to the City-Wide Garage Sale. Sales begin at 7:00 a.m., and

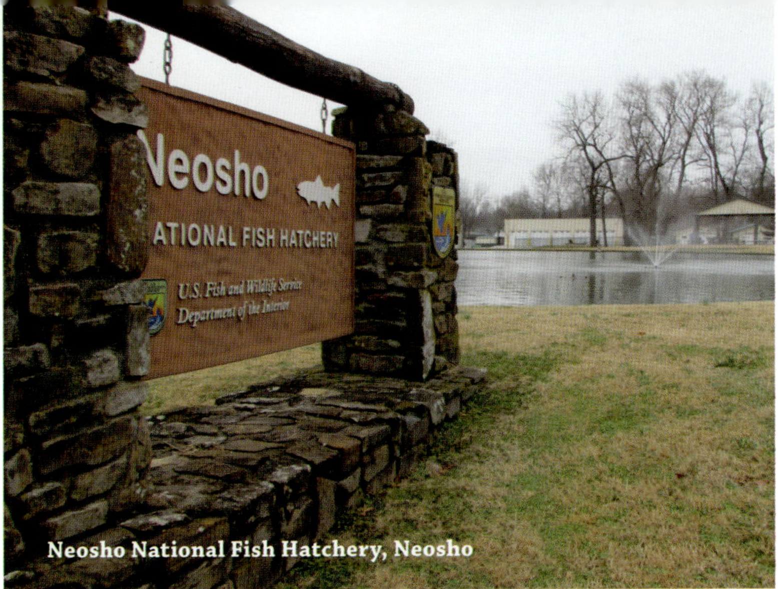

Neosho National Fish Hatchery, Neosho

the Chamber of Commerce provides downloadable maps on their website. The tip is to get an early start

The Neosho National Fish Hatchery is fascinating. This large facility sits in town and has a beautiful welcome center with interactive exhibits and aquariums. It has been created to be like a park, with walking trails, pavilions, and picnic areas. There's also free fish food to feed fish. While at the hatchery, guests have the chance to see rainbow trout, pallid sturgeon, and freshwater drum along with endangered species like Topeka shiners, Ozark cavefish, and mussels.

While in town be sure to check out the Longwell Museum at Crowder College, which features works from Neosho's own Thomas Hart Benton, a well-known painter and muralist, and aspects of the World War II Signal Corps training that was done at Camp Crowder.

## MUST NOTE

Neosho is also the hometown of the man responsible for saving European wine. A deadly louse destroyed most vineyards in France, Spain, and Portugal, but Hermann Jaegerwere found a grape that was resistant to the louse. Modern European vineyards would not exist if not for Jaegerwere. In thanks, he was awarded the French Legion of Honour, the highest honor given to civilians by France.

The engines for the Saturn 1, Saturn 1B, and Apollo rockets were built in Neosho. Also, while in Neosho keep your eyes open: there's said to be Confederate gold buried somewhere in town.

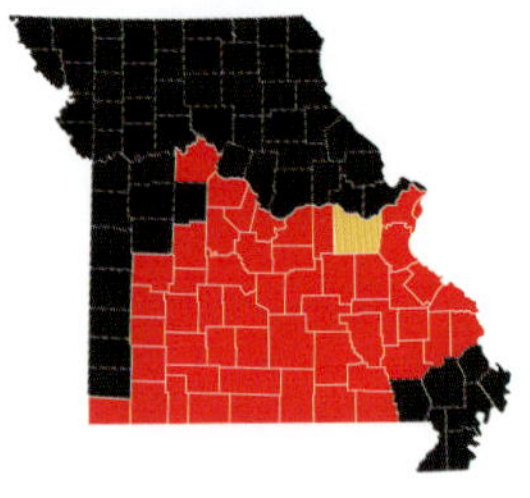

# 63

# New Haven

New Haven's website calls the town's downtown area "Missouri's Best Kept Secret." And it's definitely one of them. When you first enter New Haven, you see a typical small town and wonder if there is anything special there. But as you travels north on Miller Street or Olive Street then drop down the hill and cross the tracks, an entirely new town appears. This downtown riverfront is alive with a mix of history and art. It's basically just one block, but in it are artisan shops, stores, a bar, a restaurant, an inn, and a vintage theater. The history is anchored by the John Colter Museum and Visitor Center, and the art is anchored by the Astral Glass Studio and Hoffmann Lutherie Ukuleles.

The town was platted in 1858. First it was called Miller's Landing and saw riverboat traffic on the Missouri River. Eventually, as travel and industry began to rely more on the railroad, the name New Haven was used to reflect the city's "progress."

John Colter is recognized as the town's most famous former citizen. Long before "the world's most interesting man" of Dos Equis beer commercials, Colter was such a man. His frontiersman skills landed him a position on the Lewis and Clark expedition in 1803. After that expedition, he went on further travels and became a fur trapper. He is credited with being the first mountain man. During that time he became the first to discover Yellowstone. People did not believe his stories of geysers and called the place "Colter's Hell." He settled in New Haven for the final years of his life.

Today New Haven has become a day trip or weekend getaway for tourists, especially from St. Louis. Its close proximity to Hermann and being in Missouri's wine country contributes to its appeal. The downtown is a happening place, both on a regular basis and during the multiple special events throughout the year. The most famous event held in New Haven is Firefest.

Imagine every festival that has centered on fire entertainment meshed into one event. That's Firefest. It's a blast to attend—it has the features of a large festival, but the crowd is a manageable size. Each November since 2007, downtown New Haven and the riverfront are covered with vendors, open shops, live bands, and fun with fire. During the day, Civil War reenactors fire cannons and rifles into the Missouri River. At night the feature is the Ice House with the bonfire inside. As the fire grows, the ice blocks around it melt. But before that fire is lit, fire dancers entertain the crowd. There's typically a burning man also, and lighted flying lanterns are released. The favorite is the trebuchet that launches fiery pumpkins through the night sky and into the Missouri River.

New Haven is also home to Missouri's only short-film festival. This event is held in April at the historic Walt Theater in downtown New Haven. Beyond the special events, there's a lot more to do in New Haven than one would think.

## MUST DO

Visit downtown New Haven, especially during Firefest.

## MUST SHOP

With all the cool, quaint places in downtown New Haven, the ultimate treat is Astral Glass Studio, a working studio of professional glass blowers. The place itself is a mix of an art show, educational center, gallery, and store. First of all, the glass artwork is breathtaking. If it was merely a gallery, that would be fine, the bonus being that you can purchase it. But they also have a workshop surrounded by windows for guests to view the artists at work. It's hard to stop watching—the process is amazing and the artists do a great job of teaching and making it fun. This place cannot be recommended enough.

Also downtown is a ukulele maker. Hoffmann Lutherie handcrafted ukuleles are beautiful to see. Then there's Pickney Bend Distillery

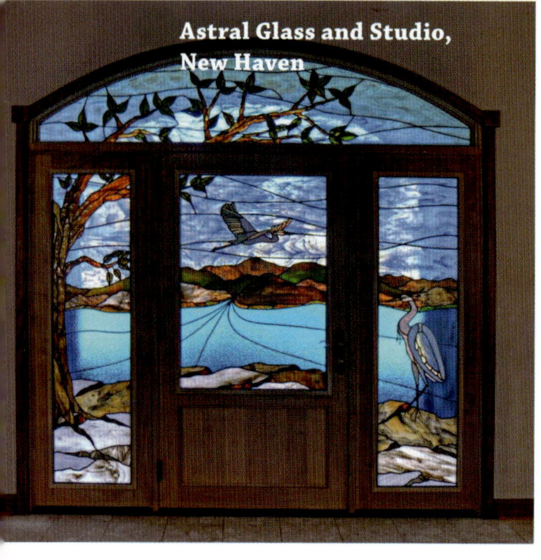
Astral Glass and Studio, New Haven

downtown and wineries spread around the area.

And once a guest has taken in the art and history, the Walt Theater is an iconic vintage theater that shows current movies at a surprisingly fair price.

## MUST EAT

Downtown New Haven is the home of Lancito's Pizzeria. These are incredible pizzas full of flavor and fresh toppings. They also have fantastic sandwiches.

## MUST STAY

Several bed-and-breakfasts are in town and nearby, but Pickney Bed and Breakfast offers a superb view and very nice rooms. It sits on the edge of a river bluff that puts it two hundred feet above the Missouri River, offering great views of the river and countryside. The view and opportunity to have a tasty breakfast out on the balcony make it a relaxing and romantic favorite.

Also in town is the Central Hotel, with a charming 1800s saloon and hotel look. Miller's Landing Bed and Breakfast has a great location by being downtown and on the river.

## MUST NOTE

New Haven's high school has one of the leading boys' basketball programs in the state. It won eight state titles between 1956 and 2001. Four of those were back-to-back.

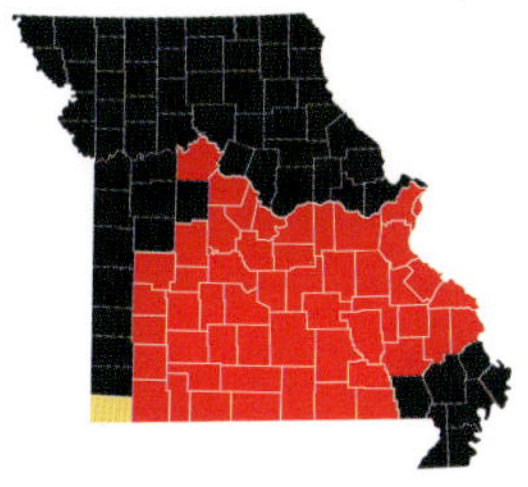

# 64

# Noel

There's lots of canoeing in the Ozarks, and multiple towns claim to be the best. Noel is one of a few that have taken on the title "Canoeing Capital of the Ozarks." Though towns farther east on the Current River might have a different opinion, the Elk River, which flows through Noel, is a worthy candidate, for it's one of the most enjoyable and safe floats in the country. It's well known in the area, but not as widely as the float warrants. Noel and nearby Pineville are hubs for camping and canoeing on the Elk. Noel is a spot for the adventurous, and there's much more than just river activities to do in the outdoors. The most exciting is the Shady Beach Zipline. If you're willing to brave the heights, then you'll experience beautiful scenic views and heart-thumping zipping.

Before more about canoeing on the Elk, one of the most fascinating historical notes on both Noel and the previously mentioned Pineville is that McDonald County, to which they belong, once seceded from Missouri and the United States. Neither the state nor Congress recognized the secession, but in 1961 the county set up a provisional government with elected officials and called the land the McDonald Territory. They sought to pursue becoming the fifty-first state. The reason for the secession attempt was that they were left off the Missouri State Highway Commission's annual Family Vacationland map. For this reason, careful steps were made to include the towns in this book—we didn't want to be the cause of another secession.

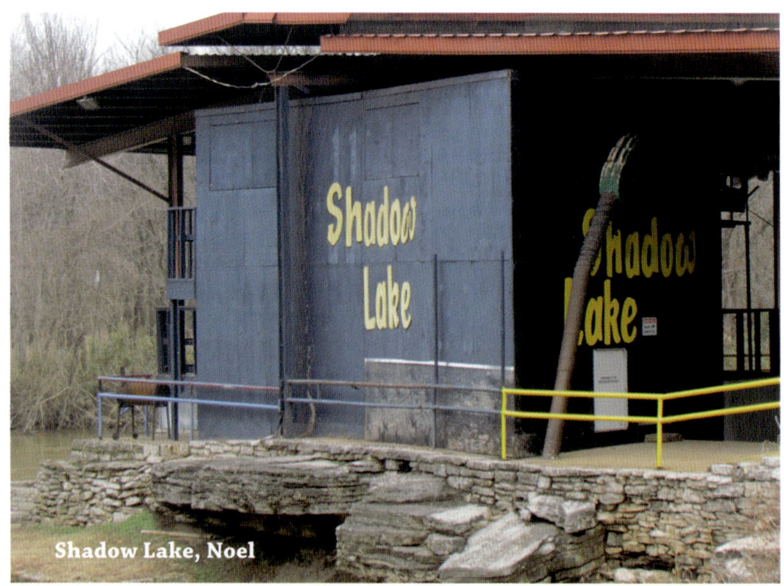

Shadow Lake, Noel

Residents of McDonald County recognize the importance of recreational river activities. It's the leading source of the county's economy. This is why a drive through Noel takes you back to the wonder of heading to summer camp. Everywhere there is a canoe or kayak—often many loaded on a trailer pulled behind a bus headed to a drop point. The river is a joyous float—enough current and bends to keep it interesting, but safe enough you're not worried about your life ending, and the difficulty level seldom rises above category two. Along the river are multiple gravel beaches on which a canoer can pull the canoe up and picnic or take a break. Deep holes dot the journey downriver, allowing for great swimming. There's the occasional well-worn bank with a quintessential rope swing. The smallmouth bass fishing in deep holes also can be good.

An Elk River float comes with a warning, though. Visitors need to know that weekends and peak season may not be best for children. If you're looking for Mardi Gras on water, you've found the place. Noel's canoeing and floating have gained quite the reputation as a party stream—men start the journey with a neck full of Mardi Gras beads and end with an empty neck, while several women make it to the destination with a neck full of beads and a stretched-out bikini top. And you're likely to see a shiny beer can in hand rather than a paddle. A tip for families and fishermen is to come midweek for your float.

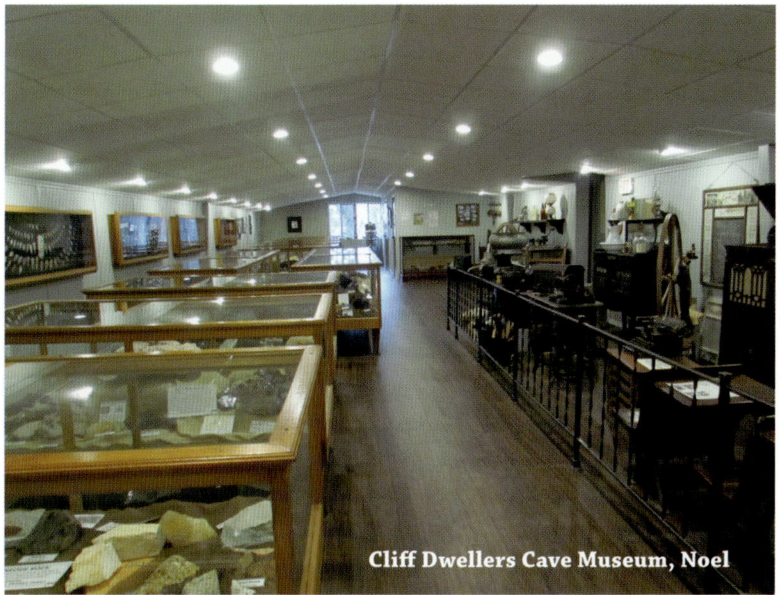
Cliff Dwellers Cave Museum, Noel

You've been warned about holiday weekends and peak season being a floating frat party. But if that's your scene—load the canoe up. You'll find the party you're looking for, and after the float, the party can continue at the Shadow Lake Surf Club, located in downtown Noel and backed up against the river. Shadow Lake has been a staple in southwest Missouri since 1925. It was established for the railroad workers to kick back and relax and still is a spot to do that, plus hear great music on weekends during the summer season.

## MUST DO

Plan a trip to float the Elk River. It's an enjoyable float, but pick your floating environment: serene during the week, or party on the weekend. Noel is the hub of activity in the southwest. In addition to river activities, there are caves to explore. Discovered the same year the Shadow Lake Surf Club opened was the Bluff Dwellers Cave. This limestone cave has yielded much information about the ancient bluff dwellers who lived in the area. Cave tours can be taken today. The cave is beautiful itself, but it also has a phenomenal story of ownership as it is privately owned and has been passed down through the Arthur Browning family. In 1858, Mr. Browning's daughter took over ownership. During her time she amassed

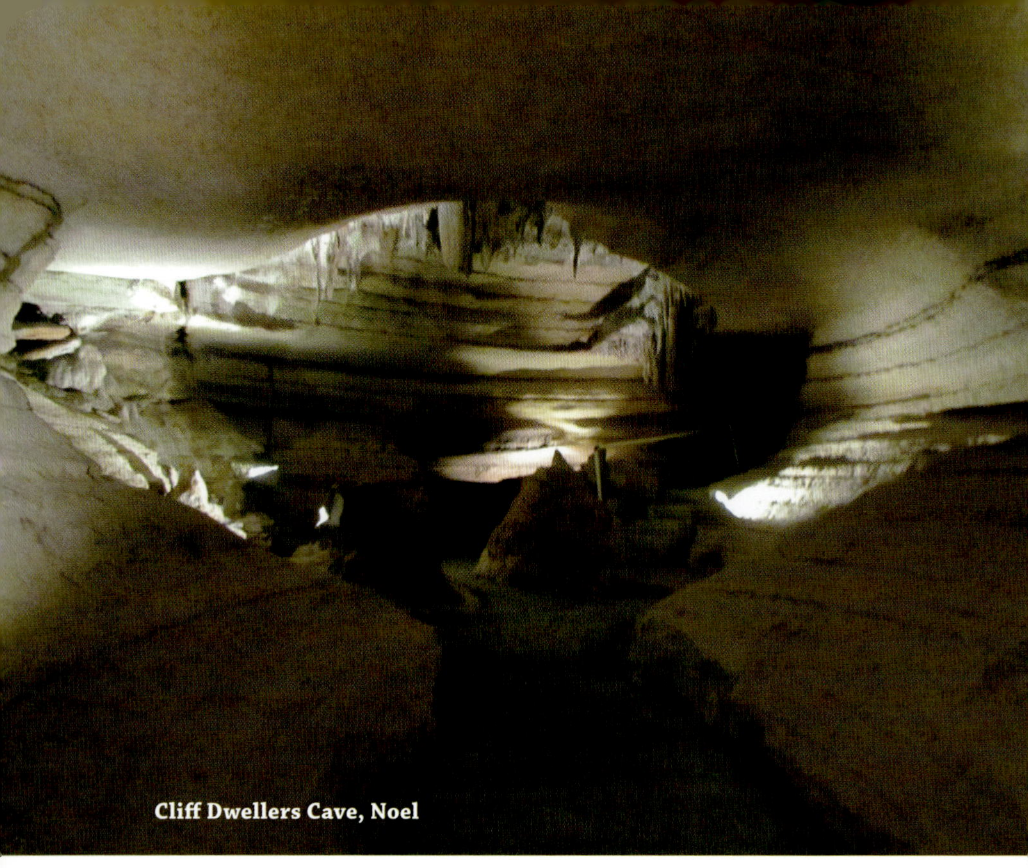
Cliff Dwellers Cave, Noel

a large collection of rocks from all over. Today a museum is on-site that displays these different types of stones, fossils, and crystals. There is even a black-light room with rocks that glow when cut open. This museum is a great feature for the place. Mr. Browning's grandson is now the owner of the cave.

Only seven miles from Noel is the Old Spanish Treasure Cave. This cave can also be toured. Old Spanish is steeped in legend, believed to be where Spanish Conquistadors hid treasure. Treasure hasn't been found, but helmets, armor, and other weapons from the era have been. During the Halloween season, you can catch a movie shown down deep in the cavern.

## MUST NOTE

One last intriguing note on Noel is that there is a large number of Somali and Sudanese refugees living here. This is why an African grocery store can be found downtown, along with a mosque, both of which are unique for a Missouri small town.

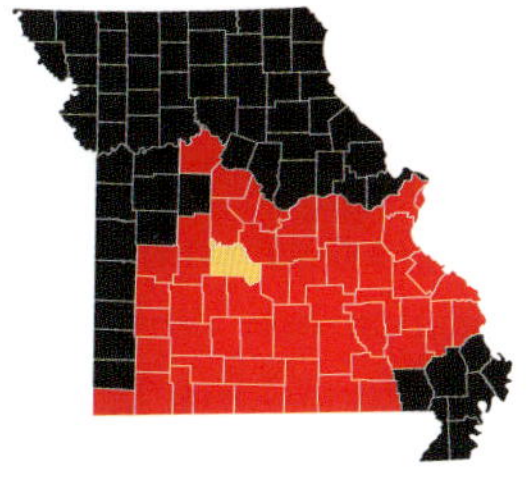

# 65

# Osage Beach

Osage Beach is the happening place on the Lake of the Ozarks. And if visitors think things are exciting now, this town had an extraordinary beginning: it was first known as Zebra. Yes, Zebra was the town's name when it was established in 1886, but Zebra ended up at the bottom of Lake of the Ozarks. So the town was moved to higher ground and renamed a less exotic name, Osage Beach, after the Osage River, which was dammed by Bagnell Dam to create Lake of the Ozarks.

Political debating and fighting almost prevented Osage Beach from becoming a tourist hub, but eventually the town got things together. And now it's the center of action on the lake.

## MUST DO

It's on Lake of the Ozarks, so the thing to do is be on the lake boating, Jet Skiing, partying, swimming, or fishing. But there are some more dry-land activities. Nearby in Brumley, in part of the Lake of the Ozarks State Park, are two classic swinging bridges waiting to be explored. If one is not too much of a chicken, they can be driven across.

The most fun resort on the lake is Tan-Tar-A Resort, which is built for families. This extremely nice stay has lots to offer. Along with a golf course and marina, there's an indoor waterpark called Timber Falls. This is just the beginning for families. At the resort there is bumper bowling, a kiddie pool, and Fin City Arcade, with more than forty games and prizes.

At the time of writing, the resort was in the process of adding eight distinct restaurants so that guests have their favorites.

For more family activities, there is Pirate's Cove Adventure Golf. In town is also Ozark Distillery, which is available to tour. They make Corn Whiskey Moonshine, Bourbon Whiskey, Premium Vodka, Apple Pie Moonshine, Blackberry Moonshine, Vanilla Bean Moonshine, and Butterscotch Moonshine.

## MUST SHOP

Osage Beach is home to the Osage Beach Outlet Marketplace, an appealing outlet mall with a rustic cabin look. There are over eighty stores such as Banana Republic Factory Store, Calvin Klein, Coach, J. Crew Factory Store, Loft Outlet, Nike Factory Store, Polo Ralph Lauren Factory Store, Under Armour, and many more.

## MUST EAT

The city is a hub for eating. There are so many restaurants that deserve to be listed, but none more so than this author's choice for the best pizza in small-town Missouri, Pappo's Pizzeria and Pub. Every aspect make each and every pizza the best, but the eye test alone proves that Pappo's is head and shoulders above all others. Even their chocolate chip cookies will become your favorite. The restaurant's numerous awards back up this being the best pizza.

There's a battle for the best barbecue in town between HalfSauced Barbeque or Wobbly Boots Roadhouse. Wobbly Boots wins for the most fun environment. But nothing will be concluded here because both are great restaurants. The beauty is that both have different flavors. Overall, Wobbly seems to edge out HalfSauced in the smoked meats, but the burnt ends at HalfSauced make it a favorite.

For lack of knowing where to list this next one, it ends up here, but Dog Days is one of the wildest places. It's as if guests get to walk into the old *MTV Spring Break* house. There are pools and connected boat slips, a swim-up bar, and beach balls galore. Even though this is a party hub, the owners have made it not too horrible for families. The large veranda is the perfect place to enjoy their lighter, breezier dishes, often with fresh fruit and veggies, and hear live music. But to be fair, their claim to fame is their frozen cocktails. Dog Days is also the venue for many annual festivals like Aquapalooza.

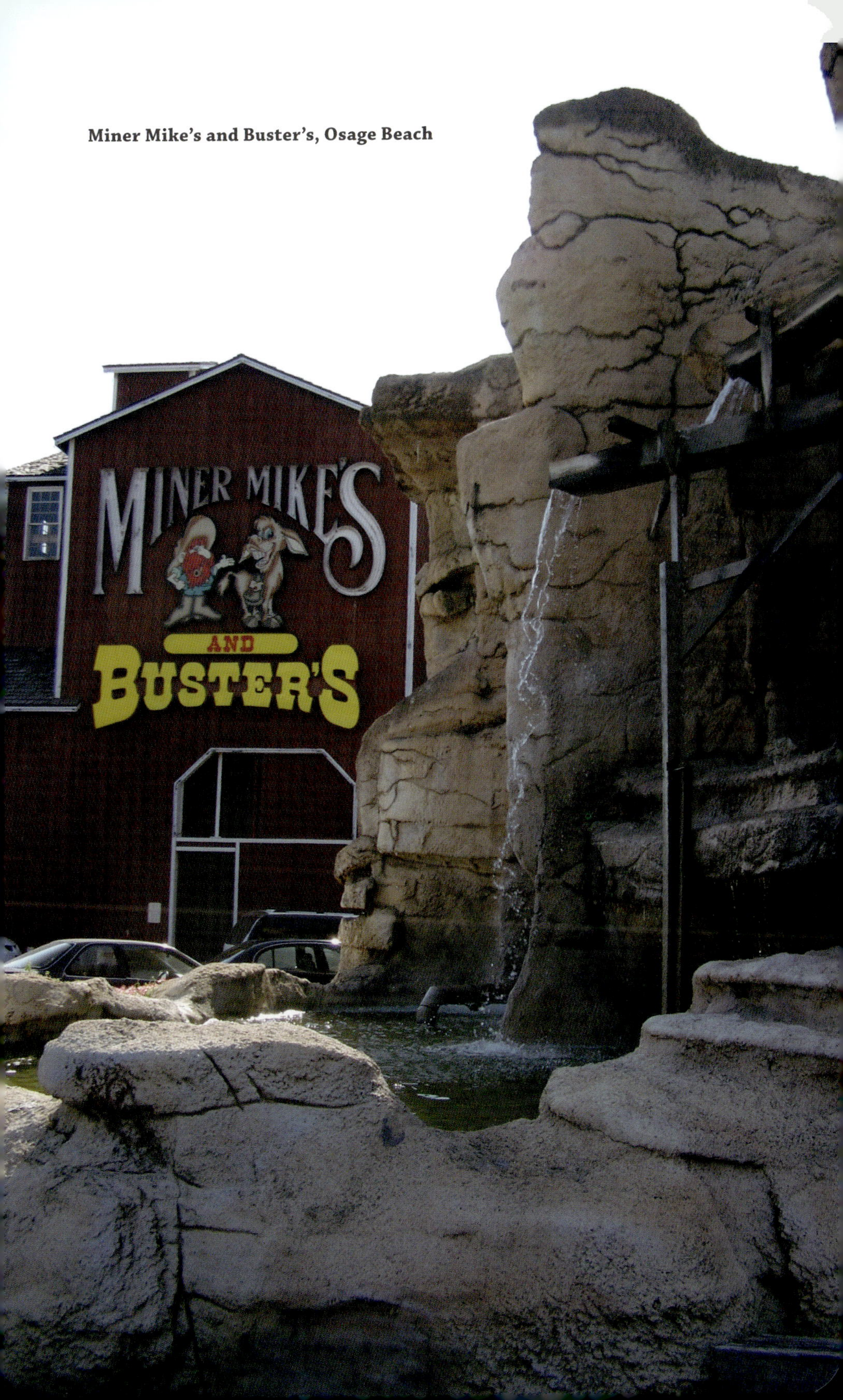


Miner Mike's and Buster's, Osage Beach

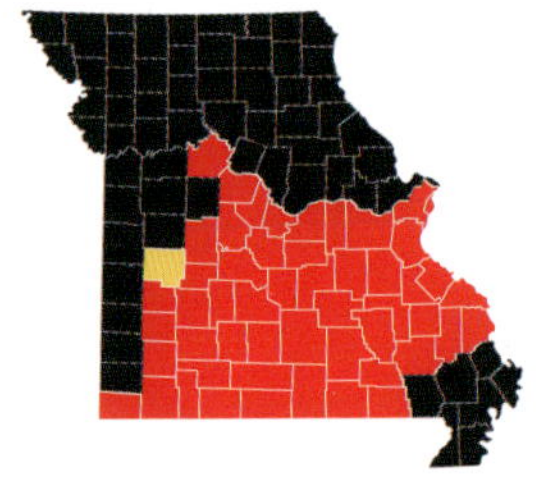

# 66

# *Osceola*

Osceola is a riverfront town along the Osage River with an eventful history that keeps appearing in popular media, politics, and sports. The draw today is not the history, but rather a giant mouse. More on the mouse to come.

The land that's now Osceola belonged to the Osage, but in treaties with the US government in the early 1800s, the land was given up. The area was first settled by European- Americans in the 1830s, and the town was established in 1838. It was named after Osceola, the Seminole chief. The town prospered leading up to the Civil War.

In 1861, Lane's Brigade (Kansas Union-sympathetic soldiers also called Jayhawkers) raided the town. During the process, they burned it to the ground, destroying almost all the homes and businesses. Osceola showed perseverance because this did not deter them, and they rebuilt. The sacking of Osceola lingers as the most historic moment for the city and continually reappears in popular culture. Clint Eastwood's movie *The Outlaw Josey Wales* was inspired by the event. And before the Eastwood film, the sacking of Osceola appeared in the 1968 novel *True Grit* and later in the movie adaptation starring John Wayne. Wayne's character, Rooster Cogburn, was from Osceola, and it was the sacking of the city that motivated him to be part of William Quantrill's raid on Lawrence, Kansas.

The destruction of Osceola has not faded from the memory of residents. In 2011, the Osceola Board of Aldermen passed a resolution urging the University of Kansas to no longer use "Jayhawk" as their mascot because the Jayhawkers had destroyed their city. Going further, the resolution asked all Missouri residents to stop using a capital "K" when writing Kansas or KU because it was "neither a proper name or proper place."

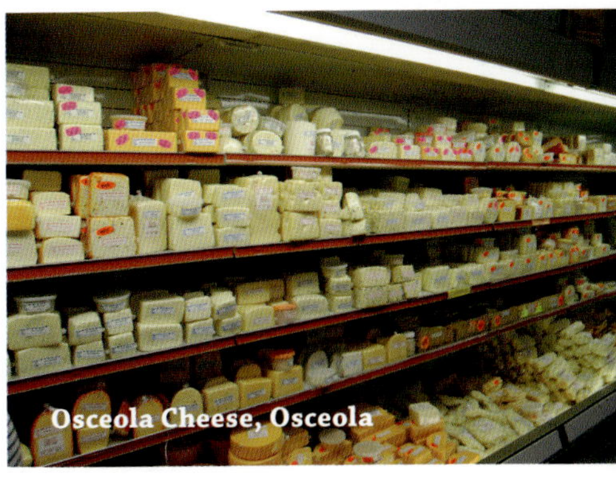
Osceola Cheese, Osceola

## MUST SHOP

Though the town's history is rich, a new landmark has become a famous icon. Osceola Cheese has become a highly popular provider of flavored cheeses, with over 275 varieties. Along with great products, their factory store is a destination in and of itself. The factory has been around since 1944. It was first located in downtown Osceola, but with the creation of Truman Lake, it moved to its current Highway 13 location.

As stated, it's a destination. It sells not just cheese but a lot of custom snacks, and a gift store has been added to the facility. But the cheese takes center stage. Visitors are able to sample almost all of the varieties. Be warned: the ghost pepper cheese will burn your nose if you breathe it in. The variety of types and flavors of cheese is mind-boggling: some are hickory smoked and some applewood smoked, and then there are the many flavors, like apple cinnamon, bacon onion, cranberry, blueberry, chipotle, garlic, and more.

You have to check this place out. Just look for the giant mouse statue sitting outside.

## MUST EAT

If somehow you're still hungry after eating all of those cheese samples, the place to go for a meal is Sugarfoot BBQ. Their smoked meats are fabulous, and credit must go to the rub they use, though their sauce is equally as good. All the meats are worth ordering, but the pulled pork seems to be the leader of the pack, mostly because of the flavor throughout the entire helping. The difficult part of a visit to Sugarfoot is deciding which side to order—Sugarfoot tater, hand-cut fries, or horseradish slaw. The Sugarfoot taters aren't something you can get just anywhere, so that may help your decision.

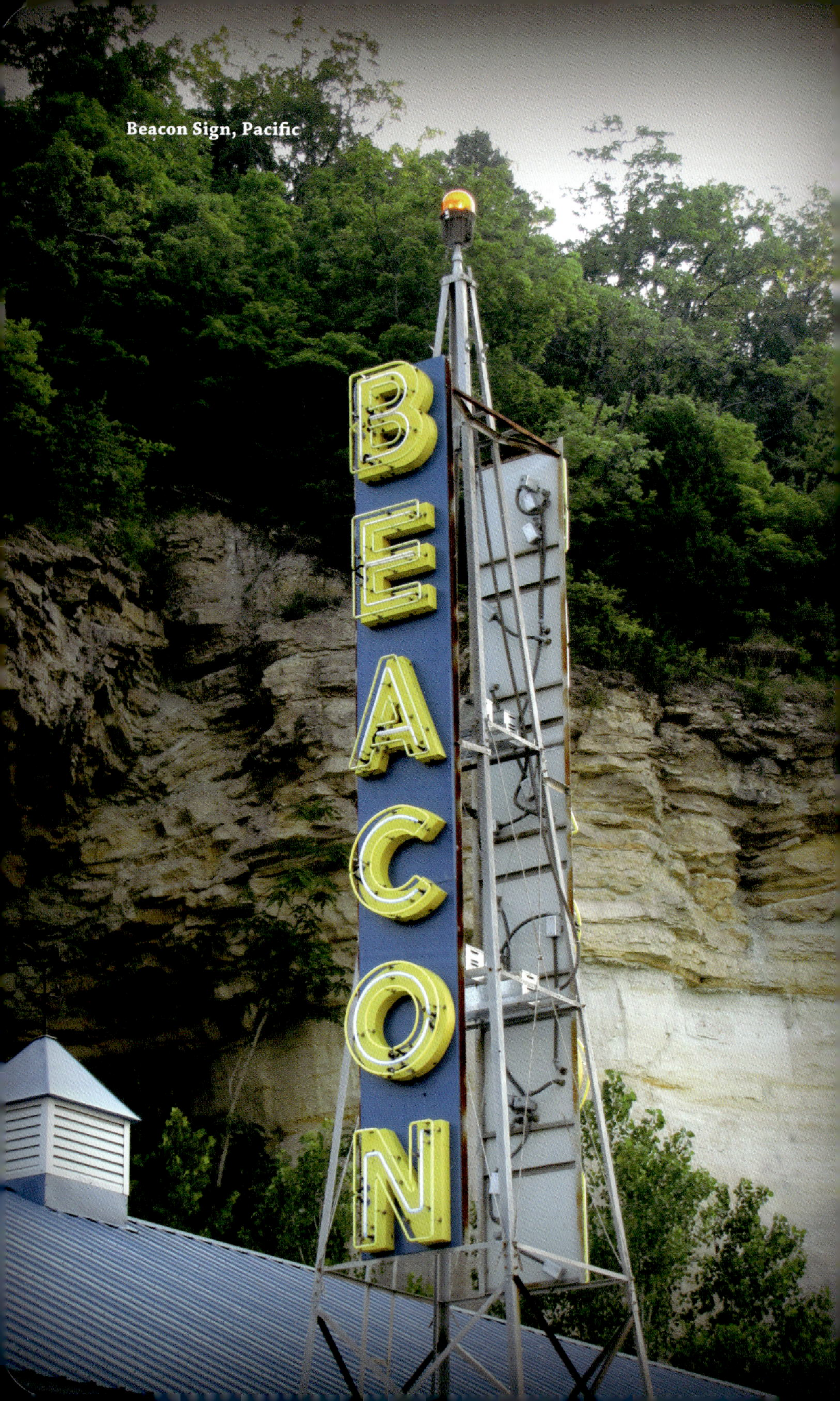

Beacon Sign, Pacific

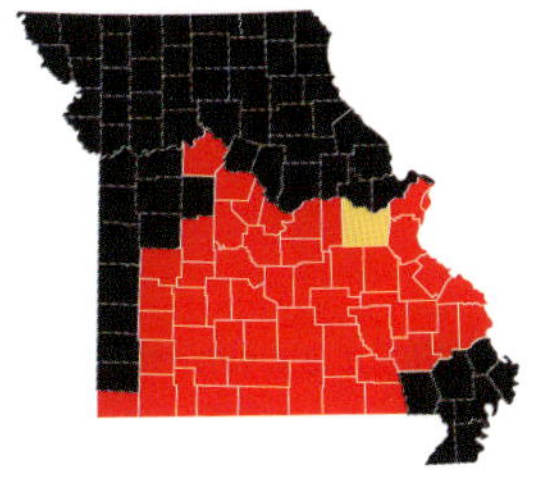

# 67

## Pacific

First a train town, then a sand town, and now home to one of the most iconic trucks in the world. Pacific can trace European-American settlement back to the first home built in 1820, but it would not be platted until 1852, when it was named Franklin. In the next year, the Atlantic-Pacific Railroad came to town, and soon the name was changed to capture that this Missouri town reached the Pacific Ocean by rail.

Pacific would host a Civil War battle that ensured St. Louis remained in Union hands. General Price's campaign of 1864 to retake St. Louis was stopped with a battle here. It's commemorated with a lone cannon on a bluff overlooking town.

Soon after the Civil War, the area was found to be a large deposit of silica. Mining began in the early 1900s and continues today. Experts project that there is enough silica for another hundred years of mining. One of the first uses of the mine's sand was for completion of Route 66, which runs adjacent to the mine. The formerly sloping Sand Mountain was cut away by miners, leaving the tall, sandy bluff that has become a symbol of the city.

A fixture on Route 66, the town and area had many connections to that historic time. The Red Cedar Inn, open from 1933 to 2005, is one of the oldest restaurants still standing on the famed highway and can be viewed from the road.

Route 66 is an iconic fixture in popular Americana, but another iconic part of history moved to town in 2015 when Bigfoot, the famed monster truck, came to call Pacific home. Bigfoot 4x4 Inc.'s shop is located in town and is open for tours.

## MUST DO

This author is a child of the eighties, when Bigfoot reigned as the world's tallest truck, so finding out that one could visit its headquarters was an exciting moment. The shop is open for free tours, and a gift shop displays Bigfoots of the past and present. If you are an eighties or nineties kid, or you have kids that like car-crushing monster trucks, this is a fun stop.

Eureka is just a few miles away and is the home of Six Flags, Hurricane Harbor, Purina Animal Farm, and more, so there's lots to do in the area.

Pacific is also home to a treasured religious site: the Black Madonna Shrine and Grottos. In 1927, a group of Franciscan missionary brothers were sent from Poland to what is today Pacific to operate a nursing home for elderly men. One of those was Brother Bronislaus Luszcz, who had a great love for Mary. In Poland, the most revered site in relation to Mary is the shrine at Jasna Gora Monastery in Czestochowa. That Mary is referred to as the Black Madonna because the painting of her and Jesus have dark faces.

Brother Bronislaus sought to replicate that shrine and did so by building multiple shrines or grottos on the grounds of that nursing home. He built these by hand, and they can be visited today, offering a unique experience.

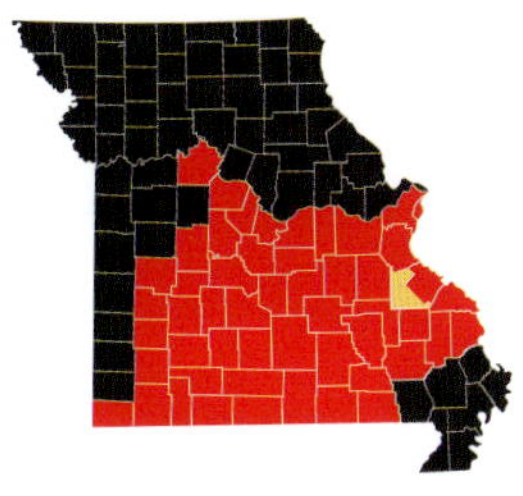

# 68

## Park Hills

Park Hills was chosen for this book because of a unique historic site, but the city is the youngest to be included. It was established in 1994 in a rather unusual way: the towns of Flat River, Elvins, Esther, and Rivermines merged and created the new city of Park Hills. A committee made up of representatives from the four towns voted on submitted entries for a new name, and the winner reflected the mountainous area and many parks nearby.

Each of the four towns, along with several others listed in this book, are part of the Old Lead Belt, an area that led the country in iron ore mining throughout the late 1800s and early 1900s. Eventually, it was considered mined out.

When the mining companies left, the land was donated to the state. On the land was Federal Mill No. 3, which operated from 1906 to 1972. In 1975, it became a historic site, which through its museum and remaining buildings, water tower, conveyor belt, and other equipment is a rare look into the history of mining. It's informative and fun to visit.

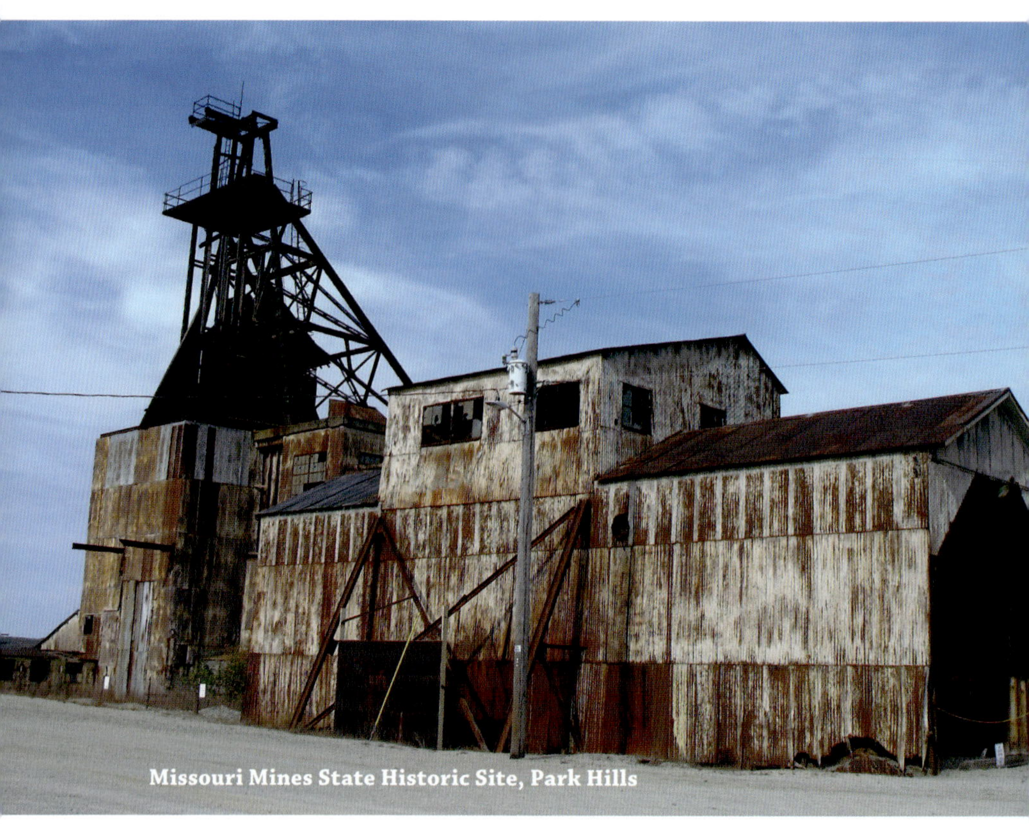
Missouri Mines State Historic Site, Park Hills

## MUST DO

Visit Missouri Mines State Historic Site and take in the history of mining in the United States.

Along with the donation of the mill, part of the land was turned into an off-road-vehicle riding area called St. Joe State Park. This park has two thousand acres of off-road trails.

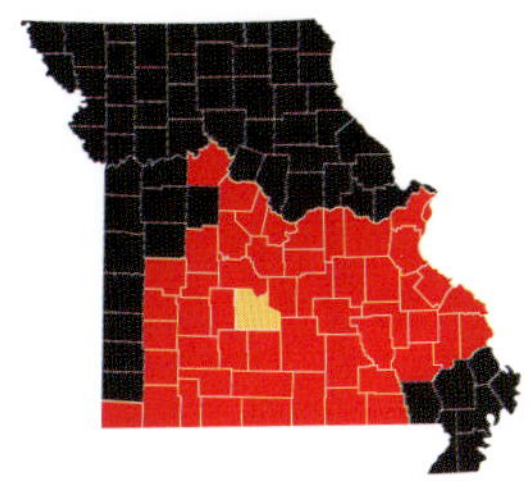

# 69

# Phillipsburg

It's known for the grand size of its two main stores, but Phillipsburg's population is quite the opposite. In this town of 202 is the World's Largest Gift Store, and next door is the large Redmon's Candy Factory. They sit alongside Interstate 44, as well as Route 66, and delight those who pass by and stop. Imagine the gifts and candy section in a truck stop and you have an idea of the merchandise, but this is a truck stop on steroids—lots of steroids.

Phillipsburg is a small community that traces its roots back to 1871 when it was established. It was named after a local merchant, Rufus Phillips. It's only twelve miles from the larger town of Lebanon. Lebanon has been a preserved stop on Route 66 and is home to the iconic Munger Moss Motel, which was built in 1946 and continues operation today. It's known by its larger-than-life neon sign. The strange name traces back to when Nelle Munger and her second husband Emmett Moss opened a restaurant near Devil's Elbow. It was bought and moved to Lebanon and along with it, the motel was built. Lebanon is also home to the Route 66 Museum. There is lots to do in Lebanon, but nowhere else in the state can claim to have a gift shop like the one in Phillipsburg.

## MUST SHOP

The World's Largest Gift Store may not be a destination in itself, but it is surely a stop that needs to be made if you are remotely close. When you

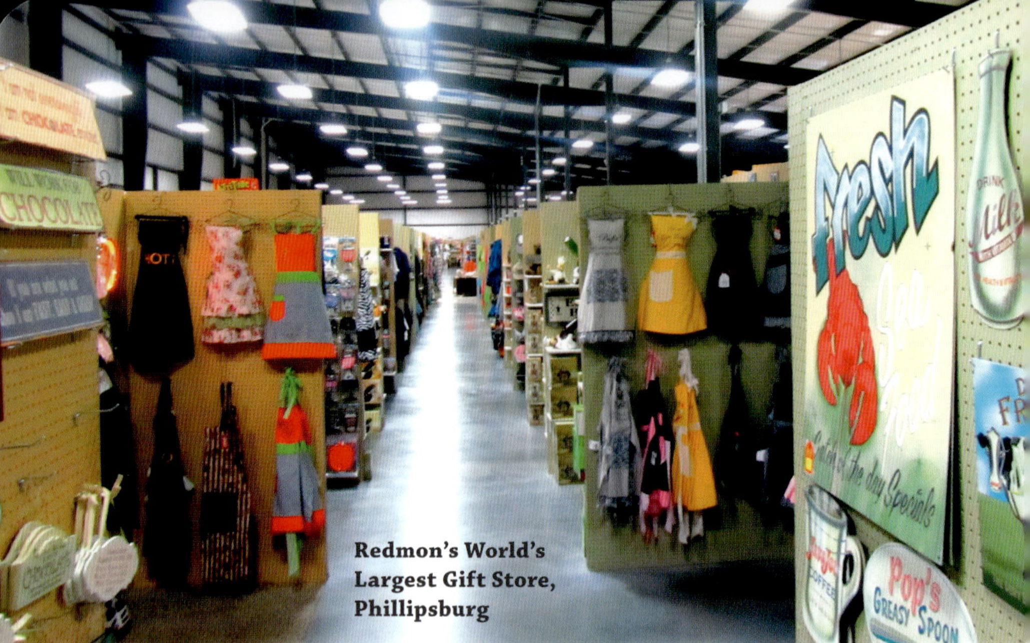

Redmon's World's Largest Gift Store, Phillipsburg

walk in, the store appears to be a large flea market with multiple sections. But each of these sections holds a particular collection, whether cartoon lunch boxes, Elvis, Route 66, stuffed animals, puzzles, Hello Kitty, and the list could go on forever. It's not just a souvenir shop but also a place for those who collect certain things. All kinds of Missouri souvenirs are for sale, and you'll find some wacky gifts as well.

Next door is Redmon's Candy Factory, a dream for children and children at heart. Over seventy different flavors of taffy are for sale, and seemingly as many flavors of fudge. The large billboards leading up to the store advertise "baskets of candy," and that's accurate. Visitors will find baskets full of candy—some of it hard-to-find nostalgic candy. There's also a large selection of sodas and other snacks.

## MUST DO

Lebanon is home to a popular trout fishery, Bennett Spring Park, which is stocked daily during the fishing season. Continuing the sporting theme, Lebanon is also home to the I-44 Speedway, a three-eighths-mile asphalt track that offers at least two race nights a month. Then there's the Route 66 Museum in Lebanon.

## MUST STAY

If one is looking for a nostalgic motel stay, Munger Moss is the place.

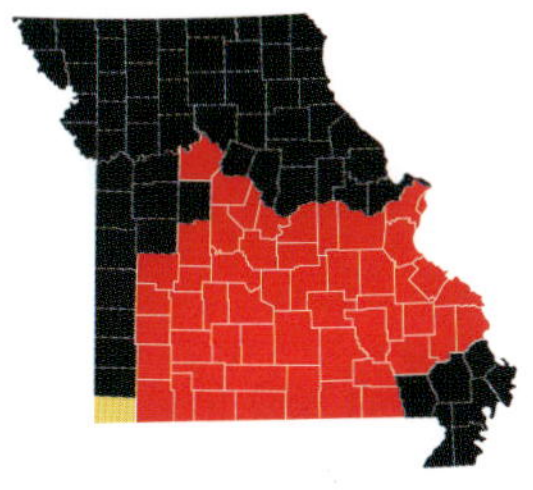

# 70

# Pineville

Most Ozark towns are places of natural beauty and outdoor adventure and rooted in histories steeped in Ozark folklore, which tends to involve moonshine or post–Civil War bandits or often both. Pineville is no exception—one of the major highlights of this town is its history and remembrance of it. The town's history can be traced back to 1847 when it was platted. At first it was called Marysville, and by 1849 it had been changed to the current name. The treasure of this town is the beautiful Elk River.

The new Interstate 49 crosses the Elk River with its rolling current and sandy beaches but shamefully bypasses the town, a town that stirs adventure when one travels through. The drive in from the south creates anticipation. Taking Highway 71 Business, you soon find yourself entering town parallel to a beautiful river reminiscent of the fur trade when Missouri was a territory. Although there's no longer a vibrant fur trade, the river and those canoes of the past are central to the town and the economy of all of McDonald County.

Soon the river turns back to the east as the town comes into focus and you pass a few stores and gas stations. Then a sight elicits your inner child and you're taken back to summer camp. Where old Highway 71 crosses the Elk, on both sides of the road are canoe camps. Big Elk Floats and Camping is on the south, and Elk River Floats and Kozy Kamp is on the north. The magic of water and water activities that surrounds the ocean

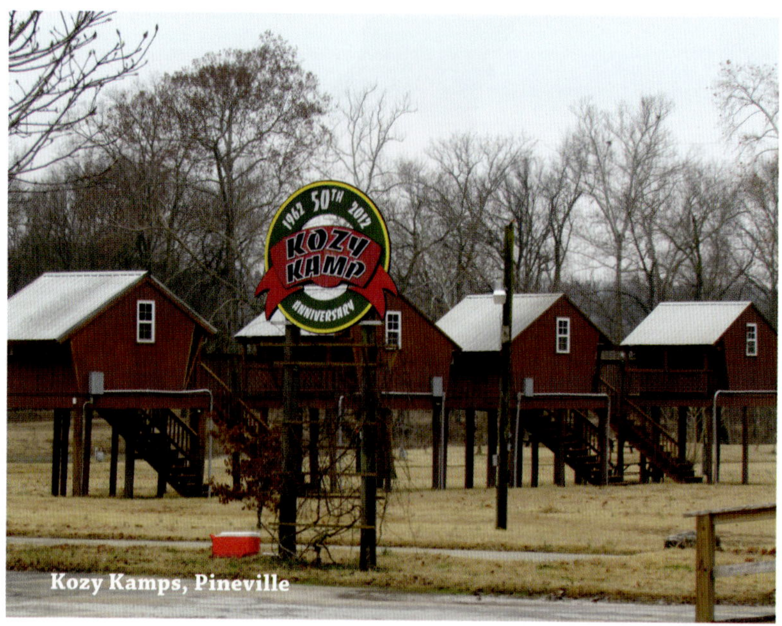

Kozy Kamps, Pineville

or lakesides hovers over this part of Pineville. From the highway, the sight of school buses pulling trailers full of canoes and life jackets brings a smile. These locations and others in the area offer overnight camping, canoe rental, and transportation to a drop-off point or pickup from another.

The standout of the two camps near the bridge is Kozy Kamp, which offers cabins built on stilts. Canoes and rafts constantly float under the bridge in the spring and early summer. Campsites are full except for late, dry summers or excessively rainy springs.

River activities are the highlight, but the history of the town is interesting. Pineville is recognized as one of the towns involved in Jesse James tales. Jesse James was a notorious outlaw from Missouri who robbed trains and banks with his brother and the Younger Gang. One local said, "There's not a town in northwestern Arkansas or western Missouri that doesn't claim James robbed one of their banks or hid out in one of their caves."

Pineville goes a step further with an annual celebration—Jesse James Days, a festival held in August with a parade and other events. A unique claim can be made by the town because the famous 1939 movie *Jesse James* was filmed here, and the town square was covered with dirt for the filming.

## MUST DO

The highlight is floating the Elk River. There are many outfitters in the area.

If you're a Jesse James fan, check out Jesse James Days.

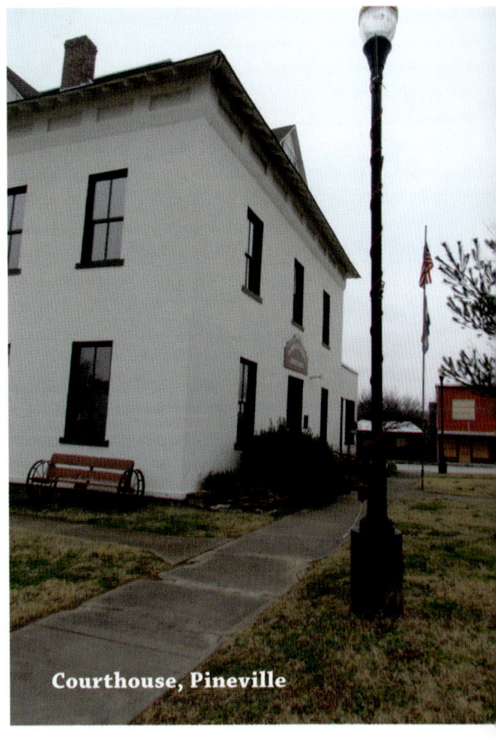
Courthouse, Pineville

## MUST EAT

There aren't a lot of restaurants in the area, but one is certainly worth the drive. Haven 55 Restaurant and Tavern offers an awe-inspiring view and food presentation seemingly too fancy for a recreational river town. The most exquisite menu choice is the unique twice-baked potato. Although the taste and presentation of the blue-cheese-sauce-covered New York strip steak gives the potato competition, the recommendation would be to pair the two. The restaurant is high on the bank of the river above an area of shoals. Visitors are able to watch canoers and wildlife. Haven's lunch menu is limited to burgers and sandwiches, which are beautiful and tasty in their own right. A full dinner menu is also available here. Oh, and how could the Frutti Di Mar be forgotten. Just one of the treats in the riverside restaurant.

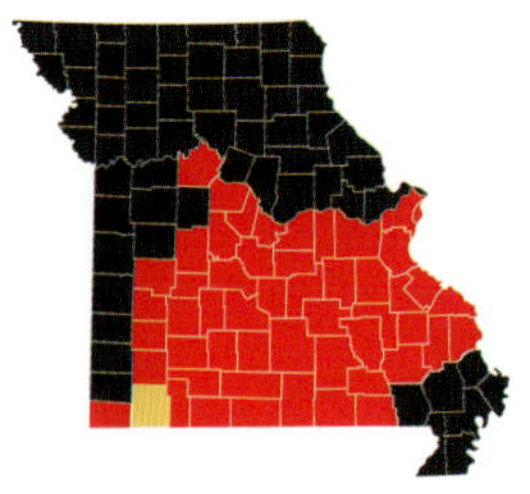

# 71

## Roaring River

Southwest Missouri is home to a hot spot for trout. Roaring River State Park is one of four trout parks in the state. These parks are designed to do all that can be done to ensure a catch and increase the opportunity to catch a trophy. This portion of the river is ideal for introducing children to fishing and creating a memorable family experience.

This pristine state park is an oasis for all ages but is especially suited for family time, whether it be a vacation, a weekend, or a day outing. The drive to the park and township from the west is an experience in itself. Highway 112 winds through the Mark Twain National Forest, a curvy road darkened by a canopy of large deciduous trees, and it'd be rare not to catch sight of a whitetail deer on the drive. Abruptly the mountain highway descends into the Seligman Hollow—prepare for your ears to pop. A similar descent is in store for drivers from the north. Once down in the river bottom, the forest gives way to life. Families and seasoned fishermen with waterproof day-use permits visible on their hats line the crystal-clear stream. Fly rods whip back and forth, and trout nets dangle from belts.

Multiple playgrounds are covered with children playing and smiling as parents look on from picnic tables. Campers and tents stretch through the forest campsites lining a portion of the river. Children play in the river swimming areas near the camps. For one just passing through, the place is a cool drink of water on a sweltering day—refreshing.

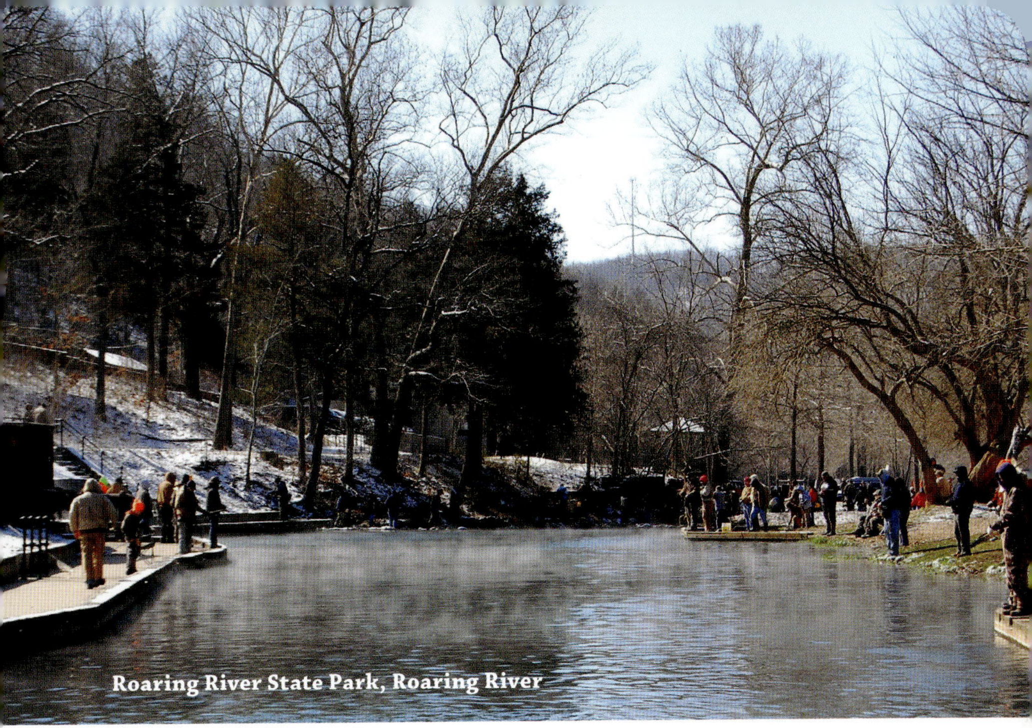
Roaring River State Park, Roaring River

You won't find much in the Roaring River township, but nearby Caseville offers most fast-food chain restaurants, Walmart, and other needed stores. Branson isn't too far from the river oasis, and Table Rock Lake is less than ten miles away.

Roaring River State Park is twenty-four hundred acres with the centerpiece being the Roaring River Hatchery. The hatchery was built by the Civilian Conservation Corps in the late 1930s. Land of the park was donated by a wealthy traveling-medicine-show man, Mark "Doc" Sayman. In 2010 the park celebrated a centennial anniversary. The hatchery sports CCC-era buildings along with holding tanks for many sizes of trout. A natural spring feeds the works. Sitting above the tanks is a beautiful, bottomless pool loaded with trophy trout—some of the biggest that one could see in the wild. There is no fishing in the pool, which extends back into a cave where the source of the spring rests. You can walk around the pool feeding the large fish and venture into the cave a short distance. A walking trail climbs the mountain above the hatchery, offering a spectacular view of the entire place. This is one of many hiking trails in the park.

The river sourced by the spring flows from the pool down through the park. All efforts have been made to create ease of fishing. Each day fish are released from the hatchery. Anglers start early because the first hour is the most exciting as hundreds of hungry fish are released. The season begins in March with much fanfare and the firing of a gun. Over 122,000 fishing trips are made to the park a year.

Three distinct zones allow the desired type of fishing for everyone. Zone one, which begins at the hatchery and extends a lengthy area, allows only artificial lures. This zone has the greatest potential for catching fish. Zone two is catch-and-release only. One seasoned angler shared that this was a perfect spot for anyone who sought a trophy-sized fish and wanted to wade in and fly-fish. This area is less crowded. Zone three allows live bait.

## MUST DO

A fishing trip to Roaring River is a blast and is guaranteed to catch some trout, but even if you're not a fisherman, feeding the trophy trout is a lot of fun. It's also fun seeing the different stages of growth in the fish. There's some great hiking as well. It's a beautiful park.

## MUST STAY

As you descend into the park from the west, before the bottom of the hollow sits a beautiful, rustic inn and conference center. The Emory Melton Inn and Conference Center offers hotel amenities right in the midst of the park. It has a restaurant and a swimming pool. Along with the inn are cabins throughout the state park, some of which date back to the CCC construction. There are also many private cabin options in the seven miles between Roaring River and Cassville. The rustic inn is a must-stay experience. Along with close proximity to Branson, the shopping in northwest Arkansas isn't too far away either.

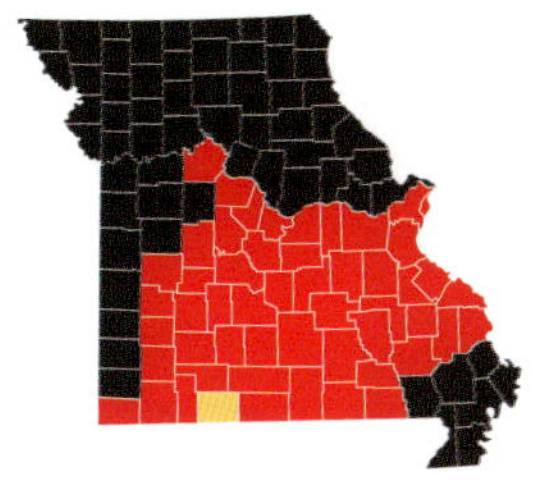

# 72

# Rockaway Beach

There was a time when Rockaway Beach would have been one of the longest entries in this book. It was billed as the first family vacation resort in the west. In 1917, Kansas City businessman Willard Merriam led the way in building a resort on the newly built Lake Taneycomo. Before there was a post office there was a resort and a sandy beach. A mile and a half on the bank of the lake became a hot spot. This continued until the construction of Table Rock Lake. While Rockaway Beach had been built on swimming and waterskiing because of the warm water, the new Table Rock Dam transformed Lake Taneycomo into a cold water lake, which crushed the resort.

Now, remnants of the resort town remain. There's still a nice sandy beach to enjoy, and the one benefit of the cold water is that it made the place prime trout habitat. The lake is one of the best trout fisheries around. There's a public pier that has free access and produces a catch of trout.

So keep in mind the sandy beach and trout fishing, but there are a couple hidden jewels that should draw visitors out of Branson and to the old resort town. One serves up some of the best pizza in the state, and the other has one of the most enjoyable atmospheres for a sip of coffee.

## MUST EAT

Don't let the descent into the basement scare you away—La Pizza Cellar is consistently considered one of the best pizzerias in Missouri and it is with

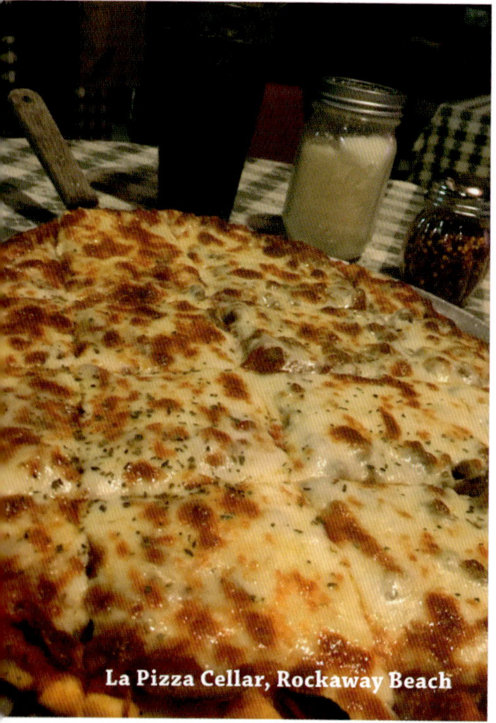

La Pizza Cellar, Rockaway Beach

good reason. From the crispiness of the crust to the loads of cheese and generous toppings, each pizza is made from scratch and is fabulous. And was "loads of cheese" said? More accurately, loads and loads of cheese. Without a doubt, it's the cheesiest small-town pizza in the state. Once the pizza brings a smile, the cellar lights up and becomes a homey atmosphere. It's this experience that has kept the restaurant going strong since 1979 and producing repeat generations of vacationers along with regional regulars. They often have families come in each year saying they came as children with their families; now they're bringing their own.

White River Coffee Company has great coffee and sandwiches, but it's the environment most of all that takes the specialty coffee drink up a notch. Inside is inviting and cozy—just plain comfortable—and outside is a spacious deck with a magnificent view. Even on a Branson vacation it's worth the short sightseeing drive to have a relaxing break on the deck.

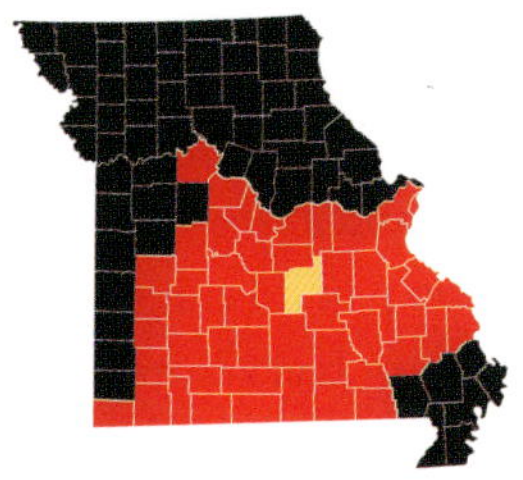

# 73

# *St. James*

It's amazing how these small towns across the state have so much to offer; many of them have enough activities to fill a whole vacation. St. James is one of those surprises. A town of only 4,216, it bears a rich history and signs of a promising future.

The town's history began in the mid-1800s with early attempts to establish it. First, it was named Big Prairie, then Scioto. Finally, in 1860 it was named St. James to honor Thomas James, who came from Ohio and created the Meramec Iron Works, which produced iron that was transported to St. Louis to be made into cannonballs and gunships. The plant used water from nearby Meramec Spring to power the machines that made the iron ore usable. The ruins of the iron works are visible at Meramec State Park. St. James was founded to be a shipping point via the railroad for viable iron. The operation ran from 1827 to 1891.

Route 66 passed through the area and helped the town grow, but recent history has shown that it's the wine industry that is bringing people back to the St. James area. It's located in the Ozark Highlands wine region. Most of the wineries throughout this book are found in Missouri's Rhineland along the Missouri River Valley, but this is a different region. Although St. James Winery has become the largest and most award-winning winery in the state, wineries here aren't a new phenomenon. Before Prohibition, over two hundred wineries were in the St. James area. Those wineries traced their roots back to European-American settlers who were mainly from Italy.

## MUST DO

St. James is the leading winery in the state, which makes it a worthy choice for a complimentary tasting and a free tour. Both are offered daily, with tours from 11:00 a.m. to 4:00 p.m. In conjunction with the Public House Brewing Company, the winery has created "The Gardens," an outdoor venue with spread-out tables, landscaping, a water feature, a fire pit, and even outdoor games. This allows a mix of St. James wines, Public House craft beers, and great Public House Kitchen food. Meramec Vineyards Winery, Three Squirrels Winery, Heinrichshaus Winery, Peaceful Bend Winery, and Ferrigno Winery are in the area as well.

Meramec Spring Park is a beautiful stop, with water that is usually clear and a beautiful blue, lots of falls, and a suspended pedestrian bridge. The Meramec Iron Works ruins are here, too, which add a historic element and help tell the story of the waterway. It's also a hot spot for trout, as it is restocked each day of the fishing season.

The Vacuum Cleaner Museum and Factory Outlet sounds boring, but it is far from it. This well-organized and well-kept museum has a collection of eight hundred vacuums—and every one of them works. Models range through the whole history of vacuum cleaners. It's absolutely fascinating. Since the focus is on one specific item, each piece allows visitors to dive deeper into the history and technology of vacuums.

## MUST EAT

St. James is home to several fine restaurants. It's rare to see such a concentration in a small town. There's one that stands head and shoulders above many restaurants in the state: Sybill's Saint James. It's hard to do justice to the food, presentation, environment, service, and beauty and overall experience of the restaurant. The only word that seems fitting is "perfect." Nothing could be done better. You're not going to have a more enjoyable, pleasant experience anywhere else. The restaurant is in a pristine southern plantation house. There's little signage or evidence that it's a restaurant. You walk up onto the wraparound porch and enter just like you are going over to a friend's home for a special meal. Inside, the atmosphere is the perfect blend of elegance and comfort. It's has the trappings of an upscale restaurant, but you're still at ease. The food is fresh, flavorful, and healthy American with Southern flair, ranging from steak, pasta, and chicken to seafood and salad.

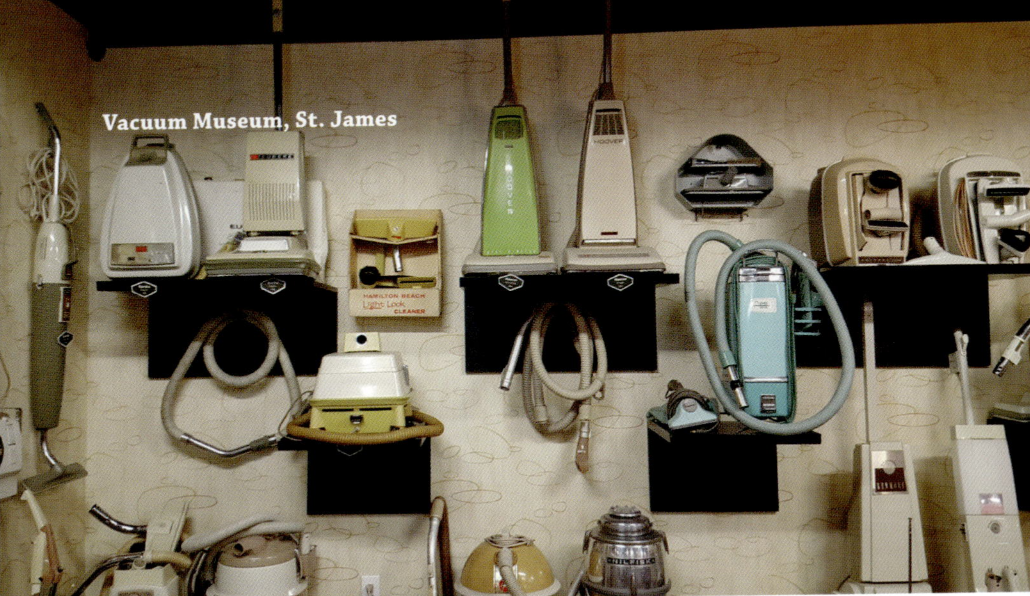

Vacuum Museum, St. James

Sybill's is the gold standard, but there are other options, such as Public House Brewing Company, which offers beautifully presented fine dining to pair with their wine, and then hearty pub food to pair with their beers.

Another honorable mention is Just a Taste, a restaurant that if in another town would be number one.

## MUST SHOP

St. James is home to not just one but two flag stores: Leo Cardetti's Flag and Flag Pole and St. James Flag Pole Co.

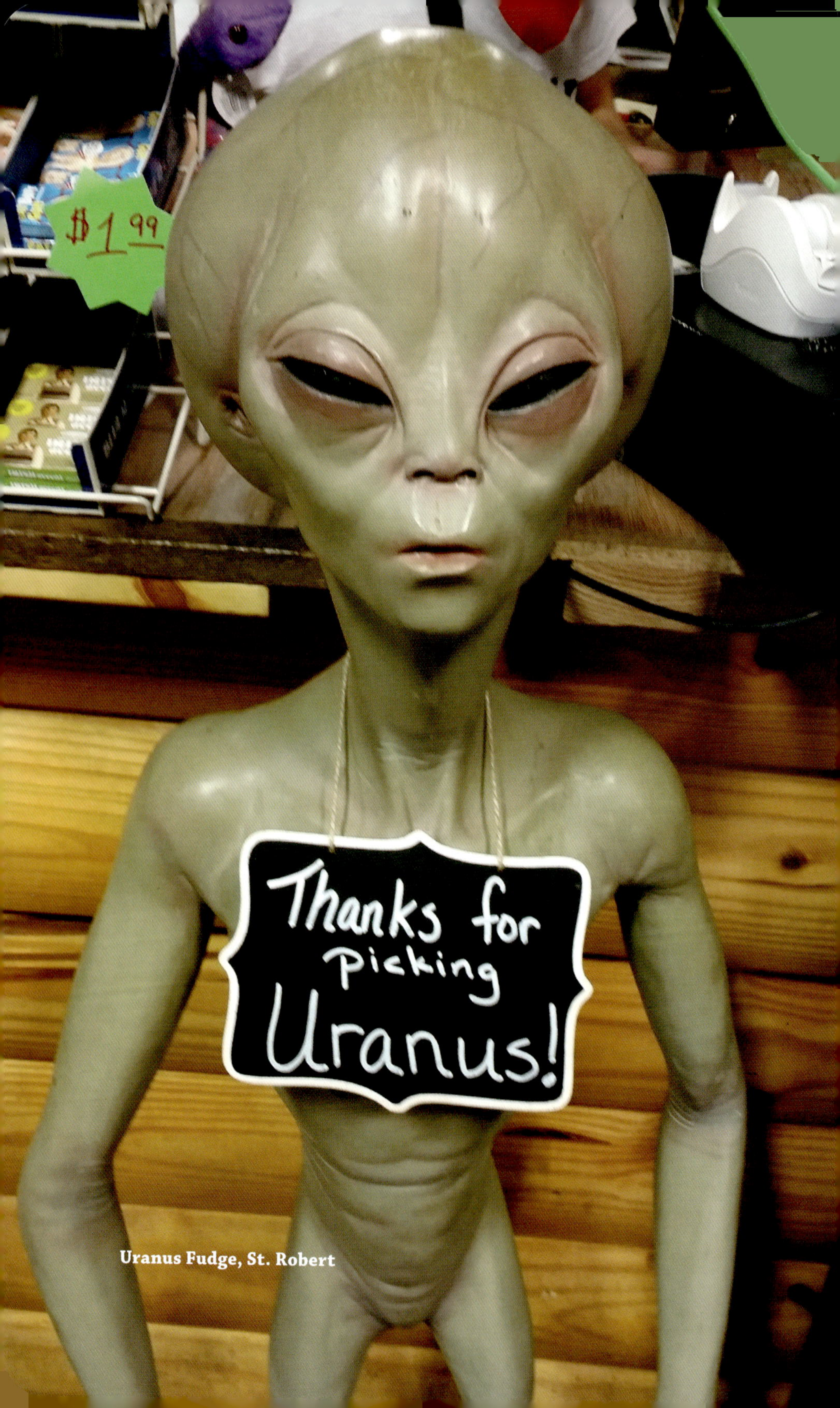

Uranus Fudge, St. Robert

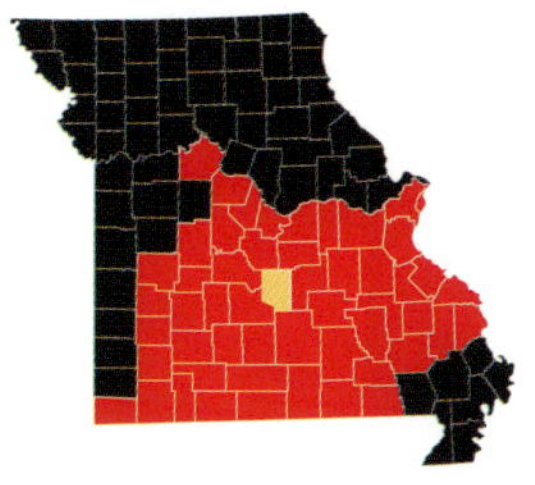

# 74

# St. Robert

The main attractions of St. Robert are two extremes: one is ultraserious, a matter of life and death, while the other is one of the funniest roadside attractions in the state. St. Robert is a relatively new town, not having been platted until 1951, but its roots go much further back. It was first a religious settlement established by members of the Church of the Brethren. They were nicknamed Dunkers or Dunkards, because they practiced baptism by dunking rather than sprinkling. At that time, the town was known as Gospel Ridge. Later it was known as Eastside because of it being east of Waynesville.

St. Robert was named after St. Robert Bellarmine, an Italian Jesuit and a cardinal of the Catholic Church in the early 1600s. St. Robert was first the name of a church and parish in the area. This church arose from the growth of the area caused by the US Army base, Fort Leonard Wood. General Wood was an army major general who served in the Spanish-American War, during which he commanded the Rough Riders with Theodore Roosevelt as second-in-command. He also served in the Apache Wars and World War I. He would later be military governor of Cuba and the Philippines.

Fort Leonard Wood is home of the Maneuver Support Center of Excellence and is where three US Army schools are based: the Engineer School; Chemical, Biological, Radiological, and Nuclear School; and Military Police School. Over eighty-two thousand soldiers are trained a year on the sixty-two thousand acres. The base is extremely active today and has been in operation since 1941. St. Robert is the gateway community to the base.

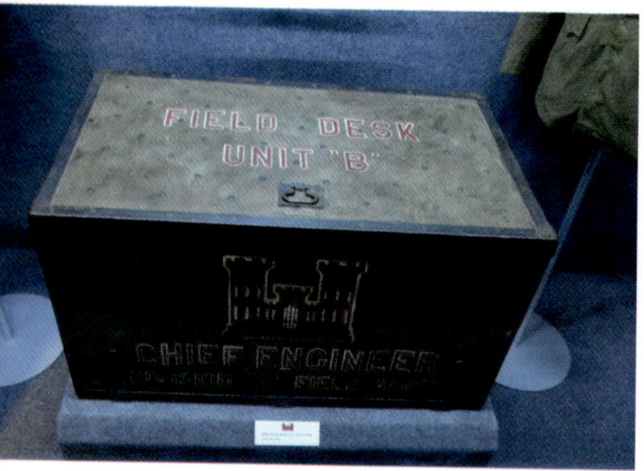


**John B. Mahaffey Museum Complex at Fort Leonard Wood, St. Robert**

## MUST DO

The base is home to three fascinating museums, one from each of the three schools on-site: the Chemical Corps Museum, Engineer Museum, and Military Police Museum. All three contain large exhibits and are focused on aspects of the US military that are not as well known. It's interesting to learn what these support divisions have done through history and prepare to do today. The Chemical Corps Museum has elements of a Ripley's Believe It or Not Museum. The equipment used in the past looks like pranks or sci-fi movie costumes. A favorite exhibit is the replica trench from World War I. Guests can actually maneuver through the trench and experience what soldiers did during that time.

Fort Leonard Wood's museums are worth the drive. They serve as the serious attraction while Uranus Fudge Factory is cracking jokes. There's no easy way to write about this place. From miles away, the jokes about Uranus start. When guests arrive at what can best be described as a shopping center, they aren't sure what they are seeing. Hopefully, most of the jokes will go over your young children's heads because there's a lot from the gutter or, well, Uranus. Your older kids will be rolling in laughter. The centerpiece is the fudge factory—yes, there's fudge in Uranus. Then there is ice cream, funnel cake, an escape room, a sideshow museum with all kinds of crazy displays, and even a tattooed woman putting a sword down her throat, an axe-throwing game, a bar, restaurant, candy store, gift shop, gun shop, gun range, and more. The kinda-historic-looking makeshift town is several rustic buildings with random vehicles and statues in between. There's a rocket, old fire truck, double-decker bus, dinosaur, and more. It's something to experience for sure. You'll be graciously welcomed to Uranus and thanked for picking Uranus.

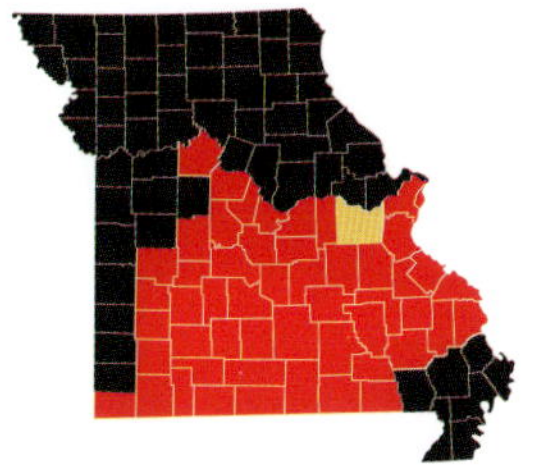

# 75

# Stanton

Stanton is home to one of the most advertised caves in America and is home to a museum built a little on history and a little on conspiracy. The town can be traced back to being established in 1857, and its name comes from a businessman, Peter Stanton, who owned a mine and made gunpowder in the area in the 1850s. Saltpeter, lead, and copper were mined in the area. During the Civil War, the area became a target because of the saltpeter available to make gunpowder.

The town is the gateway to Meramec Caverns, likely the most advertised cave in the nation. Lester Dill took ownership of the cave in the 1930s and opened it to the public. He put Meramec Caverns on the map by using "bumper signs," a forerunner of today's bumper stickers. He also had advertisements painted on the sides and roofs of barns all over Route 66. But the history of Meramec Caverns goes way back.

In 1720, a French miner discovered the cave and the saltpeter inside. It was then named Saltpeter Mine and remained under that name until Lester Dill came along. During the Civil War, the Union used the cave for mining and had a gunpowder mill in town. It was also used as part of the underground railroad that helped slaves reach freedom. In 1864, William Quantrill and his raiders destroyed the mill. One of those raiders was Jesse James, who would later become one of the nation's most recognized outlaws. A few years later in 1874, after robbing the Little Rock Express, James and his gang ran from authorities to the cave. Law enforcement

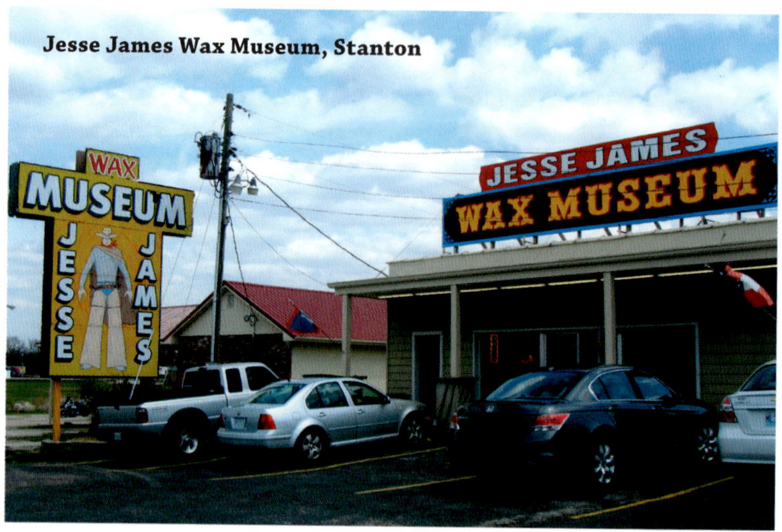

Jesse James Wax Museum, Stanton

guarded the cave's entrance to starve the outlaws out, but instead, the gang swam out through an underground river.

Jesse James left his mark on Stanton—in the cave there's an area dubbed Jesse James's hideout, and there's a wax museum in town dedicated to him.

## MUST DO

Meramec Caverns is the largest commercial cave in the state. There are several rooms that give way to magnificent geological elements. It's thought of as one of the best caves to visit.

The Jesse James Wax Museum is that aforementioned mix of history and controversy. This museum and the history of how it came to be are either a miracle, or its leaders were the victims of the ultimate con job. The story begins in 1948 when Rudy Turilli, general manager of Meramec Caverns, came in contact with an elderly man named J. Frank Dalton. Dalton lived in Lawton, Oklahoma, but after coming to believe that Dalton was actually Jesse James and that James had faked his own death, Rudy moved him to Meramec Caverns.

James was believed to have been killed in 1882, but Rudy became convinced that the death had been faked. Dalton lived in the Jesse James Cabin inside the cave until his death in 1951. He became part of the cave tour. Following Dalton's death, the Jesse James Wax Museum was built

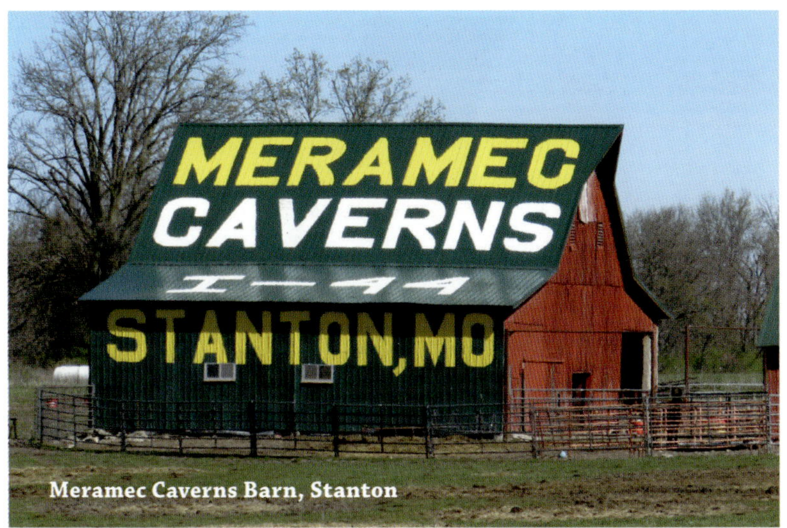

Meramec Caverns Barn, Stanton

so Rudy could continue his crusade to tell the "truth" of what happened to James. Much of the museum is dedicated to this revelation or hoax, but there are some fascinating artifacts from James's life that make this a real piece of history as well. It's worth the visit, especially for Jesse James or Old West enthusiasts. Just don't read about the 1995 DNA test of Jesse James's 1882 grave.

Stanton is also home to the Riverside Wildlife Center, which is like a zoo, but much more hands-on, allowing for a more personal connection and approach to the animals. It's known mostly for its indoor reptile exhibit, which features snakes, turtles, frogs, and others. Outside there are lions, tigers, alligators, and much more.

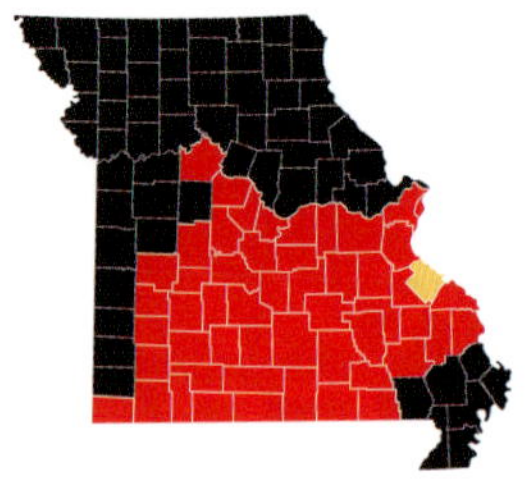

# 76

# *Ste. Genevieve*

Ste. Genevieve is the oldest European-American settlement in Missouri. Settled in 1735, it predates St. Louis by twenty-seven years. The city is loaded with history that documents the early years of Missouri while it belonged to the French, then Spanish, and then the United States. Much of that history can be explored today.

The unique name comes from the patron saint of Paris. Genevieve played significant roles in two possible disasters in Paris's history. She led an expedition for food and supplies that saved Paris in 449 when it was under siege by the Franks. Then in 451, she fasted and prayed, and God heard her prayers and prevented Attila the Hun from marching on Paris.

In similar fashion, the early settlers of Ste. Genevieve fought with the Native Americans and endured multiple floods of the Mississippi River. These first settlers were French-Canadian and utilized unique architecture, little of which remains in the United States outside of Ste. Genevieve. Through trading and marriages, early settlers were able to make peace with the native people in the area. New settlers would move in as more and more immigrants settled in the eastern United States. The fertile soil allowed for great crops. They grew wheat, maize, and tobacco. Their grain harvests were larger than St. Louis's and were used to help feed New Orleans. By the time of the Louisiana Purchase, the city was considered the wealthiest in the Louisiana Territory.

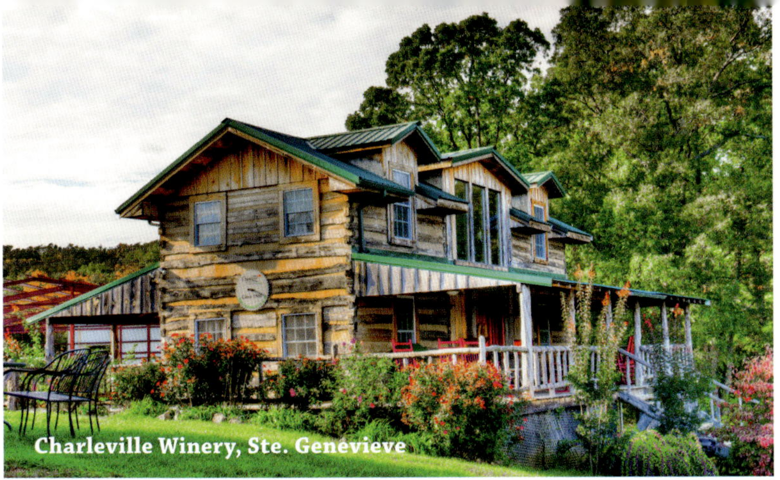
Charleville Winery, Ste. Genevieve

## MUST DO

To visit Ste. Genevieve is to embrace and explore its history, but also to enjoy its French cultural heritage expressed through its fine dining, festivals, and wineries. In a historical trip there are necessary starting points, like the Ste. Genevieve Welcome Center, the Ste. Genevieve Museum, and the Centre for French Colonial Life. A Historic Tour Passport can be purchased that includes most of the popular stops all on one ticket for one price. It's a great way to save money and make sure you view all the sites. These passports can be purchased in the visitor center.

If you have time for just one stop, visit the Centre for French Colonial Life. The Centre's museum provides a glimpse into the French settlement era and the site has historic homes from that period as well. The oldest home on the premises is the Louis Bolduc House, which dates back to the 1780s and 1790s. It's a French vertical log house. These homes have been meticulously maintained.

But there's a lot more history to take in. The Ste. Genevieve Historic District includes 646 historic buildings, and 150 of those are pre-1825. And some of those 150 are from the late 1700s. There's no way to see all of them, so here are some highlights in order of their age. The oldest structure is one of the multiple buildings that make up the Felix Valle House State Historic Site: the Janis-Ziegler House or Green Tree Tavern, which dates back to 1790. Also part of the historic site is the Bauvais-Amoureux House from 1792, a "poteaux-en-terre" or "post-in-earth" design. This distinctively French colonial design is found in only five remaining buildings in the United States, three of which are in Ste. Genevieve. There's also the Felix Valle House, which is a federal-style home dating back to 1818.

Another historic building to visit is the Guibourd House, which dates back to 1806 and is the second of the three "poteaux-en-terre" homes in town. The third is the Bequette Ribault House that dates from 1808. This one has been restored by Chaumette Vineyards and Winery and offers a truly unique experience.

Speaking of Chaumette, it's one of several wineries and vineyards in the area. A wine tour in Ste. Genevieve is a great way to enjoy the town, and paired with a stay in one of the several bed-and-breakfasts around will make your visit like a romantic Hallmark movie getaway.

## MUST STAY

Ste. Genevieve is loaded with bed-and-breakfasts as well as unique historic inns. The favorites would be Main Street Inn, an 1882 hotel; the Southern Hotel, dating from 1805; the Inn St. Gemme Beauvais, which goes back to 1848; Dr. Hertich's House, dating from 1850; and White Cliff Manor, which dates back to 1879. For a modern stay, the Villages at Chaumette would be the recommendation. The Southern Hotel tops the list of these great stays, but a truly extraordinary opportunity is to stay in a Bavarian-style castle that has a private lake and indoor pool. Check Airbnb for a stay at this genuine castle in the middle of wine country.

## MUST EAT

If staying in a castle or being treated like royalty at a historic bed-and-breakfast, you need to eat like a king or queen, too, and Hotel Audubon is the location to do this. This hotel combines history, romance, and fine dining and serves dishes made with fresh, local ingredients. It's a great mix of comfortable and fancy: linen tablecloths and nice settings without over-the-top interior decorations. The menu ranges from top-shelf steaks, pasta, and fanciful chicken dishes to build-your-own burgers, brick-oven pizza, and chicken wings. Their specialty is customizable flavor mixtures that are found in the salad ingredients, sauces, and possibilities for building your own burger. The chicken-wing sauces are the absolute highlight.

If you're looking for a more solid American menu, the Anvil Saloon and Restaurant offers hearty dishes, home-style cooking, and pub food. The Old West theme is a lot of fun. The food is quality and a favorite with visitors.

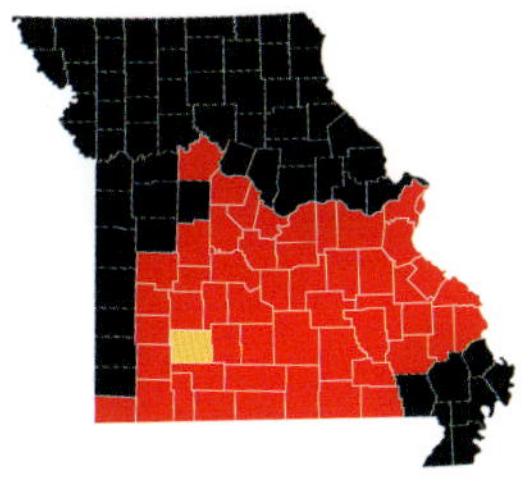

# 77

# Strafford

Ripley's Believe It or Not lists Strafford as the only town in the United States with two Main Streets and no back alleys. This feat was not accomplished by trying to make the record books, but out of necessity. When Route 66 was built, it ran parallel to the existing Main Street a block away. To keep business going, entrances were added to the Route 66 side, giving each of them two front doors.

Transportation routes have been the common thread throughout Strafford's history. They've been the reason for its existence, its industry, and its survival. First, it was established to be a stop for the railroad. It was this development that led to its 1870 platting, although settlers can be traced back to 1818. Then the Old Wire Road, or Military Road, passed through town, keeping it relevant. This would bring all aspects of history through its city limits, including Civil War soldiers. Then it would be Route 66, and later Interstate 44, that passed through town. The growth of nearby Springfield has been vital to Strafford.

These days, Strafford is home to family fun, an interesting museum, and some good food.

## MUST DO

The family fun is the Wild Animal Safari, an animal park that offers a drive-through portion, a walk-through portion, and a reptile house. This author deems it "a zoo without rules." Now, there are rules, but it's

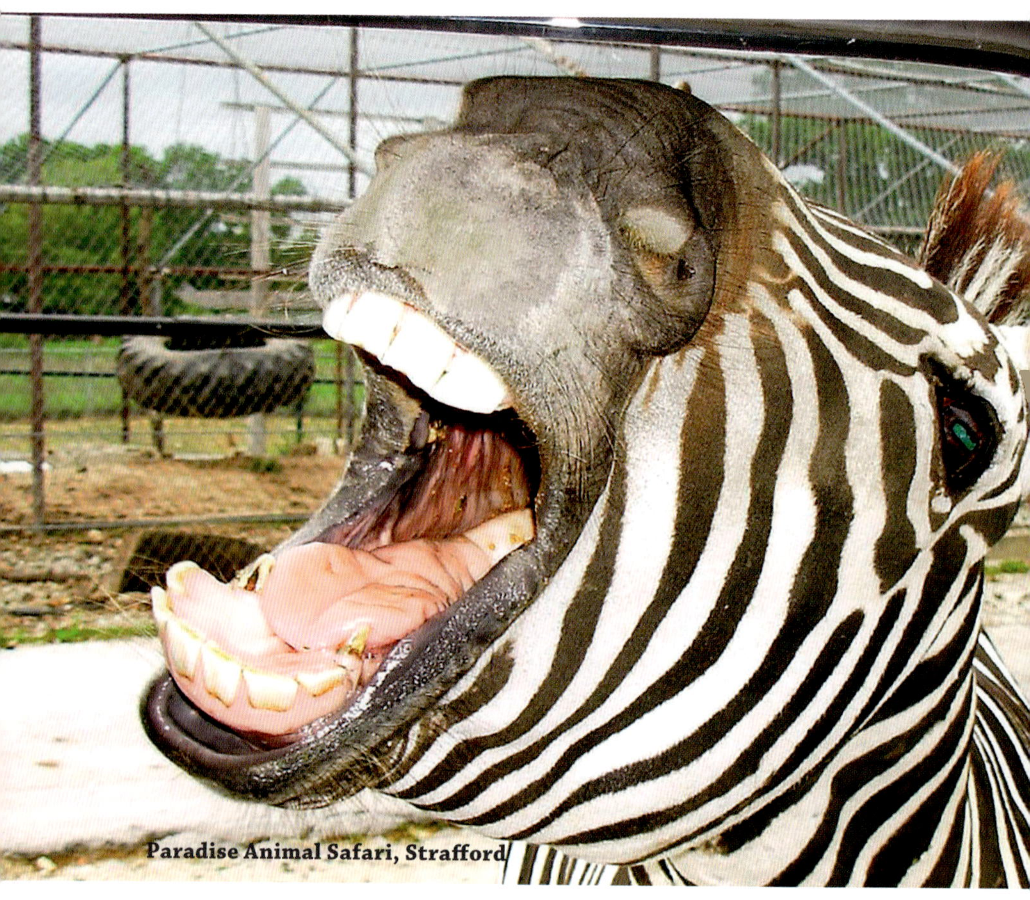
Paradise Animal Safari, Strafford

designed to get visitors close to the animals. There are over 450 animals on 250 acres. It's one of the most well-kept drive-through safaris in the country. Along with the animal exhibits, there are even rides for kids. They also offer bus tours rather than visitors having to take their vehicles. So, if you're afraid a ram might butt your side panel, you can hop on the safari bus.

Strafford is also home to a small museum that presents one form of Christianity's take on the natural history of the world—the Creation Experience Museum. Though it's just a small museum, guests have been overwhelmingly surprised at how well presented and highly organized it is. Visitors have compared it to the Answers in Genesis Creation Museum in Kentucky. Even those who don't agree with its views have found it entertaining, especially the dinosaur portion.

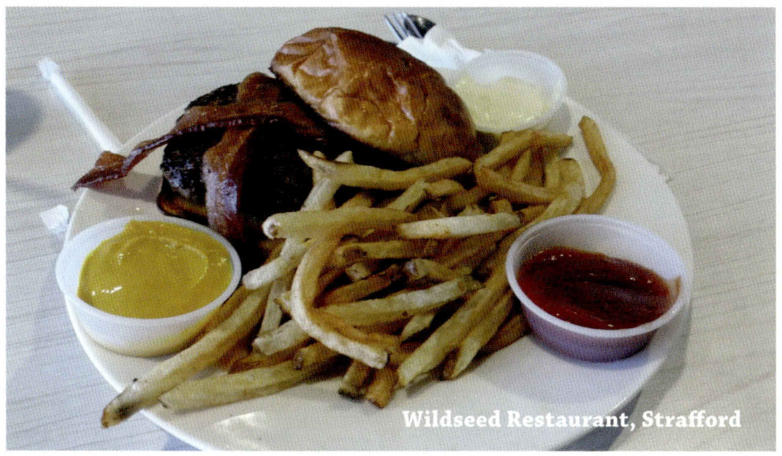
Wildseed Restaurant, Strafford

## MUST EAT

The Wildseed Restaurant and Bar is appropriately named, for it is a wild find. It's one of the many unique opportunities for fine local food, often with live music, you can enjoy throughout small-town Missouri. The Wildseed is a nice restaurant that offers a fresh, modern design and a fun dining experience and ambiance. The menu is a wide selection of hamburgers, pizza, pasta, and specialty and international dishes. They offer unique sauces that add a special taste.

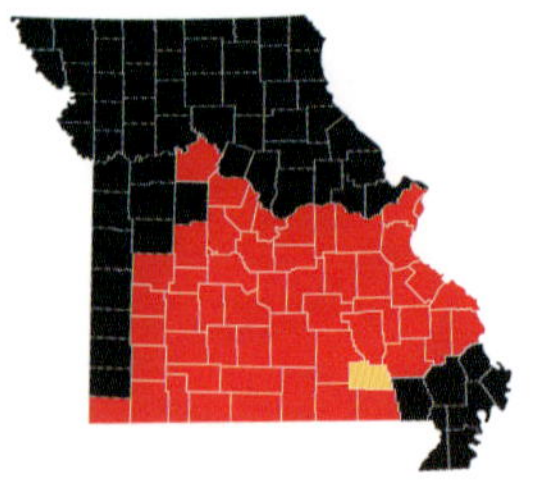

# 78

# Van Buren

Van Buren hasn't grown very much throughout its history, but that's okay for this town of 819. Its remoteness is the draw for the tons of visitors every spring and summer that come to enjoy the Ozark National Scenic Riverways and especially the Current River on which Van Buren sits. And Van Buren offers the nicest canoeing resort in the state.

The town was founded in 1833 to be the county seat of Ripley County, and it was named after President Martin Van Buren. It continued as the county seat until 1847 when the seat was moved to Doniphan. This created an exodus of residents from Van Buren. In 1859, Van Buren became the county seat of Carter County and has continued through today.

Floating, canoeing, and kayaking the Current River is the draw to the town. The river is a Class 1, the easiest and safest to float, which, when coupled with the beautiful scenery, makes it one of the most enjoyable floats around. And the Current River is just one waterway in the Ozark National Scenic Riverways.

## MUST DO

Floating the Current River is the reason to travel to Van Buren, and the Landing is the place from which to do that. There will be more about that, but there are other sights to see. Nearby is the Big Spring, one of the three largest springs in the United States. It pumps out 286 million gallons of water a day. Amazingly, the spring water first travels forty-five miles

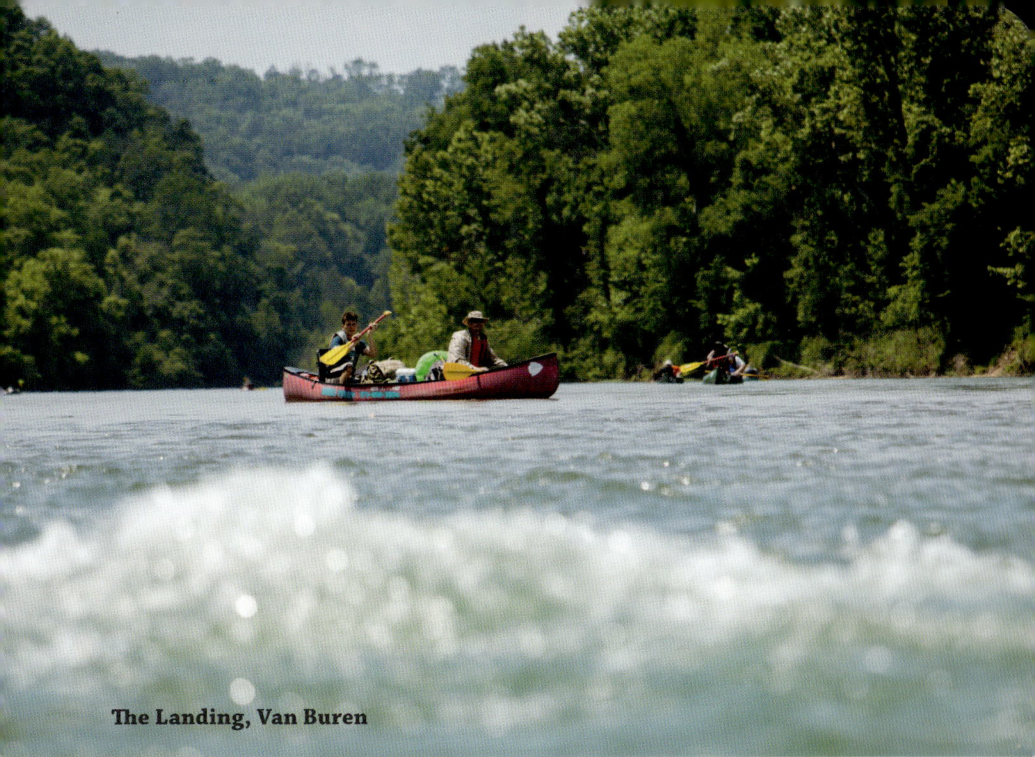
The Landing, Van Buren

through underground passages, dissolving an estimated seventy tons of limestone along the way. The draw to the spring, which also has hiking and exploring, is the beautiful turquoise water.

Nearby is Cave Spring Park, which offers a tour. It's one of the more intimate real spelunking opportunities. There's even a black-light tour. Also at the park are a zip line course, gem and fossil panning, a museum, and more.

If you want to see where history meets nature, a little exploring will yield the old Falling Spring Mill, which is a beautiful sight. But Van Buren's king attraction is floating the Current, and the Landing is the place to make it happen. The Landing is a one-stop shop for an Ozark Riverway vacation. Not only does it rent canoes, kayaks, and tubes, but it offers immaculate lodging right on the riverfront. Along with the accommodations and fine dining, they offer UTV rentals and riding. That's an adventure that needs to be checked out.

## MUST STAY

Usually, float trips or river vacations mean roughing it, but not in Van Buren. There's Rosecliff Lodge at the Landing. It's right on the riverfront, it offers unforgettable views, and the rooms are immaculate and comfortable, with everything needed to stay on the river and have fun.

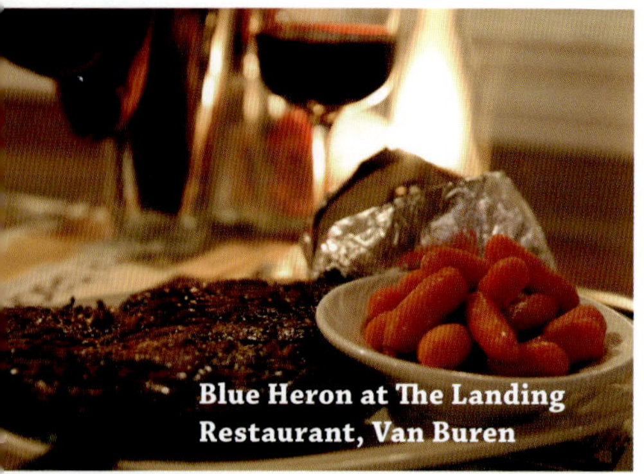
Blue Heron at The Landing Restaurant, Van Buren

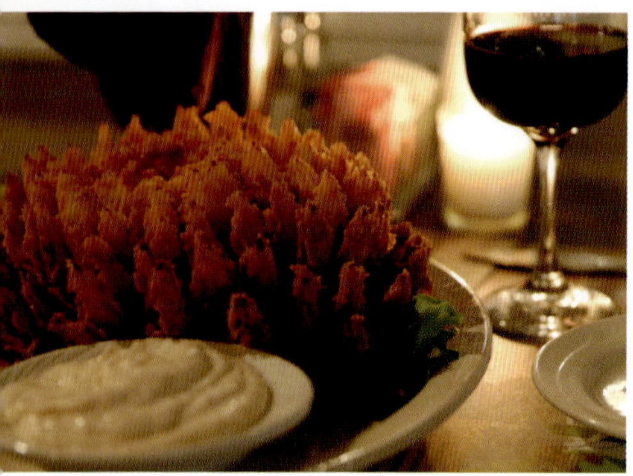

## MUST EAT

The Blue Heron at the Landing offers fine dining and beautiful views. Enjoy chef-perfected meals like steak, seafood, fish, shrimp, chicken, and more. The most unusual dish is the crab-stuffed filet, a whole new slant on surf and turf.

If more casual dining is your thing, the local staple is the Jolly Cone. This nostalgic burger drive-in has been in business since 1953 and is a great place to get a burger and especially an ice cream treat.

Jolly Cone, Van Buren

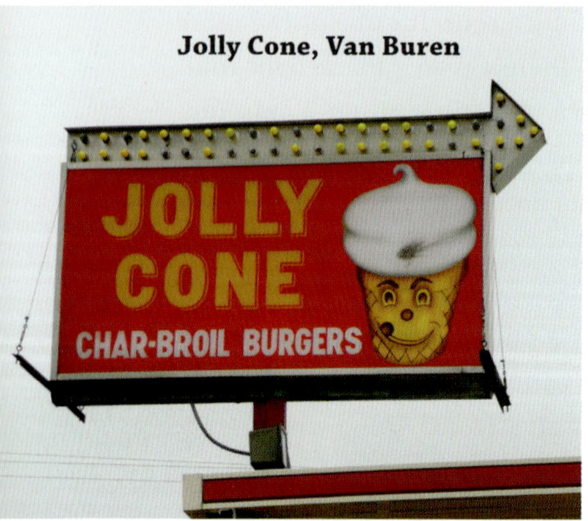

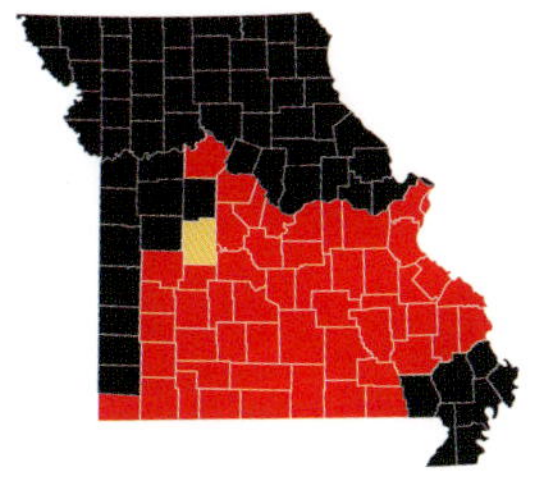

# 79

## *Warsaw*

Warsaw is a lake town with lots of outdoor fun and a quintessential small-town downtown. The Harry S. Truman Reservoir, or Truman Lake, runs from Clinton to Warsaw, with the dam located near Warsaw. It's the largest man-made lake in Missouri, just barely edging out Lake of the Ozarks. Although the town's history can be traced back to before the French settlers arrived in 1719, the completion of the lake in 1979 has had the greatest impact.

Warsaw was platted in 1837. It was named after Poland's capital city to honor the Polish Revolutionary War hero Tadeusz Kościuszko, who had also fought for independence in his homeland. In its early years it was a steamboat port along the Osage River.

There's lots to do in town, most of which is connected to the lake.

### MUST DO

The Truman Lake Visitor Center is a must-visit place. There are the traditional trappings of a state park museum with exhibits and dioramas of the lake, but the center also has a one-of-a-kind observation tour. High on a bluff above the lake is a spaceship-like round building that seriously may have been the inspiration behind Tony Stark's home in Marvel's *Iron Man* and *Avengers* movies. This round viewing platform is encircled with windows, allowing a breathtaking panoramic view of not only Truman Lake but Lake of the Ozarks as well.

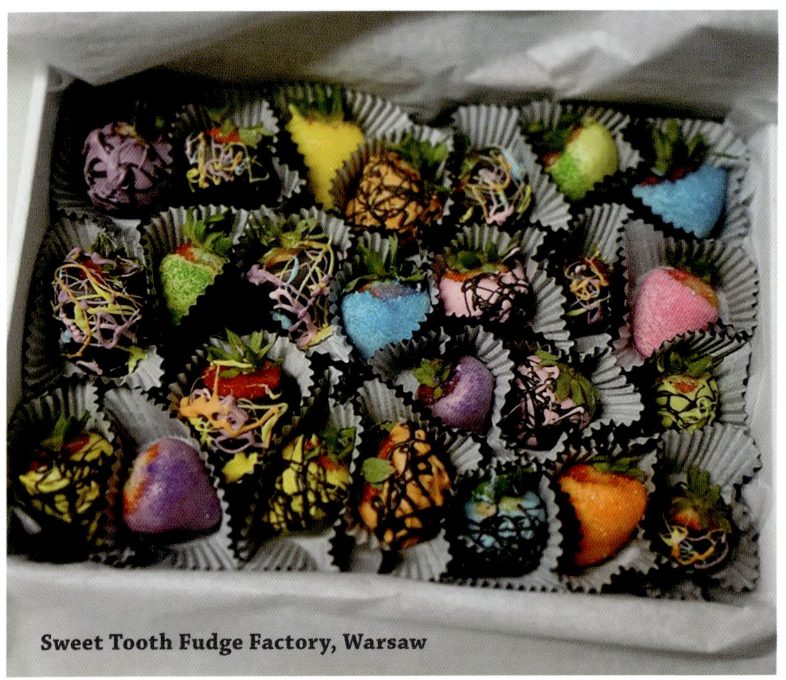

**Sweet Tooth Fudge Factory, Warsaw**

Keeping with the lake theme, Warsaw is home to the Lost Valley Fish Hatchery, the largest warm-water hatchery in the state and one of the largest in the country. This is in contrast to other state hatcheries mentioned in this book, which are cold-water hatcheries and focus on trout. Walleye, muskellunge, channel catfish, largemouth bass, striped and hybrid striped bass, bluegill, and hybrid sunfish are raised in this hatchery. The visitor center has an aquarium where visitors can get a closer look at these fish.

One of the most recognizable features near Warsaw is the Upper Bridge, or Warsaw Swinging Bridge. It's a suspension bridge on the National Register of Historic Places that spans five hundred feet from tower to tower across the Osage River.

Also near town is the riverfront park, which offers miles of trails for walking and cycling.

## MUST EAT

Lake traffic has given rise to some great eateries in the area, like Common Grounds Café and Cosmic Café.

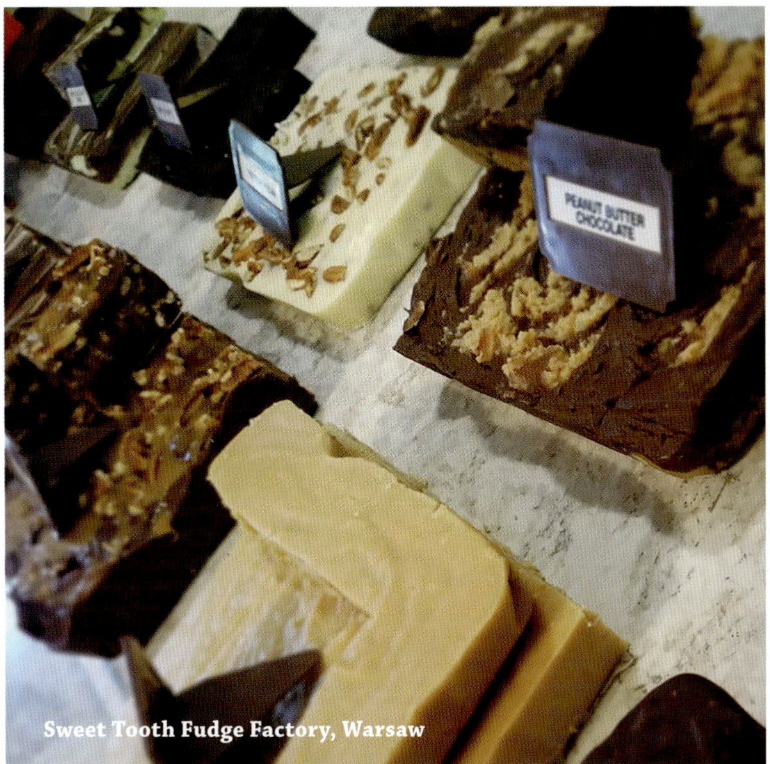

Sweet Tooth Fudge Factory, Warsaw

## MUST SHOP

The town's highlight, which is even more impressive than the swinging bridge or even the lake, is the Sweet Tooth Fudge Factory. Talk about a place that can bring a smile and light up a visitor's eyes, this store is full of treats, mostly edible, but even the gifts are great. The fantastic fudge in all its different flavors takes center stage, although the chocolate-covered strawberries might even overshadow it. Along with fudge, they have chocolate-dipped goodies, cakes, cupcakes, cookies, nostalgic candy, a large selection of other candy, and sugar-free candy. The story of the building of this local business is a powerful testament to hard work and great treats. With the sweet treats, they do have special gift ideas as well.

## MUST STAY

The hills surrounding Truman Lake are full of vacation rentals, so be sure to look them up on Airbnb and other rental outlets.

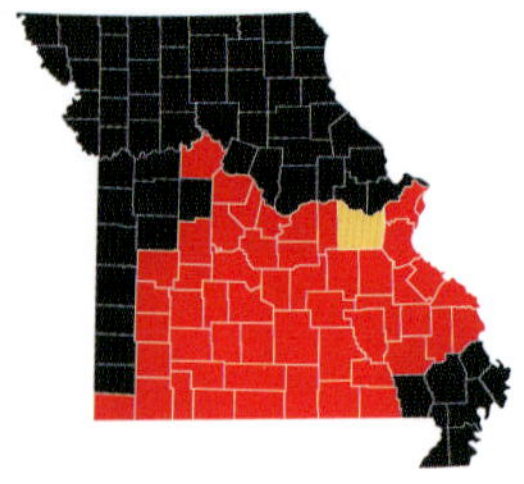

# 80

# Washington

Standing on Lafayette Street near the boat ramp in Washington, looking back toward downtown with the steeple of Saint Francis Borgia Church piercing the sky, it's understandable why Washington is becoming a regular day trip or weekend getaway for St. Louis residents. It's only an hour away, and it's much farther away with its transportive nature. Washington is recognized statewide as a historic city with its 445 buildings on the National Registry of Historic Places. And being known as the "Corncob Pipe Capital of the World" would point to it being a place of noted history as well.

Founded in 1869, the Missouri Meerschaum Company, the world's oldest and largest manufacturer of corncob pipes, is located along the riverfront in Washington. Washington was platted in 1827 and took its name from President George Washington. It was a growing town because of local industry and its function as a steamboat port on the Missouri River.

The Civil War impacted the town in several ways. Even before the war, it was a contested area, and then Confederate Major-General Sterling Price's unsuccessful campaign to reclaim Missouri for the South came through town and ransacked much of it.

Washington has lots of historic sites to offer, as well as many wineries; it's been called a gateway to the Missouri Rhineland. Numerous bed-and-breakfasts, inns, and vacation rentals make it a fun getaway.

## MUST DO

Taking in the historic sites of Washington is a must. Taking the history further back than most of the buildings is Fort Charrette Historic Village and Museum. This fun and educational French and American Indian trading post and village takes guests back in time to the 1790s. There are five log houses, one of which is believed to be one of the oldest log homes west of the Mississippi. Inside the buildings are tons of period furnishings and artifacts. It's a fun place to visit.

For kids, the Iron Spike Model Train Museum is a blast. Most train museums mentioned in this book have spectacular model trains, but none are more interactive than this one, allowing kids the freedom to play.

As mentioned, Washington is in the main stretch of Missouri's wine territory, and there are many wineries to visit.

Each August is the Washington Town and Country Fair. Now, fairs are held all across the state and nation, but Washington does dial it up a notch. Top-level music acts are brought in, and it is a large fair.

## MUST EAT

Washington is home to many special restaurants. The one that is soon to

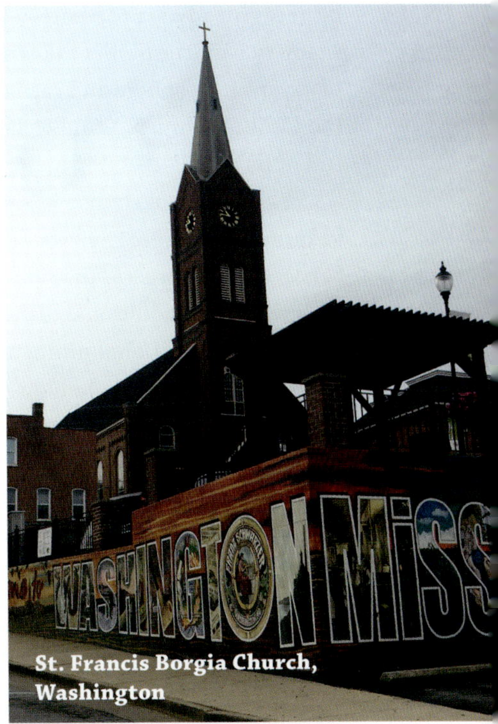

St. Francis Borgia Church, Washington

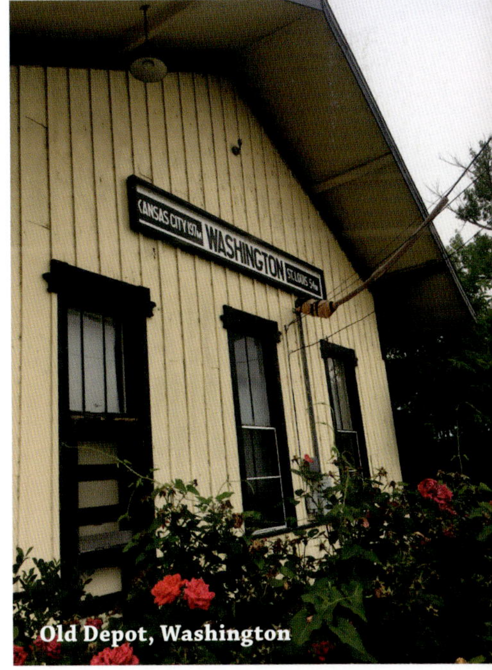

Old Depot, Washington

be recognized as a top eatery is the Tilted Skillet. Like the Town and Country Fair, the Skillet takes everything up a notch. It's a perfect blend of casual atmosphere and casual food done well. Whether it's steak, seafood, pizza, burgers, sandwiches, or salads, it comes out beautiful and full of flavor.

Sugarfire Smokehouse is another favorite for the area. It's a fun environment with great views of the river, and they offer tasty food like barbecue and burgers. The sides may take the prize, though.

Speaking of additional dishes stealing the show, Cowan's Restaurant offers more traditional dining fare and atmosphere, but their pies—oh, my! They call them "mile-high" pies, and that is accurate. The meringue on their cream pies stands nearly a foot high. That's something you don't get every day.

## MUST STAY

There are lots of great places to stay in town or nearby in wine country. Some to consider that are located downtown and offer great river views are 2nd Street Loft and the Old Dutch Hotel and Tavern. Be sure to check out the other bed-and-breakfasts. The 2nd Street Loft is in a storefront building from 1883 where downstairs was a sewing-machine store and upstairs was an apartment for the store owner and his family. The Old Dutch Hotel is also located in a historic storefront.

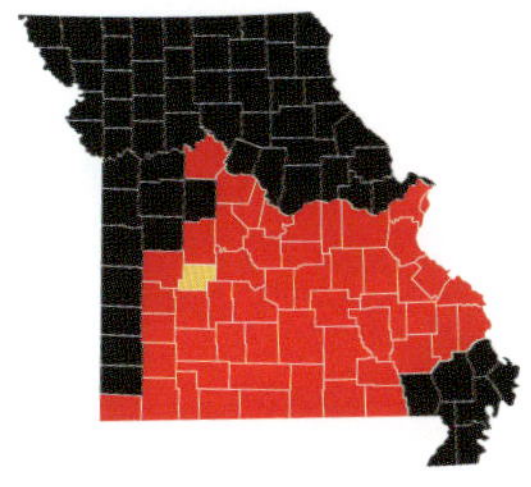

# 81

# *Wheatland*

An oasis is typically a waterhole located in the middle of an arid desert. Often these lush, green rarities can be seen from miles away as the palm trees stand in contrast to the rest of the landscape. There's an oasis of a different type in Wheatland. Rising seemingly out of nowhere in the midst of rural farmland and a small town of 371 people is one of the greatest racing facilities in the world. It hass the greatest dirt track in the world and one of the best drag-boat facilities too.

Wheatland was platted in 1869 and took on the name of President James Buchanan's retirement home in Lancaster, Pennsylvania. Buchanan had passed away a year before the town was established. From those beginnings until 2006, Wheatland remained a small, sleepy agricultural town. In 2004, the sounds of change began with the roar of bulldozers and construction noise filling the quiet air. Forrest and Charlotte Lucas, founders and owners of Lucas Oil products, had a cattle ranch nearby and wanted to build a racetrack of their own. They purchased an already popular dirt track in town and converted it into a motorsports mecca.

Lucas Oil Speedway is called the "Diamond of Dirt Tracks," and that is a mild statement. The amenities at the track include twenty-one luxury VIP suites and pits that are fully concreted with electric and water for each driver's stall. This dirt track hosts the prestigious Show-Me 100 along with other major dirt races, including all the major racing series. The complex also has a champion tractor-pull track, a go-cart track,

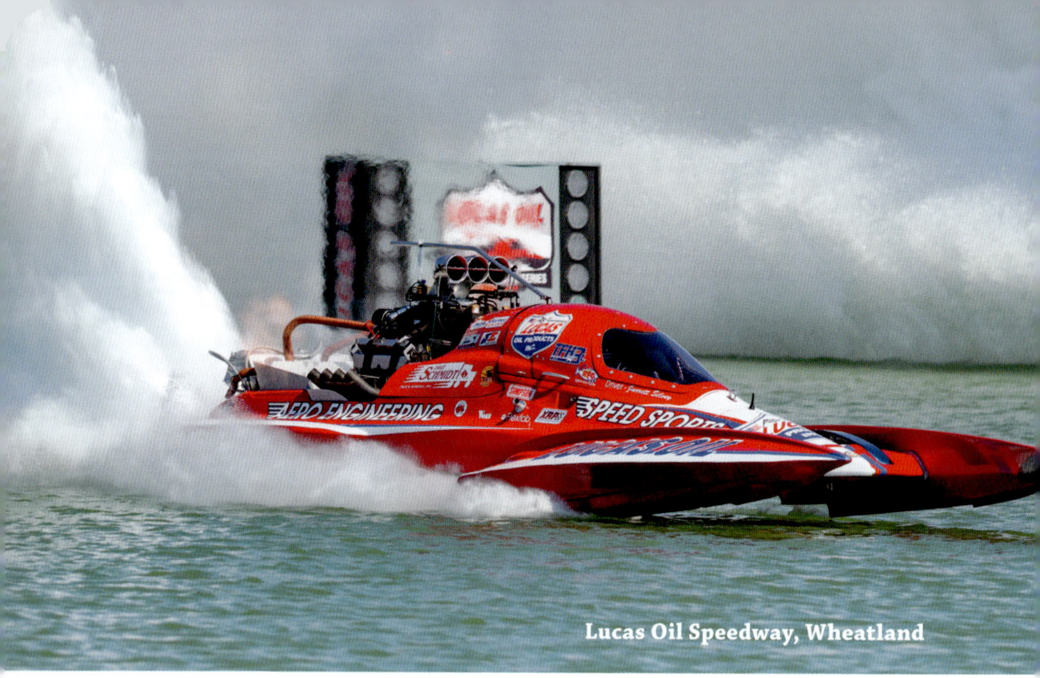

Lucas Oil Speedway, Wheatland

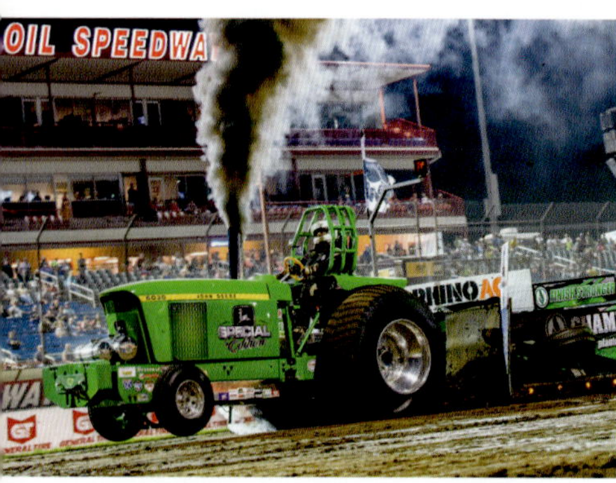


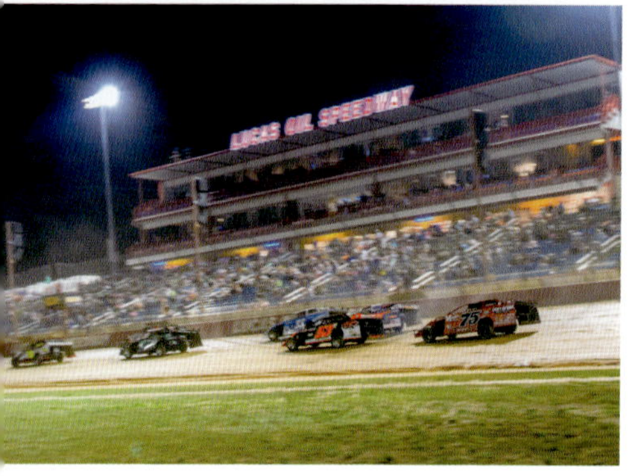


off-road truck course, and a lake for drag-boat racing. It's the only purpose-built drag-boat racing lake in the world.

## MUST DO

Catch a race or motorsports event at Lucas Oil Speedway.

# The Lowlands in the Bootheel

Dropping down from the Ozarks into the Mississippi River delta, the land flattens out and creates the lowlands that are in the bootheel, which drops into Arkansas.

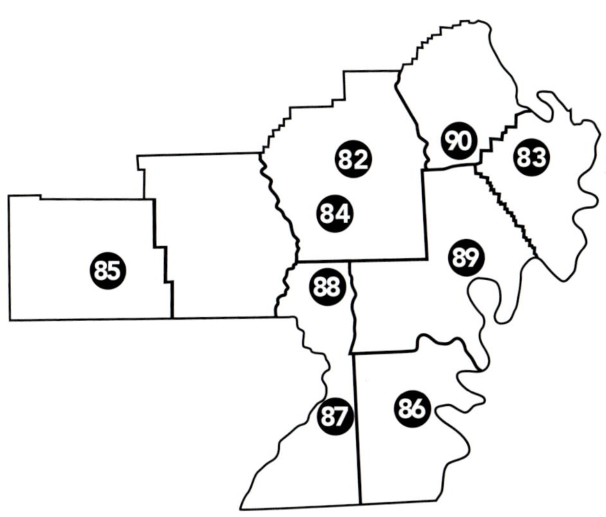


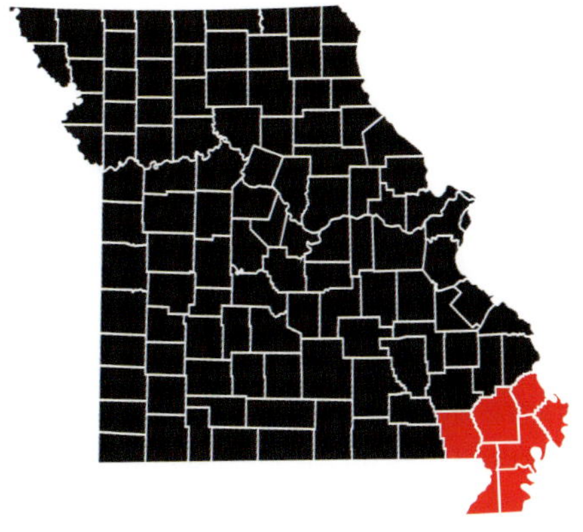

## The Lowlands in the Bootheel

82. Bloomfield
83. Charleston
84. Dexter
85. Doniphan
86. Hayti
87. Kennett
88. Malden
89. New Madrid
90. Sikeston

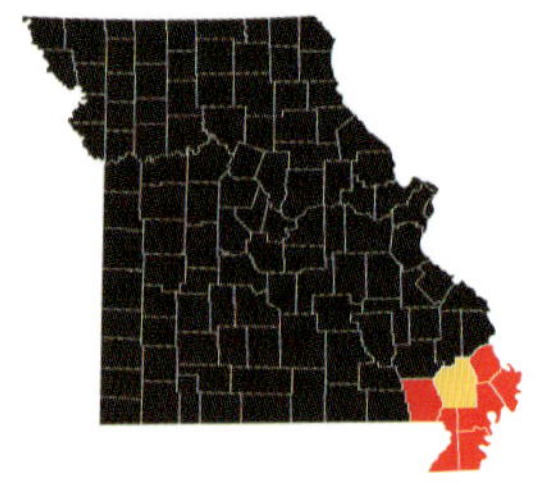

# 82

## Bloomfield

A town of nearly two thousand, Bloomfield is one of the most patriotic in the nation and a great respecter of its history. Bloomfield has taken great efforts to commemorate its history with numerous markers in town, much of that history occurring during the Civil War.

Bloomfield was established in 1824. It sits on Crowley's Ridge, a distinct geographical high ridge that rises 250 to 550 feet above the Mississippi River delta lands in Arkansas and Missouri. It runs from Helena, Arkansas, to Cape Girardeau, Missouri. On the ridge the landscape resembles the Ozark Mountains or Tennessee Hills rather than the rich farmland common to the delta area. This ridge that ranges from one mile to twelve miles wide was a major travel route since the surrounding area tended to be swampy in the early days before draining and flood control on the river. Most major cities in the Arkansas Delta are along this ridge, as well as several in Missouri. Bloomfield's placement led to it becoming a traffic area for traders, settlers, and armies during the Civil War.

The Civil War impacted the city with several skirmishes in or around it, as well as other operations during the war. One of those events was the start of the US military's *Stars and Stripes* newspaper. This long-running publication came into being by happenstance during the early stages of the Civil War. Union soldiers found a local newspaper's office empty and decided to print a newspaper chronicling the war efforts. They named it *Stars and Stripes*. Eventually the US Army would take up the idea, keeping the name and providing coverage of military action. Bloomfield is home to the paper's museum and library.

That patriotism led to Bloomfield becoming the home of the Missouri Veterans Cemetery in 2013.

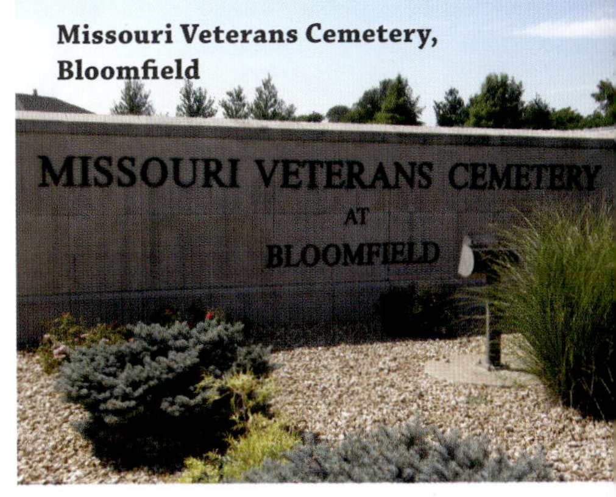


**Missouri Veterans Cemetery, Bloomfield**

## MUST DO

The Veterans Cemetery and Stars and Stripes Museum share a driveway, allowing visitors to not only see the history of this impactful newspaper but also remember our veterans. Each hour a song is played from the carillon tower inside the cemetery.

As mentioned, Bloomfield has recognized and remembered its history well. There are numerous markers in town. The two most interesting are from the Bloomfield Mutiny and the Fatal Tree. The mutiny occurred when Union soldiers garrisoned in town thought their commanding officer, Major Samuel Montgomery, was turning the post over to the Confederates. This suspicion arose after Montgomery's marriage to a local widow. The mutiny ended without action, though officers leading the rebellion were court-martialed.

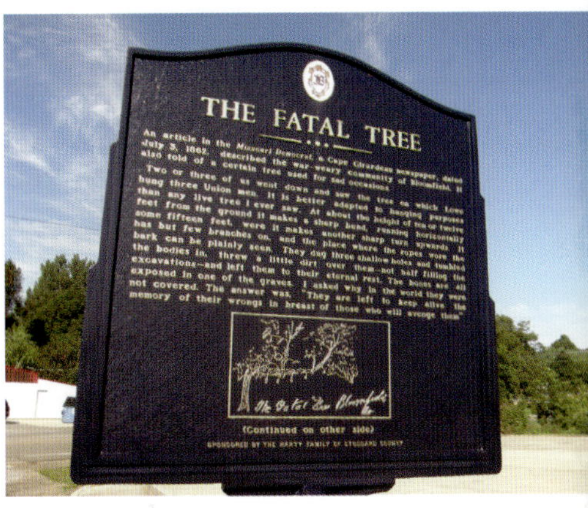


**Intersection of Routes 25 and E, Bloomfield**

The Fatal Tree marker commemorates the spot where three Union men were hung in Bloomfield during the Civil War, with two accounts of the incident on the two sides of the marker—one from a townsman and one from a Union cavalryman who wrote to his wife about the tree and its gruesome history.

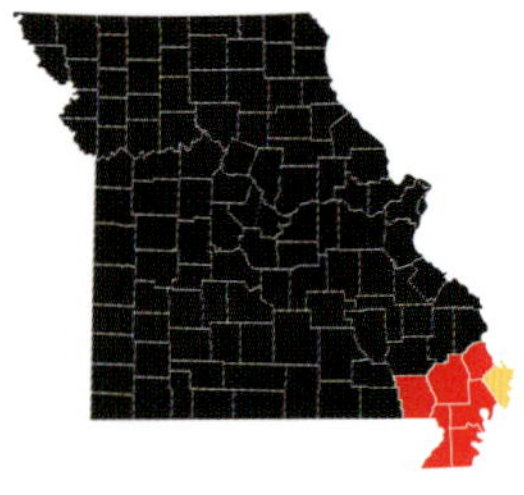

# 83

## *Charleston*

History, earthquakes, fireworks, farmland, and great food. What more could you ask for? That's what makes Charleston special. This town of nearly six thousand is the largest on the Missouri side of the confluence of the Mississippi and Ohio Rivers. Early on, this area was among the swampiest and muddiest lowlands around due to heavy rainfall and flooding. Great forests in the area attracted timber barons who cleared the lands. Then miles of levees and dikes were created, along with drainage efforts, which in return produced some of the most fertile land in the country and the world. It's been used to grow corn, wheat, cotton, and soybeans.

European-Americans first crossed the river and began to settle the area in 1805, naming the town Matthews Prairie. In 1837 it was platted, and a few years later it was known as Charleston. There's debate on where the name came from, either nearby Charles Prairie or Charleston, South Carolina.

Charleston was affected by the Civil War, with a battle taking place in town. But the most memorable moment from that time was when a Confederate general robbed a Charleston bank.

In 1895, Charleston was the epicenter of a 5.9 earthquake that damaged the whole town and was felt as far away as Indiana and Alabama. This quake was along the New Madrid Seismic Zone. Although much of the town was damaged in the quake, many historic buildings remain.

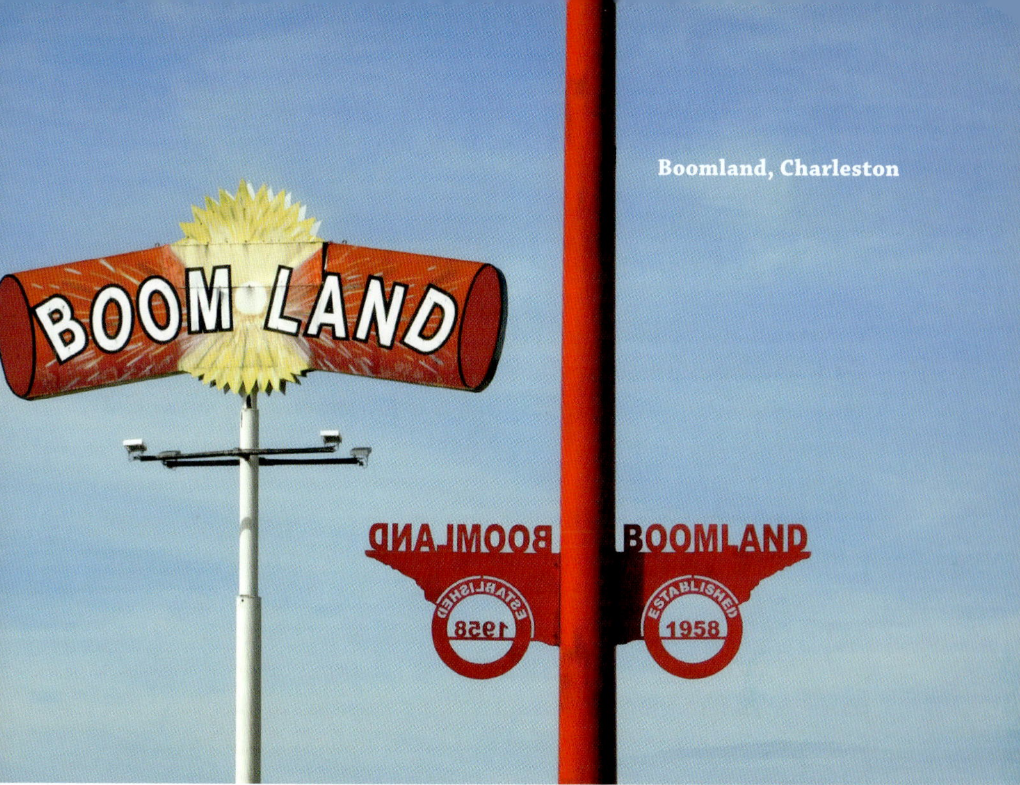

Boomland, Charleston

## MUST DO

Touring historic homes to relive the days when Mississippi River towns prospered is a great way to enjoy Charleston. There are over two hundred historic homes, and they're made noteworthy through the beautiful landscape of dogwoods, azaleas, and older trees. One of the homes available to tour is the Joseph Hunter Moore Home, built in 1899. It showcases furnishings from the period and serves as a museum for the Mississippi County Historical Society.

Another way to embrace the history of this river town is to take the ferry. The Dorena-Hickman Toll Ferry is one of the few remaining riverboat ferries in the United States and is the only operating ferry crossing the Mississippi between Missouri and Kentucky.

For a more contemporary adventure, there's Boomland, the largest supplier of fireworks in the nation. Boomland is a tourist destination in and of itself. Fireworks are available all year long, but their sixty-thousand-square-foot showroom is only open June 15–July 5. Along with the insane number of fireworks, you can visit the gift shop, get a bite to eat at the buffet restaurant, Wally's Chew Chew, or check out the snack bar for fudge, pizza, ice cream, and more.

## MUST EAT

The reason to visit Charleston is to eat at the Glenn. This has become one of the favorites, if not the favorite, of this author. Chef Adam Glenn came back home to Charleston after years in the industry elsewhere. He has brought a level of quality, presentation, and fine dining experience nearly unparalleled in the bootheel of small-town Missouri, and he's done it in an affordable way in a setting that matches local culture. It's a bit of a paradox, as the décor is woodsy and rustic, but the dining experience, especially at night, is high-end-restaurant level. The food itself is a mix of elegant preparation and down-home heartiness. There are a couple of places in small-town Missouri that have been able to create that dual-culture experience, but Adam has mastered it.

The Glenn seems like it's two different restaurants. At lunch it's a casual sandwich, burger, or plate lunch served on paper trays. At night it's transformed into a nice restaurant. It's the attention to detail and mix of flavors that make it a hit. Guests see people working hard to craft a meal that's a step above others. Also there is a focus on fresh ingredients. Each dish is superb, but the desserts may be the real gem. That attention to detail and flavor shows itself in a combination of ingredients that produces a delicious and beautifully presented product. The favorite is the s'mores tart.

## MUST NOTE

The Charleston high school boys' basketball program has won eleven state championships.

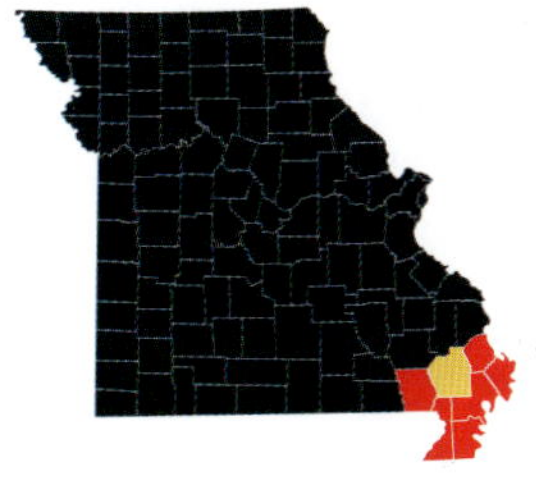

# 84

## Dexter

Dexter grew as a railroad town and shipping center. Though times have changed, Dexter has now become a location of great food. One of the area's only Mediterranean restaurants is here, and the town is home to its own brand of barbeque represented by a classic staple of the area and a chain that has multiplied throughout the region.

The town was planned by the railway. It was first platted in 1873 as Dexter City, but the name was shortened to Dexter by 1887. The story goes that the name came from the name of a horse owned by one of the early settlers. Railroad shipping brought growth to the city, but changes in shipping methods and the Civil War slowed progress. Today the Dexter Depot Visitors Center and Museum retains that railroad history.

In addition to the depot, there are other historic sites to check out, like the Heritage House, which dates back to its construction in 1870. It's been restored and serves as a park and museum.

### MUST EAT

One of the most unusual restaurants in the bootheel is Dhafer's Mediterranean Steak House, which offers fine cuisine with a Mediterranean taste. The backstory is also quite intriguing. Owner and operator Chef Dhafer Al-Makuter brings to Dexter many years of experience as a chef, but even more interesting is that before becoming a chef, Dhafer served in the US Special Forces as an interrogator and

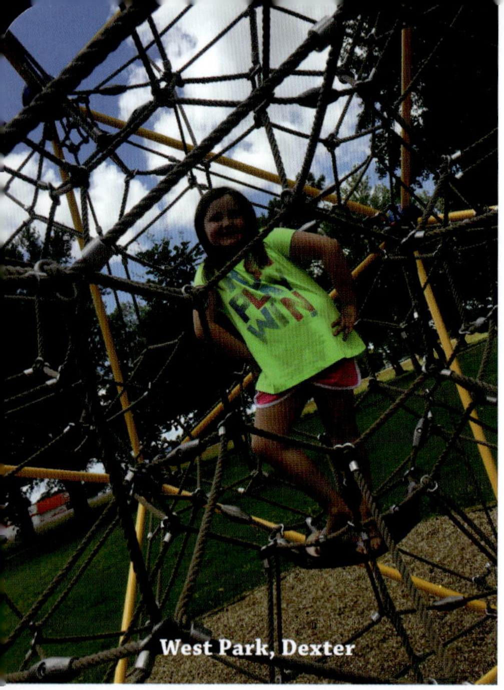
West Park, Dexter

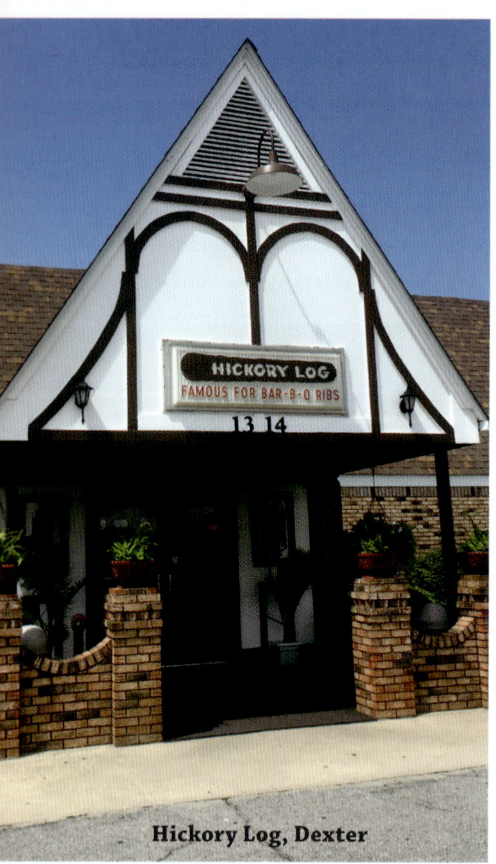

Hickory Log, Dexter

Arabic interpreter. He also spent six years with the US State Department. So if you have trouble making a decision on your order, he can get it out of you.

Dhafer's has an atmosphere, quality of dishes, and beauty of presentation that typically can only be found in larger cities. The menu offers a mix of sandwiches, burgers, and dinners. The steaks are tremendous, but the chicken dishes are done with such flavor and texture that they make even the staunchest steak man consider the white meat, especially the chicken kabob.

Dexter is also a player in the nation's kaleidoscope of barbeque. Like multiple dialects across one nation, American barbeque takes many forms: Memphis, Kansas City, St. Louis, Texas style, and so on. Dexter has a place along that spectrum. Characteristics of this barbeque are walled pits, large hickory logs, and slow cooking, along with a thin vinegar-style sauce. St. Louis–style ribs are the focal point and the meat is filled with the deep aroma of that pit smoke.

The story of Dexter's contribution to the barbeque world began in 1953 with the Hickory Log restaurant. It started out as a diner that sat 30 people but has grown into a venue that can seat 350. The Hickory Log occupies a unique building and provides a level of fine dining with

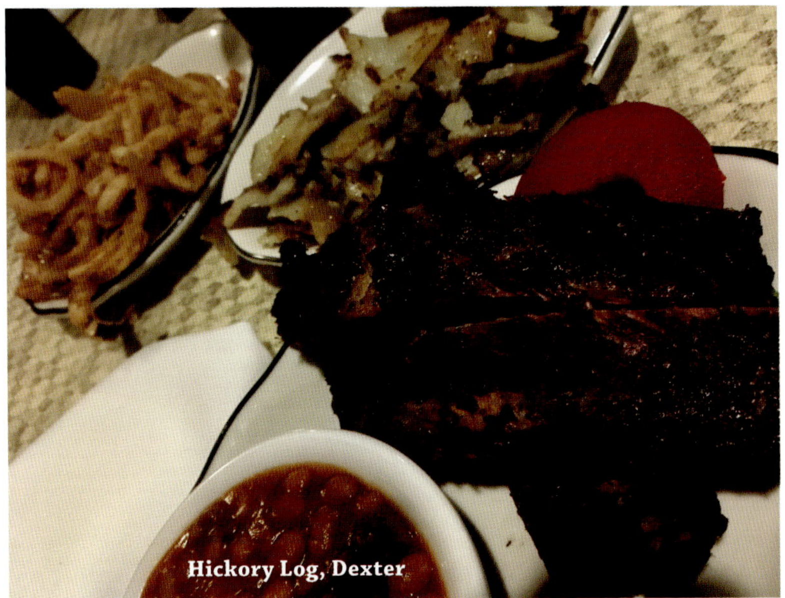
Hickory Log, Dexter

table clothes, cloth napkins, beautiful place settings, and low lighting. This is mixed with a homey comfort makes it an enjoyable experience. But it's the food that brings the most joy. The strong smokiness with a tinge of sweet makes the ribs some of the best in America. An option for a boneless rib platter or sandwich allows the enjoyment of ribs without the mess or the need for a toothpick. And it's only fair to mention that the American fries and onion rings give the barbeque a run for its money. If you travel a long distance to eat at the Hickory Log, you will not be alone as their guest book lists visitors from all over the world.

One of the area's most beloved barbeque restaurants, Dexter Bar-B-Que, carries on the Dexter barbeque dialect by providing the tastes found at the Hickory Log but presented in a more casual fast-food style. Dexter Bar-B-Que has had such success that they have now opened restaurants in five new locations.

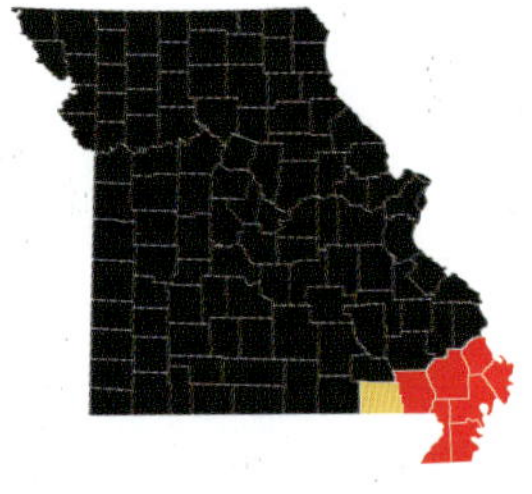

## 85

# Doniphan

Doniphan is on the edge of the lowlands but would much rather say they are in the foothills of the Ozarks. It's the end of one of the most enjoyable floats in the country on the Current River. Tubing, canoeing, and kayaking on the Current River are the things to do. Though entertainment along the Current is the main attraction to Doniphan, it has a restaurant that may be ahead of its time.

The town now has a population of nearly two thousand and was first settled in the 1840s. It was named after an attorney, politician, and war hero, Alexander William Doniphan. He is most remembered for being the defense attorney that kept Mormon founder Joseph Smith from being executed.

### MUST DO

For your float down the Current, Rocky River Resort is an outfitter to consider.

### MUST EAT

Many news outlets have reported on a transition occurring in banks, some even calling it the future of banks. Bank lobbies are being redesigned to be more café like, with gourmet coffee and free Wi-Fi. Doniphan's jewel of a restaurant, Coffee and More at the Bank, is ahead of its time, according to a *Wall Street Journal* article. In an abandoned bank built in 1903, Coffee

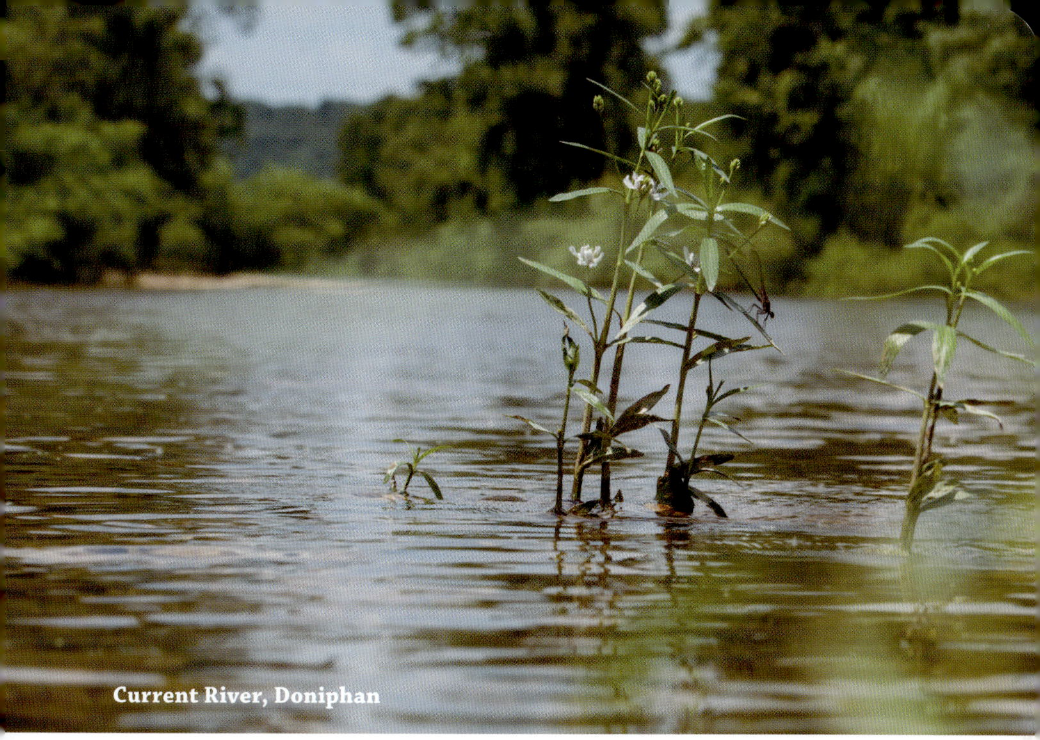

Current River, Doniphan

and More at the Bank offers coffee, comfort food, and community. The goal was to create a place where people could get good food and relax. The focus is on hearty home-style cooking. Although each dish is delicious, especially their roast, it's breakfast that is the true champion, like the amazing hash brown casserole.

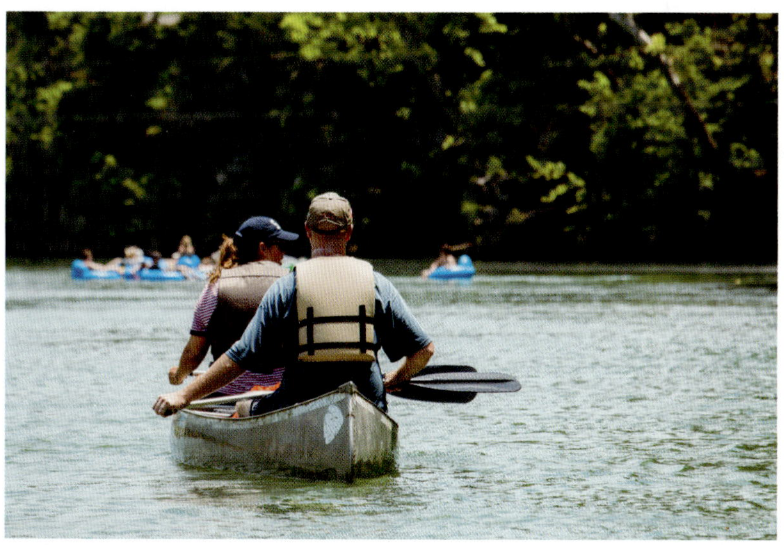

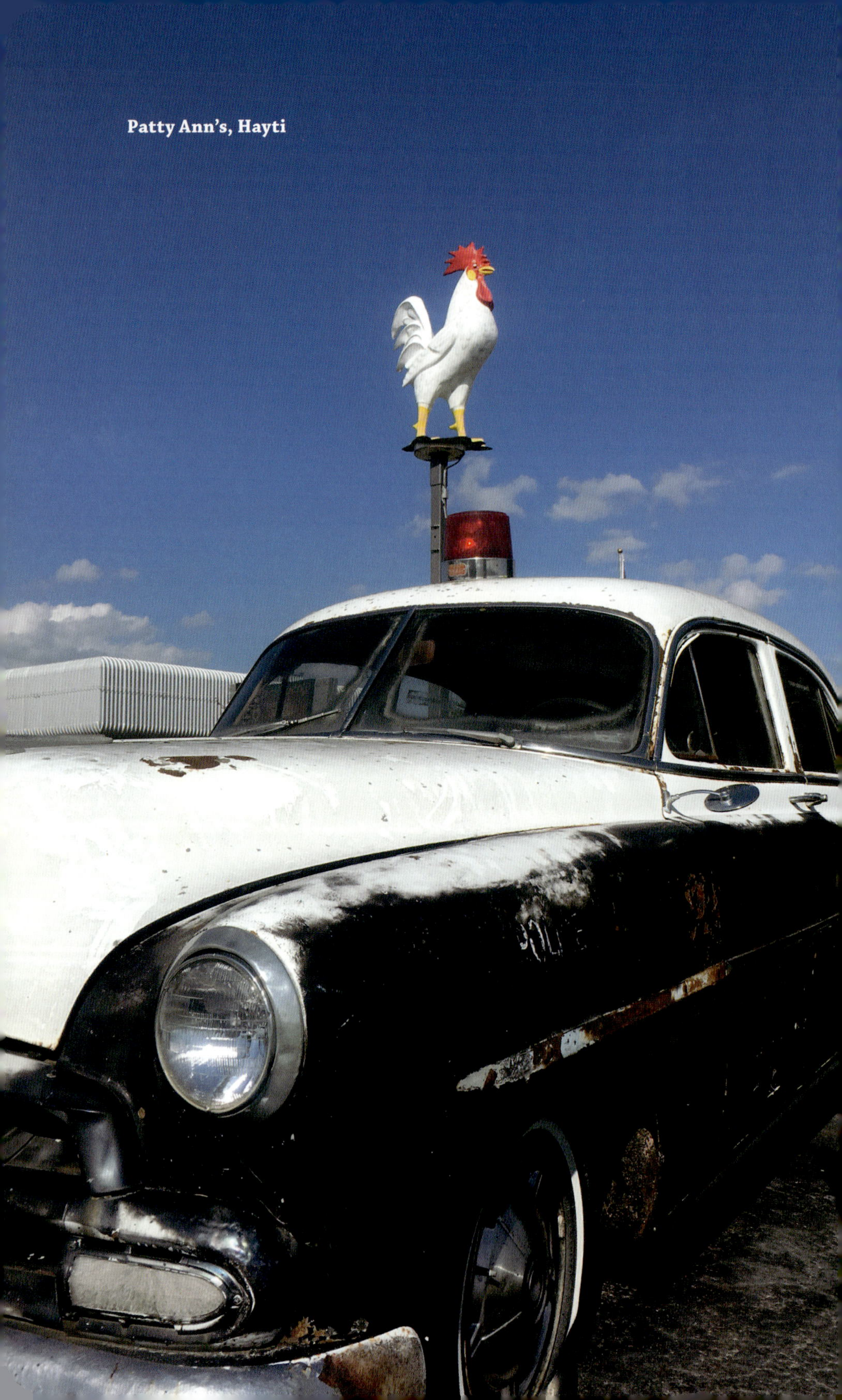
Patty Ann's, Hayti

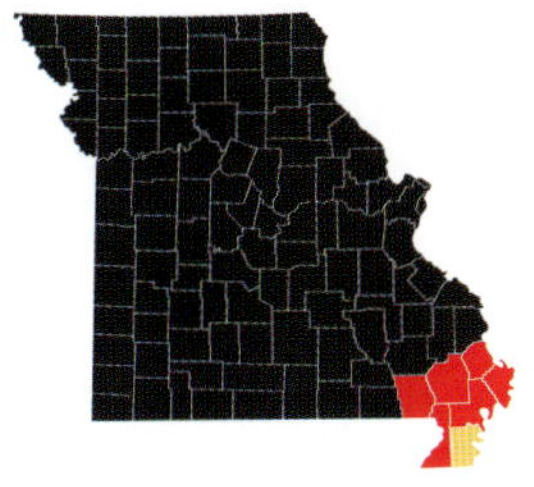

# 86

## *Hayti*

Hayti is a town of nearly three thousand located on a bend in the Mississippi River. It was platted in 1894 as a railroad town. There's a debate about where the name came from. One theory is that it came from Dr. G. Hayes, who was instrumental in the start of the town, and another is that it is from the island nation of Haiti.

Whichever origin story for the name is true, today Hayti has a couple of great places to eat. Both are a bit unassuming in appearance, but patrons enjoy every bite.

### MUST EAT

Regardless of drive time, Patty Ann's is worth it, and even just a peek in their dessert case is worth the drive. If you need a reason to smile, peer into that glass case filled with tremendously beautiful cakes and pies with mile-high meringue. The sight when stepping into Patty Ann's is surprising. Outside, it's an old Dairy Queen, but inside it's a charming country home with white tablecloths, flowers, beautiful lighting, and that holy grail of dessert cases. The country décor causes "Yes, ma'am" to roll off the tongue. Inside there is hearty, home-style food. Deciding between fried chicken, chicken fried steak, fried catfish, or something else is difficult. The homemade bread, downhome sides made from scratch, and well-crafted salads make it even better.

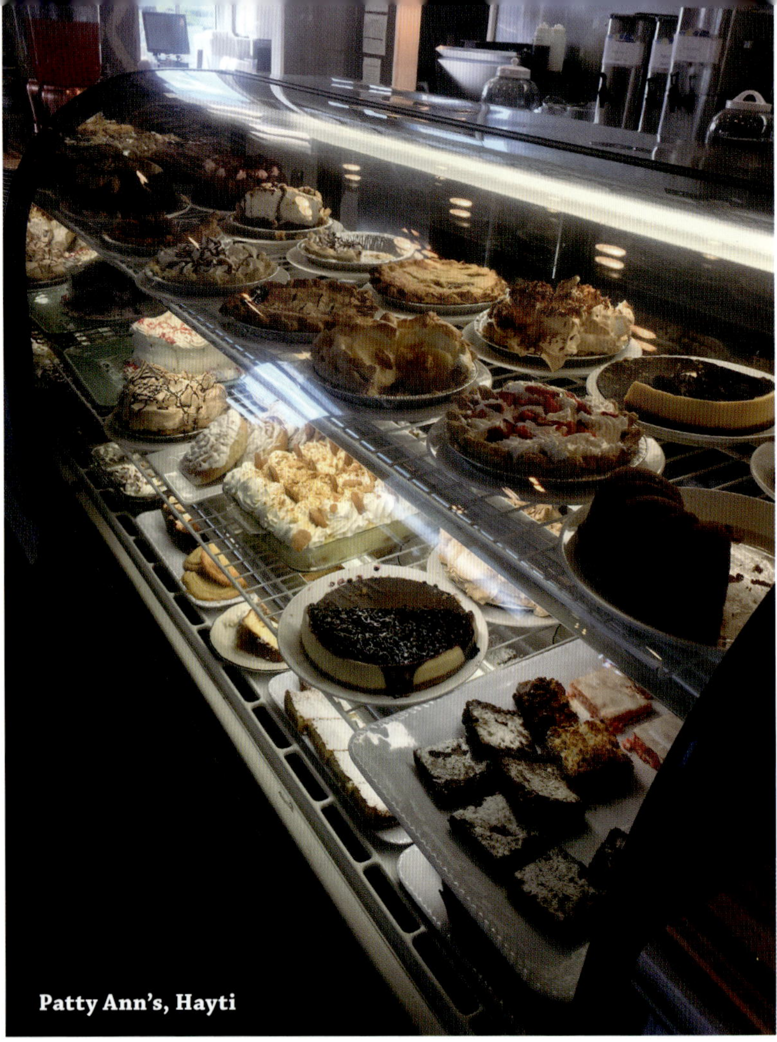
Patty Ann's, Hayti

Down the road just a little way is another hot spot. Chubby's BBQ is even more unassuming than Patty Ann's. It's a small red building, and inside there's no surprisingly charming decor, but there is some well-done food. Each piece of smoked meat is finger-licking good and, along with the sides, makes this a delicious spot. And the vinegar-based sauce is as good as the smoked seasoning in their meats.

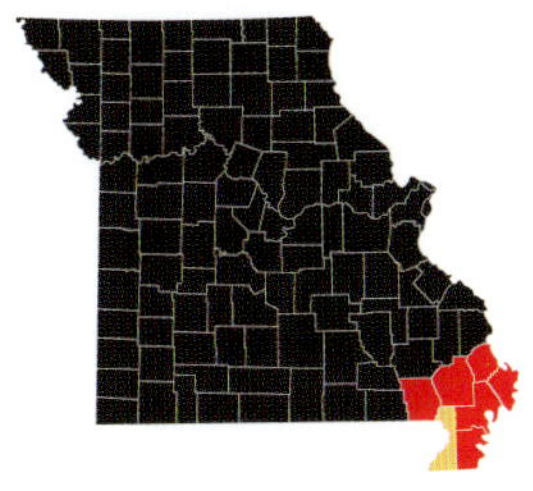

# 87

# *Kennett*

Kennett is the largest town in the bootheel. It's still a small town, but it has been the hometown of major musicians throughout the years. Settlement can be traced to the early 1800s, when the town was called Chilletecaux in honor of a Delaware Indian chief who lived in the area. Next, it was called Butler. Finally, it was named Kennett in honor of Luther M. Kennett, the mayor of St. Louis. Throughout its history, much of its growth came from the railroad. Drainage programs allowed the land to become an important agricultural area.

## MUST DO

A major piece of Kennett's entertainment history is still in use. The Palace Theater was first opened in 1916. This iconic building in downtown Kennett features a classic vertical name sign that flows into the traditional wedge marquee. It closed in 2010, but in 2014 two stay-at-home moms could not stand that their community would not have a theater, so they bought it and reopened. It continues offering first-run movies Wednesday–Sunday at 7:00 p.m.

## MUST EAT

While in town you'd do yourself a disservice if you did not stop in at Causbie Bakery. This Kennett staple offers up all kinds of baked goods, especially cookies and donuts.

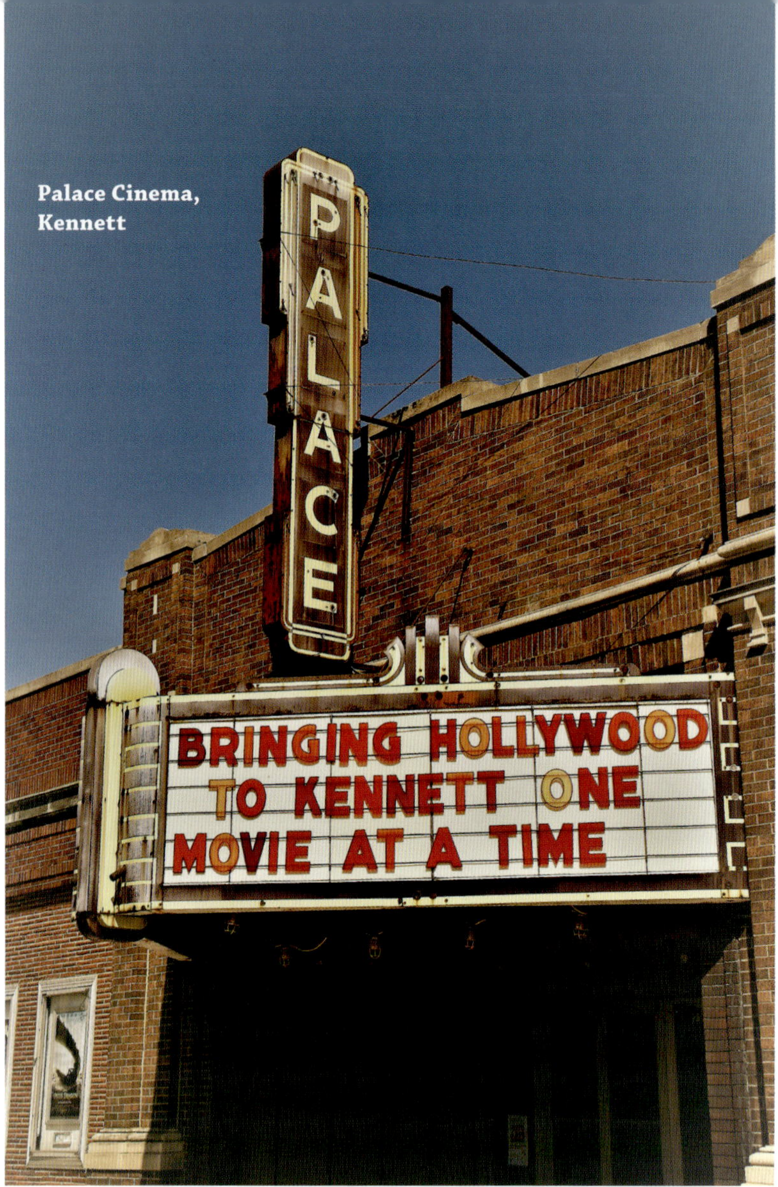


Palace Cinema, Kennett

## MUST NOTE

Kennett is the hometown of several of popular recording and performing artists. The most famous of these is Grammy-winning singer and songwriter Sheryl Crow. A welcome sign in town proclaims their famous former resident. Current popular country-music artists David Nail and Trent Tomlinson are natives. A bit different than the other artists, but it's also the home of world-renowned hammered dulcimer player Dan Landrum, who toured with Yanni.

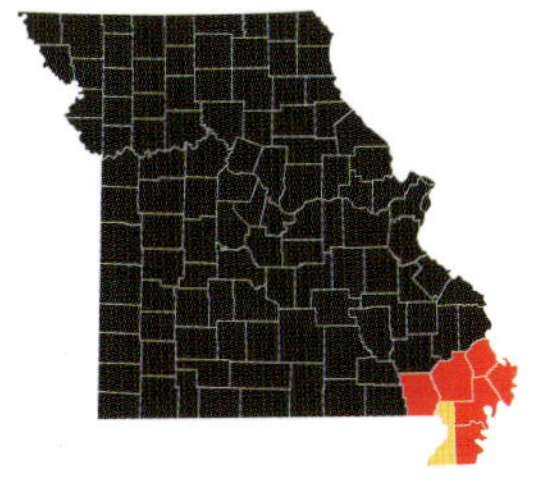

# 88

## Malden

Malden is one of the larger towns in the bootheel and is located on Crowley's Ridge. Crowley's is the unique geographical feature that rises a couple hundred feet above the rest of the land. It runs from Helena, Arkansas, to Cape Girardeau, Missouri. Malden is known for having one of the largest general aviation airports in the state.

The town was platted in 1877 to be a railway town like many of the others in the area. There's debate on where the name originated. Some believe it was named after a county judge, Colonel T. H. Mauldin, or the name may have come from Malden, Massachusetts. The large area first served as an army airfield and then as an air force base from 1942 to 1960. Pilots were trained in Malden for World War II and the Korean War.

### MUST DO

Malden is home to the Bootheel Youth Museum, a hands-on activity-based children's museum. It has been named one of the top youth attractions in America. It's a fascinating place where kids can travel into their imaginations. There are rooms decked out with equipment, décor, and costumes for children to pretend they're in a bank, medical center, country market, farm store, or construction zone. They are able to play as if they're in outer space or hanging with dinosaurs and much more.

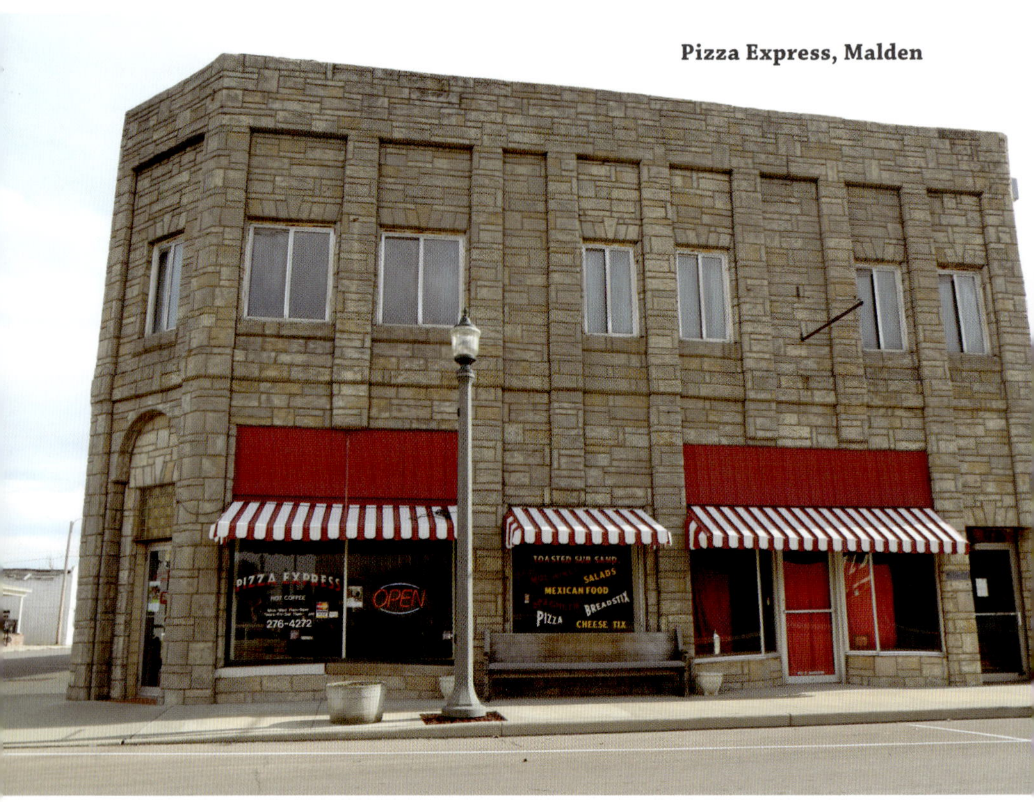


**Pizza Express, Malden**

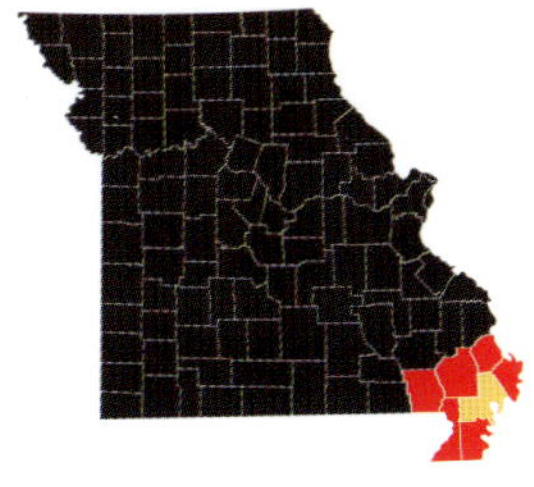

# 89

# New Madrid

New Madrid is internationally famous for the giant earthquake that occurred in 1812, and hopefully it will be a long time before the town returns to that kind of fame. But it still is the hub of the New Madrid fault and seismic activity.

The city is one of the oldest European-American settlements in Missouri. It was founded in 1778 by the Spanish governor of Louisiana, Bernardo de Galvez. Some people crossed the river to settle in the area, but they had to become Spanish citizens. By the beginning of the 1800s, there were nearly 2,000 settlers (3,116 people live there today). The United States took control of the city through the Louisiana Purchase in 1803.

Settlers would soon be challenged, as between 1811 and 1812 some two thousand earthquakes hit the area. The first three registered 8.1, 7.8, and 8.8. They're the largest earthquakes to hit the United States. They were felt as far away as New York City, Boston, Montreal, and Washington, DC. The quakes rang church bells in Boston. During the earthquake, the Mississippi River flowed backward, and it created Reelfoot Lake, fifteen miles from town.

## MUST DO

It's interesting to walk where such a huge disaster took place. There's a museum remembering the earthquake, New Madrid Historical Museum. It's more about the history of the city than the quake, but it's interesting

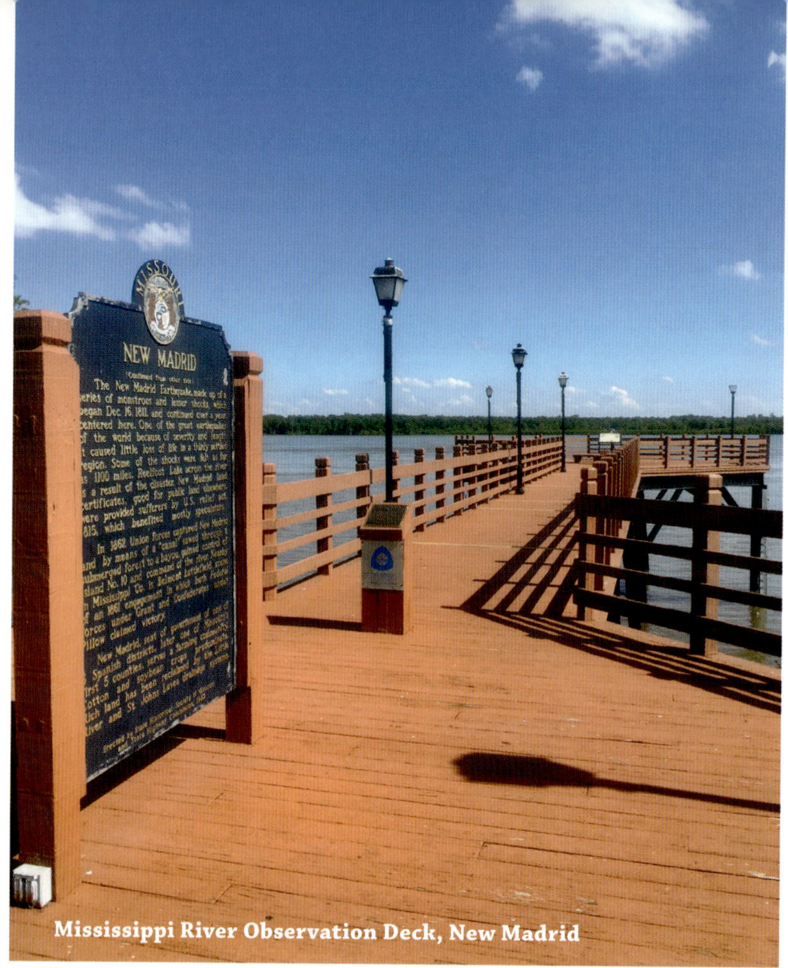

Mississippi River Observation Deck, New Madrid

to see. It's small and nicely done. At the museum there is also an observation deck, which offers a panoramic view of the river.

Another way to embrace the area's history is Hunter-Dawson State Historic Site, built around a mansion from 1860. It is a reminder of the wealth and prosperity that grew out of the Mississippi River's rich farmland. The home still has the furniture that was picked out by the house's first owner.

## MUST EAT

Good ol' delta food is needed when visiting New Madrid, and Fat Frank's is the place to get it. Formerly, this place was the popular Johnson's Fried Chicken, and Frank's serves pretty much the same fare with some barbecue. It's a downhome buffet, and the tip is to get there when they open at 10:30 a.m. and the food is fresh and hot.

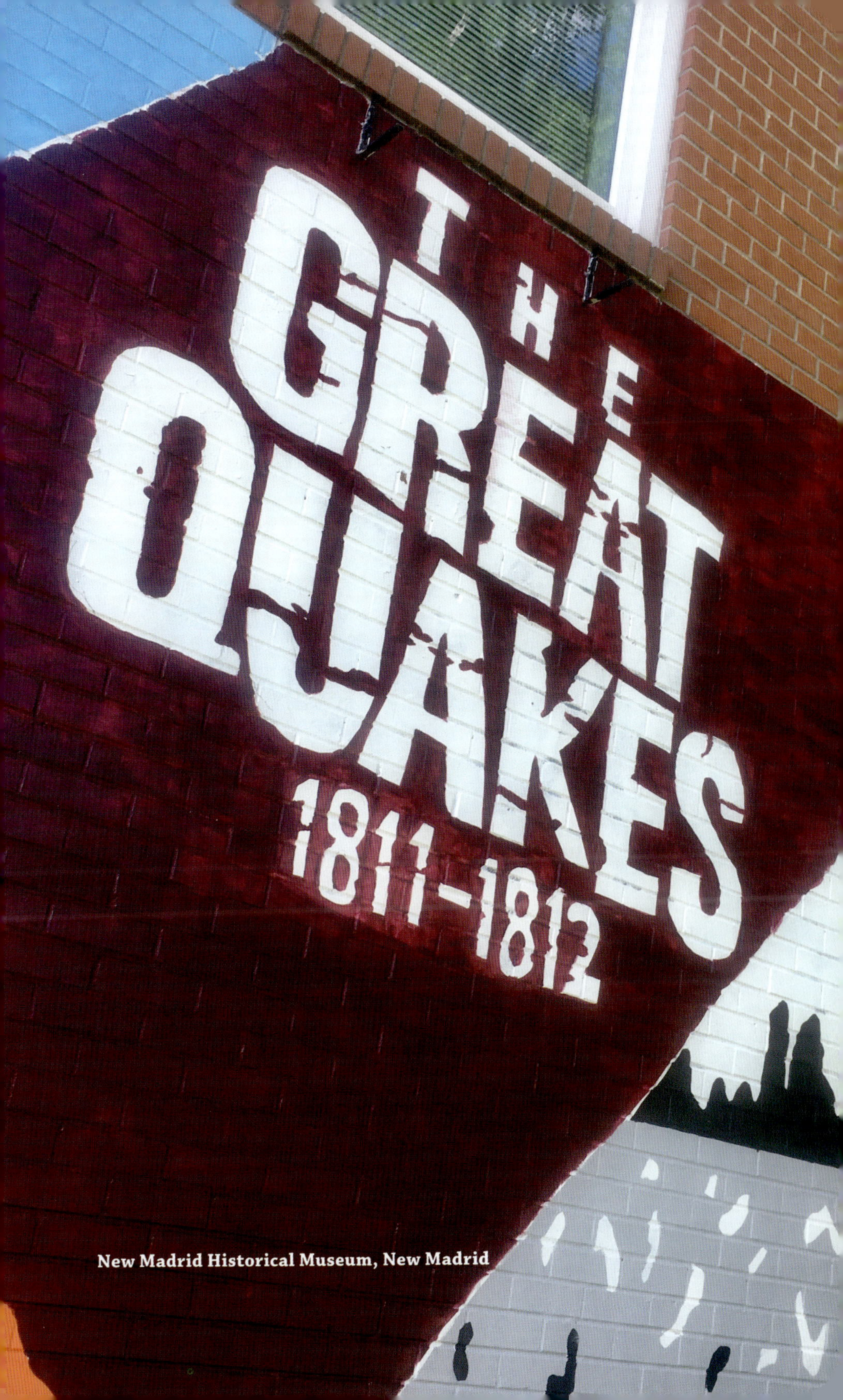


New Madrid Historical Museum, New Madrid

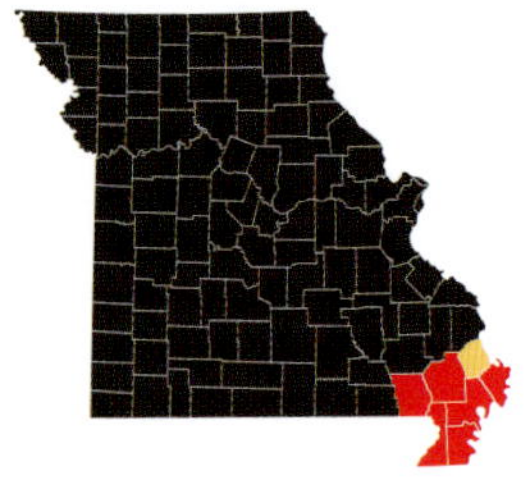

# 90

# Sikeston

Throwing rolls at dinner makes the meal better, of course. Sikeston is home to a restaurant that has come to personify the Ozarks, even though it originated in the bootheel. Lambert's Café is this destination and is known for roll throwing, which began in 1976. The restaurant itself opened in 1942. It's not the only thing in Sikeston. The city is over the target town size for this book, with a population of 16,318. That is a huge increase from the 200 residents the town had near the end of the century.

Sikeston was founded in 1860 by John Sikes, who became the town's namesake. Transportation has been important to the city. The railroad extended to Sikeston from Charleston. It also was the land route between St. Louis and New Orleans. These two transportation routes put the town in the crosshairs during the Civil War. Both sides held the city.

Growth came in 1907 with the Little River Drainage District, which allowed the heavy swamplands to become fertile soil perfect for cotton. Cotton brought prosperity to the town. Throughout the years, and especially following World War II, Sikeston became a hub of industry. It became the first location for Walmart outside of Arkansas.

## MUST DO

The town's agricultural history is preserved through the Southeast Missouri Agricultural Museum, which has the state's largest collection of antique equipment. There are more than six thousand pieces of

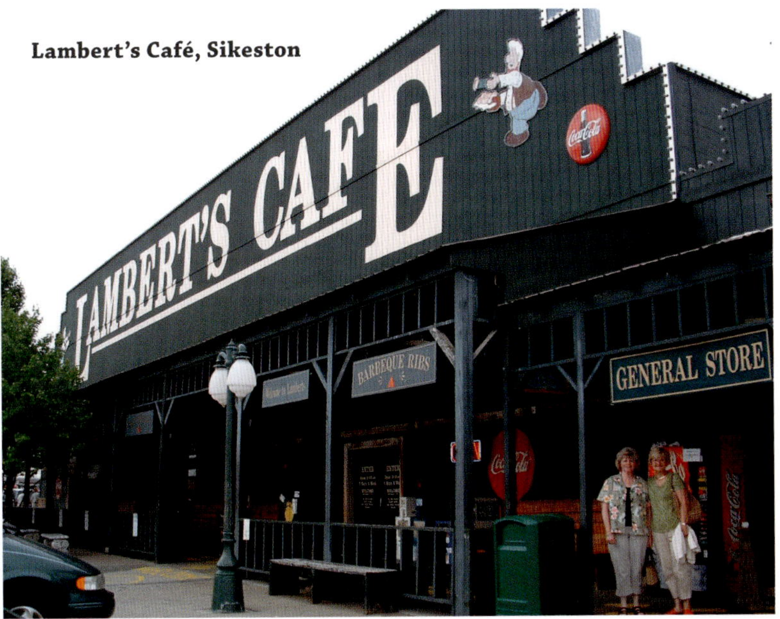

**Lambert's Café, Sikeston**

machinery all capable of performing their original tasks. Many items date back to the 1800s and include tractors, combines, and wagons.

In keeping with its agri-roots, Sikeston has been home to the Bootheel Rodeo since 1952. This event put on by the Jaycees has brought in the biggest acts in music beginning with Elvis Presley and Johnny Cash in 1955.

## MUST EAT

Again, the main attraction is the original location of Lambert's Café. It opened in 1942, but it was not until 1976 that the first roll was thrown. This has become the place's signature. Hot rolls are thrown to guests as they eat their pass-around side dishes ahead of the meal. The theme is southern home-style food, much of it fried. With the rolls, there's all-you-can-eat fried okra on a napkin before the meal comes. Once the meal arrives, there are more pass-arounds like macaroni, fried potatoes, black-eyed peas, and apple butter. There's a wide menu but southern favorites lead the way, like chicken pot pie, chicken and dumplings, roast beef, meatloaf, chicken fried steak, fried chicken, and fried shrimp. It's a fun experience, and the hot-rolls tossing doesn't lead to skimping on the food.

## MUST SHOP

The Sikeston Factory Outlet Mall is a twenty-two-store shopping center that is the only outlet center between St. Louis and Memphis.

## MUST NOTE

The city is home to Scott County High School, which has won eighteen boys' basketball state championships between 1976 and 2015. They have also won seven girls' basketball state championships.

# *Go!*

## A FINAL WORD FROM THE AUTHOR

From the prairie in the north to the Osage Plain in the southwest, from the heights of the Ozarks in the south down to the lowlands of the bootheel, Missouri is full of adventures, as you've no doubt seen. Your adventure might be a Hallmark movie–like romantic getaway in Clarksville or Rocheport or a family adventure like winter snow skiing at Weston's Snow Creek or summer Jet Skiing on the Lake of the Ozarks. Or maybe you'd like to climb unique rock formations in Sturgeon or Ironton. Your Missouri adventure could be tasting wine or great cuisine, taking a historical tour, bathing in mineral water, visiting a petting zoo, and much more. The adventures are there to be had, but one thing has to happen—you have to go. And to go, you have to plan. Do it!

As I finish this book, school is letting out for the year. Not only does that mean vacation time for my children, but also for my schoolteacher wife. And my being an author with an often-flexible schedule means Hello, Summer Adventures! My family wants to have them, but to be honest, summer has slipped up on us. We didn't plan a big vacation this year because we'd hoped to have weekly mini-adventures. The last couple of months have been extremely busy with projects for me, changes at work for my wife, and tons of children's activities, so we haven't booked a thing or planned a single outing. My wife and I know too well that if we don't plan a trip, even a day trip, it's not going to happen.

We've learned it the hard way. We love traveling, road-tripping, and exploring new places. That's what has made *Show Me Small-Town Missouri* so fun for us. We married young and were together nine years before kids. We did take trips both big and small, but not nearly enough for the amount of time we had. We both believe that we wasted time we wish had been spent together making memories. Those years and missed opportunities can't be gotten back; they're lost. All we can do is not repeat those same mistakes.

When my oldest daughter was born, I befriended fellow author Michelle Cox, who has a book and blog called *Just 18 Summers*. Her premise is that we only have eighteen summers to spend with our children, and we need to make them count. That truth captured my wife's and my hearts, and we have made it a mission to make the most of those summers, and not just summers either. Reflecting on our own experiences growing up and seeing what worked best for us as a family, we realized that outings, day trips, weekend trips, and vacations have had the greatest impact on our lives. Those were what we remembered the most from our own childhoods. The adventures are also what my kids retell the most, so we've made taking those trips nonnegotiable. The only thing that gets in the way is us not planning.

So, on the first day school was out, we loaded up and went to our favorite sno-cone stand. We got our sno-cones and pulled out a calendar. We planned our summer adventures. Now we just have to go. If we had waited a week or two, the summer would've been gone. Our time would've been stolen by something else.

I believe the same is best for you, for couples, and for families—go and see what can be found and experienced. Small towns in Missouri offer some great ideas. Those ideas are listed here. The research has been done. Now put it down on your calendar and go!

One hesitation is that there are so many ideas in this book. If you're overwhelmed, narrow your choices by deciding on the distance you want to drive. And if that's too hard, figure out what's only an hour away and just go!

# Sources

American Hauntings website. "The Hornet Spooklight." Accessed April 4, 2020. https://www.americanhauntingsink.com/devprom?rq=promenade.

City of Peculiar, Missouri website. "How Peculiar Got Its Name." Accessed April 4, 2020. http://www.cityofpeculiar.com/pView.aspx?id=6747.

Dibenedetto, David. "The Case of Old Drum: An Inspiring Story Every Dog Owner Should Know." *Field & Stream*, January 27, 2010. https://www.fieldandstream.com/blogs/hunting/2010/01/case-old-drum-inspiring-story-every-dog-owner-should-know.

Estes, Kata Pollock. "Apple Cider Slush." *417 Magazine*, October 2014. https://www.417mag.com/issues/october-2014/apple-cider-slush/.

*Ferguson, Henry.* "Jim the Wonder Dog." *Rural Missouri*, November 9, 2010. http://www.ruralmissouri.org/2010Pages/10MarchJimWonderDog.html.

Fluker, Amy. "The Grandest Charity in the Country: The Missouri Home for Confederate Veterans." *The Civil War Monitor*, April 29, 2013. https://www.civilwarmonitor.com/blog/the-grandest-charity-in-the-country-the-missouri-home-for-confederate-veterans.

Forde, Mitchell. "Where Are They Now? Joel Clinger Forged Own Path by Building His Own Zoo." PowerMizzou.com, July 7, 2018. https://missouri.rivals.com/news/where-are-they-now-joel-clinger-forged-own-path-by-building-his-own-zoo.

King, Nick. "Webb City Cardinals Football—Incomparable in Missouri." Accessed April 17, 2020. https://www.youtube.com/watch?v=kBb9umE81Wk.

Main Street Chillicothe. "Chillicothe History." Accessed April 4, 2020. http://www.downtownchilli.com/History.aspx.

McMillen, Margot Ford. *Paris, Tightwad and Peculiar: Missouri Place Names*. Columbia: University of Missouri Press, 1994.

Missouri Office of the Secretary of State. "Man's Best Friend: The Old Drum Story." Missouri State Archives. Accessed April 4, 2020. https://www.sos.mo.gov/archives/education/olddrum/StoryofBurdenvHornsby.asp.

Peake, Jason. "Webb City Went 13-1 in Stellar 2018 Season." *Joplin Globe*, December 3, 2018. https://www.joplinglobe.com/sports/local_sports/webb-city-went-in-stellar-season/article_9380d657-4609-5199-9c44-d2a7d5066e69.html.

Porkorny, Ralph. "White Grill: 75 Years and Counting." *Nevada Daily Mail*, July 19, 2013. https://www.nevadadailymail.com/story/1987308.html.

River Valley Region Association. "Lesterville, Missouri History." Accessed April 4, 2020. http://www.missourihistorictowns.com/missouri-historic-places/lesterville-missouri-history-landmarks.htm.

Satterfield, Archie. "Missouri's Rhineland." *Chicago Tribune*, May 8, 2000. https://www.chicaotribune.com/lifestyles/travel/chi-0005060041-tr-may08-story.html.

St. James Winery website. "History." Accessed April 4, 2020. https://www.stjameswinery.com/about/history/.

Taylor, Jason. "250,000 Visitors Expected for Last Weekend of Boating Season at Lake of the Ozarks." OzarksFirst.com, September 1, 2018. https://www.ozarksfirst.com/news/250–000-visitors-expected-for-last-weekend-of-boating-season-at-lake-of-the-ozarks/1411884383.

Warrensburg Convention & Visitors Bureau. "Warrensburg History." Accessed April 4, 2020. https://www.visitwarrensburg.com/590/Warrensburg-History.

Weston Chamber of Commerce. "Weston: Best Small Town in Missouri." Accessed April 4, 2020. www.westonmo.com.

The Wine Cellar Insider. "Complete Napa Valley California Wine History from Early 1800s to Today." Accessed April 4, 2020.https://www.thewinecellarinsider.com/california-wine/california-wine-history-from-early-plantings-in-1800s-to-today/.

# Illustration Credits

## NORTHERN PLAIN

### CHILLICOTHE

Silver Moon Plaza. Photo by author.
Home of Sliced Bread Mural. Photo by author.

### CLARKSVILLE

Clarksville Riverfront Park. Photo by Eugene Gamble.
State Game Refuge. Photo by Daralene Bushue.

### DEFIANCE

Chandler Hill Winery. Photo by Charles Miller.
Chandler Hill Winery. Photo by Ted Engler.

### EXCELSIOR SPRINGS

Ray's Diner. Photo by Kevin Geiss.
Hall of Waters. Photo by Kevin Geiss.
The Elms Resort and Hotel. Photo by Nicolas Henderson.

### FLORIDA

Mark Twain Birthplace State Historic Site. Photo by Mark C. Stauter.

### FULTON

National Winston Churchill Museum. Photo by John Hagstrom.
Bek's Restaurant. Photo by author.
Fulton Café. Photo by Fulton Café.

### HAMILTON

Town Mural. Photo by Jim Good.
Owl Cigar Ghost Mural. Photo by Bob Travagli-one, www.fotoedge.com.

### HANNIBAL

Mark Twain Boyhood Home and Museum. Photo by Robert Stinnett.
Mark Twain Boyhood Home and Museum. Photo by Mark C. Stauter.

### JAMESPORT

Country Cupboard Restaurant. Photo by author.
Country Cupboard Restaurant. Photo by author.

### LOUISIANA

Fat Boys Restaurant. Photo courtesy Fat Boys.
Fat Boys Restaurant. Photo courtesy Fat Boys.

### MARSHALL

Missouri Valley College. Photo by Mark C. Stauter.

### MEXICO

Mexico Train Depot. Photo by Mark Herren.

### PARKVILLE

Parkville Farmer's Market. Photo by Laura Gilchrist.

### PLATTSBURG

Greenlawn Cemetery. Photo by Aaron Mitchell.

### ROCHEPORT

Katy Trail Cave. Photo by Simon Foot.
Katy Trail Tunnel. Photo by Simon Foot.

### STURGEON

Pinnacles Youth Park. Photo by author.

### SUMNER

Sumner Community Park. Photo by author.

### WESTON

Weston Historic District. Photo by Simon Foot.
Coal House Lodge. Photo by Simon Foot.
The Saint George. Photo by Bob Travaglione, www.fotoedge.com.

### WRIGHT CITY

Big Joel's Safari. Photo courtesy of Big Joel's Safari.

## SOUTHWEST OSAGE PLAIN

### BOLIVAR

Creator Delights. Photo courtesy of Creator Delights.
Southeast Baptist University. Photo courtesy of Southeast Baptist University.

### CARTHAGE

Jasper Country Courthouse. Photo by Gordon Huggins.
Boots Court. Photo by author.
Boots Court. Photo by author.
Boots Court. Photo by author.

## CLINTON

Katy Trail. Photo by Mark C. Stauter.
Mallard's Roadhouse. Photo courtesy of Mallard's Roadhouse.
Mallard's Roadhouse. Photo courtesy of Mallard's Roadhouse.

## DIAMOND

George Washington Carver Monument. Photo by author.
Small Appliance Museum. Photo by Ken Horn.

## EL DORADO SPRINGS

Historic Downtown. Photo by author.

## GRAIN VALLEY

The Brass Armadillo. Photo courtesy of the Brass Armadillo.

## HIGGINSVILLE

Confederate Memorial State Historic Site. Photo by Mark C. Stauter.

## HORNET

E50 County Road. Photo by author.

## LAMAR

Harry Truman Birthplace Site. Photo by Gordon Huggins.

## LEXINGTON

Battle of Lexington Historic Site. Photo by Vincent Parsons.

## NEVADA

White Grill. Photo by author.
White Grill. Photo by author.
1893 Building. Photo by Gordon Huggins.

## PECULIAR

Welcome Sign. Photo by author.

## SIBLEY

Fort Osage. Photo by Mark C. Sauter.

## TIGHTWAD

Tightwad Bank. Photo by Granger Meador.

## WARRENSBURG

Retrograde Museum. Photo courtesy of Retrograde Museum.
Statue of Old Drum. Photo by Mark C. Stauter.

## WEAUBLEAU

Weaubleau Egg. Photo courtesy of Creative Commons.

## WEBB CITY

Route 66 Memorial Park. Photo by Simon Foot.
Hwy 71. Photo by Gordon Huggins.

# OZARKS

## ARROW ROCK

Arrow Rock State Park. Photo by Bruce Wicks.

## BLACKWATER

Downtown. Photo by Joe Prall.
Hotel Iron Horse. Photo by Joe Prall.

## BONNE TERRE

Depot. Photo by Robert Stinnett.
Bonne Terre Mine. Photo by Robert Stinnett.

## BOONVILLE

Depot. Photo by Robert Stinnett.

## BRANSON

Silver Dollar City, Time Traveler Rollercoaster. Photo by author.
Danna's BBQ and Burgers. Photo by author.
Silver Dollar City, Wilderness Road Blacksmith Shop. Photo by Steven Miller, www.stevenmiller.smugmug.com.
Silver Dollar City, Hazel's Blown Glass Factory. Photo by Steven Miller, www.stevenmiller.smugmug.com.
Silver Dollar City, Eve & Delilah's Bakery. Photo by author.

## BURFORDVILLE

Bollinger Mill Covered Bridge. Photo by Phil Kamp.
Bollinger Mill and Bridge. Photo by Phil Kamp.

## CAMDENTON

Ha Ha Tonka Water Tower. Photo by Ted Engler.
Ha Ha Tonka Castle. Photo by Ted Engler.

## CENTERVILLE

Reed Springs. Photo by Ted Engler.

## CRYSTAL CITY

Bridge to Underground. Photo by Larry Moore with Antonia Quest Photography, St. Louis, MO.
Crystal City Underground. Photo by Ben Moeller-Gaa.
Gordon's Stoplight Restaurant. Photo by Paul Oberle, www.dcdiscombobulated.blogspot.com.
Gordon's Stoplight Restaurant. Photo by Paul Oberle, www.dcdiscombobulated.blogspot.com.
Gordon's Stoplight Restaurant. Photo by Chris Grass.

## CUBA

Wagon Wheel Motel. Photo by Mark C. Stauter.
Amelia Earhart Mural. Photo by Sandra Tidwell.
Missouri Hicks BBQ. Photo by John Hagstrom.

## DAVISVILLE

Pine Valley. Photo courtesy of Pine Valley.

## EMINENCE

Stewart's Landing. Photo by Steven Miller, www.stevenmiller.smugmug.com.

## EXETER

Farmer's Daughter. Photo by author.
Pumpkin Patch. Photo by author.
Pumpkin Patch. Photo by Diana Elders.

## HERMANN

Stone Hill Winery. Photo by Ted Engler.
Inn at Hermannhof. Photo by Bruce Wicks.

## HIGH RIDGE

Iron Barley. Photo courtesy of Iron Barley.
Iron Barley. Photo courtesy of Iron Barley.
Iron Barley. Photo courtesy of Iron Barley.

## IMPERIAL

Mastodon State Historic Site. Photo by author.

## IRONTON

Elephant Rock Park. Photo by Ted Engler.
Elephant Rocks. Photo by Dustin Holmes.

## JADWIN

Welsh Springs Hospital Ruins. Photo by Brian Cormack.

## KIMBERLING CITY

Kimberling Bridge. Photo by Jackie Stoner.
Fourth of July. Photo by Jackie Stoner.

## KIMMSWICK

El Camino Real Monument. Photo by Mark C. Stauter.
Windsor Harbor Road Bridge. Photo by Mark C. Stauter.

## LAKE OZARK

Bagnell Dam. Photo by Glenn Rice.

## LESTERVILLE

Taum Sauk Mountain Overlook. Photo by Mark C. Stauter.

## MANSFIELD

Laura Ingalls Wilder Historic Home and Museum. Photo by Kristy Henderson.

## MARIONVILLE

Murphy Orchard. Photo courtesy of Murphy Orchard.
Murphy Orchard. Photo courtesy of Murphy Orchard.

## MONETT

Angus Branch Steakhouse. Photo by author.

## NEOSHO

Big Spring Park. Photo by author.
Neosho National Fish Hatchery. Photo by author.

## NEW HAVEN

Astral Glass and Studio. Photo by Tony Carosella on behalf of Astral Glass and Studio

## NOEL

Shadow Lake. Photo by author.
Cliff Dwellers Cave Museum. Photo by author.
Cliff Dwellers Cave. Photo by author.

## OSAGE BEACH

Miner Mike's and Buster's. Photo by Dustin Holmes.

## OSCEOLA

Osceola Cheese. Photo by Kiley Ward.

## PACIFIC

Beacon Sign. Photo by Jim Good.

## PARK HILLS

Missouri Mines State Historic Site. Photo by Mark C. Stauter.

## PHILLIPSBURG

Redmon's World's Largest Gift Store. Photo by John Hagstrom.

## PINEVILLE

Kozy Kamps. Photo by author.
Courthouse. Photo by author.

## ROARING RIVER

Roaring River State Park. Photo by Kristy Henderson.

## ROCKAWAY BEACH

La Pizza Cellar. Photo by author.

## ST. JAMES

Vacuum Museum. Photo by Robert Stinnett.

### ST. ROBERT

Uranus Fudge. Photo by Dustin Holmes.
John B. Mahaffey Museum Complex at Fort Leonard Wood. Photo by Dustin Holmes.

### STANTON

Jesse James Wax Museum. Photo by John Hagstrom.
Meremac Caverns Barn. Photo by Jim Good.

### ST. GENEVIEVE

Charleville Winery. Photo by Ted Engler.

### STRAFFORD

Paradise Animal Safari. Photo by John Hagstrom.
Wildseed Restaurant. Photo by Dustin Holmes.

### VAN BUREN

The Landing. Photo by Paul Jarrell.
Blue Heron at The Landing Restaurant. Photo by Paul Jarrell.
Blue Heron at The Landing Restaurant. Photo by Paul Jarrell.
Jolly Cone. Photo by Adam Smith.

### WARSAW

Sweet Tooth Fudge Factory. Photo courtesy of Sweet Tooth Fudge Factory.
Sweet Tooth Fudge Factory. Photo courtesy of Sweet Tooth Fudge Factory.

### WASHINGTON

St. Francis Borgia Church. Photo by author.
Old Depot. Photo by author.

### WHEATLAND

Lucas Oil Speedway. Photo courtesy of Lucas Oil Speedway.
Lucas Oil Speedway. Photo courtesy of Lucas Oil Speedway.
Lucas Oil Speedway. Photo courtesy of Lucas Oil Speedway.

## BOOTHEEL LOWLANDS

### BLOOMFIELD

Missouri Veterans Cemetery. Photo by Ken Horn.
Intersection of Routes 25 and E. Photo by Ken Horn.

### CHARLESTON

Boomland. Photo by Jack Benline.

### DEXTER

West Park. Photo by author.
Hickory Log. Photo by author.
Hickory Log. Photo by author.

### DONIPHAN

Current River. Photo by Paul Jarrell.
Current River. Photo by Paul Jarrell.

### HAYTI

Patty Ann's. Photo by author.
Patty Ann's. Photo by author.

### KENNETT

Palace Cinema. Photo by Jill Mobley.

### MALDEN

Pizza Express. Photo by Bruce Wicks.

### NEW MADRID

Mississippi River Observation Deck. Photo by author.
New Madrid Historical Museum. Photo by author.

### SIKESTON

Lambert's Café. Photo by Ken Horn.

# Index

**JAKE McCANDLESS** is an award-winning author, nationally recognized speaker, and minister who loves small towns and adventures. Being a lifelong resident of small towns and spending much time in towns off the beaten path, he decided to share his family's finds from the Show Me State with the rest of the world through his website, www.smalltownmo.com, and book, *Show Me Small-Town Missouri*. His love for making moments special was ingrained in him by his mom and his sense of adventure by his dad. Those memories and adventures have continued with his wife and partner in crime, Amanda, who is an educator and makes sure to turn each stop into an elementary science lesson, and their daughters, Andrea and Addie, who prefer the candy stores and the stops with water activities. Their beagle, Charlie, would join them more if he wasn't prone to getting carsick.